The Politics of Economic Reform in South Korea

Since the 1980s, the economic performance of the East Asian region has opened up an agenda of social science research into the directive capacity of the state. 'Institutionalist' analysis in political; science has emphasised the role of power relationships in underpinning the superior directive capacities of the East Asian state. Based on the case of South Korea (hereinafter Korea), this study will extend the political institutionalist analysis in the light of the last decade of global transition towards economic liberalisation and democratisation ('dual transition'). Set in the context of parallel changes in other former developmental states (notably those of Latin America), this volume will investigate key issues of Korea's recent experience of transition including:

- Korea's 'gradualist' or 'continuous' pattern of economic and political reform
- the variations in the rhythm and priorities of reform within the gradualist pattern of transition
- the developmental alliance of state and business as a source of both economic dynamism and vulnerability, and the endurance of that alliance despite persistent reform efforts
- the external shock and regime change of 1997 as the catalyst for decisively transforming the institutional foundations of Korean development.

This comprehensive and authoritative account of the development of the Korean economy combines an historical approach with a substantial treatment of the new economy. Its fresh analysis of the recent transition and systematic treatment of labour issues represent a significant contribution to the scholarship on the politics of development. It is an essential resource for students of comparative political economy and East Asian development.

Tat Yan Kong is Lecturer in Politics at the School of Oriental and African Studies, University of London. Educated at Newcastle and Oxford Universities, his previous publications include *The Korean Peninsula in Transition* (co-edited with D.H. Kim).

Routledge Advances in Korean Studies

1 **The Politics of Economic Reform in South Korea**
A fragile miracle
Tat Yan Kong

The Politics of Economic Reform in South Korea

A fragile miracle

Tat Yan Kong

London and New York

First published 2000
by Routledge
11 New Fetter Lane, London EC4P 4EE

Simultaneously published in the USA and Canada
by Routledge
29 West 35th Street, New York, NY 10001

Routledge is an imprint of the Taylor & Francis Group

© 2000 Tat Yan Kong

Typeset in Baskerville by Florence Production Ltd,
Stoodleigh, Devon
Printed and bound in Great Britain by
St. Edmundsbury Press, Bury St Edmunds, Suffolk

British Library Cataloguing in Publication Data
A catalogue record for this book is available from the
British Library

Library of Congress Cataloging in Publication Data
Kong, Tat Yan, 1961–
    The state and development in South Korea: a fragile miracle/
    Tat Yan Kong.
    p.   cm.
    Includes bibliographical references and index.
    1. Korea (South)—Economic conditions—1960–   2. Korea
    (South)—Economic policy—1960–   3. Korea (South)—Politics
    and government.   I. Title.
    HC467.K5885 2000
    338.95195–dc21   00-036599

ISBN 0–415–14503–1

Contents

Illustrations

Tables

Figures

Foreword

The main features of the South Korean economic 'miracle' are well known, and rightly celebrated. An outstanding record of sustained long-term growth converted a low income war-torn resource-poor economy into a major industrial and trading power within the space of a few decades. By the early-1990s, South Korea had become the world's largest shipbuilder, the third biggest manufacturer of large capacity memory chips, and a substantial player in the global automobile industry. Half a century after the Korean peninsula was divided at the 38th parallel, the southern state had demonstrated that an initially backward economy can leapfrog the international hierarchy of development and virtually eliminate absolute poverty. Moreover, according to the standard comparative indicators of income inequality, the Korea of the 1990s was relatively egalitarian, certainly not disfigured by the extremes of inequity to be found in most other newly industrialising countries, whether in Asia or still more in Latin America. In addition, from 1987 onwards this economic success has given rise to extensive political democratisation. Indeed, in 1997, the long-standing opposition politician, Kim Dae-Jung, was finally elected to the presidency at his fourth attempt.

But, as is now equally well known, the 'miracle' was also fragile. Even before Kim Dae-Jung was inaugurated, a massive financial crisis engulfed the entire banking system, the foreign exchange reserves evaporated, and the currency plummeted. The outgoing administration was forced to seek a $67 billion rescue package from the IMF, on terms that were received in a mood of national humiliation.

This volume sets out to explain both the distinctive dynamics of the miracle, and the associated sources of its fragility. It views the two as inter-dependent, and long term. The central focus is the shifting balance of power in the state–business–labour relationship, and in particular the enduring power accumulated by the *chaebol* (industrial conglomerates sponsored by the state, counterparts to Japan's pre-war *zaibatsu*). Built up under authoritarian rule they proved capable of adapting to benefit from subsequent democratisation as well, and even after the 1997 crisis their capacity for renewal commands attention.

In the course of providing his explanation, the author has also made an important contribution to the comparative and theoretical debates concerning the nature of the developmental state in East Asia, on the causes and consequences of liberalisation strategies in such contexts, and on the multiple repercussions of democratisation. The analysis is interspersed with well-chosen and often highly illuminating comparisons and contrasts between South Korean experience and parallel processes in other newly industrialising countries, both East Asian and Latin American.

A central claim about Korean development is that both economic liberalisation and political democratisation proceeded in a gradual and controlled manner, up to the 1997 crisis, thereby allowing dominant business interests to shore up their positions, even at the cost of frustrating some of the main purposes of liberalisation. Since then IMF supervision has inspired a more root and branch approach to liberalisation, but even so the author presents some compelling grounds for doubting the extent to which the Korean state can now discipline the *chaebol*, particularly the top five.

This volume provides a fresh benchmark for assessing the state of Korea's development alliance, and the country's future potential in an increasingly 'global' system, where the methods of a 'forced march' are unlikely to be sheltered, and where flexible horizontal networks are gaining competitive advantage over hierarchically organised national champions. But even though some change may be inevitable, restructuring and democratising an economic model that achieved so much success under conditions of state direction and authoritarian control is bound to be a protracted process, and may not follow standard international patterns. For example, the author suggests that the Korean state may have more of a need, and more of a capacity, to develop a social role than is acknowledged in neoliberal orthodoxy.

The immediate situation may provide some grounds for optimism about South Korea's capacity for recovery from the shock of 1997, but overall this analysis provides as much reason to identify fragilities as to anticipate renewal of the miracle. More profoundly, the volume demonstrates the longstanding way in which these two tendencies have been bound together, and why, contrary to much prevalent Western thinking, they could still prove so hard to disentangle.

Laurence Whitehead
Nuffield College
Oxford
April 2000

Preface

The character of state–business relationships shapes economic development opportunities by encouraging certain types of market activity while
discouraging others. 'Institutionalist' accounts of Northeast-Asian economic development point to the existence of state–business relationships
that encourage those activities conducive to the goals of long-term growth
maximisation and national ownership. The central component of the explanation is the superior directive capacities of the state in Northeast Asia
compared to those of other late-industrialising societies. While economic
institutionalists have focused on tracing superior economic outcomes to
governmental interventionary instruments (especially the impact of government policy on relative prices), political institutionalists explained the factors
that enabled the state to attain and sustain its dominant social position
without succumbing to the negative effects commonly associated with state
power.

Based on the case of South Korea, this study will extend the political
institutionalist analysis in light of the last decade of global transition towards
economic liberalisation and democratisation ('dual transition'). Korea's
dual transition will be set in the context of parallel changes in other former
developmental states, notably those of Latin America. Four key issues of
the recent Korean experience of transition will be investigated. First, what
factors underpinned Korea's 'gradualist' or 'continuous' pattern of economic and political reform? Second, if the Korean transition was gradual
by international standards, what accounts for the variations in the rhythm
of reform (notably in the emphasis on redistributional measures after 1987
and the turn towards accelerated liberalisation under the banner of
'globalisation' from 1993)? Third, the severe economic crises that have
punctuated Korea's overall economic success have drawn attention to the
vulnerabilities as well as the strengths inherent in the Korean development model (hence the 'fragile miracle' characterisation). This study will
explain the institutional source (located in the developmentalist alliance of
state and business) of this vulnerability and its endurance in the face
of persistent reform efforts. Fourth, if they have not reinforced the core
institutional feature of the Korean development model, the state–business

alliance, then previous external shocks (even the 1979–80 one that launched the liberalisation drive) and foreign involvement have left the essentials of that alliance untouched. Given the unique conditions of the post-1997 situation (IMF supervision, strict neo-liberal conditionalities and the unprecedented weakness of the old system), this study considers whether the 1997 crisis will prove to be the external shock that will decisively transform the institutional foundations of Korean development.

Acknowledgements

I am grateful to many friends and associates for their help and advice in the course of completing this work. James Cotton, John Enos, Dae-Hwan Kim, Arthur Stockwin, Aidan Foster-Carter, Laurence Whitehead (who also kindly supplied the foreword to the book), Victoria Smith and two anonymous referees made useful comments on earlier drafts. Many Korean scholars and officials provided me with helpful advice and research materials. The research funding provided in 1996 by the University of London's School of Oriental and African Studies enabled me to update the work I carried out as a doctoral student. The contents of this work, including any errors, are my sole responsibility.

TYK
London 1999

Abbreviations

APEC	Asia-Pacific Economic Cooperation
BOK	Bank of Korea
DJP	Democratic Justice Party
DLP	Democratic Liberal Party
DRP	Democratic Republican Party
EPB	Economic Planning Board
FEER	Far Eastern Economic Review
KDI	Korea Development Institute
FKI	Federation of Korean Industries
FKTU	Federation of Korean Trades Unions
FSU	former Soviet Union
FTC	Fair Trade Commission
HCI	heavy chemical industry
KCIA	Korean Central Intelligence Agency
KCTU	Korean Confederation of Trades Unions
KDI	Korea Development Institute
KEPCO	Korea Electricity and Power Corporation
KEF	Korean Employers' Federation
KERI	Korea Economic Research Institute
KIEP	Korea Institute for International Economic Policy
KLSI	Korea Labour and Society Institute
KSE	Korea Stock Exchange
KSY	*Korea Statistical Yearbook*
MOFE	Ministry of Finance and Economy
MOL	Ministry of Labour
MOST	Ministry of Science and Technology
MOTIE	Ministry of Trade, Industry and Energy
MRFTA	Monopoly, Regulation and Fair Trade Act
NBFI	non-bank financial institution
NKDP	New Korea Democratic Party
NPE	neo-classical political economy
NSO	National Statistical Office
OECD	Organisation for Economic Cooperation and Development

OPC	Office of Planning and Coordination
POSCO	Pohang Steel Corporation
SME	small and medium-sized enterprise
SOE	state-owned enterprise
TAFBS	Tripartite Agreement on Fair Burden-Sharing
ULC	unit labour cost
WTO	World Trade Organisation

1 Introduction
Korea in the comparative political economy debate

The character of state–business relationships shapes economic development opportunities by encouraging certain types of market activities while discouraging others. 'Institutionalist' accounts of Northeast Asian economic development point to the existence of state–business relationships that encourage those activities conducive to the goals of long-term growth maximbibliographytion and national ownership. The central component of the explanation is the superior directive capacities of the state in Northeast Asia compared to those of other late-industrialising societies. While economic institutionalists have focused on tracing superior economic outcomes to the government's interventionary instruments (especially the impact of government policy on relative prices), political institutionalists have explained the factors that enabled the state to attain and sustain its dominant social position without succumbing to the negative effects commonly associated with state power.

Based on the case of South Korea (hereinafter Korea), this study will extend the political institutionalist analysis in light of the last decade of global transition towards economic liberalisation and democratisation ('dual transition'). Korea's dual transition will be set in the context of parallel changes in other former developmental states, notably those of Latin America. Four key issues of the recent Korean experience of transition will be investigated. First, what factors underpinned Korea's 'gradualist' or 'continuous' pattern of economic and political reform? Second, if the Korean transition was gradual by international standards, what accounts for the variations in the rhythm of reform (notably in the prioritisation of redistribution measures after 1987 and the turn towards accelerated liberalisation under the banner of 'globalisation' from 1993)? Third, the severe economic crises that have punctuated Korea's overall economic success have drawn attention to the vulnerabilities as well as the strengths inherent in the Korean development model (hence the 'fragile miracle' characterisation). This study will explain the institutional source (located in the developmentalist alliance of state and business) of this vulnerability and its continuation in the face of persistent reform efforts. Fourth, if they have not reinforced the core institutional feature of the Korean development model, the state–business alliance, then previous external shocks (even the 1979–80 one that initiated the liberalisation drive) and foreign involvement have left the essentials of that alliance untouched. Given the unique conditions of the post-1997 situation (IMF supervision, strict neo-liberal conditionalities and the unprecedented weakness of the old system), this study asks if the 1997 crisis will prove to be the external shock that will decisively transform the institutional foundations of Korean development.

Institutionalist accounts of the Korean miracle

This study builds on the institutionalist approaches which have contributed greatly to the understanding of Korean development. Institutionalist approaches made their appearance in the 1980s in response to the perceived inadequacies of the market-centric (neo-classical and structural dependence) explanations of Korean economic development. By demonstrating the decisive role of positive government action in effecting favourable economic outcomes, institutionalist studies of Korea and other rapidly industrialising NICs opened up an agenda of social science research into the relationship between economic performance, the nature of government intervention and the socio-political bases of the state. After briefly summarising these accounts, I draw attention to the areas in which they can be further explored, areas that will feature in the course of this study.

Economic institutionalism

Economics-oriented institutionalist accounts attribute Korea's economic performance to the effectiveness of the state in overcoming market failure. For writers in this tradition, the East Asian growth phenomenon (of which Korea is a leading example) represents a form of industrialisation not readily explicable by standard economic theory drawn from the experience of Anglo-American societies. Alice Amsden's work stands as a seminal study of the impact of economic institutions in overcoming 'market failure' in Korea.

Amsden's explanation of Korean industrialisation is inspired by the writings on late-industrialisation pioneered by Gerschenkron (1962). She argues that neo-classical economic theory (with its faith in market forces) is derived from an Anglo-American experience of *laissez-faire* industrialisation that was historically unique. By contrast, the industrial transformations of Continental Europe and non-European countries represent examples of late-industrialisation. Rather than invent or innovate technology, late-industrialisers assimilate existing technology and make use of a variety of non-market mechanisms (notably subsidies) to stimulate productive activity. Korea and Taiwan represent ultra-successful examples of this type because of the ability of their governments to exact high performance standards from the business sector and also because of their proximity to Japan (who derived her model from the successful German one). Amsden is positive about the role of both subsidies and effective controls over business in achieving the competitiveness that could not have been generated by low wages alone (Amsden 1989: 145–6). From the Korean case study, she criticises the 'laws' of the stages of comparative advantage, one of the cornerstones of neo-classical economic theory, for neglecting the role of government in facilitating the transition from one stage to another (ibid.: 244). Based on a study of Taiwan, Robert Wade's influential account (1991) highlights the role of government leadership in generating outcomes that could not have arisen from market forces alone. He concludes that the export competitive economies of the Korean and Taiwanese types are examples of 'governed markets'.

Described as products of the 'revisionist school' by the World Bank (1991), the influential works of these authors forced the World Bank in 1991 to modify its dominant neo-classical paradigm. By incorporating aspects of the pro-intervention case into the neo-classical explanation, the Bank's 'market-friendly' view of East Asian economic development was born (World Bank 1993: 84–5; for an evaluation of 'miracle' study, see Amsden 1994b). While reasserting the staple elements of the neo-classical explanation (macroeconomic stability, human capital formation, openness to international trade, an environment conducive to private investment and competition), the Bank's 'miracle' study acknowledged that certain types of intervention were consistent with rapid growth in East Asia:

> Moreover, East Asian success sometimes occurred *in spite of* rather than because of market interventions. Korea's heavy and chemical indus- tries (HCI) drive and Japan's computer chip push did not live up to expectations. Even so, other interventions combined with export targeting apparently *were* consistent with rapid growth: quota-based protection of domestic industries in Japan and Korea; targeted indus- trial policies including directed credit in Japan, Korea, Singapore and Taiwan; heavy reliance on large state enterprises in Japan, Korea, and Taiwan; and so on. Furthermore, the successes of these three north- eastern economies compare favourably with the successes of Hong Kong, Malaysia, and more recently Indonesia and Thailand, where policy choices have been less interventionist
>
> (World Bank 1993: 86)

Political institutionalism

Politically inclined institutionalist accounts of the Korean phenomenon seek to explain the nature of the power relationships that enabled the Korean state to formulate and implement growth-enhancing policies. The socio-political frameworks that facilitated the pursuit of growth-enhancing policies in societies like Korea have been described as instances of 'state autonomy'. State autonomy describes those situations in which public officials are able to pursue policies that are at variance with the preferences of the citizens (on whose behalf they act) and organised interests that might normally be expected to have great influence over decision making (e.g. big business, organised labour). The existence of such autonomy, even in liberal democracies where formal accountability is well developed (Nordlinger 1981), can be explained by a combination of state strength (e.g. possession of unique resources like armed force, expertise) and interest-group weakness (e.g. because such groups are in an early stage of development or busy confronting each other). From a sociological perspective, while Marxists regard such autonomy as a temporary phenomenon (hence their preference for the term 'relative autonomy'), Weberians ascribe to bureaucracy a potential for autonomy that is far more wide-ranging and permanent. Long familiar to those grounded in the tradition of European social theory, the importance of the state was belatedly discovered by North American political scientists in the 1980s (leading to the launch of the so-called 'new institutionalist' research agenda heralded by Evans *et al.* 1985).

Decades of enduring state economic leadership places Korea's early experience of industrialisation closer to the Weberian version of autonomy than to a Marxist relative autonomy. The insulation of economic decision making from short-term pressures or autonomy is described as the central condition that enabled the state to formulate and implement policies conducive to long-term growth (e.g. Haggard and Moon 1983; Haggard 1990). That this capacity for autonomy was available to the states of Korea and Taiwan has been explained in terms of historical factors that saw the creation of a strong military and bureaucratic organisation prior to the rise of business and organised labour. The creation of the capitalist and working classes by bureaucratically sponsored industrialisation meant those classes remained heavily subordinated to officialdom for a long period. In contrast to Latin America, where authoritarian rule emerged as a result of capitalist crisis, in East Asia the institutions of authoritarian rule and the bureaucratic direction of the economy, having been set up by Japanese colonialism (and bolstered by US aid as a consequence of the Cold War), predated and directed the rise of capitalism. One author has referred to the emergence of an 'over-developed post-colonial state' as a result of these external influences (Jang-Jip Choi 1987: 307–10). This explains the state's control of the decisive means of economic leverage (especially in the provision of credit) over Korean business and its domination of labour right from the beginning of industrialisation (whereas in Latin America, powerful labour movements predated bureaucratic authoritarian rule).

In order that their economic projects are carried out competently, even autonomous states need the support of societal forces. Given the closure

of electoral channels, how are the goals of the state reconciled with societal expectations? In other words, how was the 'developmentalist alliance'
cemented? Here, two characteristics of the Korean experience stand out.
First, the incentives and sanctions used to discipline business, as already
described, were supplemented by a network of formal and informal consultative channels (e.g. Jones and Sakong 1980; on Japan, see Johnson 1981),
a phenomenon later referred to as 'embedded autonomy' (Evans 1994).
Second, even in the absence of active redistributive policies, the East Asian
growth rate consequent of high investment and the demand for labour
(e.g. Wade 1988: 158–60) could generate rapid improvements in mass
living standards. Third, while redistributive measures were rarely initiated,
those that were were of enormous significance (notably the Korean land
reform of 1950 and New Community Movement of 1971).

Since most statist strategies of industrialisation in the developing world
have resulted in economic failure, the economic performance of the East
Asian NICs stands out as a remarkable exception. A socio-political framework that allows government officials to exercise enormous power over
the economy without popular accountability is as liable to degenerate into
inefficiency and apathy as it is to facilitate growth. There are three aspects
to this argument: the inherent problems of planning, state predation and
rent seeking.

On the economic problems of intervention, Korean economic policies
did not escape market discipline, and Johnson's characterisation of government intervention in East Asia as 'market conforming' is appropriate
(Johnson 1988). Intervention did not place the economies of the East
Asian NICs outside of international competition (as it did in many
other late-developing countries, or LDCs) but rather helped to upgrade
competitiveness. In spite of many long-range objectives that necessitated
'getting the prices wrong' (Amsden 1989), all sectors nurtured by the
state were expected by the government to build foreign market niches, a
significant contrast with the bloated priority sectors of most LDCs. Export-
orientation gave Korean industry the benefits of international competition
and export earnings provided a crude but telling yardstick of whether the
government's intervention policies were working.

With extensive public resources at their command, and unchecked by
constitutional devices, government officials can engage in the pursuit of
their personal and bureaucratic interests to the detriment of national
development. Intellectually, the issue is not new; it has merely been revived
under the label of 'predatory state'. Marx 150 years ago described the
stifling effect of Louis Bonaparte's military dictatorship: 'this appalling
parasitic body, which enmeshes the body of French society and chokes all
its pores' (Marx 1977: 263). The distorting effect on prices of modern
government intervention was anticipated by Hayek in 1944 (Hayek 1993).
Building on this basic observation, neo-liberal critics of government intervention in economic development have generated a substantial body of

literature on the subject. It is argued that, given the resources at the disposal of public officials, those outside of the government may seek to woo officials in an attempt to gain favourable consideration or engage in 'rent seeking', a process that usually runs parallel to officials' use of their office to obtain personal benefit or corruption. Economic policy thus becomes hostage to the relationship of mutual interest between the government agents and their favoured clients. The growth of the 'political market' in governmental favours undermines the efficiency of the economic market by attracting resources away from productive investment (Krueger 1974; 1990; Colclough and Manor 1991).

Why have such problems not stifled the economic development of the East Asian NICs? Why should the state have remained committed to national development given the absence of countervailing forces? Amsden answers this by pointing to patriotism and the pressure of the student movement (Amsden 1989: 48–52). This is unsatisfactory since patriotic motives also underlie the economic policy-making of many less successful developing countries while the vocality of the Korean student movement was a sign of its political weakness rather than its strength. A point previously made by Amsden but articulated more forcefully by Kohli (1994) is the legacy of bureaucratic competence and discipline bequeathed by the Japanese colonial period when tens of thousands of Koreans were recruited into branches of the Japanese state.

By alluding to security and wider international factors, it is possible to account for the transition of Korean bureaucracy from the predatory type that existed under Syngman Rhee in the 1950s to the developmental type ushered in by the 1961 military coup. For the Korean military, the collapse of the Rhee regime in 1960 underlined the existence of a domestic security threat (arising from economic discontent) to rank alongside that posed by communist North Korea. Under military rule, the nature of governmental incentives was transformed to correspond more closely with contribution to national development as defined by GNP and export growth. Political–economic exchanges (bribery, political and bureaucratic squeeze on business) persisted under the new environment with the crucial difference that they would be tolerated only on condition of development objectives being realised. As for the role of wider international factors in exerting a favourable impact on development, one must note the role of the US. At critical junctures, US support and pressure facilitated the success of transitions that proved to be key turning-points in Korean economic and political history (e.g. land reform in 1950, the transition to export-orientation in 1961–3, the normalisation of relations with Japan in 1965, the deposing of Rhee, Park and Chun).

Recent theoretical controversies

The 'governed-market'-type explanations of Korean political economy (by authors such as Amsden and Wade) have provided informative accounts of the policy interventions and their growth-enhancing effects. Yet the empirical evidence of these works is drawn largely from the 1960s and 1970s, when state direction of the economy and society was at its most intrusive. Since then the international and domestic settings of policy have been transformed. State dominance has given way to economic liberalisation and democratisation, a tide that also swept Eastern Europe and Latin America. After 1980, external pressures and the maturation of the economy moved economic policy in the direction of liberalisation. Growing economic complexity was accompanied by an escalation of popular demands. For all its power, the Korean state was unable to prevent the tiny political openings from turning into a wider democratic break-through in 1987. Democratisation has in turn strengthened the pressure for further liberalisation from a more confident and self-sufficient big busi-ness sector. It has also opened the way for organised labour and other civic forces (such as the environmental movement) to freely advance their agendas for the first time in Korean history. Accelerated integration of the world economy (or 'globalisation') in the 1990s has intensified the pressures for a rethink of the economic policies and institutional structures (notably the collusion of government and business with the exclusion of labour) that became the hallmarks of 'Korea Inc.' in the 1970s. Korea's recent experience generates important insights into the nature of the 'dual transition' in former developmental states.

The classic institutional works alluded to above explain how the status of 'advanced NIC' was attained. The superior growth and distributional performance of the East Asian developmental state compared with those of other regions is by now a familiar story. Recent developments, however, highlight the difficulties faced by such advanced NICs in their transition to 'advanced industrial' status. The sustainability of their economic dynamism has increasingly come into question in recent years. Some commentators have questioned the appropriateness of the term 'miracle' to depict the East Asian phenomenon of rapid economic growth. For example, Paul Krugman has argued that East Asian economic perform-ance could be attributed to the extensive mobilisation of the available factors of production rather than their efficient use (Krugman 1994; and see Young 1995). The implications of this argument are twofold: that there remains a significant productivity gap between the advanced NICs such as Korea and the advanced industrialised countries; and that given their dependence on extensive growth, NICs like Korea are vulnerable to catch-up from competitors employing a similar strategy but from a supe-rior resource base (e.g. China, India, Indonesia). Such doubts lead back to the old dependency-type pessimism about the mobility prospects of semi-peripheral states in the international system, the 'squeeze' thesis and the like.

The problems of sustaining economic dynamism generated a debate about the appropriate policy response. Neo-classical commentators (espe-cially those associated with the conglomerates, or *chaebol*) alleged that the country's economic woes were the result of the slowness with which the Chun and Roh governments implemented liberalisation reforms, a critique that also gained popularity in official thinking through the 1990s (by contrast, Amsden argued that in the late-1980s, economic performance suffered because the state eased its economic leadership; see Amsden 1992 and 1994a). Beginning with the launch of the New Economy Plan of 1993, the Kim Young-Sam government accelerated the pace of liberalising reform. The new thinking affirmed that Korea's ascendancy to 'advanced' status depended on rapidly completing the liberalising transition and dismantling many of the practices traditionally associated with the old developmental state (Korea Inc.).

If there was an emerging consensus that the liberalising transition had to be accelerated, then what form did the transition take? In particular, how did the economic role of the Korean state change as a consequence of liberalising policies? In what way could its strategy and policies still be characterised as 'developmentalist' (that is, attempting to foster or prevent outcomes other than those that would arise from the free interplay of domestic and international capital)? By the early-1990s, many of the former developmentalist regimes of Latin America (the failed heterodox stabilisation programmes of Brazil and Argentina of the late-1980s represented the last gasp of the old developmentalist approach) had embarked upon far-reaching programmes of economic liberalisation. Given the poor performance record of Latin American developmentalism, Korea provides a good test case of the viability of alternatives to radical liberalisation measures. Since the outbreak of the current Asian economic crisis in late-1997, neo-classical claims extolling the virtues of the liberal politico-economic form have been powerfully reiterated (e.g. IMF 1999).

Korea's recent transition illustrates the role of democratisation and social forces in economic policy change. As in Latin America, democratisation reinforced the external and domestic pressures for economic liberalisation in Korea. By making the policy arena subject to lobbying and the pressures of electoral financing, democratisation profoundly altered the relationship between the *chaebol* and the state. The evolution of the liberalising agenda provides an indicator of the changing state–*chaebol* relationship (in terms of power distribution and degree of policy consensus) that once represented Korea's developmentalist alliance. The interesting feature about Korea, however, is that the shift towards economic liberalisation was accompanied by stronger redistributional efforts after 1980 under both authoritarian and democratic regimes.

Democratisation has also opened up the economic policy process to influence from popular forces, especially the labour unions. Apart from organised pressure group influence, the need to secure votes and the interest of political leaders in distancing themselves from the abuses of the authoritarian past have led to efforts by successive democratic governments at promoting social development (from 1987) and eradicating corruption (from 1993). At many points, the agenda of enhanced popular rights and social development conflicted with the malpractices of the *chaebol* built up with state support over three decades. Given the potential of labour's negative veto, successful economic policy change depended on the state's capacity in reconciling labour aspirations with a traditionally anti-labour business sector whose demands for flexibility and efficiency seemed to dictate further labour sacrifices. In effect, it meant reconstructing the developmentalist alliance on a consensual basis. An understanding of the capacity of the state to reconstruct the developmentalist alliance to include labour as well as business will help to clarify the nature of the Korean state's continuing 'autonomy' in the era of international liberalism.

Given that Korea is also in search of a new pattern of state–business–labour relations to replace the old authoritarian, state-dominant one, commentators have pointed to the suitability of importing Japanese-style social arrangements for the purpose of fostering social consensus in Korea (e.g. Lee and Lee 1992; Johnson 1994). Korea Inc. clearly represents a variant of the Japanese late-industrialisation model, containing both pre-war and post-war features of the Japanese original. Political authoritarianism in support of a staunchly anti-labour policy, a key feature of the Japanese colonial model also characteristic of Korea Inc., has been removed by democratisation. In light of Korea's history of late-industrialisation and the official reservations about unrestrained capitalism, Japan's post-1955 marriage of guided capitalism (based on consensual labour relations) and conservative democracy (i.e. 'Japan Inc.') looked a logical successor to Korea Inc. and found favour in Korean policy circles for much of the 1990s. Korea is in a good position to assimilate Japanese institutional forms given the cultural affinities and recent history of borrowing from her colonial 'mentor'. On the other hand, significant obstacles such as the unreformed nature of the *chaebol* and the conditions surrounding the empowerment of labour worked against Korea's capacity for imitating the social arrangements that characterised the golden era of Japan Inc.

Then there are the serious questions over the viability of the Japanese model itself (e.g. Dore 1998). The Japanese economy has been stagnant since the early-1990s while the US has rebounded strongly. The explosion of corruption scandals and corporate bankruptcies that led up to the financial meltdown of late-1997 also seemed to suggest that Korea (and perhaps other Asian countries) had perhaps assimilated too many bad practices from Japan. The neo-liberal reservations about the problems of collusive state–business relationships (which had previously been muted in the East Asian context as a consequence of the region's strong growth and distributional record) have resurfaced forcefully. They are reflected in the application of terms such as 'cronyism' (a characterisation more commonly associated with Southeast Asian-style capitalism) and in the IMF's insistence on the reform of 'corporate governance' as a condition of its 1997 rescue loan to Korea.

If the Asian economic crisis has severely tarnished the image of the Japanese-inspired growth model, the status of Anglo-Saxon model has risen commensurately. But in crisis as in boom, the East Asian economic phenomenon exposes some uncomfortable contradictions in neo-classical analysis and policy recommendations. First, the making of the Korean crisis actually coincided with the acceleration of liberalisation. Liberalising policies actually exacerbated the inherent problems of the *chaebol* and the economy's vulnerability to external shocks (e.g. Palma 1998; Wade 1998). Second, that some Asian models have been more resilient than others suggests that it is certain patterns of state–business alliance, rather than developmentalist alliances per se, that make economies prone to disruptive international shocks. Here, the relative resilience of Korea's closest competitor, Taiwan, provides a forceful case for closer examination of the reasons why the Korean pattern of state–business interaction proved to be more crisis-prone.

The present crisis illustrates the transformative potential of disruptive international shocks (e.g. Haggard 1989). I have mentioned the effects of established power structures (e.g. power of the *chaebol*) and social stalemates (e.g. hostility between business and labour) in preventing the remoulding of Korea Inc. in the image of Japan Inc. In the origins of the Korean developmental state, it was the US-imposed stabilisation programme of 1957 that opened the path to export-led growth by weakening the Rhee government (Woo 1991: Ch. 3). While the appeal of Japan Inc. itself has perhaps waned, the external-shock analogy remains, for the decisive momentum for the emergence of Japan Inc. sprang from international forces. Just as the US Occupation paved the way for the emergence of Japan Inc. from a reconstituted Meiji system (i.e. without the military), the IMF supervision of Korea from 1997 may provide a similar stimulus for institutional redesign. Given the reservations once expressed about the transferability of East Asia's successful institutions and policies to other developing country environments, one should express equal caution about the transferability of the Anglo-Saxon model to Korea and expect any institutional redesign to follow a course of gradual adaptation. These theoretical controversies can be integrated into the central questions of this study to which I now return.

Framework of this study

In formulating the main arguments of this study, I return to the guiding questions posed at the beginning of this chapter.

1   Why has Korea followed a more gradual route of economic and political reform compared to other transitional political economies?
2   How has Korea Inc. been reformed in the past two decades and, in particular, how can the variations in the rhythm of reform (in 1987 and 1993) within the gradualist pattern be explained?

3   How does the institutional framework of state, business and labour
     relations affect economic policy choice and adaptivity to external fluc-
     tuations ('fragile miracle')?
4   What is the significance of the 1997 economic shock to the Korean
     development trajectory?

Gradualist model of transition

Experience from East Asia, Latin America and Eastern Europe during the
1980s suggests that the transition from authoritarian industrialisation is
usually followed by a combination of democratisation and economic
liberalisation. The transition may take either a discontinuous or a continuous path (Martins 1986). The collapse of the authoritarian regime
represents the discontinuous path. On the other hand, authoritarian
leaders may remain in power and gradually modify their political and
economic practices (the continuous or gradualist path). In the former
path, democratisation precedes economic reform and arrives suddenly as
authoritarianism collapses amid public disapproval. This is followed by
pressure to quickly reverse the authoritarian economic agenda. On the
continuous path, however, the transformation is altogether less dramatic
as economic and political reforms are interwoven over a long period, as
the authoritarian leaders are more able to manage the pace of change.
Having initiated the beginnings of change themselves, they also develop
a positive stake in the final outcome. An important determinant of whether
a continuous or a discontinuous transition from authoritarian industrialisation occurs is economic performance. Rapid political disintegration is
normally associated with economic failure and deteriorating living standards. By contrast, those regimes that preside over economic success are
in a better position to take the continuous path of gradual reform.

On the discontinuous transition, democratisation brings with it powerful
pressures for economic reform because economic failure and its social costs
usually form one of the factors that spark political dissent against authoritarianism. At the practical level, democratisation also undermines the
bureaucratic mechanisms (e.g. the capacity to enforce unpopular distributional outcomes and pro-investment policy options that divert resources
from consumption) on which the authoritarian economic project depended.
On assuming power, democratic opposition leaders are compelled to go
along the reform route out of past promises, expedience and genuine belief.
But why should economic reform take the form of liberalisation? That the
economic failings and political costs of authoritarian industrialisation
become an indictment of government intervention per se is one answer.
Economic desperation makes the public highly receptive to the alternative (neo-liberal) agenda for economic renewal. Officials of the former
regime with many of their connections and resources intact also sense their
opportunity to get rich from the parcelling out of public resources at

discounted prices. The post-communist societies of Russia and Eastern Europe fit this scenario.

Those Latin American societies (Brazil and Argentina) ruled by bureaucratic authoritarian regimes followed a slightly different sequence from democratisation to economic liberalisation. There was a brief interregnum prior to the sea-change in public opinion towards economic liberalisation. Latin American experiments in authoritarian-led industrialisation had been justified in the name of economic efficiency, and so it was capitalism that was lacking in legitimacy, for it was associated with political repression and economic failure. Democratisation generated hopeful public expectations for governmental social intervention. As a result, the new democratic regimes came under simultaneous pressure to stabilise their economies and repay the 'social debt' that had accrued under the previous regime. This led to the introduction of the short-lived 'heterodox' stabilisation programmes (1985–7) aimed at reducing inflation without depressing popular living standards. After early successes, however, the programmes proved untenable in the face of resurgent inflation, and were abandoned in favour of orthodox stabilisation programmes and structural adjustment (Baer 1987: 1024–7; Kaufman 1991: 77–91). As in the FSU and Eastern Europe, there existed influential elements of Latin American society supportive of the neo-liberal pathway. But apart from adherents with special ideological and economic motivations (pro-US intellectuals, industrialists and middle class elements oriented to the foreign sector, public officials poised to capitalise on discounted public assets), there emerged a broader consensus favouring the shift towards liberal economics and away from the old discredited interventionism practised by authoritarian and populist regimes alike. Even the traditionally statist movements in Latin America, like the Mexican PRI and Argentinian Peronists, embraced the new doctrine (Edwards 1996; Gibson 1997).

Another explanation for the association between the discontinuous transition to democratisation and rapid economic liberalisation can be located at the international level. The conversion to free-market ideas in the advanced industrialised societies (especially the Anglo-Saxon ones) exerted a powerful role-model influence on the LDCs. But the influence went beyond the intellectual as the new norms were translated into national and multilateral policies with far-reaching consequences for the LDCs. For example, the high interest-rate policy of the US triggered the debt crisis of the 1980s, for which the Washington institutions (the IMF and the World Bank) prescribed and policed deflationary medicine on the debtor countries. Ironically, the crises for which neo-liberal solutions were prescribed were themselves either provoked or accentuated by the application of neo-liberal policies in the Northern countries.

The 'semi-periphery' was also caught up in the bigger structural changes emanating from the technological revolution in the North. Apart from justifying the painful restructuring of the Northern economies during the early-1980s, neo-liberalism reflected the emerging integration of production and finance on a world scale. Without the dismantling of national and international barriers to trade and capital flows that integration could not be completed. Based on conceptions of national political economy, the neo-mercantilistic practices of the Northeast-Asian and Latin American NICs posed barriers to international business. On the other hand, with their potential markets and their lower costs for certain stages of production, these economies also represented profitable opportunities for northern business (especially for TNCs and the financial sector). If they were to derive the international capital and technical transfers necessary for their economic recovery and further industrialisation, the NICs now also had to practise open economics with its associated risks. As a result, they came under increasing northern pressure for economic opening on the basis of conditionality for debt rescheduling (Latin America) or trade reciprocity (Korea). For the state socialist system of the former USSR, the condition for the further integration of its stagnant economy into the world economy was to be disarmament and political reform. But the rapid ideological de-escalation and softening of political control amid mass economic dissatisfaction proved fatal to such regimes. With the publics of the FSU and Eastern Europe equating the overthrow of communist rule with the impending attainment of western lifestyles, democratisation paved the way for an anarchic transition to the market. The nature of external shocks will be considered in more detail later.

Newly democratised countries that experienced repressive authoritarian rule with unsuccessful economic results would be most receptive to these international pressures for rapid economic liberalisation. In the continuous transition from authoritarian industrialisation, by contrast, the background of successful economic performance allows the authoritarian leaders greater room for manoeuvre and to implement reforms piecemeal and in a way consistent with their own long-term interests. If any sequence exists, it is a preference for economic reform first. This is based on the observation that a growing economy provides the means for the alleviation of social discontent and the belief that growth helps to stave off democratisation pressures or allows the incumbents to dilute their power at a favourable moment. If the danger of imminent political collapse is absent, then what motivates the transition from authoritarian industrialisation? In Korea's experience, authoritarian industrialisation was no longer sustainable for the following reasons: the existing policies no longer fitted the changed external environment; having achieved their initial objective, earlier policy instruments could be discontinued; and success raised new problems that called forth new policies.

Korea falls into the category of continuous transition from authoritarian industrialisation. While democratisation in 1987 was forced on the regime by mass popular protests, it had been preceded by a period of political accommodation that saw the relaxation of military control, semi-competitive party politics (there was a competitive National Assembly election in 1985) and the creation of a tentative constitutional dialogue. Economic liberalisation was announced in 1981 (when political repression was at its height), and was still continuing more than a decade later. Nevertheless, the 1980s marked Korea's transition away from the authoritarian-led industrialisation pattern established under President Park Chung-Hee in the preceding two decades and the movement towards a democratised polity with a liberalised economy. This study will explain the origins of that process, the interplay of political and economic factors in the reform process, why reform was accelerated in the 1990s and with what results.

The 1980s marked a transitional period in Korean history as the authoritarian industrialisation pattern established under President Park gradually gave way to economic liberalisation and democratisation in accordance with the three variables identified above. The pressures for change in the 1980s originated from three sources. First, international economic and political trends exerted positive and negative inducements for greater economic openness. Second, the high interventionism of the 1970s had accomplished its aim of giving Korea the productive capacity required for her future export and defence plans. The economic agenda shifted from the creation of capacity to making that capacity efficient, meaning that markets would inevitably have to play a bigger role. Third, authoritarian industrialisation unleashed popular expectations that undermined its foundations of political stability. The combination of these three factors helps to explain why Korea's authoritarian industrialisation pattern (or Korea Inc.) had become unsustainable by the end of the 1970s. Accordingly, the institutional foundations of growth (forms of government intervention, the relationship between state, business and labour, and the political regime) also had to be reformed for the Korean economy to thrive under changed circumstances.

If Korea was evolving out of the authoritarian industrialisation pattern, she was doing so in a continuous way. Continuity was reflected in the persistence of certain national priorities (sustained growth, full-range industrialisation, local ownership and ascendancy to advanced industrial status) laid down in the First Development Plan of 1962–6. These principles lay behind all government policies be they interventionist/liberalising or repressive/democratising. It was reflected also in the controlled nature of the change. For example, economic liberalisation in the sensitive domains of finance and direct foreign investment were largely deferred until the second (1990s) decade of liberalisation. Similarly, democratisation was effected only gradually. Between the fall of the Park regime and Chun's surrender to democratising pressures was an eight-year period in which the authoritarian rulers had time to prepare themselves for competitive politics. Despite their own subsequent falls from grace, Presidents Chun and Roh planted the foundations for their supporters to be peacefully incorporated into the democratic arena.

Reform of Korea Inc.

The second concern of this study is with explaining the rhythm within the pattern of gradual change, notably the emphasis on social development and redistribution (from 1988) and accelerated liberalisation and social consensus building (from 1993). The policy instruments and institutional basis of Korea Inc. have been redefined in response to the international and domestic pressures of the 1990s. On the international level, the neo-mercantilist practices that had traditionally defined the Korean developmental state could find no place in the neo-liberal global economic order that was emerging. The economic and intellectual revolution in the north, technological developments and the end of the Cold War led to a more demanding definition of 'open economy' to which NICs such as Korea had to adapt. The end of the Cold War weakened Korea's traditional bargaining counter to US pressures for economic opening. Domestic pressures for the thoroughgoing reform of economic policies and institutions also had grown. The loss of economic dynamism after 1988 strengthened the case for liberalisation within the policy community. The traditional concern of economic policy, that of industrial 'catching up' and the attainment of 'advanced status', became closely entwined with the issue of economic opening. The access to technology, finance and markets needed for the completion of catching up could not be assured without further liberalisation. Poised to benefit greatly from further liberalisation, and with their influence enhanced by growth and democratisation, the *chaebol* (Korea's conglomerates) waged a vigorous pro-liberalisation campaign. Democratisation also had loosened the state's grip on the labour movement. The labour strife of 1987–9 showed that any smooth course of economic policy change now depended on labour consent. This pointed the way to the extension of the developmental alliance to include labour.

How can the more recent transition in the policy instruments and institutions of Korea Inc. be characterised? In what way was the transition different from the 'gradual' transition towards economic liberalisation and political democratisation of the 1980s? This change can be illustrated according to three dimensions: the re-orientation of the government's economic role; reform of the state–business relationship; and the expansion of the developmentalist alliance to include labour. First, the transition of the 1990s can illustrated by looking at the official policy orientation, and the pace and scope of change. It will be seen that the terms of the policy debate became more explicitly oriented towards liberalisation, a change symbolised by the Kim Young-Sam government's guiding slogan of 'globalisation' from 1993. As for the pace and scope of economic policy reform, that the schedule for the completion of the dismantling of controls in the sensitive areas of trade and finance was accelerated did not mean an end to the state's developmental role. Instead, that role came increasingly to be redefined in terms of the market-conforming instruments of intervention, notably functional supports (R&D, infrastructure) and economic de-concentration measures (e.g. anti-monopoly and regional development measures) designed to correct the imbalances that under-pinned the economy's 'high cost and low efficiency'. It will be seen how these reforms were affected by the continuing closeness between state and *chaebol*.

Second, the 1990s also saw attempts at reform of the institutional basis of Korea Inc. in accordance with the weakening of the state's dominance and the corresponding growth of business and labour influence. With market forces now enjoying freer rein, and with the *chaebol* and labour no longer susceptible to dictat from an autonomous state, the character of the developmental alliance also needed to be redefined. This meant redefining the state–business relationship away from its established collu-sive pattern towards legally defined patterns of cooperation. Faced with the dangers of the extension of economic concentration consequent of further liberalisation, the state took measures to check the expansion of the *chaebol*. Here, in contrast to the reform efforts of the previous decade, anti-monopoly measures were also accompanied by counter-measures against the informal politico-economic exchanges (e.g. the anti-corruption campaign and real name reform of 1993) that had nullified the effective-ness of previous de-concentration measures.

Third, it was officially recognised that the economy was now facing difficult policy choices (e.g. over the adoption of flexible employment prac-tices) that could be smoothly implemented only with organised labour support. Accordingly, the developmentalist alliance had to be expanded to include organised labour as well as business. On the formal level, this was reflected in the development of structures of tripartite collaboration. This meant redressing the legacy of state collusion with business and anti-labour bias. By placing state–business relations on a transparent and legal basis, the measures against the informal politico-economic exchanges represented one aspect of the incorporation of labour on a consensual basis. Another was the expansion of the state's social development res-ponsibilities in response to the more uncertain environment that further liberalising reforms were likely to bring. This study will show how successful economic reform was constrained by the difficulties of redefining the devel-opmentalist alliance.

Korea's transition in the 1990s can be understood also with reference to comparative models of advanced capitalism. In redefining the role of the state in the economy and the institutional basis of development, Korean policy-makers came to be influenced by the recent development pathways of the advanced industrialised societies to whose status they also aspired for Korea. As previously noted, the impulse towards radical liberalisation, or the so-called 'Anglo-Saxonisation', of economics in the aftermath of democratisation was much weaker in Korea than in Latin America or Eastern Europe. For Korea, it was the Japanese political economy, with

its synthesis of liberal-democratic polity and proactive economic bureaucracy, rather than American liberalism, that represented the dominant role
model of catching up and the appropriate form of advanced industrial
economy. The potentialities of effecting a successful transition from Korea
Inc. to Japan Inc. powerfully highlights the achievements and weaknesses
of the Korean developmental model.

In spite of the differing circumstances of Japanese and Korean democratisation (defeat in war versus domestic popular pressure within a
favourable international context), the political economy of Korea's industrialisation under Park Chung-Hee had clear parallels with Japan's
post-1945 experience: a state committed to intervention in order to develop
strategic industries needing long gestation periods; and the use of direct
methods of industrial promotion. Policy instruments such as preferential
credit, trade barriers and giant trading corporations were used by the state
to promote national industry in both countries. Politically, in both countries the Left was excluded (marginalised in Japan, harshly proscribed in
Korea), and labour influence on policy was weak (incorporated in Japan,
repressed in Korea). Mikio Sumiya's observation on the problems generated by Japan's big push into heavy industry during the late-1950s seems
to bear a remarkable resemblance to the problems experienced by Korea's
'deepening' drive a generation later:

> In the US and some advanced European countries, the proportion of
> products of heavy and chemical industries in export commodities corre-
> sponds to or even exceeds their proportion in the total industrial
> output. In Japan, however, the proportion has been less than 40 per
> cent. Here is a big problem . . . The extension of the domestic market
> for producer's goods has tended to slow down because of an 'over-
> abundance' of equipment investments. In this connection, it is
> necessary for Japan to promote the export of heavy and chemical
> industry products to overseas markets. Even at the present time, the
> proportion of light industry products in the total export is still high.
> However, we have to notice that the export of heavy and chemical
> industry products is steadily increasing.
>
> (Sumiya 1963: 237–8)

Japan's instruments of direct intervention were gradually dismantled
from a position of economic strength in the 1970s. The proactive economic bureaucracy moved into indirect or functional forms of economic
promotion and regulation (e.g. technology policy, informal guidance, infrastructural development and the economic diplomacy of overseas aid).
The Japanese experience of accommodation with economic opening and
transition from the traditional developmental state was looked upon
favourably by Korean policy commentators as the least costly and most
appropriate route for Korea's conditions.

For Korea, as for Japan, the legacy of intervention remains much more deeply embedded than does the liberal impulse. In spite of the trend towards economic liberalisation, the state continues to have a high degree of pre-paredness and a capacity for economic intervention. The state–business relationship has remained strong. Indeed, the state was expected by both business and the public to use its capacity to alleviate economic distress and promote growth. The Japanese 'model' of advanced industrial society was the one favoured by Korean policy-makers, who viewed the Anglo-Saxon model as one fraught with excessive instability. For an economy, such as Korea's, that was still in the process of 'catching up', growth was as much a priority as was efficiency. On the other hand, European-style 'social capitalism' was considered inefficient and too costly. In the policy and institutional reforms of the 1990s (e.g. in the efforts to promote a coopera-tive pattern of industrial relations), one can see the attempt to assimilate key aspects of the Japan Inc. experience. Indirect intervention and the promo-tion of consensual labour–business relations were emphasised in the attempted remoulding of the developmental state that was central to the Kim Young-Sam government's 'globalisation' project.

The difficulties of replicating the Japanese experience in Korean condi-tions highlight the legacy of Korea Inc. and international circumstances shaping the opportunities for policy change. Although the Korean transi-tion towards advanced industrialised society status appeared to closely resemble the Japanese course, there also existed significant differences between the two. One stumbling-block that made the attempted Japanese-style synthesis of liberal-democratic polity with a reformed developmental state more difficult in Korea was the post-1987 activation of labour. Labour was politically excluded and repressed for almost three decades in Korea, leaving behind a bitter and confrontational legacy for democratic govern-ments to deal with. By contrast, the most intense phase of labour repression occurred during the earliest years of post-war Japan, and corporatist arrangements (e.g. company unionism) were already well established (legit-imate and delivering practical benefits to those workers included) by the time Japanese development corresponded to Korea's 1990s' level. Another was the contrast in the power of big business – strong in 1987 Korea, very weak in 1945 Japan.

Fragile miracle

The other major stumbling block in the way of Korea replicating the experience of Japan Inc. was the nature of the state–*chaebol* relationship, the institutional underpinning of both economic success and fragility. By 'fragility', I mean the economy's vulnerability to externally induced shocks. The vulnerability to external shocks is a paradoxical feature of Korean political economy, a model of development dedicated to the pursuit of national capitalism. The *chaebol*-dominated economic structure has facilitated spectacular rates of growth in periods of international expansion. On the other hand, such a structure also possessed serious inherent short-comings. It had a tendency to accumulate vast debts that would trigger serious repayment difficulties during periods of recession or uncertainty. Another weakness was the relationship of the Korean *chaebol* with their Japanese counterparts. Designed as 'national champions' with which to overtake Japan, the Korean *chaebol* are paradoxically characterised by heavy dependence on Japanese counterparts.

The nature of the developmentalist alliance of state and *chaebol* has a bearing on the major economic crises that have blighted Korea's impressive overall performance. As well as providing the basis of growth-maximising policies, the ideology and the interests behind the state–*chaebol* relationship are also responsible for the malpractices (e.g. high levels of business concentration, wasteful competition, corruption, bias against the non-*chaebol* sector) that render the Korean economy so vulnerable to externally induced shocks. Playing the role of junior partners in the developmentalist alliance under authoritarian regimes, the *chaebol* accumulated enormous influence. Attempts to counteract the influence of the *chaebol* were no more successful under democratic governments than they had been under authoritarian ones. Democratisation and economic liberalisation policies did not break the interdependence of state and *chaebol*, but had the effect of strengthening the *chaebol* and generating new forms of collusion.

This study will highlight the connection between the fragility of the Korean economic miracle and the persistence of the state–*chaebol* relationship. It will be argued that the failure of successive democratic governments to make effective inroads into the *chongkyong yuchak* (literally, the cohesion of politics and business) created serious obstacles to the badly needed reform of development policy and institutions. First, democratisation (accompanied by its anti-corruption rhetoric) not only failed to eradicate the politico-economic exchanges between state and *chaebol* but may have actually accentuated those unproductive types of exchange (so-called particularistic ties, cronyism and so forth) previously said to be uncharacteristic of the Korean experience. Second, rather than promoting competition, liberalisation in the 1990s intensified the dominance of the *chaebol*, another source of their enhanced influence. Less constrained by state power than before, the *chaebol* took full advantage of the financial liberalisation measures of the 1990s. In doing so, they deepened the traditional weaknesses of the Korean economy (e.g. disparity between the *chaebol* and non-*chaebol* sectors, high debt–equity ratios, heavy international exposure, dependence on Japanese imports). Third, the persistence of these exchanges constrained the effective reorientation of policy and institutions. Effective anti-monopoly measures could not be realised without effective control of the informal aspects of the state–*chaebol* relationship. Without the state–*chaebol* relationship being placed within a proper legal context, however, labour could not be successfully co-opted into the expanded developmentalist alliance that would enable the difficult economic reforms to be implemented smoothly. Measures vital for competitiveness, such as labour market reforms, could not be implemented, as labour and business could find no common ground. The causes of the economic crisis that engulfed Korea in the fall of 1997 can be understood only with reference to the survival of this basic institutional feature of the developmental model and its associated social impasse.

In explaining the durability of the phenomenon of state–*chaebol* collusion, the interaction of historical and structural factors will be highlighted. On the historical side, the impact of the Japanese colonial experience on later Korean development is widely recognised. In particular, the pre-war Japanese conglomerate (*zaibatsu*) provided the blueprint for the Korean *chaebol*. Another historical factor is the long-term impact of the Right's political dominance of Korea's political dynamics. I argue that the Right's dominance of the polity from the late-1940s created patterns of political competition that were conducive to politico-economic exchange. In such conditions, the radical forces that underpinned the democratic and labour movements failed to organise themselves effectively in the *political* arena. As a result, the type of democratisation that took root after 1987 lacked effective political checks against state–*chaebol* collusion. I refer to this political form as 'arrested democratisation'.

On the structural reasons for the endurance of the state–*chaebol* relationship, a key factor has been the growing weight of the top *chaebol* in the economy since the 1970s. This has corresponded with the declining capacity of the state to discipline and remould them. Alice Amsden has observed the role of the state in engineering a 'switch in industrial leadership' such that the role of spearheading the 1970s' drive into heavy industry was undertaken in many instances by newly proven companies (e.g. Hyundai) rather than by the established leaders of the traditional industries (see Amsden 1989: Ch. 10). By the end of that decade, however, the leading companies had become too entrenched to be displaced. Furthermore, their vulnerability (a consequence of rapid expansion) made it difficult for the state to use liberalisation as the means of extricating itself from support of the *chaebol*. The nature of the *chaebol* as growth-maximising entities and the state's dependence on them were reflected in the cycles of abortive reform of the 1980s and 1990s wherein the impetus for reform arising from *chaebol* failure was dissipated by their necessity to the subsequent recovery.

External shocks and trajectory change

The issue of the reformability of the state–*chaebol* relationship leads us to enquire about the influence of external forces in altering the Korean trajectory of late-industrialisation. Are the external conditions for a decisive change in the Korean trajectory similar to those of post-1945 Japan or of

Latin America in the late-1980s? Does the crisis of 1997 and the subsequent IMF-supervised restructuring represent a decisive external shock for Korea Inc.? What would the emerging trajectory of development look like? While the history of Korea has been one of high sensitivity to external shocks, the institutions and practices of Korea Inc. have endured in the face of those fluctuations. This appears paradoxical until one looks at the interaction of Japanese and American influences in the making of Korea's developmental state.

It has been observed that the superior performance of Korean late-industrialisation owed much to its Japanese lineage. External intervention was decisive in the reshaping of the Japanese political economy after 1945: reform of the *zaibatsu*; democratisation; and acceptance of the US-led liberal international capitalist order. Germany, Japan's parent model, was similarly remoulded by the post-1945 American occupation. Until it was forcibly incorporated into the sphere of US dominance by force of arms, external shocks (notably the Great Depression) led to the strengthening of the Japanese developmental state in ever more pathological directions. This suggests that external shocks, accompanied by external superintendence, provide opportune moments for radical reform of the authoritarian political structures and state–business relations characteristic of the Japanese late-industrialisation type. Given that it, too, was built by Park Chung-Hee and others schooled in pre-war Japanese economic and political methods, one would expect the Korea Inc. model to be similarly resistant to internal reform in the absence of powerful external pressure.

Responsible for creating and protecting the Korean Republic, the US exerted decisive influence in key economic and political moments of Korean history: the land reform; the turn towards export development; market liberalisation; and the fall of Rhee, Park and Chun. In spite of her undoubted influence, however, the US has not yet been able to effect an overhaul of the Korea Inc. model that she helped to create. Quite the reverse: US involvement in Korea up to 1985 tended to reinforce that model. It has been noted that the Korean military junta in 1961 'fell back into the grooves of colonial origins' (Kohli 1994: 1286). This was because American expectations of her Korean allies (loyalty in foreign policy, export orientation and a nominal adherence to liberal-democratic politics) did not impinge on the basic Japanese institutional design of the developmental state. In key moments, the US helped to strengthen the Korean developmental state: by accelerating its reconstitution (e.g. land reform in 1950, military aid from 1950, abandonment of Syngman Rhee in 1960); by extending its international opportunities (e.g. encouraging the turn to export orientation in 1961–3, opening up the Vietnam War to Korean business in 1965, supporting massive private bank loans from 1974); and by rescuing it from the brink of bankruptcy (e.g. US-backed IMF and Japanese assistance loans in 1980–3). In effect, Korea's status as a crucial

Cold War ally afforded her the luxury of US support with a high degree of economic and political autonomy. Illiberal Korean economic and political practices were tolerated by Washington if they were deemed consistent with the over-riding objective of creating a politically stable pro-US ally in Northeast Asia.

Since 1985, Korea's scope for manoeuvre within the US sphere of dominance has narrowed as a result of three structural trends: the neo-liberal economic revolution in the North; the opening up of transnational economic opportunities by new technology ('globalisation'); and the ending of the Cold War. US interests abroad now came to be represented by market democracy rather than by old-fashioned anti-communist authoritarianism. Some commentators (e.g. Cumings 1989) maintain that the US support for Korean democratisation was motivated by the economic prospect of breaking up the neo-mercantilist system of Korea Inc. Yet the dismantling of authoritarianism in Korea was not matched by a parallel neo-liberal economic revolution. While the structural changes in the international environment and in the US attitude amounted to system-transforming external shocks for such beleaguered developmental states of Latin America as Argentina and Brazil, the Korean state proved more resilient and was apparently defining its own course of adaptation to the changed international environment.

What are the external conditions favouring a decisive change in Korea's political economy? Can it be said that the recession and economic restructuring sparked by the financial crisis of late-1997 represents an external shock that will alter decisively the Korean development trajectory? Several distinctive features surrounding the post-1997 situation appear to favour such a transition. First, the effects of the current stagnation are forecast to last until 2002 (when the per capita income will recover to the 1996 level). Popular discontent with the mismanagement of the economy by the *chaebol* is therefore less likely to be assuaged by a swift return to growth, as occurred in the aftermath of the 1979–80 crisis (a factor that distinguished Korea from the major Latin American debtors at the time). Second, the December 1997 presidential election brought the first ever victory to a candidate from outside of the ruling party (Kim Dae-Jung). The new leadership pledged a sweeping reform programme that included central components of the neo-liberal model: the completion of trade and financial liberalisation; privatisation and corporate governance reform; and labour market deregulation. Third, the IMF rescue package of December 1997 was disbursed on strict condition of internationally supervised reform. This represents a significant departure, for previous reform efforts failed through domestic shortcomings in enforcement. The interplay of these three factors will be examined in an attempt to make a provisional assessment of the substance of the ongoing reform and its likely outcomes (e.g. does Kim Dae-Jung's vision of 'democratic market economy' amount to anything more than the neo-liberalisation of Korea?).

Table 1.1 Basic indicators of Korean economy 1970–97

	GNP at current prices ($ billion)	GNP per capita ($)	GNP growth rate (% pa)	Inflation rate / GNP deflator (%)	Rate of unemployed (%)	Balance of payments current account ($ million)
1970	7.99	243	7.6	12.9	4.5	-622.5
1975	20.8	591	6.8	24.6	4.1	-1,886.9
1980	60.3	1,589	-4.8	25.3	5.2	-5,320.7
1985	83.7	2,047	5.4	4.1	4.0	-887.4
1986	95.1	2,296	12.5	2.3	3.8	4,617.0
1987	133.4	3,218	12.3	3.5	3.1	9,853.9
1988	179.8	4,295	12.0	6.9	2.5	14,160.7
1989	220.4	5,210	6.9	5.3	2.6	5,054.6
1990	251.8	5,883	9.6	10.0	2.4	-2,179.4
1991	292.0	6,757	9.1	10.2	2.3	-8,727.7
1992	305.7	6,988	5.0	6.1	2.4	-4,528.5
1993	330.8	7,484	5.8	5.0	2.8	384.6
1994	378.0	8,467	8.4	5.5	2.4	-4,530.8
1995	452.6	10,037	8.7	5.5	2.0	-8,816.8
1996	480.2	10,543	6.9	3.4	2.0	-23,004.7
1997	437.4	9,511	4.9	2.3	2.6	-8,618.2

Source: EPB–NSO (several issues) Korea Statistical Yearbook [KSY]

	Major policies	Political regime type
1953–61 (Pre-developmental state)	• Reconstruction based on aid • Completion of land reform • Import substitution in light manufacturing	• Civilian dictatorship to 1960 • Democratic regime 1960–1
1962–71 (First and Second Plans)	• Export-oriented industrialisation • Expansion of key industries and infrastructure	• Military junta 1961–3 • Restricted democracy 1963–72
1972–81 (Third and Fourth Plans)	• Capital deepening via heavy industrialisation • Rural development from 1971	• Military dictatorship 1972–9 (Park's coup in office)
1982–91 (Fifth and Sixth Plans)	• Macroeconomic stabilisation • Dismantling of direct industrial supports • Social development • Internationalisation	• New military dictatorship 1980–7 • Democratic transition 1987 • Roh Tae-Woo 1988–93
1992–98 (Seventh Plan and New Economy Plan)	• Accelerate internationalisation ('globalisation') • Promote functional industrial supports • Enhance social equity and economic equity • Promote new model of labour relations • Prepare for reunification	• Kim Young-Sam 1993–8 (first non-military leader since 1961)
1998–present (IMF era of externally supervised reform)	• Stabilisation • Completion of financial liberalisation • Restructuring of financial institutions and *chaebol* • Social pact for fair burden sharing	• Kim Dae-Jung 1998–present (first ever president elected from opposition party)

Figure 1.1 Economic policy and political regime type 1953–99

Sources: Government (1962, 1967, 1981, 1992, 1993); MOFE (1998 press releases)

Summary

In the 1980s, Latin America, Northeast Asia (Taiwan and South Korea) and Eastern Europe all underwent transitions from authoritarian developmental systems to democratic pro-market systems of political economy. Of the three transitions, the East Asian path has been the most 'continuous' in sense of the gradual rate at which the economic and political practices of authoritarian industrialisation were dismantled. The broad purpose of this study is to contribute to the understanding of political and economic transition from the perspective of Korea, an exemplar of the successful authoritarian developmental type. Given the common characterisations of Korea's developmental state in terms of autonomy, highly developed political and economic capacities, institutional persistence and so forth, the term 'fragile' appears misplaced. Yet it is undeniable that Korea's record of sustained economic growth has been punctuated by severe economic crises (in 1971–2, 1979–80 and from 1997 to the present), crises that highlight both the strengths and the weaknesses of the institutional underpinning (notably the developmentalist alliance of state and business, and the exclusion of labour from that alliance) of the Korean developmental model.

The economic consequences, endurance and prospects of the Korean developmentalist alliance in the face of the 'dual transition' (of democratic and economic liberalisation pressures) will be investigated from the perspective of four key issues. First, why has Korea followed a more *gradualist* route of economic and political reform compared to other transitional political economies? Second, how did the rhythm of reform alter within the overall context of continuous transition (notably in the prioritisation of redistributive measures after 1987 and accelerated liberalisation or 'globalisation' in 1993)? Third, what distinctive features of the Korean development model made it a 'fragile miracle'? Fourth, what is the significance of the 1997 economic shock to Korea's development trajectory?

2 Pre-1979 patterns of political economy

The making of a fragile miracle

Institutionalist explanations of the Korean 'economic miracle' emphasise the role of proactive governmental intervention in overcoming the constraints to growth. Institutionalists believe that the nature of developmental constraints in Korea were such that government intervention went well beyond the neo-classical yardstick of setting the right prices for the private sector to follow. In demonstrating the role of proactive government intervention in promoting growth with national ownership, institutionalist explanations also confounded the pessimistic prognoses of the structural dependence theories (underdevelopment, dependent development). Given that the interventionist policies applied in Korea were also tried unsuccessfully in other third world countries, institutionalists have emphasised the greater rigour with which Korean governments implemented their policies. This has led to the highlighting of those institutional and socio-political factors thought to be conducive to successful economic intervention in Korea: state power in the discipline of business; bureaucratic professionalism and competence; political capacity of the autonomous state in prioritising development objectives (especially in resisting redistributional pressures while advancing overall social development); smooth relations within the policy-making community; and a set of international circumstances propitious to developmentalist practices.

Given the extensive coverage of the economic take-off period (the 1960s and 1970s) in the existing literature, the purpose of this chapter is to highlight the significance of the aforementioned institutional themes to subsequent reform efforts. In terms of the main issues around which this study is framed, this chapter will provide a historical dimension by identifying those factors that from 1981 impelled policy-makers towards reform and explain how those factors subsequently shaped reform efforts along the gradualist path. In particular, the chapter will focus on how the central problems of the contemporary Korean political economy (state–business interdependence, hostile labour relations, conservative political dominance, and vulnerability to external shocks) were defined in the formative period of the system.

The developmentalist alliance of state and *chaebol*

Work by Amsden (1989) and others have shown that government inter-vention in the Korean economy during the 1960s and 1970s went far beyond the neutralisation of the anti-export bias of the 1950s, as claimed by the neo-classicals (who believe that export incentives and deregulatory measures taken during 1964–7 resulted in a free-trade regime conducive to export activity). Numerous economic studies support Amsden's contention that the development of export and other priority industries was acceler-ated by financial incentives (as well as by administrative commands) that distorted factor prices from their market levels ('getting the prices wrong').

'Korea Inc.': mercantilism with market characteristics

In themselves, however, the interventionist measures used in Korea were not unique. Many had existed in the 1950s, under the rule of Syngman Rhee, and also in other developing countries without yielding the same impressive results. Writers from diverse ideological backgrounds have referred to the discrepancy between policy formulation and implementa-tion in LDCs as a reason for the failure of even the best plans. Explanations for this discrepancy are diverse, ranging from external manipulation and corruption of the elite (dependency) to the weakness (or 'softness') of the state at the local level (see e.g. Myrdal 1970 on India), and the self-interested nature of bureaucracies and bureaucrats nominally working in the public interest (neo-classical political economy). How then did Korean state–business relations avoid these failings during the period of economic take-off? What was the nature of the relationship established and what were its longer term consequences?

A sizeable number of Koreans had gained business experience under the Japanese. Land reform and the state's import-substitution policies of the 1950s provided further stimuli for commercial and industrial develop-ment. Funded from US aid dollars, the import substitution of the 1950s centred around the three 'white' industries (textiles, sugar refining, flour milling). Support for infant industries by protection and subsidy were already in existence. Not quite conforming to a Frankian *lumpen-bourgeoisie*, the Korean business class of the 1950s was deeply immersed in un-productive activities. The shortage situation was highly conducive to profiteering and corruption. Those businessmen, or 'political capitalists', who were well connected could get access to precious aid dollars and other American supplies (Kyong-Dong Kim 1976: 466–9). Easy profits could be made from the importation of scarce materials and their sale at inflated prices. Undertaking contracts for the US military was another profitable activity. In turn, a share of the gains would be kicked back to the bureau-crats and their political masters in Rhee's government. Many famous Korean industrialists (e.g. Chung Ju-Yung of Hyundai, 'Harry' Cho of

Hanjin) who prospered in the Park years got their initial breaks during the reconstruction. The inception of the military regime in 1961 is commonly viewed as a watershed in state–business relations. Beginning with the arrest and expropriation of the leading industrialists, the military government signalled its intent to crack down on simple profiteering (the measure had actually been passed, but not implemented, by the previous government). The businessmen's freedoms and fortunes were subsequently restored in exchange for their promise to work for national development. Having demonstrated its political commitment to development by the act of arrest and asset seizure, the military government initiated a series of incentives and sanctions that would guide the business class towards productive activity. Successful and compliant businesses would be rewarded, while others would be penalised. Of the economic instruments that gave the government great leverage over the private sector, the most powerful was the official control of the banking system. One of the first acts of the military government when it assumed power in 1961 was the nationalisation of the main commercial banks, a measure considered by the military junta as central to the fulfilment of its plans for economic renewal: 'It is indispensable, in order to successfully implement the Plan, that the crucial finance and banking sector be under government control' (Government 1962: 35).

Nationalisation of the commercial banks (and control of developmentalist institutions such as the Korea Development Bank and the Korea Exchange Bank) gave the government effective control over the regulated financial sector. Control extended also to commercial foreign loans (generated mainly from syndicates of foreign banks), whose availability was conditional upon guarantees of repayment by the Bank of Korea (under the foreign loans guarantee scheme introduced by the military government). The preferential lending rates (usually negative in real terms) offered by the official financial sector resulted in a shortage of credit relative to demand. To obtain official credit, businesses had to comply with government priorities. Companies denied official credit were forced to rely on the expensive unofficial or 'kerb' market whose interest rates were exorbitant (see Table 2.1). Other instruments of business discipline at the disposal of the government included the use of rigorous tax audits, denial of import licences for crucial inputs, and even the power (under the Public Corporation Promotion Law 1972) to force companies to go public.

In explaining the superior quality of government intervention, commentators have pointed to the Japanese lineage of Korea's bureaucracy (see e.g. Amsden 1989; Kohli 1994). Modern administration was first implanted by the Japanese and then refined by the Americans. Through Japanese colonialism, the methods of economic planning were introduced to Korea, ranging from the collection of detailed statistical data to the regulation of private industry in accordance with long-range official economic plans. In the early-1960s, all of those Koreans in senior bureaucratic positions (i.e. age 40 and over) would have spent the formative period of their education under Japanese tutelage. Even though it has been much maligned for its economic performance, the regime of Syngman Rhee maintained and extended the role of the state in long-term economic planning, beginning with the establishment of the Korea Development Bank in 1954.

These inherited skills and techniques were not fully exploited until after 1961, when the military imparted a stronger impetus for growth. Alongside the temporary arrest and expropriation of leading industrialists, the 'purification campaign' of 1961 (one of several in recent Korean history) targeted corruption and incompetence. The state's capacity for intervention was also upgraded with the formation in 1961 of the Economic Planning Board as a pilot agency for development (similar to pilot agencies in Japan and Taiwan; see Johnson 1987). Charged with pioneering economic development and with coordination between the executive and the economic ministries, the EPB was responsible for setting the macro- and sectoral-growth targets in accordance with the principle of export development and selective import substitution set by the executive. Policy instruments like the credit subsidy would then be used to ensure that the private sector fulfilled those targets. While centralising power, the state kept in touch with economic reality by integrating business leaders as junior partners in economic policy-making. Apart from incentives and sanctions, consultative mechanisms helped to convince business leaders of the state's developmental objectives. The Monthly Export Promotion Meetings, for example, included business leaders and senior government officials – up to the Deputy Prime Minister and sometimes even the President himself (Jones and Sakong 1980: 66–9).

The mixture of planning and capitalism practised after 1961 was consistent with the colonial developmental model but had an added export dimension. The private sector would be the agent of plans set by the state, as stated in the summary of the First Five-Year Economic Plan (1962–6), which announced that Korea would follow

> a form of 'guided capitalism' in which the principle of free enterprise and respect for the freedom and initiative of private enterprise will be observed, but in which the government will either directly participate in or indirectly render guidance to the basic industries and other important fields.
>
> (Government 1962: 28)

The direction and pace of industrialisation were dictated according to a series of five-year development plans, the first of which was introduced by the EPB in 1962. Apart from setting target indicators, these plans also designated new priority industries with the long-term objective of promoting the development of an integrated industrial structure. Within this long-range perspective, Korea would move beyond light industry and

Table 2.1 Cost of borrowing 1964–95 (% per annum)

	Regulated interest rates				Market rates		International rate		GDP deflator
	General loan rate	Exports	Machinery industry promotion	National investment fund	Corporate bond yield	Kerb market	US	Japan	
1964	16.0	8.0	na	na		61.8			30.0
1965	18.5	6.5	na	na		58.7			6.2
1967	26.0	6.0	na	na		56.5			15.6
1968	25.8	6.0	na	na		56.0			16.1
1969	24.5	6.0	na	na		51.4			14.8
1970	24.0	6.0	na	na		49.8			15.6
1971	23.0	6.0	na	na		46.4			12.9
1972	17.8	6.0	na	na		39.0			16.3
1973	15.5	7.0	10.0	na		33.4			12.1
1974	15.5	9.0	12.0	12.0		40.6			30.4
1975	15.5	9.0	12.0	12.0	20.1	41.3			24.6
1976	16.5	8.0	13.0	14.0	20.4	40.5			21.2
1977	17.3	8.0	13.0	14.0	20.1	38.1			16.6
1978	17.7	9.0	15.0	16.0	21.1	39.3			22.8
1979	19.0	15.0	15.0	16.0	26.7	42.4			19.6
1980	22.0	15.0	20.0	22.0	30.1	44.9	13.00	7.25	24.0
1981	17.0	10.0	11.0	16.5–17.5	24.4	35.3	12.00	5.50	16.4

Table 2.1 (continued)

	Regulated interest rates				Market rates		International rate		GDP deflator
	General loan rate	Exports	Machinery industry promotion	National investment fund	Corporate bond yield	Kerb market	US	Japan	
1982	15.0	10.0	10.0	10.0	17.3	32.8	8.50	5.50	7.1
1983	14.0	10.0	10.0	10.0	14.2	25.8	8.50	5.00	5.0
1984	10.0–11.5	10.0	10.0–11.5	10.0–11.5	14.1	24.8	8.00	5.00	3.9
1985	10.0–11.5				14.2	24.0	7.50	5.00	4.2
1986	10.0–11.5				12.8	23.1	5.50	3.00	2.8
1987	10.0–11.5				12.8	22.9	6.00	2.50	3.5
1988	10.0–13.0				14.5	22.7	6.50	2.50	5.9
1989	10.0–12.5				15.2	19.1	7.00	4.25	5.2
1990	10.0–12.5				16.5	18.7	6.50	6.00	10.6
1991	10.0–12.5				18.9	21.4	3.50	4.50	10.9
1992	10.0–12.5				16.2		3.00	3.25	6.1
1993	8.5–12.5				12.6		3.00	1.75	5.0
1994	8.5–12.5				12.9		4.75	1.75	5.5
1995	9.0–12.5				13.8		5.25	0.50	5.5

Note: all rates are nominal rates

Sources: BOK (several issues) Economic Statistics Yearbook [ESY]; kerb market figures derived from S. Nam (1992)

achieve self-sufficiency, and ultimately export competitiveness in intermediate, consumer-durable and producer goods.

In contrast to the colonial developmental state, Korea Inc. was committed to export development, a discipline that was also unfamiliar to most
third world industrialisation programmes. The initial economic programme
of the military junta paid little attention to export development. Under the
First Plan, the most ambitious growth rate was envisaged for the machinery sector rather than for light manufacturing (Government 1962: 49). The
chemical industry was designated to be the largest recipient of manufacturing sector investment funds (D.-C. Park 1996: 167). The decisive year
was 1963 in the transition to the development strategy based on the export
of light manufactures. The transition came about as a result of US pressure
(e.g. by the contraction in aid and by calls for a return to civilian rule) and
from the demonstrated growth potential of exports after 1961.

The term 'export platform' only partially conveys the nature of the
development trajectory initiated in 1963, for such a depiction does not con-
vey the interdependence between import substitution and export promotion.
The goal of heavy industrial self-sufficiency was never abandoned. Indeed,
the Second Economic Development Plan (1967–71) envisaged the changing
of the percentage ratios of light to heavy industry from 72 : 28 to 66 : 34
(Government 1967: 4). The Third and Fourth Plans envisaged even more
ambitious secondary import substitutions. Korean development planners
seemed to be well aware of the necessity of continuous industrial upgrading
(by means of public ownership, if necessary, as in the case of steel) and the
weaknesses of the industrial structure based on labour-intensive sectors:

> [The] export structure is greatly dependent on the country's export
> competitiveness based on low wages, because the bulk of Korean
> exports consist of labour-intensive light industrial products. This makes
> it difficult for the country to improve its terms of trade. . . . the dis-
> equilibrium in the balance of payments results basically from Korea's
> industrial structure itself. *This situation calls for stepped up efforts to build
> a resource-saving industrial structure, while developing greater self-sufficiency in
> raw materials and capital goods.*
>
> (OPC 1977: 141–2 [italics added])

While this type of analysis had much in common with the justifications
for heavy industrialisation efforts launched elsewhere (e.g. with ECLA-
inspired formulations for Latin American ISI), Korean heavy industrialisation was far more strongly committed to creating export winners out
of target industries:

> [The] most basic task of the nation will be to develop the most suit-
> able plans for developing the right kinds of heavy and chemical
> industries in order to establish a self-reliant industrial structure and

reduce external dependence. Toward such an end, it is important to give priority to international competitiveness, in consideration of inter-industry relations, Korea's comparative advantages, the sizes of developable markets, technological requirements, and the availability of capital. *Accordingly, it will be necessary to develop technology-intensive indus-tries needed to produce domestic substitutes for imports used for export production, thereby increasing the ratios of net foreign exchange earned through exports. To further improve the balance of payments position of the country, it is also desir-able to re-orient existing industries toward export markets.*

(OPC 1977: 149 [italics added])

The export of light manufactures represented the means towards the development of an integrated industrial structure. The designation of new priority sectors and continuous secondary import substitution was a policy consistent with export promotion. Foreign exchange earnings from exports would support the nascent heavy sectors. These new sectors would in turn reduce the import content of exports, and would be pushed to become export winners themselves. Light manufacturing exports owed their origin to the import substitution carried out in the 1950s, and a similar path was envisaged for heavy industry. The effect of continuous import substitution after 1961 was such that by 1978, heavy industry accounted for the major share of manufacturing output and value added. The long-term nature of most of the import-substitution projects of the 1960s and 1970s points to the plan-driven nature of Korean industrialisation. Premised on the belief that comparative advantage was not something that spontaneously emerged but had to be actively fostered by the state, Korean planning and inter-vention represented a latter-day form of mercantilism with market characteristics.

Economic concentration, non-productive activities and corruption

In the Introduction I mentioned that the emergence of neo-liberalism from the late-1970s not only restated the traditional economic critiques of inter-vention but was supported by an analysis of the state based on the methodology of neo-classical economics (so-called 'neo-classical political economy', or NPE). The assumptions about private interest maximisation leads on to the NPE assertions about the likely abuse of bureaucratic power. The potential for bureaucratic abuse points to the undesirability of government economic intervention (see e.g. Bates 1981; Olson 1982). From this line of reasoning, the exercise of so much economic power by the Korean state should have resulted in a developmental disaster rather than a miracle.

The problems of cronyism and corruption associated with state power so stylised by the NPE were already diagnosed by Syngman Rhee's US advisers in their analysis of the Korean banking system of the early-1950s. The list of irregularities included loans to unreliable borrowers with collaterals inadequate to their borrowings, loans for speculative purposes, and loans for 'obscure purposes' (Bloomfield and Jensen 1951: 68–9). The striking feature of the Korean developmental state is that growth was maintained and living standards transformed in spite of the existence of many of the distortions attributed to intervention by the NPE: economic concentration; non-productive activities; and corruption. So how can these paradoxes be resolved? What were the countervailing tendencies in favour of economic growth? Let us consider each distortion in turn.

Intervention in Korea was associated with the growth of economic concentration. The incentive system poured subsidised credit into those companies that were exporting successfully. On the basis of their proven records, many of those same companies were selected for import substitution in heavy industry through which they received massive subsidies, especially in the 1970s when capital-intensive projects received top priority. This combination of subsidy and diversification gave rise to today's conglomerate-dominated economy. By 1977, the top thirty conglomerates, or *chaebol*, accounted for one-third of mining and manufacturing shipments. The rise of the *chaebol* was the logical outcome of an incentive system that rewarded the successful. It sprang also from the practical needs of planning. If the state was to direct industrialisation effectively, then, apart from the public ownership path of Taiwanese heavy industry, the most sensible choice was to concentrate resources behind the most successful industrialists. In line with the claims made by the critics of intervention, the official policy of economic concentration did produce distorting effects, notably the squeezing of small and medium-sized industries, growing income inequality and the targeting of unsuitable industries (more of which below).

However, such symptoms of uneven development appeared within a context of sustained growth and rising incomes. So why was the deliberate favouritism shown towards officially designated 'national champions' compatible with sustained growth in Korea, when similar strategies of concentration failed elsewhere? In contrast to the experience of most LDCs, the policies of concentration did not eliminate the dynamic of competition among the recipients of state favour. Apart from having to compete on world markets, the *chaebol* competed fiercely with one another for official favour. Many of the top *chaebol* of the 1960s lost their prominence a decade later as state support was switched to more dynamic companies (e.g. the decline of Samwha to the third tier compared to the meteoric promotion of Daewoo to the first), a phenomenon described by Amsden as a 'switch in industrial leadership' (1989: Ch. 10). Export targets provided the state with a crude but effective yardstick for selecting the entrepreneurs most worthy of subsidy. Another contrast with other LDCs that tried unsuccessfully to select national champions was that Korean policy drew on a successful colonial precedent. The colonial economy was dominated by a small number of officially favoured Japanese conglomerates, or *zaibatsu*, such as Mitsubishi, Mitsui, Sumitomo. These were forerunners of the *chaebol* that emerged in 1960s' Korea. (The terms *zaibatsu* and *chaebol* are written using the same Chinese characters.) Contemporary Japanese export promotion policies, such as the creation of General Trading Companies, were also emulated by the Koreans.

Unproductive forms of money making is another economic distortion associated with intervention by the NPE. I have previously outlined the structure of incentives and sanctions used by the Park regime to steer the business sector towards productive activities after 1961. However, that is not to say that all non-productive activities were eliminated under the new developmentalist regime. Indeed, the structure of incentives and sanctions in operation after 1961 opened up new avenues for profiteering. Soft loans could be partially re-lent on the unregulated (kerb) financial market at much higher rates of interest. Exporters could also overestimate the amount of imported materials required for export production and then sell the surplus on the domestic market at a profit. But the crucial point is that after 1961 the opportunity to exploit such loopholes was open only to those who were fulfilling the government's development targets, and especially of export growth. In effect, non-productive activities would thrive only on the basis of successful industrial performance.

Related to the debate about the association of intervention with the rise of non-productive activities is the issue of corruption. As described in the Introduction, one of the central claims of the NPE is that special interests target politicians and administrators in order to generate preferential policy formulation and implementation (or, put in another way, the market for discretionary favours expands). It is then argued that the more the state is enmeshed in the economy the stronger is the incentive for lobbying and the more resources are diverted towards such 'rent seeking' and away from productive use. Corruption was rife under the regime of Syngman Rhee, whose import-substitution policies accorded great discretionary power to public officials. In such an environment, businesses wishing to prosper needed to bribe the right officials and, crucially, make donations to Rhee's ruling Liberal Party. From NPE, one would expect the dynamism of the Korean economy after 1961 to have been associated with the reduction of the state's discretionary powers over business. But, as we have seen, such powers actually grew under the Park regime. Moreover, rapid growth and the transformation of living standards coincided with the existence of considerable corruption. For example, President Park's Democratic Republican Party became the principal beneficiary of (compulsory) business donations. Korea's experience indicates that corruption may lubricate as well as block the engine of growth.

If corruption survived after 1961, then what accounts for its transition from 'sand' to 'oil' in the engine of development? Here, the executive's commitment to achieving export targets needs to be re-emphasised. For businessmen seeking official favour, after 1961, bribery alone would no longer suffice, and contribution to national development had to be demonstrated. Compared to its predecessors, the Park regime had consistent and easily measured economic targets, and its rule enforcement was perceived to be more formidable. The effectiveness attributed to state capacities was indicated in a survey cited by Jones and Sakong in which 78 per cent of respondents thought it impossible to avoid compliance with the directives of the Park government, whereas only 3 per cent thought likewise of the Rhee government (Jones and Sakong 1980: 137).

Economic nationalism

The history of Korean industrialisation has been that of a determined response to perceived external threats with the ultimate objective of enhancing the nation's room for manoeuvre in an inhospitable international system. To the North Koreans' doctrine of *juche* (being the master of one's fate) stands the South Koreans' usage of similar terms, such as *chaju* (autonomy) and *chalip* (standing up for oneself). The modernisation effort of the 1960s and 1970s represented the latest chapter in Korea's long history of adaptation to her powerful neighbours. Historically, Korea has emulated and indigenised foreign social models: traditional Korea and the Chinese Confucian bureaucratic state; South Korea and the Japanese developmental state; and North Korea and Stalinism–Maoism. Such duplication in part reflected the foreign powers' influence over the Koreans, but imitation of foreign social models has also been the result of Korean nationalist attempts to build a stronger state, one more resistant to external domination. This accounts for the zeal with which the imported foreign social systems have been applied. And so the authoritarian state-driven pattern of industrialisation was not only the product of foreign influence (Japanese colonialism and US containment policy) but also of the Korean impulse towards self-strengthening. The nationalist orientation of the Korean developmental state should be set against this historical background.

Commentators have identified the role of economic nationalism in shaping the course of Korean industrialisation strategy towards rapid growth with the minimisation of direct external influence. Historically, economic nationalism is associated with projects of late-industrialisation. Korea in the 1920s and 1930s became the scene for the initiation of such a project by an alliance of the Japanese state and monopoly capital (Zo 1978). As Japanese colonial subjects, the Korean populace suffered terribly for the most part but thousands of the luckier ones got administrative and technical jobs under the colonial order. (Korea's leading universities were established during the Japanese period.) Of the hundreds of thousands conscripted for the Imperial Army, a small number were recruited into the officer corps. One such trainee was Park Chung-Hee (aka Lieutenant

Minoru Okimoto). If Japanese colonialism exploited Korea and left the local population divided, it also created a stratum of military and civilian bureaucrats with experience of administering a modernising economy. Japanese economic development demonstrated to Korean leaders such as Park what could be achieved by a society with a similar cultural background and equally limited natural resource endowments.

Apart from Japanese colonialism, another intellectual source of bureaucracy-led modernisation, or developmentalism, came to Korea from the US, especially in the form of military training. From the outbreak of the Korean War in 1950, the peninsula was deemed vital to US strategic interests. American assistance transformed the Korean military into one of the largest in Asia, and imbued it with US doctrines of anti-communism and the national security state. From the vantage point of these doctrines, the conditions of 1960–1 (mounting popular dissatisfaction with Syngman Rhee and his replacement by a weak democratic government in 1960; faltering economy in contrast with rapid North-Korean industrialisation; and the radicalisation of sections of the student movement) fully justified the military intervention and necessitated policies that would revive economic growth.

Aside from security, economic development would serve another purpose, to build support for a military regime lacking legitimacy. In spite of the failures of the Chang Myon government, there was little overt popular enthusiasm for the military takeover. Pressure to return to civilian rule came also from the US (with which Chang was closely associated). It was clear to the coup leaders that direct military rule would have to give way to a civilian form of government involving some degree of political contestation. To placate the US, the military junta established the Democratic Republican Party (DRP) (a name indicative of Korea's attachment to the US) as its civilian front, and Park Chung-Hee was chosen as the DRP's candidate for the 1963 presidential election. Park and the DRP came to be defined by their commitment to economic development, a stance that would yield substantial electoral rewards during the 1960s (when conservative opposition parties lacked an alternative programme of economic and social regeneration). The military's self-appointed task of national revitalisation was explained by President Park himself:

> [We] must liberate the people from poverty and establish a self-reliant economy. Because our people have been exhausted by poverty, there is among us a tenacious habit of thinking that this condition cannot be changed. The people have never seen the formation of national capital; political brokers overran the nation . . .
>
> (Park Chung-Hee 1970: 120)

Without being explicitly informed by the most fashionable theoretical advice on escape routes from the periphery (cf. the role of the ECLA in Latin American development), Korean development strategy demonstrated a remarkable capacity for capitalising on international opportunities while avoiding the associated traps. Export promotion and domestic market protection enabled Korean producers to realise the benefits of open economics, without succumbing to its dangers (e.g. penetration by TNCs, collapse of infant industries, capital flight, wastage of foreign exchange through luxury imports). The emphasis on export promotion enabled Korea to avoid the worst excesses of ISI. By contrast, those developing countries that implemented ISI without a strong export orientation found themselves lumbered with inefficient industrial structures after the early 'horizontal' industrialisation spurt, a condition that paved the way for the direct entry of TNCs (both Brazil and Argentina moved in this direction in the mid-1960s as a result of the contradictions of their ISI programmes).

Whereas TNCs played an active role in concurrent developmentalist projects elsewhere and helped to foster 'dependent' forms of industrialisation (e.g. on Brazil, see Cardoso 1973 and Evans 1979), Korea's developmentalism took on a highly nationalistic form. The strong nationalist inclination of economic policy was apparent from the earliest policy documents of the Park regime that called for the creation of heavy industry and 'guided capitalist development'. Even though autarkic development (as espoused by some junta members after 1961) was rebuffed by Washington, nationalist economic goals could still be accommodated within the export orientation required by the US. As it turned out, export development proved to be highly conducive to the goal of industrial upgrading. Apart from the commitment to developing an integrated industrial structure, economic nationalism was defined by the predominance of domestic ownership. The concern with domestic ownership led to a preference for foreign savings (as domestic savings could not keep up with the high investment rate) in the form of commercial loans rather than direct investment.

The exclusion of foreign companies and of those imports directly competitive with domestic products was designed to promote Korea's own 'national champions', the *chaebol* (this did not preclude access to foreign finance and technology deemed crucial to national industrialisation, which was facilitated by the state). Korea's ability to maintain a high growth rate while minimising foreign ownership was praised by western dependency theorists. In a perverse way, Korea's avoidance of the typical 'dependency traps' associated with foreign capital penetration (e.g. entry of TNCs and the subsequent suffocation of nascent domestic producers) could be taken as the exception that proved the rule: successful national industrialisation would take place only under special circumstances.

What, then, were the special circumstances that enabled Korean industrialisation to assume a national rather than dependent form? A combination of international and domestic forces pushed Korea's developmentalism in a highly nationalistic direction, with significant consequences for reform in later decades. Given the association between late-industrialisation and military security, an obvious source of economic nationalism was the necessity of establishing a self-sufficient local defence industry to deter communist attack. The 1961 coup took place against the threatening backdrop of North Korea's industrial recovery. The coincidence of unfavourable security circumstances helps to explain the decision to accelerate heavy industrialisation in 1973. Another external source of Korean economic nationalism was the historic relationship with Japan. While Korean industrialisation was facilitated by the transfer of finance and techniques from Japan, it was undoubtedly driven also by a desire to turn the tables on the former colonial oppressor. In effect, Japan's national industrialisation provided Korea with a concrete pathway to emulate whereas Latin American projects of national development could draw only on the abstract benchmarks of ECLA models.

From an economic perspective, the imperative of developing an integrated industrial structure could be traced also to the logic of export development. The import-intensity of light manufacturing exports and rising labour costs created pressures for capital deepening. From a class-interest perspective, economic nationalism coincided with the economic and political interests of the developmentalist alliance of bureaucrats and big business. The policy of national ownership was functional to regime maintenance. For a regime eager to bolster legitimacy, industrial self-sufficiency fostered national pride as symbolised by Park Chung-Hee's comment that 'steel equals national power'. Commentators on capitalist late-industrialisation (e.g. Moore 1984: 441–2) have remarked on the role of nationalism as a device for attenuating class tensions. In the case of Korea, the equation of industrial self-sufficiency with national power was particularly important given the illegitimate origins of modern bureaucracy and capitalism (as appendages of Japanese colonialism) and the existence of a rival nationalist Korean model (in the shape of North Korean *juche*). Reliance on domestic companies enhanced the state's overall control of the economy and brought benefits to the regime, as grateful companies would kick-back money to the ruling party. As for big businesses, the drive to self-sufficiency enabled them to expand into sectors that would otherwise have been dominated by TNCs. By undertaking the projects most strategic to the state, the industrialists would build up their own indispensability and political leverage.

International factors facilitating neo-mercantilism

Both the US and Japan were crucial to the resourcing of the Korean industrialisation effort. Each imparted peculiar characteristics to Korea's development trajectory. The US shaped the general direction after 1953: who would rule Korea; how they would rule; and how the country would pay its way in the world. The most powerful organisation in Korean society, the military, was also the one most sensitive to US pressure. The influence of Japan, on the other hand, was manifested in the shape of economic policy: the policy instruments; the economic institutions; and as a pointer to future stages. The two influences meshed together in the 1960s when US policy in Asia shifted towards lessening her own burden by according a greater role for a re-industrialised Japan in the economic support of Taiwan and Korea. Within this arrangement, Korea would be revived by Japanese aid. One political casualty was Syngman Rhee, who incurred American displeasure (e.g. aid was slashed by one-third in 1957) by resisting this grand design.

The US, while disapproving of specific actions and even facilitating the fall of both Rhee and Park, had the impact of reinforcing the Korean developmental state, especially during its formative first decade. While the initial inclination of the military junta for economic autarky was blocked by US pressure, this did not scupper the quest for industrial diversification. Instead, it forced the Koreans into realising the goal by more efficient means. The Vietnam War (1964–73) was another source of US transfer to Korea. Relations were strained in the 1970s as Park's ever-more overt authoritarianism and ambitious heavy industrialisation drive (funded by petro-dollars after 1973) were unpopular with the US. Even so, the economic vitality of Korea could not have been maintained without the benign attitude of the US in both military aid and trade. In spite of growing concern at the trade threat posed by Japan and the NICs during the 1970s, only mildly restrictive measures were adopted by the industrialised countries under US leadership (e.g. in the form of the Multi-Fibre Agreements). The demand for full trade reciprocity did not emerge until well into the 1980s, and when it did it marked the turning-point for the developmental state.

The evolution of the world economy and of the regional economy was also favourable to Korean-style industrialisation. World trade in manufactures was expanding at an unprecedented rate. The rules of international trade allowed the more nationalistic features of Korea's development strategy to escape sanction on the basis of 'infant industry' arguments. The industrialised countries' transition from, first, light and then capital-intensive forms of industry created new niches for ambitious industrialisers such as Korea. In this way, the nationalistic aims of Korea's development strategy – industrial deepening and diversification – were congruent with the international restructuring of core capital. Having recovered her position as a major industrial power by the mid-1960s, Japan would exert both a facilitating and a limiting effect on Korea's quest for autonomy.

A move orchestrated by the US, but also favoured in Seoul and Tokyo, the normalisation of relations in 1965 resumed the flow of Japanese funds and technology into Korea after an absence of twenty years. While there was a shared US and Japanese interest in the economic revitalisation of Korea, their differences over the specifics provided space for the Park regime to manoeuvre its development strategy in a highly nationalistic direction. Whereas the US attitude to Korea was inclined towards cautious-ness and pessimism (e.g. the local US commander, General Wedemeyer, dismissed the feasibility of Korean industrialisation in 1957), Japanese capital would play a pivotal role in supporting ambitious Korean plans. While international advisers dismissed the feasibility of Korean plans for the building of a steel mill in 1968, Japanese suppliers stepped in to furnish the finance and technical know-how. Similarly, the industrial diversifica-tion drive of the 1970s was based on the import of Japanese inputs. The US looked on the Korean plan with scepticism, but for strategic consid-erations refrained from using her full power (e.g. with international financiers) to bring Seoul back into line.

The US pressure in forcing the normalisation of Korean–Japanese rela-tions was motivated by the need to find outlets for Japanese capital as well as the need for Korean recovery. Economically, the Japanese returned to Korea in strength after 1965. Just as they had exploited former colonies more thoroughly than had the Europeans, Japanese government and capital had far more systematic plans for the maximisation of econ-omic benefits in Korea in 1965. The means (e.g. in the provision of supplier credits at highly concessionary terms, the cementing of deals with bribes that reportedly got kicked-back to the ruling DRP) by which it supported the Korean economic take-off of the 1960s ensured for Japanese capital a pivotal role in future Korean development plans. Thus the turn towards industrial diversification and deepening, initiated by Park Chung-Hee in the late-1960s and accelerated in 1973, complemented Japanese plans for the export of machinery and critical components to Korea. The endurance of the Japanese relationship in the quest for economic autonomy represents one of the paradoxical consequences of what I call 'hyper-developmentalism' (see below).

Authoritarianism and development

The administrative instruments and intellectual climate that enabled the state to redefine state–business relations according to exacting perform-ance standards were based upon effective coercive capacities. The Park Chung-Hee regime could be characterised as a Myrdalian 'hard' state capable of formulating and implementing policies according to long-term and rational criteria. The military coup led to the development of the state's coercive and control capacities as well as its economic ones. The military junta's determination to override all political opposition to its poli-cies was symbolised by the formation of the Korean CIA and the passage of the Anti-Communist Law in 1961 (on top of the tough provisions of the National Security Law of 1948, on the pretext of which Rhee executed a political opponent in 1958 – a former prime minister no less).

How, then, was the coercive power of the new military-based regime translated into 'autonomy' in economic policy-making, and why did such autonomy have positive effects on growth? A civilian political regime would have found it more difficult to discipline the business community towards a new economic agenda. Syngman Rhee's regime was unwilling to disrupt the existing cosy relationship between the politicians, bureaucrats and businessmen based on the allocation of aid dollars. The idea of export promotion had actually emerged under the Chang Myon regime but his government was too bogged down with immediate problems to initiate any long-term development strategy. Moreover, Chang's Democratic Party drew on similar social elites (privileged businessmen, former landlords) for support as had Rhee's Liberals. In contrast to their civilian predecessors, the military was unencumbered by previous ties to business and could redefine the state–business relationship on its own terms. The anti-corruption purge, initiated soon after the military assumed power, sent a signal to the civilian bureaucracy of the new political masters' commitment to national development. The improved performance of the economic bureaucracy has to be seen against this changed political background as well as that of institutional reorganisation. The temporary expropriation and arrest of leading tycoons soon after the military took power sent a similar signal to the business community. Enrichment would now be conditional on increasing national wealth and on compliance with official objectives. Significantly, during the period of semi-open politics (1963–72), the state maintained its autonomy from the business sector. The latter was unable to dominate the state through its financial support for the governing Democratic Republican Party (DRP). While the DRP served to legitimise the regime, the basis of Park's power continued to be the coercive agencies.

In spite of the transition from direct military rule in 1963 (to placate American opinion), the institutions of the authoritarian state remained in place and were ready to intervene at the behest of President Park. By paving the way for funding and technology transfers, the normalisation of diplomatic relations with Japan in 1965 was a key turning-point in Korean economic history. In spite of widespread opposition to reconciliation with the former colonial power, the treaty was successfully concluded. Street demonstrations that had toppled Syngman Rhee just five years earlier were now quelled by Park's martial law troops. Although electoral success of the DRP made governing easier, the capacity for authoritarian rule was highly developed, and the regime was not beholden to electoralism, as events after 1972 demonstrated.

The industrialisation project imposed the psychological cost of normal relations with Japan; but there were also material costs: on farmers suffering from the effects of urban bias; on workers having to endure exploitation by the capitalists; and on the social marginals uprooted from the land but without stable employment in the cities. Writers on Latin America have attributed the political crises of the 1960s to the early appearance of strong distributional demands, the effect of which was said to be the over-burdening of the state during the wealth-creation stage of early-industrialisation (Hirschman 1979). By contrast, the presence of a strong state and other factors ensured that popular organisations and the redistributional agenda would advance slowly in the course of Korean industrialisation.

Labour exclusion

The quiescence of labour relations during that decade reflected the difficult conditions under which the formation of the working class proceeded. Rapid growth in the 1960s was accompanied by the corresponding formation of an industrial working class recognisable by its standard objective traits: non-ownership of the means of production; acquisition of the means of livelihood by waged labour; and employment under factory conditions involving cooperation and mechanisation. The collective identity and organisational capacity of Korean labour, however, were weakly developed. In part, this reflected the common problems of labour organisation associated with early-industrialisation. For example, being recent arrivals from the countryside, most workers had relatively modest expectations, with few ideas about labour rights or unionisation. To this were added such special Korean features as the sequencing of industrialisation, the nature of Korean proletarianisation and the state's anti-labour orientation.

Industrialisation in Korea occurred under the auspices of a strong state. As a result, business and labour emerged under the dominance of a highly developed authoritarian state, a climate that was inhospitable to labour organisation. They did not enjoy a period of political consolidation akin to the populist import-substitution periods of the Latin American countries (*c.* 1945–65). The history of unionisation in industrialised societies demonstrates the receptiveness of labour aristocracies (relatively well-paid, predominantly male, employed in heavy industry) to collective and socialistic appeals. By contrast, proletarianisation in Korea and other East Asian countries was dominated by light industry employing female labour and rural migrants. This resulted in the emergence of what Deyo (1989: 210–11) called the 'hyper-proletariat'. Although recognisably 'proletarian' in objective terms, such a stratum could not easily unionise. The simple skills used in light industry meant that workers were readily replaceable (especially in light of the labour surplus that existed in the 1960s) while traditional patriarchal norms reinforced the subordinate status of women workers. For the most part, enterprises tended to be non-unionised. In the interests of maximising growth, the state tolerated unscrupulous and arbitrary (sometimes violent) managerial behaviour (even though *on paper* Korea's labour laws contained some very liberal provisions), and intervened in disputes on behalf of employers.

The state's anti-labour orientation dates back to the labour-repressive practices under Japanese rule, practices common to the late-industrialisation model but manifested in a particularly militarised form in colonial Korea. Correspondingly, the history of labour protest dates back to the independence movement, a lineage that has given labour protest legitimacy. After Liberation in 1945, the official repression of popular forces resumed with the American installation of a right-wing authoritarian regime. The labour movement was brought under the control of the state. From 1946, the only legal mass labour organisation was the state-founded Federation of Korean Trades Unions (FKTU), an organisation that had originally been established with the aim of expanding right-wing political influence in the immediate aftermath of Liberation (FKTU 1979: 347–97). Later, as the focus shifted to growth, the official trades unions were geared primarily towards supporting the state's economic priorities (e.g. by promoting enthusiasm for production targets) rather than towards protecting members' rights (Jang-Jip Choi 1987: 317–21). The weakness of the labour organisations in the 1960s was reflected in a study that noted the deferential way in which union officials behaved towards the management (Ogle 1974: 23–56). To all intents and purposes, labour was effectively 'excluded' from input into economic decision-making at all levels during the period of Korea Inc.

The transformation of living standards

In a quasi-democratic and then an openly authoritarian guise, President Park managed to remain in power for almost two decades. Political discontent, while vocal at times, did not succeed in derailing the economic strategy or the foreign confidence in the Korean economy. But, in contrast to other cases in the developing world, where political longevity was associated with economic failure, Park's regime coincided with a period of development. Apart from enforcing economic priorities and repressing redistributional demands, the Korean state also succeeded in motivating public enthusiasm for development. It did this by following a growth strategy that opened up economic opportunities for broad swathes of the population. While labour as a collective entity was excluded, there existed opportunities for individual economic advancement. Just as high standards of business performance depended on incentives as well as sanctions, so coercive capacity had to be complemented by effective appeals to economic instrumentalism.

It was logical for the military, lacking intrinsic legitimacy, to cultivate popular support on the basis of superior economic competence. For the developmentalist ideology to have any credibility, however, mass living standards had to be improved. The period between 1962 and 1978 witnessed such improvement. As much as for the achievement in sustained growth, Korea earned lavish praise from development commentators for the accompanying transformation of living standards. In spite of the criticism over the widening of social disparities in the 1970s (see below), the striking feature of industrialisation in Korea was its economically inclusive nature. Compared to the NICs outside of East Asia, Korea's experience of industrialisation was distinguished by the extent to which the poor were integrated into the modern sector. The Korean drive, modelled on that of Japan, to maximise the economy's potentialities ('endogenous modernity') has been contrasted with the much less ambitious nature of Latin American industrialisation ('showcase modernity'). According to Fajnzylber (1990: 334–5), the latter's contentment with reproducing the 'American way of life' for the middle and upper classes (rather than aiming at all-out economic transformation) meant the bypassing of the interests of the excluded majority.

The basic strategy for the reduction of poverty was that of absorbing surplus labour by promoting industrial growth. The impressive growth of per capita GNP and manufacturing wages was accompanied by the reduction of urban unemployment and rural underemployment which had plagued the economy in the early-1960s. Absorption of surplus labour was shown by the declining rate of unemployment – it fell from 7.4 per cent in 1965 to 4.5 per cent in 1970 and to an all-time-low of 3.2 per cent in 1978 (official sources defining as 'employed' those working more than one hour per week). Employing a more rigorous definition of employment (as over 18 hours of work a week), an alternative estimate quoted by Hamilton put the rate of unemployment at around 15 per cent in 1965, falling to about 8 per cent by the mid-1970s (estimate by Wontack Hong, quoted in Hamilton 1986: 42–3). Even on the basis of the more rigorous measure, unemployment was still halved, meaning that labour-intensive industrialisation pulled a large section of the population from the edge of starvation and into gainful employment, a view supported also by data on declining levels of absolute poverty (e.g. from 40.9 to 9.8 per cent of households between 1965 and 1980: see Leipziger *et al.* 1992: 7) and by case studies of poor urban localities' emergence from the 'culture of poverty' (e.g. observations by Brandt of Seoul and Inchon from 1969–72 to 1976–7,

Table 2.2 Trends in income distribution 1965–96 (whole country)

	Bottom 40% (%)	Top 20% (%)	A/B	Gini Index
1965	19.34	41.81	46.3	0.344
1970	19.36	41.62	46.5	0.332
1975	16.85	45.34	37.2	0.390
1980	16.06	45.39	35.4	0.389
1985	18.91	42.72	44.3	0.345
1988	19.68	42.24	46.6	0.336
1990	21.60	38.80	55.7	0.295
1993	22.20	37.60	59.0	0.282
1996	21.16	38.01	55.7	0.295

Source: NSO (several issues) *Social Indicators in Korea*

cited in Repetto *et al.* 1980: 108–9). By international standards, the income differential between the top 20 and the poorest 40 per cent of households in Korea was indeed very narrow and led to the description of Korea's experience of development as a case of 'growth with equality', a term especially popular with international observers.

The 'growth with equality' depiction has been criticised for its reliance on official survey data that failed to include the highest income brackets (e.g. Steinberg 1982: 101–2). In spite of the favourable international comparisons, the overall trend in Korean income distribution in the 1970s was towards a widening of income disparities (see Table 2.2). After 1970 overall disparities widened, driven by the key divides: professional and blue-collar, heavy and light industry, *chaebol* and non-*chaebol*, the industrialising Seoul–southeast regions and the impoverished southwest. Only in the urban–rural divide was there a trend towards income equalisation after 1970 (a consequence of active redistributional measures).

While it was content to rely on the welfare-enhancing effects of growth, the Korean state, however, was capable of making significant distributional adjustments for the sake of its broader political and economic objectives. In two areas it was forced to implement forceful interventionary measures to redress excessive disparities. The first was the widening rural–urban divide caused by the urban bias of the grain-pricing policy. In response to President Park's loss of rural support in the 1971 election, the previous discriminatory pricing of farm products was reversed and a system of positive pricing introduced. Under the new two-tier pricing system (the Grain Management Fund), the farmers got better prices while the government continued to subsidise urban consumption. The average rate of protection for rice rose from minus 26 per cent in 1960–9 to 39 per cent in 1970–9 and 74 per cent in 1980–4. The percentages for beef in the corresponding periods were minus 20, 40 and 112. Not surprisingly, this became a major deficit item in the government budget (Moon and Kang: 1989: 200–6). On top of the reversal of the discriminatory pricing policy, the government launched the New Community Movement (*Saemaul Undong*). Under the scheme, the condition of the countryside was improved by the transfer of construction materials (especially cement, of which there was a production glut).[1] By subsidising programmes for the improvement of rural livelihoods, the New Community Movement helped to keep the rural electorate supportive of the regime. For example, in the 1978 legislative election, the DRP avoided defeat because of its success in the over-represented rural constituencies.

The other major intervention was the 3 August (or '8-3') 1972 Presidential Emergency Decree for Economic Stability and Growth, a measure designed to counteract the effects of the underground financial market (or 'kerb' market) on the real economy. The existence of the kerb was itself a by-product of financial repression. The setting of official interest rates at below market prices encouraged the formation of an underground market linking savers looking for better returns with companies unable to obtain credit from the official sector (which, being heavily subsidised was oversubscribed). In 1972, the government acted to alleviate the debt burden on the manufacturing sector at the expense of the kerb market. Reported kerb market loans were converted to long-term soft loans with three-year grace and five-year repayment periods. While the 8-3 measures demonstrated the state's commitment to industrial development over the interests of informal finance, the episode highlighted a central feature of the fragile miracle, namely, the link between the strategy of directed credit and the vulnerable financial structure of Korean business.

Although the Korean state of the 1960s and 1970s systematically excluded labour from any decision-making influence, the social implications of its development strategy were broadly inclusive. The repression of labour rights has to be seen against the existence of a broader growth environment that created powerful material incentives (employment generation, rising wages and the opening up of high-pay sectors like heavy industry and construction) for individual workers. The state was forced into making two significant distributional adjustments in the early-1970s (farm pricing and the 8-3 measures), but there was no broader shift towards active redistributional measures. It was determined that growth would lead (and lead to) welfare. This accounts for the paradox between the reality of rising living standards and the widely felt perceptions of maldistribution that oppositional forces increasingly capitalised on during the second decade of the Park regime, perceptions that have persisted despite the transformation of livelihoods in the ensuing two decades. The labour unrest of the 1979–80 period was a watershed for social development. From that point onwards (and especially under democratic governments), integrating redistributional and growth objectives in a mutually complementary way became a major concern of all regimes.

The making of a fragile miracle

Consequences of a tight state–business relationship

The foundation of Korean economic performance was, as noted by many authors, the close state–business relationship. In order to effectively guide the private sector towards national objectives, incentives were concentrated in a small number of proven exporters. By the end of the 1970s, the most successful of those favoured business groups had developed into highly diversified conglomerates, or *chaebol*. Some of these groups (e.g. Samsung, Lucky) were already well established on the local market at the inception of the military regime. Others (notably Hyundai and Daewoo) were selected by President Park as 'national champions' for their enterprise. They rose meteorically as a result. All *chaebol* were dedicated to aggressive expansion, a feature reinforced by official support. For example,

the chairman of Daewoo (Kim Woo-Choong) began with an initial investment of $18,000 in 1967; by 1983, the group had become one of the top
four conglomerates with a turnover of $4.3 billion and a workforce of
77,240 employees (Aguilar and Cho 1989: 458). Two quotes from statements made by the Daewoo chairman exemplify the drive for expansion
(by acquisition, if necessary) characteristic of the super-*chaebol* which
emerged in the 1970s:

> I know my strength as an entrepreneur; I also know my weakness as
> an organizational builder. I can be an asset for Daewoo so long as it
> grows rapidly and a liability when it needs to be stabilized.
>
> (Aguilar and Cho 1989: 470)

> Since we had little money, the only way for us to grow was to rescue
> seriously troubled companies.
>
> (ibid.: 467)

The 1970s represented the decisive stage in the formation of the *chaebol*.
Amsden (1989) has noted that in the late-1960s the state engineered a
'switch in industrial leadership' whereby many established leaders of light
industry were bypassed for the role of pioneering heavy industrial development. Responsibility was instead accorded to groups with high-growth
potential like Daewoo, or with previous experience in capital-intensive
industry (e.g. Samsung's long history in electronics). Participation in the
heavy industrialisation programme provided the selected groups with mani-
fold opportunities for expansion. The selected groups all diversified into
several heavy industries, behaviour consistent with the state's policy of
ensuring dynamism by encouraging competition between rival groups
seeking official favour (by contrast, Taiwan's heavy sectors were dominated by state-owned enterprises). For each individual *chaebol*, rapid
diversification was a sensible option, as cheap credit provided a cost-free
opportunity to become established in the 'frontier' industries. From the
perspective of business competition, a *chaebol* could not forgo the opportunity of low cost expansion into new areas since rival conglomerates were
doing the same. Leading business groups of the 1960s that were not selected
to play a leading role in HCI found themselves consigned to the third-
tier by the end of the 1970s. Non-compliance with government wishes
also brought sanctions. And sometimes acquisitions of failing companies
were encouraged by a state that wanted to avoid the loss of jobs and
capacity (with the result that the acquiring group would get even bigger).
The 1980s would see further acquisition of unviable companies forced on
reluctant *chaebol* by the government.

Many of the economic and social distortions commonly associated with
the Korean *chaebol* originated during the 1970s' period of expansion. In
terms of their overall size (Jones 1981: 98–100, 101), the largest of the

chaebol had risen to become world-class companies by the end of the decade. On the other hand, Korean groups also tended to be far more diversified than western TNCs. The individual subsidiaries of the *chaebol* tended to be small and technologically backward compared to their far more specialised TNC counterparts, a serious weakness in sectors where wages constituted only a small fraction of production costs. The dynamic of inter-*chaebol* competition in heavy industrial development meant that each *chaebol* (especially those in the top-tier) tried to do almost everything but did nothing particularly well.

Another defining feature of the Korean *chaebol* is fragile financial structure. Very high debt–equity ratios and the heavy burden of non-perfoming loans on supporting banks originated in the resourcing of HCI. The *chaebol* grew on the basis of debt rather than share capital or foreign direct investment. Expansion on the basis of debt reflected the owners' priority of maintaining familial control. It was also consistent with the state's priorities of rapid growth and keeping ownership Korean. Without the state's recourse to the *chaebol* and debt finance, heavy industry could not have developed as rapidly as it did. As in other strategic projects, it is likely that the risk and long duration of HCI would have deterred private investors (in any case, nothing approximating a developed private financial structure existed in Korea at the time). Moreover, private investors would not have tolerated the internal structure of the *chaebol*, where profitable subsidiaries supported marginal or even loss-making ones through their infancy. Controlled by the government, domestic financial institutions were required to make subsidised loans in support of the *chaebol*. Direct foreign investment was strictly limited but foreign loans played a vital role in funding the HCI drive. This was reflected in the high foreign savings' share of investment (Table 2.3).

It has been remarked that the dependence on borrowed technology forces third world business groups to expand laterally, often into unconnected areas of activity (e.g. Amsden 1989: 125–7). In theory, the conglomerate structure spreads risk and supports the entrance of affiliates into new activities. The development of the Korean *chaebol*, with their system of mutual support between affiliates, seems to accord with this line of reasoning. There was another aspect. Far from spreading financial risk, the diversification of the conglomerates and the indebtedness of their affiliates were major sources of economic instability. Given the connectedness between affiliates (e.g. by means of internal loans and cross-holding), the insolvency of one over-extended affiliate threatened to trigger chain bankruptcies throughout the group.

Diversification and debt-financed growth were also transforming the nature of the state–business relationship. As well as being the high point of direct government intervention in the economy, the HCI drive also proved to be a watershed in state–business relations. Paradoxically the economic weaknesses of the *chaebol* mentioned above also gave the major

Table 2.3 Ratio of investment to GNP (%) and foreign investment ($ million) 1976–97

	Gross investment ratio	Gross domestic investment ratio	Ratio of net lending to rest of the world
1976	25.4	26.5	−1.1
1979	29.4	35.8	−6.4
1980	23.4	31.9	−8.5
1985	29.4	30.3	−0.9
1986	33.5	29.2	4.3
1987	37.2	30.0	7.2
1988	38.8	31.1	7.7
1989	36.1	33.8	2.3
1990	36.2	37.1	−0.9
1991	36.1	39.1	−3.0
1992	35.3	36.8	−1.5
1993	35.3	35.2	0.1
1994	35.0	36.2	−1.2
1995	35.4	37.4	−2.0
1996	33.8	38.8	−5.0
1997[p]	33.6	35.3	−1.8

Source: EPB–NSO (several issues) *Major Indicators of Korean Economy*

chaebol potential leverage over the state, since the collapse of one such group (with a domino effect on smaller suppliers and sub-contractors) posed unacceptable costs in terms of lost production and jobs. Fearful of such consequences, the state has always avoided the ultimate sanction of allowing failing *chaebol* to go bankrupt. Instead, the state supported the takeover of failing groups by healthy ones (making the absorbing group bigger but more financially vulnerable – in effect, replicating the problem on a higher level). Because of the massive investments tied up in the *chaebol* that spearheaded the HCI drive, the state had less autonomy in selecting which businesses it would support (or destroy) thereafter. In effect, it became far more difficult to engineer another 'switch in industrial leadership' akin to that made in preparation for HCI. The leading industrialists had been established: they could not be dislodged without unacceptable costs to the state. This would impede subsequent official efforts aimed at industrial rationalisation, redistribution and counteracting corruption. The completion of HCI marked the beginning of the transition from state dominance of business to interdependence.

The 'reciprocal relationship' extended beyond the formal incentive structure and included the state's acceptance of domestic monopolies, unproductive forms of money making (property, recycling of funds through the kerb market) and corruption. Far from being eliminated, such activities functioned as informal incentives that motivated industrialists and public officials behind the developmental priorities. Tolerated on condition of the business sector's fulfilment of development tasks assigned by the state, such informal incentives augmented the low profit margins of many of the *chaebol*'s mainline manufacturing activities. While such activities provided informal incentives in oiling the engine of development (in contrast to the predictions made by NPE), they also highlighted the tightness of the relationship between the state and selected industrialists and the costs that were imposed on less favoured sectors of society.

The existence of informal incentives sprang from the government-driven allocation of credit. Very low rates of interest meant that there was credit rationing, which resulted in the losers (smaller companies lacking collateral and those lacking government backing) having to borrow at very high rates (20–50 per cent per annum) from the unofficial financial market or kerb market (see Table 2.1). Not only did the high-risk, high-return kerb market attract private savings but financial repression raised the potential for abuse through the re-lending of official funds on the kerb. Credit diversion (or 'credit fungibility') was calculated to be very high across the manufacturing sector, with the exception of the steel and cement industries, sectors which were directly government-run (foreign loans were not so susceptible to such diversion) (Hong and Park 1986: 173–80). Alternatively, there was the option of investing in Seoul real estate – land values there were growing at a much faster rate than the economy as a whole (Jones 1981: 167–8).

The dynamic of *chaebol* expansion, their growth at the expense of the small and medium-sized sector (elements of which were potentially more efficient and innovative but lacked the resources of the *chaebol*), and households, and lopsided industrial structures raised efficiency and equity questions about the nature of government intervention. In effect, the costs of *chaebol* expansion were being socialised and imposed on households and small businesses (e.g. by way of monopolisation, spiralling property prices and regressive taxation). These illegitimate activities helped to highlight the relative disparities generated by the state's developmental policies (an issue that gained salience as absolute poverty was reduced). The structural interdependence of state and *chaebol* cemented by the HCI drive, as well as the individual benefits derived by public officials, would hamper future efforts to counteract the illicit political–economic exchanges. The difficulties encountered by the post-1987 democratic regimes in their attempts to broaden the developmentalist alliance to include organised labour had their origins in the state's attachment to business.

Hyper-developmentalism

If economic nationalism helped to steer Korea clear of the typical dependency traps, it also contributed to some of the heavy industrialisation excesses that so preoccupied the reform agenda of the 1980s and 1990s.

The promotion of 'national capital' was taken to extremes in the 1970s and was manifested in the worsening of problems that nationalism was designed to overcome, namely, vulnerability to external shocks; techno-logical dependence; and the lack of integration. The shifting of industrial promotion into overdrive, or 'hyper-developmentalism' as I have labelled it, has its roots in the regime insecurities of the 1970s. A key enabling factor was the congruence between Korean and Japanese economic objec-tives, and US political aims. The economic relationship with Japan has re-ignited debates about the extent to which Korean development was genuinely 'autocentric' or nationally oriented.

In contrast to other NICs, Korea's economic performance was impres-sive in the face of the oil and debt shocks of 1979 and 1981 respectively. Led by exports, GNP growth rebounded strongly in 1981 after a year of contraction in 1980. Although Korea became the developing world's fourth biggest debtor in 1985 (behind Brazil, Mexico and Argentina), the growth of exports kept debt-servicing ratios at manageable levels, and there was never any serious danger of default. Previously plagued by under-utilisation of capacity, the heavy industrial sectors promoted during the 1970s[2] were also showing strong signs of recovery by 1985, such that their earlier prob-lems were regarded by some commentators as those typical of industries in their growing stage. Reflections on the HCI drive generally pronounced a favourable verdict and the initiators were praised for their foresight (see e.g. Amsden 1987; for a more qualified endorsement, see Stern *et al.* 1995).

While Korea clearly outperformed Latin America, the claim that the HCI programme contributed to the Korean economy's post-1980 recovery is by no means uncontentious. First, the recovery was led by the tradi-tionally competitive labour-intensive sectors (subjected to even tougher labour controls by the new military regime from 1980). Second, the reversal of the oil prices and the lowering of interest rates brought about a general world recovery from 1983. Third, in spite of the existence of highly favourable conditions after 1983, the most capital-intensive sectors (e.g. petro-chemicals, heavy machinery) promoted under the HCI drive failed to become competitive. They burdened their supporting banks with bad debts ('non-performing loans') and became the subject of numerous state-financed restructuring programmes. Meanwhile, those ('national champions' or otherwise) that achieved international competitiveness could not escape the technological dominance of their Japanese suppliers.

Structural weaknesses of hyper-developmentalism

In retrospect, it can be seen that the seeds of many of the problems of the contemporary Korean political economy were actually sown by the HCI programme. A striking characteristic of the Korean trade structure has been the persistence of trade deficits with Japan, a reflection of Korean producers' dependence on their Japanese suppliers for machinery and critical components. Historical and logistical factors gave Japan a pivotal role in assisting the relaunch of the Korean economy after 1965. From the very beginning of the economic take-off, Japanese advice, money and technology were deeply embedded into Korean development plans (e.g. reparation aid in the form of supplier credits). Some leading Korean industrialists (e.g. Samsung's Lee Byung-Chull) were well connected with the Japanese before 1961. The effect of HCI would be to deepen Korean technological dependence on Japanese suppliers. The latter were ideally placed to assume the role of purveyor to Korean technological needs. Beginning with the integrated steelworks proposals of 1968, the US was less than enthusiastic with Korea's ever-more ambitious HCI plans. By contrast, Japanese suppliers, already familiar to their Korean counterparts, were always prepared to furnish mature technology at competitive prices (and in turn deepen the dependence on Japanese sources).

Besides Park's familiarity with Japanese methods and US strategic preference, the return of Japanese capital into Korea suited the objectives of both sides. In the Koreans' dash for growth, Japanese resources were crucial. For a Japanese economy that was just completing its own heavy industrial drive, Korea, Taiwan and (beyond that, Southeast Asia) were logical areas for expansion. Korean protectionism and preference for national ownership restricted the opportunities for Japanese direct investments and exports of finished consumer goods. On the other hand, the Korean government subsidised domestic companies' importation of inputs for exports and heavy industrial production. That these imports (except raw materials) were largely of Japanese origin demonstrated complementarity between Korean economic nationalism and the Japanese objective of exporting capital goods to emerging Asian exporters (and, in the process, boosting indirect exports to third countries). The essential components of the Korean-owned industrial structure were literally made in Japan.

The Korean industrialisation effort was motivated in part by the desire to catch up with the former colonial oppressor, and so the Korean state was not unaware of the dangers of over-reliance on Japanese suppliers. It was no coincidence that the two most successful business groups under the Park regime, Hyundai and Daewoo, advanced because they were promoted as 'national champions' in rivalry with the Japanese connected groups, Samsung and Lucky–Goldstar. The Korean state responded with its own initiatives in anticipation of the increasing reluctance of Japanese suppliers to transfer crucial technology for fear of boomerang effects. It is certainly possible to point to Korean successes in technology acquisition and development. To maximise technology transfer from their Japanese suppliers, Korean companies encouraged bids from rival foreign firms. This strategy enabled the successful development of the government-owned steel company, POSCO, nurtured first on Japanese and then on European technology (after the Japanese became reluctant to support a potential rival) into one of the world's premier producers of steel. Successful

Table 2.4 R&D expenditure at current prices 1971–96

	R&D (billion won)	R&D/GNP ratio (%)	Government sector share of R&D (%)
1971	11	0.31	62.2
1975	43	0.42	66.7
1980	212	0.57	49.8
1985	1,237	1.56	24.6
1990	3,350	1.88	19.4
1991	4,158	1.94	19.4
1992	4,989	2.09	17.2
1993	6,153	2.32	16.7
1994	7,895	2.60	16.8
1995	9,441	2.71	19.8
1996	10,878	2.81	22.8

Source: EPB/NSO (several issues) *Major Statistics*

technology acquisition was also noted for other industries (see e.g. Enos and Park 1988 on petroleum refining). The 1970s saw the beginnings of the country's independent scientific infrastructure, and Korea's R&D expenditures have compared favourably with those of other developing countries such as India (e.g. Lall 1990).

The narrowing of the per capita GNP gap between Korea and the advanced industrialised countries suggests that the disparity in capacities to fund technological development should also narrow correspondingly. While the expansion of heavy industrial capacity was impressive, technological capability lagged behind. For example, R&D in the 1970s remained at under 1 per cent of GNP (Table 2.4). While Korea's technological base might have compared favourably with other LDCs, the drive to make Korea a world competitor in HCI required massive and sustained investment in technological infrastructure. Japan's R&D spending, at 2–3 per cent of GNP (twenty times the size of Korea's GNP in 1979), already amounted to half of Korea's total national output. It has also been argued that the perpetuation of long-term technological dependence was a conscious aim of Japanese suppliers in their dealings with Korea and other Asian trade partners. The cheapness and familiarity of Japanese technology inputs made it difficult for Korean business groups ('national champions' alike) to turn to alternative suppliers. In effect, Japanese suppliers would facilitate the development of new industrial sectors in Asia but would maintain their dominance of the high value-added stages of production across all sectors (Bernard and Ravenhill 1995). This was manifested in the Asian countries' persistent trade deficits with Japan.

The structural impediments to industrial 'catch up' were made worse by the regime's deliberate policy choices in its promotion of HCI. One such choice was the preference for conglomerates over state-owned enterprises. Based on SOEs, Taiwan's HCI promotion avoided the duplication of capacity that was caused by inter-conglomerate competition. The success of the government-owned steel giant POSCO suggests that the state enterprise route, or at the very least, a stricter division of labour between the *chaebol* would have yielded superior results (e.g. in terms of focused R&D, avoidance of non-performing loans and duplication of capacity). Rationalisation of the *chaebol* into their appropriate areas of specialisation would remain an unresolved problem two decades after the HCI drive. The policy of encouraging the *chaebol* to develop several heavy sectors simultaneously also diverted resources from the SME sector. The skewing of the official lending policy in favour of the conglomerates starved SMEs of affordable credit, forcing many firms to turn to the kerb markets, where exorbitant rates applied (even though a Small and Medium Industry Bank had existed since 1961, with the expressed aim of supporting smaller firms). Potentially dynamic small exporting firms were being crowded out by the superior financial access of the *chaebol*. Another consequence was that many of the parts (the exporting of which Taiwan excelled at) that could have been domestically manufactured by SMEs were instead having to be imported or produced inefficiently inhouse by the *chaebol*. Weak SMEs was a feature that distinguished Korea from both Japan and Taiwan (Ohtsuka 1981).

In contrast to Taiwan, Korea's HCI was driven by the far more ambitious objective of becoming a world leader in HCI products. The Taiwanese strategy of producing parts for established producers was considered and rejected in favour of exporting finished items under Korean brand-names. The aim of turning Korea into a second Japan, however, was based on unrealistic assessments of Korean capabilities. Korea's HCI of the 1970s bore a resemblance to the earlier stage of Japanese heavy industrialisation in the 1950s in the industries targeted and the instruments used to promote them. In other respects, there were significant differences. I have already referred to the self-generating nature of Japanese technological capacity versus the dependent nature of the Korean one. Another significant difference was domestic market size. Due to Japan's larger population (three times that of Korea) and a higher level of prior development, the domestic market could absorb a far greater share of Japanese heavy industrial output in the 1950s than could Korea's two decades later. Although rising real wages in the 1960s underpinned the expansion of Korean light industry, similar conditions did not apply to heavy industry in the 1970s. In key products such as consumer durables, the domestic market was still not affluent enough to absorb output to any great extent. For example, spending on basic wage goods (food, drink, tobacco, clothing) still accounted for 61.4 per cent of domestic consumption expenditure in 1979 (compared with 68.6 per cent in 1971).

The plight of the car industry at the end of the 1970s was indicative of the dilemma. Owing to its linkages with other sectors (e.g. steel,

electronics), the development of this industry was a key target of the deepening programme. This resulted in an expansion of output that outstripped
the domestic capacity for absorption. To realise economies of scale, the
car industry had to produce around 250,000 units per annum while the
domestic market could absorb only about half of the 112,000 units
produced in 1979. Or, to put in another way, at Korea's level of per
capita income, the domestic market could support only *one* major domestic
producer. Yet there were already three by the end of the 1970s (Hyundai,
Daewoo, Kia).[3] Having established production facilities for the export of
heavy industrial products on a world scale (in apparent imitation of
Japanese practice), leading Korean *chaebol* would find themselves vulnerable to such downswings in the world economy as occurred between 1979
and 1983. In spite of the painful lessons of the 1970s, this basic formula
for the promotion of leading sectors (inter-*chaebol* competition leading to
the development of huge plants dependent on scale economies) persisted
(e.g. semi-conductors and steel both slumped in the 1990s because of over-
crowding).

Explaining hyper-developmentalism

The hyper-developmentalism of the HCI drive can be explained as the
response of an ambitious modernising regime under conditions of external
and domestic threat. By 1972, there had developed a deep sense of vulnerability and a realisation of Korea's continuing economic limitations in spite
of her accomplishments over the previous decade. The high import content
of light-manufactured exports was cited as a central weakness of the
development based on light manufacturing exports:

> The Korean economy has grown rapidly since the latter half of the
> 1960s, chiefly through the expansion of foreign trade. For this reason,
> within the national economy or in various fields of the economy, the
> realignment of the economy has yet to be realised. Moreover, because
> of its heavy dependence on foreign capital, the economy has a very
> weak adaptability to development in the international economic situ-
> ation.
>
> (OPC 1973: 139–40)

There were other inter-related dimensions of vulnerability. The exhaus-
tion of the growth potential (as a consequence of limited scale, insufficient
domestic demand, backward technology) in the import-replacement industries evident in Latin America and elsewhere was also identified by Korean
planners:

> With the passing of the boom in automobile, television and refriger-
> ator manufacturing industries and in the construction industry as

demand for their products is now increasing at a much slower tempo than before, the growth of these and related import-replacing industries appears to have reached its limit.

(OPC 1972: 200)

And then there were the unfavourable developments in the international environment. These included: the running down of a costly war in Vietnam that had netted Korea over $1 billion of foreign exchange (a sign of America's unwillingness to involve herself in further wars in Asia); the emergence of China and other cheaper exporters of light manufactures; and the reappearance of protectionist practices among the industrialised countries (on the impact of the changing international division of labour, see Dae-Hwan Kim 1987). The solution to all these problems seemed to converge on one policy: accelerated self-sufficiency in intermediate and capital goods. Inputs hitherto imported could be provided domestically, while new export sectors would arise:

In the export field, the present method of exporting goods which are processed domestically after the direct import of machines and technology from advanced countries should be ended. *The export method should be converted into an active one of developing technology by ourselves and exploring new strategic export items so that the nation may not lag behind others in the keen competition waged on the world market.*

(OPC 1973: 140 [italics added])

Meanwhile, a heavy industrial capacity would assuage Korea's sense of military vulnerability in the wake of America's Vietnam debacle and yield other economic linkages:

An industry dependent on science and technology, the munitions industry will help develop machinery and special metal-working, chemical and petrochemical industries in the course of producing weapons, explosives and ammunition. It will also help achieve industrial integration in similar lines of industries and inter-industrial cooperation.

(OPC 1972: 210)

Domestic political pressures were also impelling the regime towards overt authoritarianism and HCI. The popular challenge to President Park's rule intensified in 1971. Park won a fraudulent victory over Kim Dae-Jung in the presidential race while the Chun Tae-Il incident signalled the beginning of labour activation. Because capitalism and bureaucracy lacked legitimacy owing to their colonial origins, developmentalism was a crucial legitimising factor for the military-based regime between 1961 and 1979. The overtly authoritarian Yushin system was installed in 1972 in response to the regime's loss of its electoral mandate the year previously. From

1972, the regime relied instead on security and breakneck industrialisation for its legitimation.

Labour exclusion and activation

Amsden's assertion that: 'Paternalism in Korea since the military coup in 1961 has witnessed almost three decades of relatively peaceful labor relations' (1989: 325) overstates the stability of Korean labour relations during the period of Park's rule. In contrast to the 1960s, the acceleration of heavy industrialisation in the 1970s was marked by a turn towards labour activism and strikes. This occurred despite the intensification of labour controls that accompanied the transition to authoritarianism in 1972 (e.g. the banning of strikes in foreign-invested enterprises). The political turning-point came in 1971, when a young worker called Chun Tae-Il burned himself to death in protest at the state's failure to enforce labour rights. (The labour code ostensibly contained some very liberal provisions.) In the same year, a Special Law on National Security was enacted, a law which tightened the restrictions on labour (e.g. banning strikes, making government intermediation binding and final). The stronger position of labour during the 1970s arose from a combination of market and institutional factors.

The abundance of labour became a thing of the past as the rate of unemployment dropped to an all-time-low of 3.2 per cent in 1978. It has been argued that by the mid-1970s, Korea had reached the Lewisian turning-point in which the unlimited supply of unskilled labour was exhausted (Bai 1982). The manpower shortage was not confined to technical sections. Growing rapidly on subsidised credit, heavy industry could afford to pay skilled workers well. Wages were driven up by the *chaebol* in the scramble for skilled workers (for individual companies, poaching skilled workers trained by others made economic sense). In addition, the post-1974 overseas construction boom helped to exacerbate the domestic labour shortage by employing about 250,000 Koreans. The shortage of skilled labour was exacerbated also by the gender segmentation of the labour force that kept women out of the high-paying domains reserved for men. Women were excluded from white-collar supervisory and technical roles as well as from most capital-intensive blue-collar work (Cho 1986: 165–8).

One reason for the tightening of the labour market was the slowing down of rural out-migration after the government's introduction of price supports in 1971. The continuous rise in manufacturing unit labour costs was not determined by the labour market conditions alone (e.g. rural migration to the cities accelerated from 67,000 in 1976 to 252,000 in 1977 and 430,000 in 1978, see Park and Castenada 1987: 16): the rise was determined also by the changing institutional context in which wage bargaining took place. Foremost among these changes was the development of labour consciousness and solidarity. This was evident from labour's

Table 2.5 Industrial disputes and their causes 1975–97 (by number of disputes)

	Total disputes	Workers involved ('000s)	Working days lost ('000s)	Wage bargaining	Delayed wages	Unfair labour practice	Better labour conditions	Others
1975	133			42	22			
1976	110	7	17	31	37	8	4	30
1977	96	8	8	36	30	6	2	22
1978	102	11	13	45	29	2	—	26
1979	105	14	16	31	36	3	—	35
1980	407	49	62	38	287	—	14	68
1981	186	35	31	38	69	4	32	43
1982	88	9	12	7	26	—	21	34
1983	98	11	9	8	35	—	19	36
1984	113	16	20	29	39	7	14	24
1985	265	29	64	84	61	12	47	61
1986	276	47	72	75	48	16	48	89
1987	3,749	1,262	6,947	2,613	45	65	566	460
1988	1,873	293	5,401	946	59	59	136	673
1989	1,616	409	6,351	742	59	10	21	784
1990	322	134	4,487	167	10		2	143
1991	234	175	3,271	132	5		2	95
1992	235	105	1,528 (132.1)	134	27			74
1993	144	109	1,308 (111.3)	66	11			67
1994	121	104	1,484 (120.7)	51	6			64
1995	88	50	393 (30.8)	33	—			55
1996	85	79	893 (68.5)	19	1			65
1997	78	44	445 (33.6)	18	3			57

Note: data in parentheses under 'working days lost' denotes rates of days not worked per 1,000 workers

Source: MOL (several issues) *Yearbook of Labour Statistics*; EPB/NSO (several issues) *Major Statistics of Korean Economy*; ILO (1998) *Yearbook of Labour Statistics*

preparedness to strike (see Table 2.5). In effect, as industrial employment grew, proletarianisation in the subjective sense was also taking shape. Between 1971 and 1978, production workers in the total workforce grew from 19.5 to 29.3 per cent. Deyo attributes Korean labour's capacity for defiance to the existence of 'stable proletarian employment systems' of relatively privileged workers brought about by heavy industrialisation (Deyo 1989: 211), a feature that distinguished Korea from Taiwan and the city–states of Hong Kong and Singapore.

Labour demands for a minimum wage grew during the course of the 1970s. Beneath the rapidly growing wages for which Korea was internationally famed lurked vast pockets of subsistence pay (e.g. Jang-Jip Choi 1989: 300–4), endured especially by women workers in the mass export sectors such as textiles, garments and electronics. Pay and conditions in the foreign invested free-trade zones also became a matter of controversy (e.g. Committee for Justice and Peace of South Korea 1976; AMPO 1977). Macro-data conceal the even worse plight of the 'social marginals' (composed primarily of recent arrivals from the rural sector) who were underemployed or were forced to work in the informal sector under squalid conditions (Chang-Soo Kim 1977: 28–30). A KDI report found that the majority of those living below the poverty line consisted of the 'working poor', usually temporary and casual production and agricultural workers with inadequate incomes (Sang-Mok Suh 1980: 361–2). The declining poverty gap (i.e. the amount that had to be spent in order to bring the poor to a level above the poverty line) to GNP ratio highlighted the growing capacity of the government to alleviate the problem (ibid.: 352).

Labour expectations of relative equality advanced with the overall modernisation of society. In the initial phase of industrialisation, urban employment facilitated political stabilisation by improving the living standards of rural migrants (who also remitted money back to the country-side). But as absolute poverty declined, the issue of relative poverty emerged, as criteria such as GNP growth, the dangerous and degrading conditions of work as well as the material progress made by other sections of society (such as employers and senior government officials) rather than subsistence increasingly shaped workers' perceptions of their condition. The official ideology of patriotic labour was being eroded by the practices of unscrupulous employers sanctioned by the government (Jang-Jip Choi 1989: 70–1, 73–4). In spite of their links to the government, the unions helped to transform workers' conception of the minimum wage: from individual subsistence to the level required for the maintenance of a family (ibid.: 281).

The advance of proletarianisation was also the consequence of deliberate educative efforts of progressive groups. There were also deliberate attempts by radical organisations, especially church-based ones (such as the Protestant Urban Industrial Mission [UIM] and the Catholic Young Christian Workers), to campaign for workers' rights and heighten consciousness.

Government concern about the UIM suggests that these radical forces exercised growing influence in the workplace despite strict official sanctions. One source noted the emergence of 'core' groups (consisting of: charismatic individual leaders and their close associates; production line team leaders associated with the UIM; union leaders educated by the central unions or the Christian Academy; and student turned workers) at the head of worker protests in the 1970s (Jeong-Taik Lee 1988: 146–7). The growth of the union movement in the 1970s may have reflected the state's attempt at incorporation, but the effect of such organisational absorption was to advance workers' expectations and their capacity for collective action in support of their interests.

Korea Inc. employed systematic and repressive labour controls administered directly by the state or by employers with state support. The effect of this was to poison labour relations, creating the basis for the explosion of labour discontent in the immediate post-democratisation years. Rapid industrialisation based on the *chaebol* and the repressive labour policies that went with it left a confrontational legacy that would make subsequent reconciliation difficult. The situation of labour shortage that had emerged by 1978 was an early indicator that labour relations would have to change towards a more consensual pattern. Instead, the coercive model was prolonged for another decade. Both labour and business came to be thoroughly socialised into the mentality of confrontation as a result. This would inhibit democratic government attempts to implement much-needed labour market reforms on the basis of consensus. Although living conditions improved immeasurably under authoritarian regimes, the way in which this was achieved did little to bolster political legitimacy. Improvements in living standards were delivered by an economic strategy oriented towards growth and employment generation rather than by redistribution (this explains the turn towards more positive redistributional policies from 1981, a trend greatly accelerated after 1987). On the other hand the potential for organised labour resistance was also enhanced by the high level of economic concentration and heavy industrial bias that favoured the development of 'stable industrial proletariat' more akin to the Latin American pattern (Deyo 1987: 196). Another factor inhibiting the development of consensual relations was the existence of the unpopular political–economic exchanges (e.g. corruption) that reinforced the state's image of being pro-*chaebol*.

Sources of social discontent

The accentuation of the issues of relative income and sectoral inequalities during the 1970s was a product of the state's industrialisation policies, especially the very rapid expansion of heavy industrial development and overseas construction after 1973. The Korean state was committed to improving living standards by growth and employment generation. The direct alleviation of poverty by redistributive measures received low priority. For example, that only half of those deemed to be in absolute poverty were in receipt of government assistance showed the low priority accorded to redistribution during this period (even if the *scope* of social assistance widened, particularly in the 1970s). That the share of public expenditures devoted to health, education and welfare in Korea was well below international norms was the result of deliberate policy (Bahl *et al.* 1986: 219). Corresponding to the reduction of absolute poverty, the issue of relative disparity came to the fore. The state's adherence to its basic strategy for poverty reduction by growth promotion enabled its opponents (politicians opposed to the DRP, civic organisations and radical labour activists), to mobilise popular support on the basis of redistribution after 1971.

The egalitarianism controversy

Korea's egalitarianism has been widely praised from a comparative perspective. Export development promoted equality during the 1960s by reducing the high levels of unemployment through the creation of labour-intensive employment (e.g. Rao 1978). Distribution became more uneven after 1970 (see Table 2.2). A study using three measures of distribution (decile distribution, the Theil index, Gini coefficient) indicates that the slight improvement in distribution in 1965–70 was reversed thereafter (Choo 1980: 288–9). The overall pattern of income distribution was driven by developments in the urban sector (the narrowing of the rural–urban gap between 1971 and 1976 actually coincided with an overall deterioration of income distribution).

The gap widened between white-collar (especially the 'new middle class' of educated personnel such as managers, administrators and engineers) and blue-collar workers, between heavy and light industrial workers and between large and small businesses. That the declining income share for the lowest 40 per cent of employer households was being matched by concentration in the top 30 per cent was an indicator of the rise of the *chaebol* (Choo 1980: 293). Trends in income disparity reflected the tight labour market for skilled labour (as discussed above), the higher productivity of capital-intensive sectors and also the high male concentration in HCI and top white-collar posts. By contrast, pay in many sections of light industry (where plants tended to be smaller and female concentration higher) remained below the manufacturing average. In effect, a gap was opened up on the basis of education and also between those employed in the priority sectors and those in the rest of the economy.

Social development

Social development and the existence of relative poverty became a more sensitive political issue in the 1970s as the persistence of social deprivation contrasted with rapid economic growth. Consistent with its priority of growth first, government expenditure on economic development out-stripped spending on social development. Such an ordering of preferences was not surprising. In a semi-industrialised country like Korea, social expenditures diverted scarce resources from industrial investment. In con-trast to other semi-industrialised societies, the Korean government kept social expenditures strictly under control. Not only did unsustainable levels of social expenditure contribute to the fiscal crises typical of the Latin American populism but the absence of social provision was an incentive to household saving. Having never been subject to populist pressures, the Korean government could keep social expenditures under tight rein. In spite of the priority accorded to promoting economic development, the government nevertheless presided over a rising share of GNP devoted to social expenditure and it also extended the scope of social provision in the 1970s. The political problem it faced had to do with expectations.

In fact, some social problems grew markedly worse while the public had reason to expect the government's problem-solving capacity to have been enhanced as a consequence of economic growth. One intractable and politically sensitive social problem was the housing crisis, which got worse with urbanisation. The supply ratio of housing to households indi-cated that construction failed to keep up with demand in spite of the more active role played by the government (Table 2.6). The housing shortage

Table 2.6 Housing construction and supply 1966–96

	Housing units constructed ('000s)	Public (%)	Private (%)	Housing investment rate to GNP (%)	Housing supply rate (%)	
1966	93	12	81	1.8	75.3	(63.1)
1970	115	12	103	5.9	78.2	(58.2)
1975	180	63	117	6.1	74.4	(56.3)
1980	212	106	105	5.9	71.2	(59.2)
1985	227	132	95	4.4	69.8	(57.8)
1986	288	153	135	4.4	69.7	
1987	244	167	78	4.2	69.2	
1988	317	115	202	4.7	69.4	(60.2)
1989	462	162	300	5.4	70.9	
1990	750	269	481	8.2	72.4	
1991	613	164	449	8.9	74.5	
1992	575	195	381	8.1	76.0	
1993	695	227	469	8.6	79.1	
1994	623	258	364	7.7	81.7	
1995	619	228	390	7.2	86.1	
1996	592	232	360	6.8	na	

Note: Figures in parentheses in final column denote the supply rate for cities

Source: Korea Housing Bank (several issues) *Housing Finance*

was particularly acute in the cities, where the supply ratio was only 59.2 per cent in 1980.

While the large companies provided basic dormitory accommodation for their employees, rapid urbanisation forced many families into makeshift housing (shanty towns on the outskirts of major cities) or into shared accommodation (with relatives or in the rented sector). Mills and Song (1979: 137–8) quote a government estimate that there were 218,000 illegal households in 1973 (of which 70 per cent were in Seoul and 22 per cent in Pusan, Taegu and Inchon), making up 4 per cent of the total population and 8 per cent of the urban population. Even for the bulk of the country's middle classes, the absence of mortgage facilities for home purchase meant that the acquisition of property was difficult. Government control of the regulated financial sector and credit rationing meant that lending for industrial purposes invariably got first priority. Loans from the kerb market, being high interest and short term were unsuitable for potential home-buyers (ibid.: 136). On the other hand, property provided generous pay-offs for those with the resources to enter the market, be they wealthy individuals looking for a sound investment or *chaebol* engaged in land acquisition (since land ownership improved their borrowing status with the banks). Official land development programmes designed to free up more land to those of limited means often resulted in the sale of property to speculators rather than end-users because of the government agencies' desire to recover their investments quickly (Song and Stryuk 1977: 131–2). The ability to purchase property became an obvious difference between the disadvantaged and well-to-do. The housing crisis was a potent symbol of the contradictions of Korean development: the deterioration in the provision of a basic need amid unparalleled economic growth; and profiteering by the powerful at the expense of the poor and ordinary people (this accounts for the first post-1987 democratic government's priority on housing construction). The rapid appreciation of the land price (at many times the rate of GNP growth) penalised those non-owners forced to pay rent; housing costs were more burdensome for those households on low income. The difficulty of property acquisition also frustrated middle-class material aspirations (until the rise of the stock market, home ownership was the principal means of accumulation for those of moderate means).

In other basic areas of social development, healthcare and industrial safety, a similar gap had opened up between society's capacity for provision and a worsening situation. Superficially impressive expansions of health insurance and industrial-accident coverage were not matched by public resource inputs.[4] A study of Korean healthcare in the 1970s found that while Korea was not suffering from the stark starvation that blighted the masses of most developing countries, the general population was suffering from many of the debilitating illnesses associated with undernourishment (Chong-Kee Park 1980a: 144). The same source noted that the under-utilisation of the country's medical resources was not a result of oversupply, but was rather due to the lack of purchasing power among needy sections of the population (ibid.: 108).

In facilitating investment, hard work and saving, low spending on social development represented one of the cornerstones of Korean development. From the experience of the East Asian NICs, Wade and others have observed that, provided there is rapid employment generation and investment growth, governments need not accord high priority to social development (Wade 1988: 159). The low priority accorded to social development highlighted one of the contradictions of the authoritarian industrialisation pattern. If restricted social expenditure contributed to a faster rate of growth, it also had a politically de-legitimising impact on the regime, as growth and rising levels of relative inequality fostered popular expectations for more proactive social development policies.

The political limits of state capacity

The policy choices and performance of the developmental state were shaped also by its political capacities. In spite of its reputation for 'hardness' and autonomy in economic policy-making, the regime of Park Chung-Hee was constrained by institutional and ideological weaknesses. These constraints enabled an effective opposition to authoritarian rule to emerge during the 1970s. The democratisation movement of the 1980s was also built on this oppositional base. Regime weakness was one factor pushing development strategy on to a more accommodationist path after 1980 (i.e. more emphasis on redistribution versus all-out-growth).

Institutional weaknesses

While it was common to compare Korea's authoritarian developmental state with its forerunner in Japan and contemporary in Taiwan, the Korean model was characterised by distinct weaknesses in terms of regime structure and societal penetration. This could be traced to the process of authoritarian regime creation. Historically, the instruments of the authoritarian state in Korea were gradually assembled under Japanese and US influence. Taiwan was ruled by a cohesive party–state organised on the Leninist model (entailing politicisation and domination of the military and government bureaucracy by a single party). By contrast, by the time of the inception of the military regime in 1961, conservative political parties (from which sprang leaders like Kim Dae-Jung and Kim Young-Sam) were already well entrenched in Korean society. In terms of capacity for political control, the Korean state resembled the bureaucratic authoritarian type of Latin America whereas the Taiwanese state tended more towards monism.

Writers on Korean politics have noted the lateral weakness of the Korean state in relation to its US sponsor (e.g. Cumings 1989). Important changes in policy course (e.g. the transition to export orientation 1961–3, leadership changes 1960, 1979 and 1987) could be traced to changing US preferences. The lynchpin of the authoritarian regime in Korea, the military, was the branch of the state most sensitive to this influence. This was due to its US training, its integration with the US forces, and its recognition of the US as the ultimate provider of security. In line with its wider strategic concerns in Pacific-Asia, however, US interventions in Korea between 1945 and 1985 tended to reinforce rather than weaken the Korean developmental state. The price of US support was Korean obedience in foreign affairs. In return, the US would give Korean regimes some space for manoeuvre in economic affairs and domestic politics. Even so, there existed ambiguities in the US–Korean relationship that would define the policy choices open to the developmental state.

These ambiguities were rooted in the contradiction between the ideals of American capitalist liberal-democracy and the means used for its global defence. First, there was tension between the US commitment to liberal democracy and its expedient support for undemocratic anti-communist regimes. This would periodically manifest itself in friendly guidance (e.g. in persuading the military to return to civilian rule in 1963 or to commute Kim Dae-Jung's death sentence in 1981) or in sterner admonitions that could determine the survival of the regime in Seoul (e.g. Carter's human rights rhetoric, belated US support for democracy in 1987). This tension has obviously facilitated societal challenges to the authoritarian state. Second, tension existed also between the US commitment to open economics (which became more strident in the 1980s) and Korean economic nationalism. For the period up to 1985, this potential divide was suppressed under shared strategic interests and cosmetic liberalising reforms implemented by the Koreans (e.g. the financial liberalisation reforms of 1965). After 1985, the intensification of the US scrutiny of Korean economic practices was a factor forcing the reform of the developmental state. It has even been suggested that US support for Korean democratisation in 1987 was motivated by the need for market access (see e.g. Cumings 1989) (though US–Korean trade disputes, notably those over agriculture, could be guaranteed to rally even the most radical Korean dissident elements to the defence of their government).

The evolution of opposition

The crushing of organised left-wing forces by the anti-communist assaults of 1945–53 left a political sphere dominated by Syngman Rhee's Liberal Party and the opposition Democratic Party, both conservative groupings that drew their support from the former landlords and business elites. As in Japan, the land issue on which the communists had built support after 1945 was defused by a series of land reforms starting in 1949. The harsh experiences of war and communist occupation between 1950 and 1951 also discredited moderate forms of left-wing opposition. With left-wing political parties proscribed and unpopular, more radical forms of resistance to authoritarian rule evolved away from the organised political arena. Instead it came to be based on the urban groups of high traditional social standing (notably students, teachers, writers). They led the first successful uprising to authoritarianism in 1960, when Rhee was toppled and replaced by the Democratic Party.

The 1960 uprising marked a high point of radical dissent. The entry of the military into politics ushered in a barren decade for the opposition. Not only did the military introduce more effective instruments of social control but its practical developmentalist ideology caught the public mood, as demonstrated by the electoral success of President Park and the DRP between 1963 and 1971. In spite of its successful appeal to economic instrumentalism and nationalism, the developmentalist alliance (bureaucracy, military and leading industrialists) could not overcome the intrinsic illegitimacy of its non-Korean origins. Whereas the original nineteenth-century developmental states (Germany, Japan) were home-grown, the Korean state owed its creation to Japan and the US. By contrast, popular forms of opposition such as the student movement and the nascent labour movement (that was minuscule in the 1960s) based their legitimacy on their nationalist and anti-colonial past.

Industrialisation would create the conditions for the emergence of a broad popular alliance in opposition to authoritarianism and its economic model. Oppositional politics in the 1960s was marred by its lack of a credible alternative project to the regime's developmentalism. Kim Dae-Jung's vision of a 'mass democratic economy' (Dae-Jung Kim 1985) marked the emergence of just such an alternative. By promising political democracy and fairer distribution without sacrificing growth, such a populist programme could attract widespread inter-class support, as demonstrated by Kim's performance in the 1971 presidential election (commonly believed to have been stolen by Park). Park's response was to dispense with the semi-democratic system and install in its place an overtly authoritarian regime (the Yushin constitution) in 1972.

The need for accelerated heavy industrialisation in the face of an ever-more threatening international environment became the official justification for authoritarian rule. Capital deepening was deemed instrumental to the achievement of both growth and security. However economically functional authoritarianism was to deepening (it certainly stamped out economic alternatives), the background to its emergence ensured that mass support for the Yushin republic would remain limited (e.g. the narrow victory for the DRP in the December 1978 elections was secured on the basis of over-representation of the ruling party's strongholds).

Superficially, the transition to the Yushin regime in Korea closely resembled the transitions to bureaucratic authoritarian rule concurrently taking place in Latin America. The dictatorships that emerged in Latin America during the 1960s and 1970s were underpinned by their appeal to big business and the middle classes (authoritarianism's mass base), forces menaced by the distributional implications of popular mobilisation (O'Donnell 1973). Facing an even more potent external communist threat, Korea appeared to be fertile ground for the consolidation of authoritarianism of the Yushin type. But despite the existence of very strong coercive institutions, the conditions for the consolidation of open authoritarian rule did not exist in Korea. In the absence of solid middle-class support, authoritarianism lacked its mass base.

There were apparent structural affinities between pre-Yushin Korea and the pre-coup situations in the Latin America cone. Popular mobilisation was expressed in student dissent, incipient labour organisation and widespread electoral support for Kim Dae-Jung's redistributive political platform, trends that ran counter to the project of rapid capital deepening. But, irrespective of the objective economic requirements, the *political impulse* towards authoritarianism was much weaker in Korea. The most significant difference was that popular assertiveness in Korea unfolded against a background of fragile but nevertheless rising prosperity. This ensured that redistributional pressures would not assume the Latin American pattern of zero-sum conflict between the working and middle classes that drove the latter to support authoritarian rule. By 1972, the political climate had not deteriorated to the extent that the Korean middle class would wholeheartedly support the authoritarian cause. On the contrary, the opposition leaders and other notables representative of middle-class interests (especially clerics) became more aware of and sympathetic towards the plight of labour through the 1970s. By 1977, traditionally conservative civic and religious leaders were expressing their support for labour reform (Sohn 1989: 132–6). The security argument for dictatorship was unconvincing given the existence of already very powerful institutional safeguards (such as the Anti-Communist Law and the KCIA). The abuse of executive powers served to reinforce the public view that the Yushin constitution was a vehicle for perpetuating President Park's personal power. One manifestation of the abuse of power was the notorious People's Revolutionary Party case in which the seven accused were hanged (Amnesty International 1977: 33–44).

In contrast to Latin America, where populism's failure led the middle classes to embrace authoritarian alternatives, populism had not been tested in Korea and so remained a credible alternative. There was agitation for fairer social arrangements coming from another quarter. Due to popular anti-communist sentiment and tight political control, Korea was not fertile ground for socialist opposition. Instead, radical social protest was articulated by the church-based organisations (of which the Urban Industrial Mission was one example). Apart from providing organisational support to workers, the church also fulfilled an educative role in raising the consciousness of both labour and the wider public (Committee for Justice and Peace 1976: 58–69). Since authoritarian rule prohibited open discussion of political affairs, proposals for constitutional reform took on a radical significance and became a common platform behind which government opponents (from conservative democrats to student radicals) could unite, a phenomenon that would reappear in the 1980s' struggle for democracy. The student movement cohered with the principles of 'democracy, nationalism, people and unification' as espoused by the broader reform movement (Sohn 1989: 144).

The process of the evolution of opposition to authoritarianism would condition the course of the future democratic transition. Opposition to authoritarianism evolved on two distinct levels: the official political arena through the conservative politicians displaced by the military in 1961; and the non-communist radical reform movements such as the labour unions and the students. The latter, while being effective at mobilising opposition to the regime at the grassroots level, were unable to translate their issue-based support to the national political level. This could be explained by the prohibition and unpopularity of left-wing political parties as a result of anti-communism. Instead, they had to encourage their supporters to back the conservative opposition parties (whose most progressive representative was Kim Dae-Jung). Riding on the anti-authoritarian platform, conservative opposition politicians dominated the national political arena. This dominance would preclude the emergence of a viable Centre–Left in the post-1987 democratic era. The dominance of personalities and regionalism (symptoms typical of low ideological differentiation) that characterised the first democratic decade (1988–98) could be traced to the two-level evolution of opposition in the 1970s. The squabbling that broke out between Kim Dae-Jung and Kim Young-Sam soon after the demise of Park Chung-Hee in October 1979 was an early sign of the dynamics of the future democratic polity.

Conclusion

Korea's economic and political liberalisation began with the 1979–80 crisis. That crisis had its origins in the institutional features of the high-growth economic model (Korea Inc.): the close developmentalist alliance of state and business; the ideological driving force of economic nationalism; and the authoritarian political system that enforced the anti-labour and pro-investment policies. The first part of this chapter showed the origins of these institutional features and how they interacted in favour of high growth and the transformation of mass living standards. My discussion broadly coincides with the economic and political institutionalist critiques of the neo-classical and dependency interpretations of the Korean development experience. Institutionalist accounts, however, have tended to understate the significance of two points raised by the neo-classical and dependency approaches: the economic distortions associated with the state–business relationship; and the nature of the relationship with Japan.

First, institutionalists (e.g. Jones and Sakong 1980; Amsden 1989) emphasised the importance of state discipline over business in ensuring that the economic distortions (business concentration, non-productive activities and corruption) associated with governmental intervention would not undermine growth performance (as would be expected according to NPE-type reasoning). However, this tended to overlook the weakening of the state's disciplinary powers that sustained *chaebol*-oriented growth would bring. For example, by the end of the 1970s, the state was no longer capable of enforcing new patterns of industrial specialisation among the *chaebol* akin to the restructuring in preparation for the HCI drive (what Amsden called 'the switch in industrial leadership'). While the high-growth model brought improvements to mass living standards, its associated distortions sharpened the conflict over relative inequalities, and de-legitimised the regime in the process.

Second, the dependency effects of relations with Japan were obscured by the evidence of sustained growth, the prevalence of local ownership and by equitable (by third world standards) income distribution. Even western dependency theorists themselves (e.g. Foster-Carter 1987) have pointed to Korea as the exception that proves the rule. While acknowledging the crucial role of Japan in the historical and recent formation of Korean capitalism, established institutionalist accounts (e.g. Amsden 1989; Woo 1991) have emphasised the Korean capacity for autocentric industrialisation. With historically the highest rates of growth, Korea was set to catch up with Japan, just as Japan had caught up with the West in the mid-1960s. A persistent feature of the Korea–Japan relationship neglected by institutionalist accounts is the technological dependence on Japanese suppliers. From the beginning of the Korean economic take-off, Japanese capital has used its proximity and familiarity to gain a lucrative niche in the Korean market as the supplier of technology and critical components. In so doing it successfully capitalised on the obsession for industrial 'self-sufficiency' that defined Korean economic nationalism. The dependence was consolidated by the HCI drive and was manifested in the permanent trade deficits with Japan (and the corresponding need for surplus trade with third countries, notably the US). While facilitating high growth and industrial diversification, the HCI drive also deepened technological dependence and vulnerability to trade fluctuations with third countries (e.g. to shocks emanating from US trade policies), phenomena that the programme was ostensibly designed to counteract. I have referred to this as 'hyper-developmentalism'.

The second part of this chapter argued that even at its apogee (*c.* 1978), this political economy of success revealed an economic and social underside that would make the Korean miracle a fragile one. Two aspects (the effects of a cohesive developmentalist alliance and the paradoxes of economic nationalism) have already been discussed. A third aspect was the political contradictions of the anti-labour and pro-investment policies.

The socially 'inclusive' nature of development could be traced to the government's growth policies rather than to proactive redistribution. The economic success of these policies could be seen in the growth of employment and the transformation of mass living standards. By transforming the social structure and social expectations, the policies would create the very conditions of their own de-legitimisation. The extent of support for Kim Dae-Jung in the 1971 election was an early sign of the popularity of redistributional alternatives to the regime's developmentalism. Besieged by unfavourable domestic and international conditions, Park's response was to install an openly authoritarian form of government and to launch the HCI programme. The goals of security and breakneck industrialisation became the twin ideological pillars of the regime. But the HCI programme would sharpen political contradictions by accentuating relative inequalities (especially in favour of the *chaebol*) and by enhancing labour's capacity for defiance through proletarianisation. Resistance to the regime was expressed on two levels: at the level of the national political arena, by the re-invigorated conservative opposition; and at the grassroots level, by the non-communist radical groups.

The contradictions discussed above defined the agenda of reform for the 1980s and 1990s. The turn towards liberalisation and business de-concentration measures (Chapter 3) was spurred by the inefficiencies associated with the *chaebol* and the subsidy system. Similarly, the turn towards redistribution and labour accommodation from 1987 could be traced to the contradictions that originated with the anti-labour and pro-investment policies of Korea Inc. described in this chapter. The ensuing chapters explain why reform proceeded in a gradualist manner in Korea (when parallel changes occurred at a much faster pace elsewhere) and with what consequences.

3 Gradualist pattern of transition

Korea Inc. after the 1979–80 crisis

The economic and political instability of the late-1970s exposed the limits of state-led industrialisation and opened the way for economic liberalisation. In 1981, the economy recovered from a brief but painful experience of negative growth. The year marked the beginning of a sustained recovery characterised by high growth and low inflation. The IMF-backed stabilisation measures implemented by the Chun government (two standby arrangements in 1980–2 and another one in 1983–5) were praised by external commentators for laying the basis of the transformation (e.g. Aghevli and Márquez-Ruarte 1987). There were other significant indicators of improvement. First, dependence on external finance, a factor that made Korea vulnerable to international interest rate movements, was sharply reduced by four consecutive years of current account surpluses between 1986 and 1989. Second, beneath the macro-economic indicators, structural reforms appeared to be taking root in key areas of the economy (e.g. the financial system) that had previously defined Korea Inc. Third, the role of the state in development also appeared to have shifted markedly away from neo-mercantilism and towards a pro-market stance. Another aspect of the changing orientation of the state after 1980 was its more proactive role in social development (at a time when many other developing countries were being forced to make deep cuts in such expenditure), the affordability of which symbolised Korea's transition to 'advanced' status. The hosting of the 1988 Olympic Games was equally symbolic in this respect. Fifth, the character of Korean society also had undergone a profound transition. The rapid growth of personal incomes and the purchase of consumer durables goods seemed to signal the arrival of a middle-class society. By 1988, the country appeared to be entering the 'mass consumption' stage of the modernisation sequence. To put it another way, Korea was now apparently leaving the late-industrialisation model and joining the liberal–capitalist mainstream.

Focusing on the 1980s, this chapter will argue that Korea's experience of economic reform falls within a pattern of gradual transition to liberalisation. That reform took a gradualist course will be illustrated by an examination of policy change in three defining areas of Korea Inc.: the financial system; business concentration; and labour reform. In all three areas, reform did not result in a weakening of the dominant priorities or interests forged under Korea Inc. In that sense, it can be said that the developmentalist alliance of state and *chaebol* remained the institutional foundation of Korean development by the end of the Chun regime in 1988. As before, labour and small businesses remained the perennial outsiders. Within the developmentalist alliance, power shifted in favour of *chaebol*. This could be explained by their indispensability to economic recovery and the continuing mission of national industrialisation. The selective manner in which reform unfolded also helped to strengthen rather than to discipline the *chaebol*, the entities most favourably placed to take advantage of the opportunities opened up by liberalisation. These factors, together with the fact of strong recovery from the 1979–80 crisis, would restrain the far-reaching structural reforms that were implemented in NICs elsewhere (where the policies and institutions of late-industrialisation had been discredited). While this gradual and selective approach to liberalisation enabled Korea to avoid the economic and social instability consequent of a sudden lurch towards the market, a price was paid in the perpetuation of economic concentration and other structural inefficiencies (weaknesses that made the Korean development model a 'fragile miracle', such as vulnerability to external shock and structural dependence on Japanese suppliers) that would return to haunt policy-makers in the 1990s.

Emergence of the liberalisation agenda

In the response to the economic crisis and social unrest that had deepened since the assassination of President Park in October 1979, the military six months later reasserted its control over Korean society. The new military-led government (under the control of Chun Doo-Hwan and other three-star generals) boldly redefined the economic development strategy in a liberalising direction. In one of its earliest policy formulations, the government signalled its intention of carrying out structural economic reform:

> In striving to reach the goals envisioned in the Fifth Plan, however, Korea will depart from the quantitative target-oriented methods, as were the primary tactics of the past four Plans. The present Plan, in its place, relies mainly on the structural reform of economic institutions and policies, working toward, among others, import liberalization, autonomous banking operations, an efficient industrial incentive system, and a competitive market mechanism.
>
> (Government 1981: 12–13)

In effect, the policy statement was announcing a major policy switch consistent with the prevalent neo-classical intellectual climate. The process of planning itself would now assume an indicative rather than compulsory character. The institutions and policies of intervention established since the 1960s were also set to undergo reform driven by the the neo-classical agenda of market-led, internationalised growth (Michell 1981; C. Moon 1988; Jung-Ho Yoo 1989: 21–3).

In an apparent conversion to the neo-classical outlook on development, the new government criticised the excessively interventionist practices of the past. The Fifth Five-Year Economic Plan (1981–6) strongly reflected the influence of the neo-classical economists of the Korea Development Institute now influential at the Blue House (e.g. Kim Jae-Ik, Kim Mahn-Je, Sakong Il, Park Yung-Chul). Their appointment and subsequent imprint on policy design were indications that real reform was under way.

The reformulation of the developmental agenda in a liberalising direction could be traced to the domestic and international pressures confronting the new regime. The agenda for liberalisation actually predated the Chun regime. Even under President Park, the case for economic restructuring towards market-led development was already being made by a growing number of economists within Korea. The arguments were acknowledged by the president and resulted in the announcement of the Comprehensive Stabilisation Plan of April 1979, a policy that would set the economy on a less interventionist course (EPB 1979; Amsden 1987). The plan, however, was not followed through as a result of the second oil shock and the political crisis that led to the assassination of Park himself. The emergence of another strong regime in 1980 provided fresh opportunity for the stabilisation programme to be launched. Faltering economic performance greatly strengthened the course of market-oriented reform being urged by domestic economists, notably those associated with the KDI, the think-tank of the Economic Planning Board. For political reasons, the new military rulers were also receptive to the promises of the new economic doctrines. The new military regime came to power in far more violent circumstances than had the Park regime, and was more desperate for economic success as a result.

The turn towards a liberalising agenda also has to be seen against the background of external changes. If the state had enjoyed a sort of 'relative autonomy' over society in Korea, its relationship with the wider international economy could be seen in similar terms. While the state could moderate the impact of international economic forces (e.g. by integrating the foreign sector into national priorities) in the pursuit of national developmental goals, those goals nevertheless needed to be congruent with the broader economic and political evolution of the international capitalist system to which Korea belonged. The 1980s was a period of accelerated international change, and this created pressures for policy change in Korea.

The second oil shock of 1979 undoubtedly contributed to the Korean economy's experience of slow-down and negative growth. Apart from raising production costs, the oil price rise helped to push Korea's principal export markets (US and Europe) into recession. In contrast to the aftermath of the first oil shock, the industrialised countries responded with deflationary policies. This reflected a transition in economic thinking that had profound consequences for the conduct of economic policy in Korea, which became one of the first developing countries to encounter strong external pressures to conform to the emerging neo-liberalism of the US.

The reaffirmation of market principles by the new US government in 1981 (whose interest rate policies actually helped trigger the Latin American debt crisis in 1982) was echoed by multilateral development institutions such as the IMF and the World Bank. Development assistance and support for re-financing packages involving commercial banks both became conditional upon stabilisation and structural reform. Korea was exposed to the sea-change in international economic opinion. With her high export:GNP ratio, Korea had long been praised for economic openness by neo-classical commentators. A World Bank Report had cautiously welcomed the HCI programme (Westphal 1979: 279–80). The subsequent Bank Report, however, blamed the problems of the early-1980s on the interventions of the past (e.g. World Bank 1984: 8–15). Forced to turn to the IMF for an emergency loan in 1981, the Korean government promised to implement a stabilisation programme. The government also had to demonstrate its commitment to dismantling the growth instruments of the 1970s (e.g. interventionist industrial policies, financial repression, over-valued exchange rate, tolerance of high inflation) that were at variance with the new orthodoxy.

Before assessing the extent to which liberalising measures replaced interventionist ones, it is worth pointing out that the liberal development agenda of 1981 was not as inconsistent with past practice as it first appeared. To placate influential international advisers eager to see signs of neo-classical conformity, previous Korean governments had announced liberalisation measures.[1] In practice, however, liberal policy measures were either not implemented or were neutralised by other measures. That the Korean government expressed a preference for liberalisation as an ultimate goal could not be interpreted as the green light for sweeping liberalisation.

There were other indicators that the developmental state was set for retrenchment rather than dismantling. First, the announcement of liberalisation as the guiding objective did not conflict with the objectives of industrial policy. By 1980, the most ambitious HCI projects had been largely completed and the agenda turned towards making that newly acquired capacity internationally competitive (e.g. by reforming the incentive structure and by technological upgrading). Second, in line with previous economic plans, maintaining a high growth rate was a principal objective of the Fifth Plan. While world recession and high oil prices made the projections modest by Korea's past standards, the targets for growth and investment were nevertheless highly ambitious by international standards.

The ambitious official targets (even if planning had now become 'indicative') for development in the 1980s highlighted not only the commitment to growth but the favourable background conditions enjoyed by Korea in her transition to liberalising reform. In spite of the problems of HCI, Korea possessed a competitive labour-intensive export base that kept debt-servicing ratios manageable. Broader international conditions also favoured Korea. International tension put Korean stability high on the US agenda in the early-1980s (e.g. Japan made a $4 billion soft loan to Korea – equal to 10 per cent of Korea's total external debt – at US encouragement in 1983).

The financial system

The foundation of Korea Inc. was state control of the financial system. On the basis of that control, the state exchanged subsidies for business compliance with officially defined development goals. While it facilitated very rapid growth rates in target industries and companies, serious economic distortions could also be attributed to the system of subsidised credit. These included financial repression (one consequence of which was the flourishing underground financial market); misallocation of resources; and the rise of a monopoly sector of officially favoured business groups weaned on easy credit. Previous programmes of financial liberalisation (notably the 1965 programme proposed by a US advisory team; see Gurley *et al.* 1965: 58–9) were soon put on hold once they came into conflict with the government's growth priority. In the wake of the 1979–80 crisis, the case for financial reform was officially acknowledged:

> Other efforts will be made to promote the efficient operation of financial market. Special attention will be given to deregulation and development of financial institutions. Financial deepening should accelerate, increasing the flow of funds through non-bank financial institutions and the securities market.
>
> (Government 1981: 39)

While the liberalising direction of reform was apparent, the actual process of reform in this sensitive area was a very gradual one and lends support to the view that the developmental state was retrenched rather than dismantled in the 1980s. The course of financial liberalisation illustrated the changing nature of power relations within the developmentalist alliance. Despite their financial weaknesses, the *chaebol* were in a strong position to derive benefits from liberalisation. The most radical measures of financial liberalisation (e.g. the sale of domestic banks to foreign buyers) could not be applied to correct *chaebol* failings because the biggest groups had to be protected for the sake of the national economy. From the security of this safety-net, the *chaebol* could extend themselves into those domains vacated by the state. By the end of the decade the *chaebol* were strong enough to lobby vocally for faster liberalisation in the financial sector.

Selective financial liberalisation

Two key reforms in 1981–2 signalled the shift in the direction of official policy towards liberalisation. First, the ownership of the banks was privatised as the government sold its shares in the national commercial banks (the 'city-banks'). Second, an interest rate reform was implemented with the aim of ending the system of lending exchange rates biased in favour of certain categories of borrowers while penalising others. The significance of these developments is further discussed below.

There were other notable features of financial liberalisation in the early-1980s: the reduction of preferential finance in the share of bank credit; the rise of new private banks; a deepening of the financial structure, as seen in the development of the secondary financial institutions; the cautious encouragement of foreign participation in Korean portfolio investment (e.g. the establishment of the Kor-Am Bank in a joint-venture with the

Table 3.1 Internal and external funding of the business sector 1970–94 (%)

	1970–74	1975–79	1980–84	1985–89	1990–94
Internal funds	na	23.0	22.0	38.3	28.4
External funds	na	77.0	78.0	61.7	71.6
Total	100.0	100.0	100.0	100.0	100.0
Composition of external funds					
1 Indirect financing	30.1	35.2	37.2	36.0	39.0
a Bank loans	(21.7)	(22.6)	(17.6)	(19.8)	(17.3)
b Non-bank loans	(8.4)	(12.6)	(19.5)	(16.2)	(21.7)
2 Direct financing	13.7	20.4	31.0	42.8	42.6
a Stocks	(12.1)	(13.6)	(16.0)	(23.7)	(15.9)
b Bonds	(0.9)	(5.1)	(10.7)	(12.3)	(21.2)
3 Commercial paper	(0.7)	(1.7)	(4.3)	(6.8)	(3.4)
4 Foreign borrowing	11.4	11.1	4.4	1.7	3.4
5 Others	44.7	33.3	27.4	19.6	15.1
Government loans	(2.3)	(1.3)	(2.0)	(0.2)	(0.2)
Total	100.0	100.0	100.0	100.0	100.0
Preferential credit					
Share of bank loans	47.8	40.9	49.1	39.3	47.5
	(1972)	(1975)	(1980)	(1985)	(1990)
Share of non-bank loans	60.1	52.4	43.9	30.2	12.7
Share of total credit	50.4	43.5	47.4	35.3	28.1

Source: EPB–NSO (several issues) *Korean Economic Indicators*; Asia-Pacific InfoServ, Inc. (1996 VII: 28)

Bank of America in 1983, the Korea Fund for channelling foreign port-folio investment in 1984); and the replacement of bank lending limits by reserve requirement. Preferential finance (loans allocated to projects by government fiat) as a proportion of total domestic credit was reduced from 47.4 to 28.1 per cent between 1980–4 and in 1990 (Table 3.1). Development of the secondary financial sector or non-banking financial institutions (NBFIs) actually began in the 1970s as a form of domestic saving mobilisation by offering savers more attractive rates than the banks (which offered low or even negative rates) without the risks of the high-yield kerb market. NBFIs were also designed as alternative lending institutions to the banks which were shackled to heavily leveraged *chaebol*. The growth trend of secondary financial institutions can be seen from the increasing share of NBFIs in financial market composition from 22.4 to 33.2 per cent between 1980–4 and 1990–4 (Table 3.2). For the years 1982–4 in particular, the growth of the NBFIs was exceptionally rapid, reflecting the riskiness of the kerb market after the scandal of 1982.[2] Another sign of financial deepening was the growing weight of the privately owned investment finance companies and savings institutions while the officially controlled Development Institutions declined.

Like other NICs, Korea's foreign borrowing requirements intensified in the early-1980s, a consequence of international recession and higher interest rates. The heavy industrialisation of the 1970s had relied strongly on overseas borrowing. Crucial to the foreign willingness to lend was the Korean government's role as guarantor (through institutions such as the Korea Development Bank). With the government playing such a decisive role, foreign loans, like domestic credit, became the instrument of indus-trial policy. Motivated by the burden of heavy debt servicing and by the vulnerable financial structure of Korean business, alternative forms of

Table 3.2 Financial market composition 1970–94 (%)

	1970–74	1975–79	1980–84	1985–89	1990–94
1 Financial institutions	38.0	40.7	45.6	48.7	52.5
Banks	(29.2)	(26.2)	(23.2)	(20.3)	(19.2)
2 Non-banks	(8.8)	(14.5)	(22.4)	(28.4)	(33.2)
3 Securities market	11.1	15.6	20.0	27.1	27.0
Stocks	(9.7)	(11.1)	(11.9)	(16.4)	(11.4)
Bonds	(1.3)	(4.5)	(8.1)	(10.7)	(15.6)
4 Commercial paper market	0.5	1.4	3.2	4.7	4.0
5 Foreign capital market	13.5	13.3	6.0	0.2	2.2
6 Other finance	36.9	29.0	25.2	19.3	14.4
Total	100.0	100.0	100.0	100.0	100.0

Source: Asia-Pacific InfoServ, Inc. (1996 VII: 29)

Table 3.3 Foreign debt and investment flows 1970–97

	Total foreign debt ($ million)[1]	Short-term debt : total debt (%)	Total debt/ GNP (%)	Debt-servicing ratio (%)	Direct investment ($ million)	Portfolio and other investments ($ million)
1970	1,911	–	22.3	20.4		
1975	6,234	–	30.0	11.6		
1980	29,480	35.8	48.7	20.2		
1985	47,133	22.8	52.5	27.3	−358	2,082
1990	46,976	48.5	18.7	10.8	−263	3,159
1991	53,641	46.8	18.4	7.2	−309	7,050
1992	57,466	43.9	18.8	7.8	−433	7,428
1993	62,802	44.3	19.0	9.4	−752	3,967
1994	94,038	42.7	24.9	7.9	−1,652	12,384
1995	115,030	51.3	25.4	8.6	−1,776	19,050
1996	131,740 (164,340)	49.9	27.4	9.4	−2,345	26,270
1997	143,373 (158,060)	37.5	32.8	8.6	−1,947	7,974

Note
[1]Total foreign debt 1996 and 1997 in parentheses includes debt contracted by external branches of Korean financial institutions (excluded from ratio of short-term : total debt)

Source: World Bank (several issues) *World Debt Tables* and *Global Development Finance: Country Tables*; NSO–EPB (several issues) *Major Statistics*

foreign savings were developed during the 1980s. More responsive to profitability, such alternative forms included direct investment and the opening up of the Korean stockmarket to indirect foreign participation. The development of alternative forms of foreign saving to loans can be seen in Table 3.3. The growth of foreign portfolio investment and direct investment reflected the trend towards selective liberalisation. That the opening of the domestic financial sector to direct foreign participation would not become a serious matter for economic debate until the 1990s was an indication of the gradual nature of the liberalising reform.

There were other trends towards reduced reliance on the banks in the 1980s. Apart from the growth of the NBFIs, already mentioned, the business sector started raising more funds from equity and corporate bond issue. The growth of these instruments was encouraged by the government in its aim of improving corporate financial structures. For example, the interest rate on non-guaranteed bonds was deregulated in November 1984. One significant effect of these developments was to attract into the organised sector funds that would otherwise have gone to the unofficial kerb market (which disappeared by the early-1990s). The phenomenal growth of the stock and corporate bond markets in the latter half of the 1980s (Young-Ki Lee 1992) was also associated with the boom conditions in the economy from 1986 (Table 3.4). The effects of these changes and

Table 3.4 Indicators of the stock and corporate bond markets 1980–98

	Stock price index end of year (4 January 1980 = 100)	Value of corporate bonds outstanding (billion won)	Corporate bond yields (%)
1980	106.9	1,839	30.1
1985	163.4	7,396	14.2
1986	272.6	8,747	12.8
1987	525.1	10,116	12.8
1988	907.2	11,886	14.5
1989	909.7	16,321	15.2
1990	696.1	24,068	16.5
1991	610.9	31,382	18.9
1992	678.4	35,384	16.2
1993	866.2	39,890	12.6
1994	1,027.4	47,928	12.9
1995	882.9	61,287	13.8
1996	651.2	76,327	11.9
1997	376.3	90,102	13.4 (24.3% Dec. 97)
1998 June	297.9	95,516	16.6

Source: Korea Stock Exchange (several issues) *Stock*

of the real estate boom were to improve the internal financial structures of the *chaebol* sector and alert them to the potentials of further financial liberalisation as government support declined.

Continuities within the change

The financial reforms of 1982, the denationalisation of the city-banks and the interest rate reform were landmark reforms in that they signalled the liberalising direction of policy. But there was to be no rapid financial liberalisation. The government exercised a strong guiding hand over the financial sector through the 1980s. In spite of the government's divesture of ownership (the number of private commercial banks increased to ten by 1990), lending rates in the banking sector remained within narrowly defined official limits, and so the financial sector's scope for discretionary action (in which the interest rate is set according to the banker's perceptions of the risk and profitability of a particular project) continued to be restricted. Moreover, formal equalisation of lending rates did not eliminate the officially sanctioned biases in favour of high-priority activities and borrowers.

High inflation meant that borrowing was effectively subsidised in the 1970s. After 1980, however, the pattern was reversed by the coincidence of high nominal rate of interest with falling inflation rate (see Table 2.1). For example, the real rate of interest on loans for export use rose from minus 9 per cent in 1980 to 2.9 per cent in 1982. This was perhaps the first time that exporters (and other favoured borrowers) had had to pay any real interest. The reform of 1982 was designed to equalise the nominal rate of interest (at 10 per cent) for different categories of borrowers (whether a large exporter or a small company serving the domestic market) across all lending institutions within the official financial sector. The decree applied to the commercial banks and development institutions such as the Korea Development Bank and the Small and Medium Industry Bank. After 1982, the rate of bank lending for export use was held at 10 per cent whereas the lending rate for other purposes fluctuated within a narrow band of 10–11.5 per cent, meaning there was still a slight bias in the lending rate in favour of exporters.

While the interest rate reform helped to equalise the attractiveness of different forms of production (e.g. between exports and the domestic market), it did not correct the biases surrounding the allocation of credit. The government still controlled interest rates and borrowing from the controlled financial sector remained very cheap in comparison with the market rates. Consequently, credit continued to be oversubscribed, making rationing necessary. The cheapness of mainstream credit was reflected by the fact that the real rates of the kerb market never fell much below 20 per cent during the 1980–5 period (Table 2.1). Oversubscription meant that lending decisions continued to be influenced by criteria other than profitability: borrower's collateral, bureaucratic connections, compatibility of project with government priorities. Government control over interest rates was maintained precisely to ensure that the officially targeted sectors got the necessary resources.

Although declining, preferential finance still accounted for one-third of domestic credit in the period 1985–9 (Table 3.1), indicating the continuation of significant state support for target sectors and companies. Being heavily leveraged or saddled with 'non-performing assets', the commercial banks were dependent on the support of the Bank of Korea. This, together with the directive powers of the government, led to the commercial banks being easily swayed on lending decisions (Amsden and Euh 1990: 11, 13–15). Irrespective of their newly 'privatised' status, banks had only limited discretion over lending policy. They remained susceptible to 'informal guidance' from the government, a process facilitated by the official appointment of senior bank personnel. The persistence of dual financial markets and the difference between regulated and market rates (kerb and bond markets) meant that all the recipients of credit from the former sector were in effect receiving preferential finance. The turnaround in profitability during the 1986–8 boom reduced the *chaebol*'s dependence on subsidised finance. Nevertheless, even during this period of exceptional performance, the government played an active role in supporting industrial restructuring using policy loans. Under the guidelines of the Industrial Deliberative Council created under the Industrial Development Law, financial institutions

allocated 9.8 trillion won (*c.* $12.3 billion) to assist seventy-eight corpora-
tions in the period 1986–8 (Nam 1992: 37–9). Making such loans to troubled firms at the behest of the government undoubtedly contributed to the
commercial banks' problem of non-performing loans.

In a bid to accelerate financial reform, a five-year capital market liberalisation plan that included the deregulation of interest rates was announced
in December 1988. Among those interest rates that were liberalised were
most bank and non-bank interest rates and some long-term deposit rates.
Excluded were rates on some policy loans, as also were short-term deposit
rates. Restrictions (e.g. ceilings on financial institutions' volume of transactions) were maintained to prevent a flight to liberalised assets. The
deregulation of 1988 failed to free up interest rates, as the government,
fearful of a drastic interest rate increase, tacitly consented to (or may even
have encouraged) the collusion by financial institutions to keep rates down
(Nam 1992: 13).

For the World Bank, Korea represented a model of financial liberalisation (World Bank 1989: 126). Liberalisation reform, however, did not
appear to have fundamentally altered the basic rationale of the financial
system, namely, to funnel low-cost credit to officially favoured projects.
The Ministry of Finance continued to wield formidable regulatory instruments ('window guidance' and the official appointment of key personnel
remained intact at the beginning of the 1990s) that ensured the financial
institutions' compliance with the overall aim of lending to target sectors
at favourable rates of interest (Amsden and Euh 1993: 381–4). The same
authors saw the phenomenal rise of the stockmarket in the late-1980s as
an alternative means of mobilising savings instead of higher interest rates
achieved through deregulation (ibid.: 384). Commenting on the 1980s'
experience of financial reform, a respected authority on the subject noted
that despite expansion of the financial sector (as measured by the growth
of financial assets to GNP), he was unable to

> identify any significant changes in the behaviour of financial institu-
> tions or markets that indicate attempts to adjust to a changing financial
> environment. Nor do I see indications of changing relationships
> between the government and financial institutions.
>
> (Park 1994: 170)

Chaebol *entry into financially liberalised domains*

The 'big bang' approach to liberalisation was ruled out for Korea. Apart
from its unacceptable costs, such an approach (involving the speedy dismantling of subsidies, trade and financial liberalisation, and the privatisation
of state-owned enterprises) would have put an end to the ambitious plans
for national industrialisation. As in other developing countries where this
approach was tried, inefficient domestic monopolies would probably

have been replaced by the dominance of TNCs. That the fate of the *chaebol* was intertwined with that of the national economy dictated a cautious approach towards liberalisation. The selective liberalisation that characterised economic policy in the 1980s worked to the advantage of the *chaebol*. Shielded from serious foreign competition in the domestic market, and with their enormous size, the *chaebol* were well positioned to occupy those domains vacated by the state. This was evident from the effects of financial liberalisation.

Financial liberalisation had been initiated with the aim of improving the efficiency of credit allocation (e.g. by making borrowing more accessible to promising non-*chaebol* companies). De-nationalisation of the banks, however, allowed the *chaebol* themselves (the very entities that financial liberalisation was designed to check) to become major shareholders in the banks. As early as 1984, the presence of the *chaebol* in the big five city-banks was already formidable (Table 3.5). Their degree of control over the city-banks in 1984 was probably an underestimate given the prevalence of financial transactions (e.g. share holdings and bank accounts) conducted under assumed names and intermediaries. (A 'real name' financial reform had been suggested in the aftermath of the 1982 kerb market scandal, but was not implemented given its potential threat to the entrenched interests of politicians, bureaucrats and businessmen. Instead a voluntary system was recommended; see BOK 1982: 33.) In any event, even by keeping within the legally permissible 8 per cent limit on ownership (which excluded ownership by *chaebol* financial institutions such as the fledgling insurance institutions), the *chaebol* could influence banks' lending and other decisions. As for local banks, there was no legal limit whatsoever on ownership. *Chaebol* control over finance extended also beyond the monetary institutions into the secondary financial sector. For example, a KDI report found that 11 out of 26 stockbroking companies were owned by a single conglomerate (Kyu-Uck Lee 1986: 7).

Instead of furthering competition, the selective financial liberalisation measures strengthened the consolidation of monopoly status by the *chaebol*

Table 3.5 Shareholdings of the city-banks by major companies in 1984 (%)

	Cho Heung	Korea First	Hanil	Commercial Bank of Korea	Bank of Seoul and Trust
Daewoo	nil	14.4	n	n	n
Hyundai	2.4	10.3	17.5	n	12.0
Samsung	10.3	6.5	n	16.6	n
Lucky	n	8.5	7.4	n	n
Ssangyong	6.0	n	n	n	n
Others	16.2	n	31.0	n	34.1
All *chaebol*	34.9	39.7	55.9	16.6	46.1

Source: Adapted from Mabe (1984b: 19)

(Amsden 1989: 134–6; Amsden and Euh 1990). The alternative of full and equal foreign participation in the financial sector, on the other hand, would have posed an unacceptable threat to the survival of local financial institutions (and the manufacturing firms dependent on them), and the government was not prepared to see its long-term industrial goals jeopardised for the sake of efficient financial intermediation.

Reform of the *chaebol*

The problems and policy responses associated with the monopolisation by powerful business groups date back to the so-called Three Powders Scandal (flour, sugar and cement) of 1963. Closely modelled on Japan's pre-war *zaibatsu*, Korea's conglomerates or *chaebol* epitomised both the successes and the weaknesses of the Korean industrialisation model. Their meteoric rise to international status was achieved at the expense of small and medium-sized industry and on the basis of fragile financial structures. The economic distortions that led to the 1979–80 crisis dictated that these unruly giants be reformed. The *chaebol* dynamic of expansion in all directions had to be checked. The *chaebol* had to be streamlined in accordance with their strengths instead. Practices such as the crowding out of smaller firms and vast property investment diverted money that could have been spent productively in strengthening the *chaebol*'s core areas of activity (especially by developing R&D). Monopolisation and nebulous activities such as land acquisitions bred political resentment as well.

In the promotion of a more market-oriented economy, financial liberalisation measures were complemented by the extension of regulatory controls on the *chaebol*. These controls were designed to curtail the non-productive activities of the *chaebol* as well as to check their expansion into sectors more suited to non-*chaebol* enterprises. In spite of the regulatory measures passed, the *chaebol* were even more dominant by the end of the 1980s. That the de-concentration measures failed to arrest the expansion of the *chaebol* highlighted the constraints imposed by the growth-first priority and the potential costs of *chaebol* failure. As a result, the power within the developmentalist alliance continued to shift in the *chaebol*'s favour. *Chaebol* non-reform followed a familiar course during the 1980s and 1990s, namely, that an economic setback traced to *chaebol* malpractice provokes widespread calls for structural reform; then the realisation sinks in that effective structural reform would have to deepen economic pain in the short-term; favourable cyclical factors plus some limited adjustments by the *chaebol* themselves promote recovery; once the recovery is under way, the momentum for structural reform evaporates.

The trend towards concentration

In theory, the previous regime already possessed formidable instruments for checking the problem of economic concentration. These included: direct price controls provided under the Price Stabilisation Act of 1972; the 'main bank system' set up in 1974 to scrutinise the *chaebol's* borrowing requirements, investment lines and property purchase (see Nam and Kim 1993: 6–8); and the power of the government to compel companies to go public (dating as far back as the Law on Fostering the Capital Market of 1968). But these measures lacked effectiveness because the objective of reducing the economic power of the *chaebol* was subordinated to the priority of growth, especially of heavy industry. With a liberally inclined economic team newly ensconced at the Blue House as well as the demonstrated disadvantages of the *chaebol*, the policy environment of the 1980s should have favoured the successful implementation of de-concentration measures. The military government acted immediately in 1980 by passing the Monopoly, Regulation and Fair Trade Act (MRFTA), the legislative foundation of all subsequent anti-monopolisation measures. This was followed by restrictions on credit availability to the *chaebol* in 1984–5 and by the 1986 amendment to the MRFTA.

In spite of the introduction of ostensibly tough policies, the decade was marked by further business concentration. In 1975, the largest of these groups were the eight accorded the status of General Trading Companies (GTCs), parallels to the *sogo shosha*, the trading arms of the Japanese business groups. Through them, much of the country's trade was conducted. Of these, the most powerful were the Big Four consisting of Samsung, Daewoo, Hyundai and Lucky–Goldstar, namely, the groups most active in the HCI drive. While the product diversity of the Big Four immediately springs to mind, the phenomenon of participation in multiple activities was typical of all the thirty or so recognised *chaebol*, with the lesser ones branching out into activities entailing lower entry costs. This was evident from their number of member companies (which for most of the top groups grew during the 1980s) (see Table 3.6). The production methods of the *chaebol* were highly capital-intensive and unsuited to the absorption of the rapidly growing labour force. By 1990, the top thirty *chaebol* accounted for 35 per cent of manufacturing shipments and 30 per cent of value-added, but only 16 per cent of employment.

The diversification of the *chaebol* was accompanied by financial vulnerability, a weakness manifested in the groups' high levels of indebtedness and low profit margins. During the early-1980s, the debt–equity ratios of the *chaebol* were much higher than was that of the manufacturing sector as a whole, an indication of the *chaebol's* expansion based on massive borrowing. Indeed, it was not uncommon for *chaebol* subsidiaries to have debt–equity ratios of over 500 per cent. The Kukje group, one of the top eight *chaebol* (with General Trading Company status), went bankrupt and

Table 3.6 Indicators of the top *chaebol*

	Sales in 1991 (billion won)	Debt–equity ratio 1991 (%)[1]	No. affiliates 1981	No. affiliates 1986	No. affiliates 1991	No. affiliates Feb. 1998
Hyundai	23,401	443.4	30	43	42	63 (30)[2]
Samsung	23,169	323.6	21	31	48	65 (40)
Lucky–Goldstar	12,196	355.1	30	43	42	53 (30)
Daewoo	9,938	298.1	25	25	24	41 (10)
Sunkyung	6,813	244.2	16	13	26	42 (20)
Ssangyong	5,685	173.4	13	16	22	
Kia	4,144	328.7	12	7	10	
Hanjin	3,838	1,411.3	13	12	22	
Korea Explosives	2,277	290.6	16	20	27	
Hyosung	2,177	317.0	27	19	14	
11–20 largest (1991)	15,366	–	–	–	175	
21–30 largest (1991)	5,570	–	–	–	118	
Manufacturing sector	–	310.3	–	–	–	
GDP	214,240	–	–	–	–	

Notes:
[1]Debt–equity ratio = ratio of borrowing to equity; net profit = operating profit minus interest and other charges; [2]figures in parentheses indicate the target number of affiliates under the 1998 restructuring programme

Sources: Data on business groups derived from Nam and Kim (1993: 19, 34); manufacturing data from BOK (1991) *ESY*; group affiliates February 1998 obtained from MOFE (12 February 1998)

was dismantled in 1986, a move designed by the government as warning to the failing *chaebol* (the alleged cause for the withdrawal of official financial support being the refusal of the group chairman to donate to the governing party). Until they realised substantial surpluses from 1986, the *chaebol* operated on a financial knife-edge, with low ratios of net profitability. Even by the end of the 1980s, the debt–equity ratios (of around 300 per cent) of the *chaebol* remained very high by international standards (it was below 200 per cent for Taiwanese companies).

Passed in December 1980 by the military junta, the MRFTA was the first comprehensive anti-trust law of its kind in Korea. The intention of the act was to stem the growth of market dominating power by prohibiting combinations deemed likely to accentuate concentration. The MRFTA was followed by the establishment of a new agency responsible for its implementation, the Fair Trade Commission, in 1981. Effective implementation of the MRFTA was obstructed by resistance from the forces tied in with the traditional growth-first orientation of the developmental state. Through their peak organisation, the Federation of Korean Industries, the *chaebol* warned that the tightening of regulation would jeopardise the fragile recovery taking place, a stance that was echoed in the economic ministries. From the beginning, then, the MRFTA and other de-concentration measures (for the background to the 1986 amendment, see EPB 1984) were constrained by the ethos that had justified concentration in the two previous decades.

In an attempt to enforce financial discipline on the *chaebol*, the government adopted a more restrictive credit policy towards the top 30 *chaebol* in 1984. The government's decision allowing Kukje (one of the top ten *chaebol*) to be dissolved and absorbed by rivals was intended to serve as a warning to the business sector that flagging companies could not expect to be supported indefinitely (*Business Korea* 1985 and 1986b). If this was a signal of the government's resolve to restructure the *chaebol*, its limits were also apparent. Because of its size, recipients had to be found for the various Kukje subsidiaries which the government was not willing to abandon to market forces. The need to find recipients set limits on the number of financially unsound companies that could be 'disciplined'. The difficulties (political as well as economic) raised by the collapse of one of the Big Four would have been insurmountable. Sure enough, the Bank of Korea stepped in to rescue a number of over-extended city-banks on the brink of collapse from supporting the Big Four's move into the new areas of export production such as electronics and cars (e.g. Daewoo Electronics' debt–equity ratio reached a staggering 1,150 per cent in 1985).

The direct approach to restructuring was attempted in 1980 when the military tried to enforce some specialisation by dividing heavy industry between Hyundai (passenger cars), Kia (trucks) and Daewoo (heavy machinery). This could not be maintained. For example, Daewoo and Kia returned to car assembly while Samsung had not abandoned its plans to enter the industry at some future date (a goal that it realised on the eve of the 1997 crisis). During the 1980s, Daewoo and Hyundai moved into consumer electronics and high-tech goods despite their lack of experience in those fields. A number of problems made compulsory restructuring of the 1980 variety unworkable. Since the groups had become involved in so many products, it was very difficult to distinguish between their *core* and *peripheral* activities. To saddle one group with another's loss-making subsidiaries might jeopardise the viability of the recipient unless generous incentives were provided by government (as occurred with the case of Kukje's receivers). In fact many of the shaky subsidiaries belonging to *chaebol* were acquired as a result of previous government encouraged takeovers. While the 1985 Development Law was passed to facilitate government disengagement from direct intervention in industry (e.g. stricter criteria would apply to government assistance for industry), the government found itself giving subsidies to keep troubled *chaebol* afloat in the mid-1980s. Even the massively state-subsidised restructuring of 1986–8 (see above) did not result in the *chaebol* becoming more streamlined; nor did they alter their expansionary strategies. The tight mechanisms of credit control on the *chaebol* were also relaxed in 1991 in response to the economic slow-down. Corresponding to the easing of controls, the problem of credit diversion from core to peripheral businesses reappeared (Nam and Kim 1993: 35–6).

Similarly, the amendment to the MRFTA, passed in 1986, ran up against some of the traditional constraints. Designed to control the *chaebol*'s artificial expansion of their capital base by means of cross-payment guarantees, the regulation was hedged with exceptions (e.g. for groups undergoing industrial rationalisation or deemed vital to international competitiveness) (FTC 1996: 14–15). That the volume of guarantees amounted to 44,130 trillion won in 1988 was an indication of the extent of the problems (*Business Korea* 1991: III-3). These problems resulted from the groups' strategy for expansion. They showed up the contradiction between the government's claim of promoting a competitive market mechanism and other imperatives like nurturing the conglomerates for the sake of social stability and the development of leading sectors. For the official objective of establishing Korea as an independent producer in the frontier industries (e.g. high-tech and consumer electronics, transport equipment) to be achieved, it made sense to concentrate financial resources in the *chaebol* (especially the Big Four) in view of their proven record and expertise. Moreover, the problems of debt-servicing meant that successful exporters, invariably *chaebol* subsidiaries, had to be given maximal financial encouragement. Anti-concentration measures were overshadowed by the dominant culture of industrial priorities that prevailed in the economic ministries (Jong-Won Choi 1993: 42–6). Such considerations precluded the more drastic measures of restructuring and also put a brake on determined measures to curb the *chaebol*'s unproductive activities such as land speculation (see below). Even during the period of the authoritarian regimes, the *chaebol* organised effective lobby groupings against the state's land policies (Jung 1994: 317–8). The peculiarities of the Korean *chaebol* (e.g. private ownership, internally centralised, highly extended financially and along product lines, financially interconnected subsidiaries) made them less amenable to the standard liberalisation techniques being implemented throughout the developing world (e.g. privatisation after appropriate rationalisation).

Explaining chaebol *expansion*

Having explained the weaknesses of de-concentration measures in checking the expansion of the *chaebol*, the question remains: why did the top *chaebol* diversify into so many activities (a process described as 'octopus-like'), often at a loss, instead of specialising in a few profitable ones like their Japanese or Taiwanese counterparts? A tentative answer might be that such expansion helped to spread the risk, allowing the slack in one sector to be compensated by upturn in others. But instead of spreading risk, the *chaebol* subsidiaries were so intertwined (e.g. through cross-holdings) that the collapse of one was likely to provoke a domino effect throughout the group. Another reason may have been the desire for vertical integration within the group to ensure the supply of critical parts. This was the reason given by the chairman of the Lucky–Goldstar conglomerate (Amsden 1989: 126). For example, it may be feasible for a group producing a range of finished items to have its own network of distribution. Thus, the activities of the Lotte group in the food industry (it had been started by a Korean–Japanese chewing gum salesman) and retailing could be thought of as an instance of complementarity. Since the typical *chaebol* consisted of subsidiaries in totally unconnected industries, from noodles to industrial machinery, expansion could not be fully explained by the benefits for integration or complementarity. The reason given by the *chaebol* themselves was that they were relatively small compared to the TNCs of the industrialised countries and so needed to expand to a critical level in order to become world-competitive. Such a 'kindergarten' theory was also unconvincing since the development of diverse unrelated sectors only diverted resources away from a group's core activities and weakened its competitiveness against much more specialised foreign competitors.

A more sophisticated explanation depicts the state together with the *chaebol* as representing a form of *quasi-internal organisation*. According to this view, the large size of the *chaebol* and the supports provided by the state allow the competitive disadvantages that characterise developing economies (e.g. underdeveloped capital markets, small firm size, information costs) to be overcome. In effect, the *chaebol* and the government acting together replicate the effects of market processes absent in LDCs. Provided the outward-oriented development strategy is maintained, then the quasi-internal organisation is subject to financial discipline, and there is the incentive for resource misallocations to be corrected (Chung H. Lee 1992: 187–97). Yet this broad restatement of the rationale of the developmental state in the language of organisation theory does not adequately account for the *chaebol*'s motivations for their expansionary tendencies, and it also overestimates the responsiveness of the quasi-internal organisation to economic mistakes.

If financial security and efficiency could not adequately explain the dynamic of *chaebol* expansion, what other factors should be brought into the explanation? Perhaps size and even a shaky financial structure were factors which worked to the groups' advantage. First, the integrated structure of the groups facilitated expansion. The establishment of subsidiaries and the intra-group trading which this entailed helped to inflate a group's overall size and bolstered its borrowing level. The transfer of capital around the group, which inter-subsidiary cross-holding involved, enabled expansion on the basis of very low equity. Serving as collateral for loans, real estate holdings fulfilled a similar function (plus the value of land grew at a much faster rate than the economy as a whole).

Second, the conglomerate structure suited the owners' aim of maintaining familial control. Since the Korean *chaebol* rose from medium-scale family concerns into companies of world rank in a single generation, the influence of the founders and their descendants remained pervasive. As a result, the groups were characterised by tightly knit internal structures of control (Kuk 1988: 126–30). A means of perpetuating this influence was through the reliance on alternatives to public flotation such as borrowing and cross-holding (the government was theoretically empowered to compel companies to go public under the 1972 legislation). By relying on borrowing, the founding family could control a large group on the basis of very low equity. Within the shaky financial structure of Korean business, the trend has been for larger firms to have the highest debt–equity ratios. For example, one study found that for the period 1984–6, 37 per cent of the top decile of firms had equity ratios of below 5 per cent (E. Han Kim 1990: 347).

Ownership outside the founding family extended only very slowly. For example, a KDI report in 1986 found that up to 60 per cent of a given *chaebol*'s shares were owned by an individual shareholder (i.e. the founder) directly or through subsidiaries also controlled by the same individual. The same report found that only 91 of the 402 subsidiaries of the top 30 *chaebol* were listed on the stock exchange, reflecting the prevalence of familial control (Kyu-Uck Lee 1986: 7–8). It was also estimated that the *chaebol* themselves owned at least 50 per cent (but perhaps as much as 70–80 per cent) of stockmarket capitalisation (FEER 1986: 63). Ownership was concentrated, with those owning over 10,000 shares (representing 1 per cent of shareholders) accounting for almost 80 per cent of all shares owned in 1990 (see Table 3.7). Forcing the *chaebol* families to divest their control was not easy. For example, it took twenty-eight official requests before the chairman of Hyundai, Chung Ju-Yung, agreed to allow Hyundai Engineering and Construction to become a publicly listed company. In the event, only 30 per cent of the company's shares were offered for sale on the stockmarket (*Business Korea* July 1984: 54). The extent of public ownership of the country's major companies remained undeveloped in Korea compared to other East Asian economies during the first half of the 1980s (although the situation would alter considerably after 1986). For example, it was estimated that in 1985, the value of stockmarket capitalisation was about 12 per cent of GNP in Korea compared with 75 per cent for Japan and 100 per cent for Hong Kong (FEER 1986: 64). Another estimate put the average equity ratio for all non-financial firms listed on the Korean Stock Exchange at 16 per cent between 1977 and 1986, in contrast to the 40–50 per cent range for US and Japanese firms. The finding also seriously qualifies the common belief that Japanese firms tend to be as heavily leveraged as Korean firms (E. Han Kim 1990: 354).

While the low profit margins of the *chaebol* reflected the financial vulnerability of their legitimate activities, they prospered from non-productive

Table 3.7 Share ownership by size of portfolio 1975–96

	No. share-holders ('000s)	Under 10 shares	10–49 shares	50–99 shares	100–499 shares	500–999 shares	1,000–4,999 shares	5,000–9,999 shares	Over 10,000 shares
1975	290.6								
1980	753.2	26.3	29.1	14.9	19.6	4.3	4.6	0.7	0.6
		(0.19)[2]	(1.34)	(1.93)	(8.07)	(5.23)	(17.49)	(9.32)	(56.43)
1985	772.5	32.9	21.8	8.9	19.7	6.8	7.8	1.2	1.1
		(0.08)	(0.49)	(0.61)	(4.10)	(4.48)	(13.54)	(7.90)	(68.75)
1986	1,410.5	33.8	29.2	10.0	16.3	4.3	4.5	1.1	0.9
1987	3,102.3	14.5	29.7	20.1	26.4	4.3	4.0	0.5	0.5
1988	8,541.3	35.1	29.0	10.4	19.5	3.0	2.5	0.2	0.2
1989[1]	19,014.0	37.5	38.1	8.2	12.6	1.9	1.5	0.1	0.1
1990	2,418.3		38.4	10.4	31.3	8.8	8.9	1.2	1.0
			(0.65)	(0.37)	(3.71)	(3.06)	(9.21)	(4.21)	(78.80)
1991	2,150.4		41.7	8.6	27.8	9.0	10.3	1.5	1.2
1992	1,741.2		32.6	9.8	31.2	10.5	12.4	2.0	1.5
1993	1,485.9		27.7	9.4	32.1	12.0	15.2	2.0	1.6
1994	1,706.7		32.0	8.8	28.6	11.7	15.4	2.0	1.6
1995	1,548.4		23.6	9.7	31.0	13.2	17.9	2.6	2.1
			(0.13)	(0.13)	(1.49)	(1.81)	(7.40)	(3.58)	(85.44)
1996	1,464.7		30.2	15.6	26.4	10.2	13.8	2.0	1.9
			(0.27)	(0.36)	(2.03)	(2.28)	(9.14)	(4.38)	(81.55)

Notes: [1]The method of accounting was changed in 1990 from each company's shareholder (up to 1989) to each shareholder (since 1990); [2]Parentheses denote the shares owned as a percentage of total shares

Source: KSE (several issues), Stock

sidelines such as land acquisition. Because the shortage of residential and commercial space in Seoul was far more acute than for the rest of the country, land holding in Seoul was very lucrative. Land values appreciated at a rate much faster than the growth of the economy as a whole. The Kukje conglomerate, which went bankrupt in 1985, was found to have amassed considerable property holdings in Seoul. One opposition legislator estimated (or more probably, underestimated) the size of the *chaebol*'s real estate (land and buildings) holdings to have been worth around 3.4 trillion won (about $4.2 billion) in 1985 (FEER 1985a: 71). Measures to force the *chaebol* to relinquish their land holdings had been tried at the beginning of the military regime in September 1980 (and before that by the Park regime in 1974 – see Jones and Sakong 1980: 282–5) when indebted conglomerates were required to declare and sell off their non-business holdings. Hampered by the problem of definition and by the priority of resuscitating growth, the measure was not very successful. According to another source, having disposed of 300 billion won's worth of real estate by the government deadline of April 1982, the *chaebol* had amassed 1 trillion won's worth by the end of 1984 (Mabe 1984a: 29). Once the economy was revived in the mid-1980s, the *chaebol* started buying back the land they had earlier relinquished to the government at favourable prices and used that asset to bolster their collateral and secure more borrowing (Jung 1994: 307–9). The anti-land speculation policies carried out by the Roh Tae-Woo administration in 1990 was to encounter similar problems (see Chapter 4) (Jung 1994: 309–10).

The intractability of the *chaebol* problem highlighted the conflict between the attempt to control some aspects of *chaebol* expansion and an industrialisation strategy dependent on those very same entities. It was unlikely that alternative forms of finance to the targeted subsidy (e.g. retained earnings, capital markets) could have financed as rapid a rate of growth or could have allowed very long-term investments to be undertaken. For their part, the *chaebol* took advantage of this interdependence and consciously pursued a policy of expansion to enhance their economic and, ultimately, political clout by linking their survival with that of the national economy. That size helped to boost the political importance of the group was not lost on the *chaebol*. Their maze of interlocking subsidiaries, and the possibility of wholesale collapse emanating from the failure of the weakest link, gave enormous potential leverage to the leaders of the most powerful business groups *vis-à-vis* the government (and explains the government's intervention to rescue the troubled city-banks in 1985).

Labour in the developmental model

Labour policy during the Chun regime exemplified the continuity of the development model. While potentials for disagreement were beginning to open up between the state and *chaebol* elsewhere (e.g. over monopolisation), there was a strong consensus within the developmentalist alliance for the maintenance of the anti-labour policy, which was intensified in 1980. Although it was economically effective in the short term, the perpetuation of the labour-repressive model would undermine future democratic governments' prospects for building consensual industrial relations.

Reliance on the labour-repression strategy sprang from the constraints of the development objectives and from the insecurity of the regime. In contrast to other developing countries, the Korean state made every effort to sustain economic growth in the face of stabilisation pressure. The fragile structure of the *chaebol* groups ruled out harsh deflationary policies. De-industrialisation and unemployment consequent of such policies would have undermined the Chun regime's tenuous legitimacy still further. Instead, Korea would have to grow her way out of economic crisis, with the export sector playing the lead role. Export competitiveness in the early 1980s continued to depend heavily on the labour-intensive sectors (e.g. textiles still accounted for 30 per cent of export earnings in 1979). In this ordering of priorities, it was not surprising that the state intensified labour repression in 1980.

The trends for real wage and productivity growth shown in Table 3.8 do not clearly illustrate the impact of the anti-labour policy. Given the dependence of Korean competitiveness on manufactured products, the relative decline in manufacturing wages after 1979 is probably a more accurate pointer to the regime's wage containment policies (i.e. contained in line with productivity growth rather than 'compressed' in the sense normally associated with bureaucratic authoritarianism). Another significant development for export competitiveness was the decline in dollar-denominated unit labour costs (the currency in which the Korean trade is conducted), a trend highlighting the importance of the devaluation of the won against the dollar (from 484 to 861 won per dollar between 1979 and 1986). Falling ULC after 1979 was attributable to the deceleration of wage increases, a trend explicable by the reversal of the market and institutional factors that favoured labour during the 1970s. That wage repression depended on institutional controls could be seen from the spiralling of real wages that occurred after the democratisation of 1987.

Labour market conditions

The return to labour repression was facilitated by labour market trends. The rapid growth of industrial wages and tight labour market conditions in the 1970s led economists to talk about the ending of Korea's 'Lewis phase' of industrialisation based on unlimited labour reserves (Bai 1982; Lindauer 1984: 2–3). Conditions of labour shortage coincided with the advance of labour's organisation and capacity for resistance. By contrast, labour market changes of the early-1980s suited the intensification of the

Table 3.8 Comparative wages in manufacturing industry 1976–96

	Nominal monthly wages: industrial average (1,000 won)	Manu- facturing wage to industrial average (%)	Real wage increase: all industries (% pa)	Productivity growth: all industries (% pa)	Ratio of female to male wage in all industries (%)	Estimated minimum wage (1,000 won per person per month)
1976	64.3	85.4	17.4	1.8	43.9	
1977	77.4	84.5	19.8	5.7	43.9	
1978	104.1	85.1	18.1	14.0	43.4	
1979	146.4	84.9	8.6	6.5	42.3	
1980	173.2	83.7	−4.2	−2.7	42.9	
1981	209.6	83.0	−0.6	11.5	44.5	
			(7.9)	(6.8)		
			(76–81)	(76–81)		
1982	244.8	82.7	8.1	1.6	44.0	
1983	271.2	82.9	7.4	8.9	45.2	
1984	295.0	82.7	6.2	7.3	45.9	
1985	314.2	82.2	6.7	2.1	46.7	
1986	345.2	82.2	5.3	8.3	48.0	
			(6.7)	(5.6)		
			(81–6)	(81–6)		
1987	378.6	83.1	6.9	7.3	49.2	
1988	446.8	87.3	7.8	10.1	50.4	111.0/117.0
1989	524.6	90.2	14.5	7.5	52.8	144.0
1990	616.8	91.3	9.4	12.8	53.4	165.0
1991	733.5	93.2	7.5	13.9	54.1	192.7
			(9.2)	(10.3)		
			(86–91)	(86–91)		
1992	866.5	90.9	8.4	11.0	53.8	209.1
1993	956.5	92.7	7.0	8.0	54.6	227.1
1994	1,047.7	93.6	6.1	10.2	56.8	245.2
1995	1,196.0	93.8	6.4	10.5		264.4
1996	1,352.0	93.7	6.6	12.2		288.2
			(6.9)	(10.4)		
			(91–6)	(91–6)		

Sources: EPB/NSO (several issues) *KSY* (several issues); minimum wage data from Korea Labour Institute (1996) *Labour Statistics 1996*: 127 (in Korean)

traditional anti-labour policies. The renewal of out-migration from the countryside and the changing pattern of workforce participation brought new entrants into the urban labour market. The successful revival of labour repression was helped by these one-off changes in the labour market. The revival of the labour-repressive policy, however, did not prepare industrial relations for a return to the conditions of labour scarcity that sustained recovery would bring.

The agricultural price-support system introduced in 1971 slowed migra- tion from the countryside to a trickle by the mid-1970s. With almost one-third of the population left on the land, there was still much scope for further rural out-migration. Out-migration (predicted farm population minus actual farm population) regained momentum after the poor harvest of 1978. The decline of the farm population took place at a staggering rate of 5.2 per cent per annum between 1980 and 1985, reaching a high of 12 per cent in 1984 (EPB, KSY: several issues). This change could be traced to the deterioration of agricultural prices, slashed as a result of the government's stabilisation programme. After 1980, the state set about reducing agricultural subsidies. The reduction of agricultural subsidies after 1981 was a source of renewed out-migration from the countryside (Song and Ryu 1992: 151). Another was the endemic weaknesses of Korea's equitable structure of rural land holding (e.g. the difficulty of applying expensive inputs due to fragmentation) which limited the prospects for profitable agriculture. Consequently, the young and the able-bodied migrated to the cities.

The other trend affecting the urban labour market was the changing pattern of workforce participation.[3] Although overall participation rates declined, this was not a uniform trend across all age and gender cohorts. Female participation rates actually increased in the 25–29 and 30–34 years-of-age cohorts. As suggested by the participation rates, more married women were being drawn into industrial employment where they tended to be concentrated in the low-wage labour-intensive sectors (A.-S. Kim 1990: 31). The composition of female employment for a number of key industtries in 1986 was as follows:

- 41.8 per cent (total manufacturing);
- 63.7 (textiles);
- 74.9 (garments);
- 64.2 (footwear);
- 18.4 (industrial chemicals);
- 8.3 (petroleum refining);
- 6.7 (iron and steel);
- 14 (machinery);
- 51 (electronics);
- 9.3 (transport equipment);
- 10.8 (construction).

Working at typically half the male wage (see Table 3.8), women's contribution to the recovery of the mass export sectors was considerable.

Intensified anti-labour policy

Declining unit labour costs and falling strike and unionisation rates were signs that the institutional conditions of wage bargaining had shifted back in favour of employers between 1980 and 1987. The early-1980s coincided with the most repressive period of the new authoritarian regime.

Public sector wages were frozen while the private sector was given firm guidelines on pay. For example, the Bankers' Association of Korea was instructed to restrict credit to firms that were unprofitable or which had granted wage increases in excess of productivity growth (Chong-Soo Kim 1994: 214). Tough measures were meted out against the labour unions, which led to the purge of both independent activists and those in the official hierarchy appointed during the Park era. The long-term policy of control was to be one of dissolution of national organisations into company-based units which could then be easily controlled or incorporated by the state-backed management (see Chapter 4).

From the data on the official labour union movement (the one legally permissible umbrella organisation being the Federation of Korean Trades Unions), the period of the Chun regime was one of organisational decline for the labour movement. Some striking trends are worth pointing out. From the peak unionisation rate of 24.3 per cent in 1977, membership fell drastically between 1980 and 1986 (see Table 3.9). In spite of rapid industrialisation, the unionisation rate reached a low of 16.8 per cent in 1986. Only 311,000 women workers belonged to a union in 1986 compared to 365,000 in 1979 at a time when female participation was on the increase. The depletion of union membership points to the intensity of the state's anti-labour policy, a policy that emphasised coercion (whereas a policy based on incorporation would have sought to recruit workers into officially licensed organisations like the FKTU). It suggests that the approved union organisations were so emasculated that workers found little point in joining them. Reports from human rights and labour monitoring groups alluding to the numerous case studies of workers attempting to form independent labour unions support this point (more on the fate of state incorporation in Chapter 4).

The origins of industrial disputes during the 1980s are revealing about the state of industrial relations and the source of tensions between workers and capitalists (see Table 2.5). These tensions would contribute to the impasse in labour relations that confronted the later democratic governments. That far fewer strikes originated from wage negotiations during 1982–4 suggests that employers were in a stronger position to fix wage deals consistent with productivity growth. A major source of industrial disputes was *delayed wages*, a mechanism whereby companies attempted to pass the burden of slack business on to their workers by withholding wages (just as the *chaebol* passed the slack on to dependent sub-contractors by delaying payments). This accounted for 70 per cent of the disputes in 1980, and continued to be an important source of trouble thereafter. Labour reports detail instances of workers (usually in the labour-intensive industries) confronting companies over the issue of back-wages. Another source of tension involved dismissals and working conditions (over which disputes increased after 1985).

The sharp reduction in the number of industrial disputes between 1980 and 1985 attest to the short-term effectiveness of the anti-labour policy.

Table 3.9 Unionisation levels 1970–97

	Union membership ('000s)	Unionisation rate (%)
1970	473	20.0
1975	750	23.0
1976	846	23.3
1977	955	24.3
1978	1,055	24.0
1979	1,088	23.6
1980	948	21.0
1981	967	20.8
1982	984	20.2
1983	1,010	19.4
1984	1,011	18.1
1985	1,004	16.8
1986	1,036	16.8
1987	1,267	18.5
1988	1,707	19.5
1989	1,932	19.8
1990	1,887	18.4
1991	1,803	17.2
1992	1,735	16.4
1993	1,667	15.6
1994	1,659	14.5
1995	1,615	13.8
1996	1,599	13.3
1997	1,484	12.2

Source: Ministry of Labour (several issues) *Yearbook of Labour Statistics*

Its impact was not only on direct production costs but in the area of flexibility, one aspect of which was longer working hours. In spite of the rising capital intensity of Korean manufacturing, the trend in the 1980s was towards a longer working week of up to 60 hours (up to 70 in manufacturing), perhaps the longest in the world (see Table 3.10); and so the maintenance of productivity growth of the 1980s was attributable to longer hours as well as technical advance.

Harsh labour repression after 1980 put the workforce in a weak bargaining position over wages or to resist management dictates over other impositions, such as the lengthening of the working day or the withholding of wages as a cushion to cover slack periods. Labour repression was not inconsistent with rising wages (which resumed in 1981). Rather its most significant effects were the keeping of wage increases in line with productivity growth and the enhancement of managerial flexibility. Another factor that affected wage demands was inflation, as the spiralling cost of living fuelled massive wage demands in 1979–80. The control of inflation after 1981 (a principal objective of the anti-labour policy) in turn helped to moderate the pressure for wage hikes.

Table 3.10 Average length of the working week 1970–94 (hours per week)

	Average length of the working week (hours)		Proportion of workers working 54 hours per week and over (%)		Ratio of female to male hours
	All industries	Mining and manufacturing	All industries	Mining and manufacturing	All industries
1970	48.3	53.6	37.0	49.1	
1975	53.0	58.9	50.6	70.0	102.5
1980	54.0	56.8	50.4	62.8	103.5
1981	53.7	55.7	49.0	59.6	104.9
1982	56.0	58.7	55.7	70.6	103.9
1983	55.5	58.2	54.1	69.2	104.3
1984	55.3	57.5	54.6	68.8	103.0
1985	55.2	57.2	53.8	67.0	102.7
1986	53.8	55.3	50.8	61.9	103.3
1987	55.5	56.8	55.3	66.8	102.1
1988	55.8	56.8	56.7	67.3	100.4
1989	54.5	55.0	53.7	61.9	100.0
1990	53.8	54.4	51.9	59.8	100.4
1991	53.2	53.5	50.9	56.9	99.6
1992	52.4	52.4	48.1	52.2	99.2
1993	52.6	52.5	48.0	50.9	98.7
1994	52.3	52.3	46.7	49.0	98.7

Source: EPB/NSO (several issues) *KSY*

The collapse of wage controls in 1987 underlined the extent to which labour control depended on the authoritarian state. In fact, the resurgence of labour activism (e.g. in the rising frequency of disputes and the number of lost working days) had begun before democratisation. It coincided with the first signs of political opening in 1985. The revival of labour protest after 1985 was associated also with the pressures built up during the early-1980s when the Chun regime repressed union activity to an artificially low level. The revival of labour disputes after 1985 showed the limits of a policy of labour control based on coercion. Labour repression was dependent on the unsustainable conditions of authoritarianism and labour abundance. Adherence to the labour-repression policy facilitated economic recovery in the short term but only at the cost of delaying the formation of the accommodatory structures consistent with the conditions of labour scarcity and democratisation.

The underside of the recovery

In spite of its professed enthusiasm for market-driven growth, the Chun regime failed to make significant inroads into the dominance of the state–*chaebol* relationship. In any case, the post-1980 economic recovery seemed to vindicate the controversial investment decisions of the 1970s (e.g. Amsden 1987). Recovery also demonstrated the formidable leadership role of the Korean developmentalist alliance of state and *chaebol*, at a time when the failure of other developmental states reinforced the neoliberal case for 'government failure'. If the state–*chaebol* alliance led the Korean economy out of the crisis, it did so at the cost of perpetuating the structural weaknesses identified in the previous chapter. Some of these costs have already been discussed in the present chapter (e.g. insinuation of the *chaebol* into newly liberalised financial sectors, market domination and non-productive activities, dependence on labour repression). Another dimension was the deepening of the external weaknesses of the economy, weaknesses that define the fragile nature of the Korean miracle. It is to these that I now turn.

Structure of export dependence

The aim of the HCI programme of the 1970s was to reduce dependency on the export of light manufactures (which carried the looming threat posed by lower wage competitors) and the dependence on imported intermediate and capital goods. In the transitional period, however, the prioritisation of investment for the heavy sectors would create all kinds of discontinuities: accentuated imports of technology and machinery; diversion of resources from the traditional foreign exporters (thereby weakening their capacity to earn the foreign exchange on which all sectors depended); and over-capacity of the nascent heavy sectors because of domestic market size and entry barriers in markets for sophisticated products. These problems of transition were exaggerated by the over-ambitious targets of the HCI drive.

By the mid-1980s, the transitional period appeared to be successfully completed. In spite of beginning from a much weaker domestic market base than Japan (smaller population and lower per capita income), Korea had made the difficult leap into the export of heavy industrial products (just as she had done with light manufactures two decades earlier). That heavy industry was making headway into export markets was apparent from the changing composition of Korean exports in the 1980s. By 1986, heavy industrial products accounted for 50 per cent of exports. The most important products here were electronics (which accounted for one-quarter of heavy industry exports in 1986). Basic metals (especially steel) were another export success while transport equipment (ships and cars) were emerging on the horizon.

The emerging export profile was revealing about the effects of the HCI policy and, by extension, the nature of the leadership of the state–*chaebol* alliance, and the degree to which Korea had 'escaped' from its external vulnerabilities (the original aim of the HCI programme). First, the recovery was powered by a few industries (i.e. electronics, ships and cars) that were approaching global over-capacity. Set up on an even bigger scale, the new export winners were perhaps even more dependent on buoyant international conditions than the labour-intensive sectors they were supplanting. The collapse of semi-conductor prices from 1996 would spark the second collapse of the economy. Second, like their predecessors, the new export winners continued to be highly dependent on imported machinery and components (see below). Third, apart from steel (which was directly government owned and managed) the new export winners were located at the labour-intensive end of the heavy industrial spectrum. As such, Korea had not escaped vulnerability to competition from the new wave of NICs like those of China and ASEAN. The very capital-intensive sectors built by the *chaebol* at the behest of the state during the 1970s (petrochemicals, machinery) failed to prosper into major exporters by the end of the 1980s (machinery was so plagued by over-capacity it had to be taken into government ownership in 1980). At the very least it cast doubt on the wisdom of relying on the *chaebol* if not on the original decision to go ahead.

To reduce the economy's vulnerability to external fluctuations, the development of the domestic market was targeted by the government as the 'second engine of growth' for the 1980s. The domestic market was also a source of monopoly profits for Korean businesses exporting at very thin to non-existent profit margins (a strategy for securing foreign market share). Export dependence peaked in 1986 (the export : GNP ratio was 36.5 per cent). By the end of the decade, there were unmistakable signs of the development of the domestic market in consumer durable goods, a trend evident from the rapid growth of car ownership[4] and the growing share of household expenditure devoted to consumer durables. Of course, the development of this 'second engine' of growth also brought with it further external pressures for market opening.

With respect to the country of destination, the US became more important than ever as the main recipient of Korean products (see Table 3.11). By 1986, the US absorbed 40 per cent of Korean exports, or the equivalent of 14.6 per cent of Korea's GNP. The dependence of Korean exports on the affluent markets of the advanced industrialised countries was not surprising. Much more interesting was the uneven relationship with these trading partners. The structure of trade was skewed towards one supplier of technology (Japan) and one market (US). The massive deficits with Japan mirrored the consistent surpluses with the US. Korea's trade position with her two leading trade partners highlighted the economic relationship between the three in which Korea purchased machinery and parts from Japan to produce finished goods for export to the US. To put it another way, Korea was an indirect channel for Japanese exports to the US (in effect, compensating for the appreciation of the yen negotiated by the G5 under the Plaza Agreement of 1985). It was a sign that Korea had not escaped the traditional dependence on imported producer goods

Table 3.11 Balance of trade by region 1976–97 ($US million)

	Total	*Japan*	*US*	*Other countries*	*Export/ GNP (%)*
1976	−1,059	−1,297	530	768	26.9
1980	−4,788	−2,819	−283	−1,686	29.0
1985	−853	−3,017	4,265	−2,101	36.2
1986	3,131	−5,443	7,335	1,239	36.5
1987	6,261	−5,220	9,553	1,928	35.5
1988	8,885	−3,925	8,647	4,163	33.8
1989	912	−3,992	4,728	176	28.3
1990	−4,828	−5,936	2,418	−1,310	25.8
1991	−9,655	−8,764	−335	−556	24.6
1992	−5,143	−7,859	−197	2,913	25.1
1993	−1,564	−8,452	209	6,679	24.8
1994	−6,335	−11,867	−1,026	6,378	25.4
1995	−10,061	−15,557	−6,273	11,769	27.7
1996	−20,624	−15,682	−11,635	6,693	27.0
1997	−8,452	−13,065	−8,356	12,969	31.1

Source: EPB/NSO (several issues) *Major Statistics*

that was the aim of the HCI programme. It would also make Korea a target of US pressures for market opening.

The 'three blessings'

Korea's continued sensitivity to external fluctuations was underlined by the changes in the international economy after 1983. This time, however, the changes were favourable, and they aided economic recovery. The projections made by Korean economic planners during the early-1980s proved to have been over-cautious, as the international economy recovered strongly after 1983. By 1986, the Korean economy was benefiting from a set of favourable external circumstances known as the 'three blessings', all of which greatly boosted Korean exports. In 1986, the country's balance of payments recorded its first ever surplus. From the depths of the debt crisis in 1985 (when total indebtedness reached $50 billion) the country's financial position was transformed by four consecutive years of surpluses. International factors played an important role in this turnaround.

First, the price of crude oil fell from $28.14 per barrel in 1985 to $15.35 per barrel the following year. As a result, the crude oil share of total imports fell from 17.9 to 10.6 per cent (it was as high as 25 per cent in 1982). Apart from improving the trade balance, the collapse in the oil price also lowered production costs, especially for energy-intensive industries. Second, while the won had been depreciating in relation to the dollar, the Japanese yen appreciated under the terms of the Plaza Agreement (reflecting inter-governmental attempts to rectify the US–Japan trade imbalance). The nominal rate of exchange of the won to the dollar between

1980 and 1986 had depreciated by about one-quarter, while the yen had appreciated by 34.5 per cent over the corresponding period. This made Korean products particularly competitive in the labour-intensive sectors, as well as in such emerging sectors as basic steel products where Korea was now in direct competition with Japan. Third, international interest rates had also fallen to new lows, thereby lessening the burden of Korea's debt-servicing commitments. By 1986, Korea started to reduce her debt in absolute terms.

On the other hand, the three blessings and export recovery also high-lighted the continuing imbalances in Korea's trade structure. Korea's high dependence on the US market had serious implications for the future conduct of trade relations. Korea shipped 40 per cent of her exports to the US in 1986, and reaped a trade surplus of $7.3 billion, a figure which grew to $9.5 billion the following year. Pressure from the US to reduce the country's trade deficits led to much closer scrutiny of the trading prac-tices of the surplus countries. Japan was deemed an exponent of unfair practices, followed by NICs such as Korea and Brazil. This view was rein-forced by a number of dumping suits brought against Korean companies in the US. In spite of the rhetoric of liberalisation used in official Korean circles, non-tariff and other informal barriers continued to keep out foreign consumer goods or to price them out of the reach of Korean consumers in areas deemed strategic to local industry (Allgeier 1988: 90–1). US pres-sure for the opening up of the Korean agricultural market to imports such as beef and tobacco posed a serious political problem for the Korean government, since the plight of the country's farmers was a sensitive polit-ical issue with nationalist overtones (after democratisation, the Korean government was more sensitive to domestic pressure). Primary products represented the tip of the iceberg of further liberalisation pressure in other sensitive sectors (e.g. financial services, entertainments). Currency appre-ciations, previously forced on Japan, were also applied to Korea and Taiwan in order to reduce their trade surpluses with the US (a change that sparked the outflow of Northeast Asian investment to Continental Asia).

While the World Bank and neo-classical economic commentators were happy with Korea's formal steps towards trade liberalisation, the US government clearly was not, and criticisms of Korean protectionism became more strident in the 1980s. This stance was not unrelated to the waning of the Cold War. The US had previously overlooked the economic protec-tionism of her Northeast Asian allies for the sake of high politics. In effect, the US indulgence of Korean neo-mercantilism, a defining feature of the US–Korean relationship for the previous thirty years, was now nearing its end. In contrast to Japan, Korea was encountering retaliatory pressures from her protector at a far earlier stage of industrialisation, and conse-quently had far less leverage (e.g. Japanese purchases of US treasury bonds helped to fund the US federal deficit) to withstand protectionist pressures.

The technology gap

The deepening of technological dependence on Japanese suppliers (as reflected in the persistent trade deficits) was a paradox of the economic nationalism of the 1970s. In an effort to avoid being caught in an intermediate position between low cost and advanced producers, Korea's R&D expenditure increased rapidly after 1981. In particular, the private sector played a far more substantial role in technological upgrading (see Table 2.4). At 1.9 per cent of GNP in 1989 (and more in the priority sectors), it was quite respectable by the standards of developing countries, but the Korean economy was now competing in sectors dominated by producers from the industrialised countries. Korean engineers managed to fabricate a number of sophisticated products which, combined with cheap labour, became internationally competitive. By the end of the 1980s, Korea was internationally competitive in a limited number of heavy and advanced sectors: cheap household electronics, basic semi-conductors chips, cheap cars, basic steel products, ships. But although the country had made considerable efforts in technological development during the 1980s, the gap between Korea and the advanced countries remained wide. Moreover, the pattern of technological dependence on Japan, established in the 1960s and 1970s, persisted. The persistently big trade deficits (even through the boom years of 1986–8) with Japan were symptomatic of the dependence on the foreign sector for technology transfer as well as the burden of having to import technology. As a 1988 discussion paper found,

> transferred technology is mostly associated with a mature stage of the product-life cycle, and very few cases of state-of-the-art technology transfers are found. . . . The study on the pricing of technology shows that the monopolistic rents portion of the technology supplier is high. In other words, technology is transacted in a monopolistic or oligopolistic environment.
>
> (W.-Y. Lee 1988: 203–4)

Technology was becoming increasingly difficult to acquire (unless it came in the form of a direct investment, which the government was still reluctant to liberalise) as leading producers began to perceive Korea as a potential threat, a threat that they were increasingly prepared to counter with litigation. Lawsuits were brought against prominent Korean companies accused of copyright violations. For example, Samsung was forced to pay Texas Instruments $90 million for a patent violation (FEER 1988: 59). Realising the Korean challenge, the Japanese side became reluctant to pass on its know-how, and disputes over technology transfer resulted in the collapse of a number of joint-ventures. That a Bank of Korea report of 1986 found companies were spending more on entertainment than on

R&D was a worrying sign, for it suggested the private sector was placing greater emphasis on lobbying than R&D (ibid.: 59).

The dependence on foreign technology allowances showed up the still significant shortcomings in domestic research capacity in the light of the ambitious developmental goals. From the Normalisation Treaty of 1965, Japan had been Korea's leading supplier of technology. The reluctance of Japanese suppliers to transfer vital technology (the picture tube for colour televisions being a celebrated case in point), as well as their tendency to off-load outdated plant to recipient countries, prompted Korea to look to other sources. The Japanese refusal to meet what they considered to be excessive Korean demands for technical transfer led to the collapse of the proposed joint-ventures between Daewoo and Toshiba, and between Samsung and Ishikawajima–Harima in the early-1980s (Mabe 1984b: 14–19). Korean insistence on technology transfer and the Japanese reluctance for fear of boomerang effects has been a recurrent factor affecting cooperation ever since. Yet, after a long period of reliance on Japan, diversification of the sources of technology procurement could not be achieved quickly. The trade deficits with Japan (regardless of the overall trade balance) were a sign of the persistent pattern of technology dependence established during the 1960s and 1970s, in spite of the Koreans' own intensified R&D efforts (e.g. on micro-electronics, see Schive 1990).

All this did not imply that Korea was incapable of making progress. Indeed, Korea had made impressive strides, as shown by the progress of the steel industry. The point is, however, that it was extremely difficult for an NIC to make inroads into the frontier industries dominated by its principal purveyor of technology, especially one that had an active strategy for perpetuating dependence (see e.g. Bernard and Ravenhill 1995). In spite of the intensified domestic R&D efforts, it was recognised that foreign technology would continue to play an important role. The relaxation of regulations governing foreign direct investment, and the joint-ventures with foreign TNCs and other moves aimed at stimulating much-needed technology transfer, would characterise the 'globalisation' project launched in 1993.

Uneven industrial structure

While the growth record showed that conglomerate-centred development possessed great strengths, there were also serious flaws associated with over-reliance on the *chaebol*. First, the activities of the *chaebol* had parallels with the behaviour for which TNCs have been commonly criticised. By virtue of their financial clout, the *chaebol* were able to monopolise areas of production in which they were not necessarily the most efficient. Their ability to pay the best wages also led to a monopolisation of talents that could have been better deployed elsewhere. Using highly capital-intensive production methods, they contributed less to job creation and social equality. Their dominance and involvement in non-productive activities bred much political resentment.

Second, being centralised family-owned organisations, the *chaebol* were capable of making long-range decisions that profit-driven corporations would have found risky (e.g. the rapid advance into the former Eastern Bloc after 1991 being a case in point). On the other hand, being oriented to economies of scale derived from the mass production of standardised items, the *chaebol* lacked the flexibility in responding to market shifts that typified smaller, more specialised, companies. The *chaebol* were slow to respond to the rapidly changing consumer preferences in affluent sophisticated markets (which placed great onus on quality and product differentiation). By contrast, East Asian competitors were highly attuned to these trends (e.g. specialist Japanese companies like Toyota and Sony, and Singaporean and Taiwanese companies with TNC connections).

Third, another consequence of the pro-conglomerate bias was the weakness of the parts and components side of Korean manufacturing. Instead of being produced locally by SMEs, such parts and components tended to be either imported from Japan or manufactured inefficiently inhouse by the conglomerates themselves. By contrast, Korea's closest rival Taiwan excelled in this area. The point made earlier about the neglect of R&D by the *chaebol* is also underlined by a study showing that even the financially hard-pressed SME sector had higher R&D to sales ratios (e.g. 2.57 and 3 per cent for 1989 and 1990 compared to 1.93 and 1.9 per cent for *chaebol*) (Soh 1997: 248).

One of the stated aims of the Fifth Plan was to reverse the skewed allocation of credit that had worked against the development of small and medium-sized enterprises (Government 1981: 69–70, World Bank 1987a: 123–4). Such reforms included the stipulation that the city-banks and foreign banks must make, respectively, 35 and 25 per cent of their lending to SMEs. Data supplied by the Bank of Korea suggest that the conditions necessary for SMEs to thrive (e.g. access and cost of borrowing) had improved after 1981.[5] Data point to the growing SME share of manufacturing employment, output and value-added during the 1980s. Since such data refer to all enterprises with less than 300 workers, it is difficult to differentiate between independent small and medium-sized enterprises versus those controlled by the *chaebol*. There was also a widening of the productivity (and wage) gap between the SMEs and the large enterprises. The launching of another 'localisation' programme in 1986 as part of the Sixth Economic and Social Development Plan (1987–91) attested to the continuing deficiencies of SMI (Business Korea 1986a: 15–18). These deficiencies were also evident from the growing trade deficits with Japan, as the appreciation of the yen raised the cost of imported parts and machinery.

There is also other contrary evidence. According to the World Bank study of 1987, the financial crisis facing the conglomerate sector by the mid-1980s was such that the pro-SME policy had to be reversed (World

Bank 1987a: 92–3). There was a long way to go before Korean SMEs matched the dynamism of their counterparts elsewhere in East Asia. The large enterprise (LE) sector (companies employing more than 300 workers) in Korea was much bigger in terms of total manufacturing employment and output. For example, the share of manufacturing employment in enterprises of less than 300 employees in 1985 was 49 per cent for Korea, compared to 70 per cent for Hong Kong, 75 per cent for Japan, and 98 per cent for Taiwan (FEER 1985b: 76–7). This suggests that the weight of the *chaebol*–LE sector in Korea was the outcome of a distinct type of late-industrialisation strategy that was unique even in East Asia.

International versus domestic market trajectories

From its minuscule base, the domestic market for consumer durable goods grew rapidly during the latter half of the 1980s. The growth of the internal outlet for consumer durables pointed to the rising purchasing power of Korean consumers (especially the growing middle-class in Seoul), and it had the potential to become the 'second engine of growth' if the rate could be maintained. But it did not amount to the arrival of a prosperous middle-class society or the similarities with 1960s' Japan which such a depiction would denote. Far from generalised affluence, the Korean situation was marked by the persistence of certain types of inequality and the neglect of basic needs (see Chapter 4).

By the late-1980s, the domestic market for new high value-added products (e.g. cars, household electricals, semi-conductors) was growing rapidly. In spite of this, the existence of massive productive capacity and the need to earn foreign exchange (for the purposes of debt servicing and technology importation) meant that the products of those sectors would depend heavily on foreign markets. For example, as early as 1984, Samsung alone had the capacity to manufacture 6 million 64K semi-conductor chips, against a maximum domestic requirement of 4 million, while other *chaebol* had equally ambitious plans in this area. The collapse of chip prices would trigger the economy's undoing in 1997. The fierce rivalry between the *chaebol* was responsible for their tendency to diversify into each and every frontier sector.

While generating very rapid growth, the Korean industrialisation trajectory was unevenly developed between the modernised state-favoured *chaebol* sector (oriented towards foreign consumers and creditors) and the rest of the economy. The imperative of concentrating on the export-oriented sector accounts for the contrast between the 'advanced' and 'backward' aspects of Korean development: an industrial capacity that ranked alongside those of the OECD countries in a selective number of products existing alongside human development indicators (e.g. housing, access to clean water) characteristic of semi-industrialised status (e.g. Wade 1992: 275–6). This is a paradoxical feature of Korean development. In a bid to avoid dependence, the strategy of fostering national champions had exaggerated some of the social and economic disparities characteristic of dependent development.

Conclusion

The macro indicators of the 1980s showed that the Korean economy experienced both structural change and impressive recovery from its crisis of 1979–81. The retrenchment of the developmental state carried out under the Chun regime set the scene for a new boom at the peak year (1988) which the economy grew by a staggering 12 per cent. The structural transformation was evident from the success of a new wave of Korean products on world markets such as cars, consumer electronics and information technology components. Korea's congruence with the neo-liberal international trends was also visible from the official commitment to price stabilisation and the liberalisation of the trade and financial sectors (e.g. bank de-nationalisation, promotion of the secondary financial institutions) and the scaling down of direct industrial supports.

Economic reforms were set within the confines of a gradualist pattern of transition. The key objectives of the economy were set by the state in close cooperation with the *chaebol*. The state still maintained powerful instruments with which it could ensure the compliance of private agents. Being the principal executor of the state's development priorities, the *chaebol* continued to enjoy favoured status. It was within these confines that selective financial liberalisation policies and business de-concentration policies were implemented. In financial reform, even though the state had relinquished its ownership of the city-banks, it still determined the most important decisions over lending and appointments. This ensured that priority industries would continue to receive preferential access to bank credit. The sectors that emerged to become the export winners of the 1980s continued to receive credit on favourable terms from 'privatised' banks that were themselves financially beholden to the government. Those outside of government favour still suffered under this climate of financial repression. The government's determination of a company's worth (i.e. by its contribution to national development) still held sway over financial decisions. To achieve the breakthroughs in the target sectors necessitated continuing reliance on that proven agency of Korea's economic success, the *chaebol*. The difficulty of restructuring the *chaebol*, or of restraining their unproductive and anti-competitive activities (e.g. gobbling up weaker companies, real estate acquisition, bureaucratic lobbying), was a sign of their indispensability to the development priorities of the 1980s. The direction of economic policy and institutional reform was clearly one of liberalisation, a shift made in recognition of the existence of the neo-liberal international economic environment. But the process of change was also gradual and accommodated within the overall objective of growth. There would be no economic free-for-all. By the end of the decade, it was clear from the extent of institutional and policy reform that the developmental state had been retrenched rather than dismantled.

The 1980s coincided with the consolidation of the economic power of the *chaebol*. This resulted in a shift of power in favour of the *chaebol* within the developmentalist alliance. Their financial fragility and their impor-tance to the achievement of ambitious industrialisation goals made the *chaebol* indispensable to the state, and precluded the state from taking radical liberalisation or business de-concentration measures. Shielded from foreign competition in the domestic market, the *chaebol* were poised to take advantage of the opportunities opened up by piecemeal liberalisation. In the area of financial liberalisation, for example, far from promoting the development of a more competitive market mechanism, liberalisation led to the extension of the *chaebol*'s influence over the financial institutions in the 1980s. Where the government withdrew, the conglomerates stepped in, extending their control over the banking and secondary financial insti-tutions alike. Their expansion into the financial sector was symptomatic of their importance to the economy as a whole and their growing power in relation to the state. Apart from their enormous share of national output, only the *chaebol* had the know-how and the infrastructure to realise the ambitious plans for the development of the frontier industries. The prac-tical difficulties raised by the high-profile dissolution of insolvent *chaebol* (notably Kukje) also revealed the limits of the state's capacity for indus-trial restructuring. The 1980s was a period of transition in the state–*chaebol* relationship from state dominance to interdependence, a transition hastened by the end of authoritarian rule in 1987 (see Chapter 4).

Repressive anti-labour measures were reactivitated in the early-1980s. Here, the state and the *chaebol* were in full agreement. Being at the basic end of the heavy industrial spectrum, the frontier industries targeted for development during the 1980s were the ones most appropriate to Korea's comparative advantage. The new 'export winners' were industries (e.g. consumer electronics, steel, cars, ships) that remained highly sensitive to changes in unit labour costs. Helped by one-off labour market changes, the system of labour repression was temporarily restored. By suppressing strikes and dissent, repression helped to boost export competitiveness, as witnessed by the flattening out of unit labour costs in the first half of the decade. Although it was a crucial component of economic recovery, the repression unleashed on labour did not sow the conditions for the most articulate sections of labour to be peacefully incorporated on the Japanese pattern. It did nothing to prepare industrial relations for democratisation and the impending return to conditions of labour shortage. Not surpris-ingly, labour disputes spiralled out of control in the immediate aftermath of democratisation in 1987. The culture of confrontation that remained deeply etched in Korean industrial relations hindered the emergence of a cooperative approach to common problems (e.g. policy towards declining industries, reconciling of labour rights with efficiency needs). This legacy would undermine economic restructuring efforts in the 1990s.

The state-sponsored export development of the Korean type was geared towards growth maximisation by incorporating the advantages of intervention and international competition. The process of gradual adaptation (as opposed to the 'big bang' transition to the market) to the neo-liberal international environment, which I have referred to as the gradualist model of transition, was consistent with those principles. Successful though this approach was in maintaining growth and avoiding the painful economic and social consequences of rapid liberalisation suffered by other developing countries, it failed to reform and even exacerbated certain aspects of the authoritarian industrialisation model, most notably the problems of confrontational labour relations and business concentration, problems that would ultimately affect Korea's drive for advanced industrialised status. It is worth restating the main aspects of these problems.

First, while labour control was particularly vital to the early decades of Korean industrialisation, the legacy of coercive controls and the unwillingness of the state and management to countenance any form of independent union activity meant that all parties were inexperienced at working out compromises to industrial disputes. By the late-1980s, however, the erosion of authoritarian labour controls and the emergence of cheaper sources of labour (from China, ASEAN, India), made it all the more important for labour and business to reach some form of accommodation.

Second, the ambitious nature of Korean development necessitated a high degree of centralisation in order to realise scale economies and to create companies with comparable resources to match the western and Japanese TNCs. In contrast to other NICs, such as those of Taiwan, Hong Kong and Singapore, which established niches in specialised light manufacturing and components (and even services), the Korean policy-makers sought to compete with the leading multinationals in their own market niches. It meant heavy reliance on the *chaebol*, making the more harmful and unpopular aspects of their activity (e.g. land holdings, corruption, the squeezing out of small and medium-sized businesses) impervious to reform. It was also becoming apparent that the push into the frontier industries could not be successfully accomplished without more extensive foreign interactions (the *chaebol* themselves were aware of this as they mounted pressure for faster liberalisation from the late-1980s), a path that would transform the national champions into genuinely internationalised business groups far less amenable to state direction (and less oriented to conceptions of national interest).

Third, while enabling Korea to avoid common dependency traps (e.g. penetration of TNCs, capital flight) and to stand up for herself in the international economy, the priority of building national champions dedicated to export success created dependency-type effects. Internationally, these were manifested in the continuing vulnerability to external shocks and the

skewed trading patterns with the US and Japan (whose calculated technological dominance of Korea was deeply embedded), when the *raison d'être*
of HCI was the freeing of Korea from such constraints. Domestically,
economic and social disparities characteristic of dependency-type situations were also in evidence. Such disparities were manifested in the business
concentration (and underdevelopment of SMEs and specialist firms) already
discussed as well as in regional and sectoral concentration, and the underdevelopment of the social infrastructure (notably, public housing). In spite
of the recovery of the 1980s, the constraints imposed by these three factors
contributed to the stressful nature of Korean development.

4 From autonomous state to consensual development?

The impact of democratisation

Within the course of the gradualist reform initiated in 1981, the strategy of development experienced two important shifts. One was the emphasis on redistributional policies from 1987. This included the reversal of many aspects of the authoritarian state's anti-labour policies. The other was the acceleration of structural economic reform from 1993 under the slogan of 'globalisation' (see Chapter 5). This chapter will deal with the origins and consequences of the post-1987 shift towards redistributional measures from three perspectives. First, this chapter argues that the successes and tensions of the Korea Inc. model of development facilitated the emergence of democratic opposition. On top of the dissatisfaction with the political constraints of authoritarianism being felt by an increasingly advanced society (modernisation theory), the regime also suffered from the de-legitimising effects of *chaebol*-dominated economic development. Discontent over labour and equity issues (e.g. social development, housing, business corruption) represented the political underside of the economic model. The shift towards redistributional and other reform policies after 1987 was a response to the political pressures unleashed by democratisation (e.g. direct action by labour, the need for public officials to secure votes).

Second, this chapter shows how the legacy of the developmental state structured the form of democratisation and helped to constrain the opposition within moderate confines. While the political and social costs of rapid growth took their toll on the authoritarian regime's legitimacy, the conditions of democratisation favoured continuity in political leadership. Continuity was manifested in the dominance of opposition politics by conservative professional politicians, the electoral survival of Roh Tae-Woo in 1987, and the conservative merger of 1990 which produced another successful presidential candidate for the regime (Kim Young-Sam) in 1992. While playing a crucial role in activating public opposition to authoritarianism, the more radical forces (e.g. students) were unable to translate their influence into a viable political alternative (e.g. in the form of a Centre–Left party) to the conservative politicians who dominated the electoral arena. This conforms to the point about the evolution of democratic opposition on two distinct levels made in Chapter 2.

Third, this chapter examines the balancing of the demands of redistribution and of growth. From 1987, the Korean state took a more pro-active role in addressing social development and equity issues. This marked not a dismantling but a re-defining of the developmental state to include redistributive functions. Government policy pronouncements linked the reduction of social disparities and their associated grievances to economic performance. In effect, the shift towards redistribution was designed to widen the developmental consensus (by giving the previously excluded a stronger stake in development) beyond the traditional confines of the state and business elites. This intent was most explicit in the attempts to co-opt labour into tripartite arrangements that would help secure future changes in sensitive areas such as labour market reform. It will be seen how redistributive policies (expenditure on which was substantial) helped to ingratiate the new conservative democracy with the middle classes (e.g. in areas such as housing and share-ownership).

On the other hand, by the end of the first democratic government (1988–93), state efforts to integrate labour into cooperative tripartite arrangements had largely failed. Another failure was the inability of the state to reverse the advance of business concentration. Democratisation and economic recovery further strengthened the leverage of the *chaebol* in their dealings with the state. The uneasy interaction of activated labour, weakened state and monopolistic *chaebol* meant that the institutional basis of Korean development remained far from consensual, a deficit that made Korea significantly different from Japan Inc., whose institutional basis of development (of business deference to administrative guidance, cooperative labour relations rooted in company unionism and so forth) was considered a role model in Korean policy circles. In the failure of the state to successfully integrate labour into the developmentalist alliance, or to effectively counteract the trend towards the *chaebol*'s continuing advance (with all the social and economic inefficiencies that entailed), the persistence of the institutional features of the 'fragile miracle' becomes clear.

Sources of democratic change

The mass demonstrations which culminated in Roh Tae-Woo's Democratic Declaration of 29 June 1987 ended 26 years of military based authoritarian rule. The immediate cause of the mass protests that swept the authoritarian regime aside in the summer of 1987 was the decision by President Chun Doo-Hwan to hold the forthcoming presidential election under existing rules designed to favour his nominee, Roh Tae-Woo. (The previous mass uprising had occurred in 1960 when Syngman Rhee tried to rig an election.) Chun's only possible option for survival in the face of overwhelming popular opposition, martial law, was prevented by a number of factors: divisions within the leadership (especially from Roh, who saw in electoral competition a means for his own political survival); military unwillingness to launch further intervention; US approval of the democratic opposition; and a common reluctance to jeopardise the forthcoming Olympiad to be held in Seoul in 1988.

Crucial to the success of the democratic protest was the participation of those sections of society whose material stake might have led them to acquiesce in the maintenance of authoritarianism. The fact that managers, professionals and clerical workers joined with students and workers on the streets of downtown Seoul made clear the public's disapproval of Chun. The growth-plus-coercion formula that sustained authoritarian rule in previous decades could no longer contain popular expectations. The changing climate of public opinion (from acquiescence to mass defiance of authoritarianism) reflected the structural changes in Korean society. Such changes enhanced the scope of popular protest and at the same time shaped the parameters of political contestation in the post-democratic period.

The social context

Many of the associations of economic development with democratisation identified by modernisation theorists were also present in Korea. The mass base of the Park regime was the countryside. A consequence of land reform was the transformation of the rural sector into a bastion of conservative support, a support reinforced by a combination of moderate subsidies, political control and orchestrated participation. Not surprisingly, the countryside was politically over-represented. Political dissent was concentrated in the cities (an indication of higher standards of education and more exposure to political alternatives and international influences). The erosion of agricultural employment was the inevitable consequence of industrial development. It was indicative of the extent to which Korea was still semi-industrialised at the beginning of the 1980s. Between 1980 and 1985, the rural sector's share of total employment declined from one-third to one-quarter (see Table 4.1). In contrast to the situation faced by President Park a generation earlier, the erosion of the peasantry meant that Korea's leaders of the late-1980s could no longer rely on a political base whose support could be so easily manipulated. By engendering urbanisation and the expansion of the 'modern' strata (the middle and working classes), accelerated industrialisation increased the political influence of the cities. Urbanisation was a development favourable to the oppositional forces.

One of the most significant social changes brought about by accelerated industrialisation was the transformation of the class structure and the rise of Korea's middle class. A striking aspect of this transformation was the growth of the 'new middle class', consisting of educated white-collar workers. Educational expansion in response to the growing technical composition of industry pointed to the further expansion of this social stratum. By

Table 4.1 Composition of the labour force 1970–95 by occupation (%)

	Prof., tech., admin., managers	Clerical and related workers	Sales workers	Service workers	Agriculture	Production, machinists
1970	4.7	5.9	12.3	6.5	50.3	20.3
1975	3.5	6.3	12.9	7.2	46.1	24.1
1980	5.3	9.3	14.5	7.9	34.0	29.0
1985	7.3	11.5	15.5	10.8	24.6	30.3
1990	8.7	13.0	14.5	11.2	17.8	34.8
1993	10.3	15.0	15.9	12.3	14.6	31.9

By new classification after 1994

	Senior public officials, managers, professions	Technical, associate professions	Clerks	Service, shop workers	Agri-culture	Craft and related trades	Plant and machinery operators and other assemblers	Elemen-tary occupa-tions
1995	7.4	9.0	12.3	21.9	11.7	15.8	10.7	11.2

Source: MOL (several issues) *Yearbook*

1985, as Table 4.1 shows, skilled white-collar and clerical workers combined accounted for almost one-fifth of the total workforce.

Classical theories of social change and modernisation theory associate democratisation with economic growth and improvements in the quality of life. This link is supported by findings from a number of developing countries which show positive correlations between rising incomes, urbanisation, educational attainment and the emergence of popular expectations for enhanced political participation (see e.g. Lipset 1959). Even the alternative structuralist theory of Barrington Moore (1984) associates the middle class with democratisation, arguing that under the non-democratic routes to modernisation, the bourgeoisie was either subordinated ('revolution from above') or non-existent (communist industrialisation). Being a principal beneficiary of economic growth, and in a good position to look beyond the difficulties of daily survival, the middle class (white-collar workers and small proprietors) was identified as the section of society likely to be at the forefront of democratic agitation. Thus, as the middle class expands (and the conservative rural stratum declines), the greater the likely pressure for democratisation (see e.g. Cotton 1989). The emergence of highly repressive forms of authoritarian rule in Latin America during the 1960s and 1970s, however, underlined the dual role of the middle class as a mass base for authoritarian rule as well as democratic change in nascent capitalist societies (O'Donnell and Schmitter 1986: 51–2). This has led some to emphasise the role of labour as the decisive democratising force (e.g. Rueschemeyer *et al.* 1992). In Chapter 2, it was noted that the conditions of intense social polarisation and the resultant perception of the 'threat from below' (e.g. from organised labour, left-wing and populist parties) generated by economic crisis that swung the middle class behind military dictatorships in Latin America did not prevail to the same extent in Korea (although there was arguably quiet acceptance for Chun's suppression of popular protest in 1980; see Sung-Joo Han 1990: 328). Having never been menaced by popular mobilisation to the same degree, the Korean middle class was less reticent about supporting the introduction of democracy than its counterparts in Latin America (see e.g. Stepan 1985 on middle-class insecurity and the perpetuation of authoritarianism in countries like Chile).

There has been much debate about the nature of the middle class (and even if it constitutes a 'class') among Korean sociologists (see Kyong-Dong Kim 1993). In spite of the disagreements over the middle class's exact composition and political orientation, all studies point to its growing size and periodic challenges to authoritarian rule (see e.g. Sang-Jin Han 1988 and 1993). By the mid-1980s, the conditions for the Korean middle class to act as a democratising force were in place. Although growth with low inflation during the 1980s brought greater prosperity (e.g. luxury items such as cars now became affordable) and stability to the expanding middle class, the authoritarian regime was unable to capitalise politically on an appeal to economic instrumentality. With economic prosperity restored, the costs imposed by authoritarianism became less acceptable. Articulate sections of the middle class (led by professionals in education and the media, and, of course, students) suffered particularly under a regime that eradicated political choice, practised intimidation and imposed tight restrictions on expression, association and travel. In continuity with the past, the traditionally high-status educated groups were again at the forefront of the opposition to authoritarianism.

Government appeals on the basis of middle-class economic instrumentality were doomed to failure given the existence of credible alternatives, as conservative opposition leaders (notably Kim Young-Sam) promised to secure economic prosperity by democratic means. It has been observed that protection of the material interests of the beneficiaries of authoritarian rule (often in the form of a formal pact) is an important facilitator of democratic transition (O'Donnell and Schmitter 1986: 45–7). While challenging the regime on its weak points, namely its illegitimate origins and authoritarian record, the opposition promised continuity to those who had prospered under authoritarian rule. On substantive issues such as internal security, inter-Korean relations, foreign policy (where they reaffirmed their support for the US alliance and disavowed the nationalistic militancy of the student movement) and the appropriate model of development there was little difference between the government and mainstream non-radical opposition leaders. Even the more reformist of the opposition figures, Kim Dae-Jung, accepted the prevailing social and economic arrangements to a large degree in his political programme. On the economy, he explicitly repudiated socialism as an alternative model of development, and in his specific criticisms of the pattern of development the *underreliance on market forces* was singled out for criticism (Dae-Jung Kim 1985: Chs 4–6). In fact, Kim's critique of specific aspects of the export platform, together with his approval of the overall strategy, showed a remarkable affinity with the official assessments of the economic mistakes committed during the 1960s and 1970s. By attacking the economic distortions brought about by intervention over previous decades, the opposition could also appeal to those aspiring sections of society held back by the workings of the state–*chaebol* nexus (e.g. small business owners denied credit, aspiring property buyers frustrated by the spiralling costs, workers aggrieved at arbitrary management practices). Paradoxically, its ideological affinity with the regime on substantive issues placed the opposition in a good position to prise away the regime's target supporters, those who had a stake in the existing economic order. In promising political reform without jeopardising growth, the opposition politicians were continuing the theme powerfully articulated by Kim Dae-Jung in 1971.

While sustained capitalist industrialisation was responsible for the strengthening of the modern social strata in relation to the regime, democratisation could not have been achieved in the absence of a conservative opposition that appealed to the middle class, the economic beneficiary of authoritarian industrialisation. This neutralised the most effective issue (economic stability and growth) on which the authoritarian regime could maintain popular acceptance. Instead, the opposition dictated the political agenda by focusing attention on the social and political costs of dictatorship. Given that their panacea for the ills of the authoritarian system – constitutional reform – offered to expand the political and economic opportunities for many sections of society (including big business) without jeopardising any section's vital interest, the opposition leaders were in a position to build a mass pro-democratic following.

The dynamic of political liberalisation

Just as the resumption of electoral politics (within carefully controlled limits) gave legitimising force to the military junta after 1961, President Chun's hold on power could be consolidated only on the basis of a credible electoral mandate. If it was difficult (and ultimately impossible) for President Park to rule on the basis of economic success during the 1970s (in spite of there being a tense security situation and with the balance of power between state and civil society loaded firmly in favour of the state), Chun's long-term prospects looked even more precarious. Not only had the structure and the outlook of Korean society become less receptive to authoritarianism in the ensuing decade, but the violent origins of the regime accentuated its illegitimacy. Given the absence of a powerful 'threat from below' that solidified the middle-class basis of authoritarianism in Latin American countries such as Argentina and Chile, regime consolidation in Korea depended on its capacity to elicit consent. To do this, the blanket closure of the political system imposed in 1980 needed to be partially reversed. In effect, a measure of controlled liberalisation had to be implemented: political controls had to be relaxed sufficiently for the regime to secure a popular mandate – but not to the extent that regime survival would be threatened. This depended on permitting a return to political competition, but a competition that would be controlled within safe limits maintained by the executive's ultimate recourse to the military.

The façade of constitutional process that ratified the new Fifth Republic regime in 1981 could not disguise its illegitimate foundations. Most of the opposition were in jail or banned from political activity when Chun was indirectly 'elected' to the presidency in 1981. The attempt to legitimise the regime began with the formation of the Democratic Justice Party (DJP) in 1981, with President Chun at its head (just as the previous military junta had founded the Democratic Republican Party two decades earlier). Liberalisation got under way in 1983 as the repression unleashed in 1980 was scaled down. The ban on politicians of the pre-coup era was lifted, control over college campuses was relaxed and political prisoners were released in substantial numbers. But, even then, censorship and the harassment, intimidation and torture of opponents (measures continuously meted out to student and labour radicals) remained regular features of Korean political life.

The exclusion of Kim Dae-Jung and Kim Young-Sam from the list of politicians whose bans were lifted demonstrated that there were clear limits to how far the Chun regime was prepared to liberalise politically. Political exclusion would continue to apply not only to radicals but to any proponent of genuine constitutional reform. The aim of the limited opening was to co-opt those prepared to work within a constitutional order suited to the DJP and to allow those in power to dictate the pace of constitutional change.

In its first test of public opinion in 1985, the DJP received 35 per cent of the votes cast.[1] The support of one in three voters may have been seen as respectable, given the party's recent authoritarian lineage, and the result was better than that achieved by President Park's DRP in its first electoral showing in 1963. Yet the parallels with Park could not be taken too far. The DJP failed in its stated objective of winning 38 per cent of the votes cast. In spite of its minority support, the DJP's maintenance of its majority status in the national legislature (through a bonus system that rewarded the party with a simple plurality) only highlighted the electoral system's lack of genuine representation. The result was also disappointing from the DJP's point of view because of the financial and organisational advantages the DJP enjoyed over opposition parties hurriedly put together after the ban was lifted. Whereas the legislative opposition to Park in the 1960s was divided into a dozen warring parties, the New Korea Democratic Party (NKDP) emerged from the 1985 election as a coherent opposition.

Government efforts at sowing opposition discord (e.g. gestures to elements of the main opposition party NKDP after the 1985 election[2]) yielded little success. Instead, the policy of limited liberalisation had the opposite effect, as those allowed back into the political process made common cause with those very forces the government had hoped to marginalise. Substantive constitutional reform (e.g. the widening of the right of participation, replacement of the rules of political competition obviously loaded in favour of the DJP) was an issue around which all oppositional groups, whether moderate or radical, could unite (see P.-S. Chang 1985). As is evident from the 1985 election results and from surveys, the existing constitution (indirect elections and the allocation of 'bonus' seats to the largest party) had little popular credibility, and so there was much to be gained from opposing it (Ahn *et al.* 1988: 103–5, 138–40). The government's dissatisfaction ratings in the polls broadly coincided with the election figures.[3] Furthermore, with President Chun having committed himself to standing down in 1988 after a single term of office, there was strong incentive for opposition parties to maximise agitation in the period leading up to the transfer of power.

The DJP's electoral disappointment illustrated the difficulty confronting authoritarian regimes once they embark on the liberalisation route. If they remove too many obstacles to participation, then the process becomes uncontrollable; while an insufficient opening may highlight constitutional shortcomings and so strengthen oppositional demands (on Brazil, see Martins 1986). Such regimes face difficulties in establishing their preferred version of the 'rules of the game' (Kaufman 1986: 93–6). The results of Korea's 1985 legislative election belonged to the latter scenario. Legitimacy (and with it the rulers' long-term guarantee of political survival) would be denied the DJP so long as the rules of political competition remained fixed in its favour and key opponents excluded from participation. The ban was ineffective as well as unpopular, since Kim Dae-Jung and Kim Young-Sam jointly managed the NKDP from behind the scenes. The regime was in a dilemma here: the participation of the Kims represented its greatest threat, but their continued exclusion made a mockery of the official claims to political reform. The government continued to brand Kim Dae-Jung as a dangerous subversive (he was seen by hardliners in the military as a virtual communist), while the threat from the other Kim was much more subtle: he appealed to the middle class (a constituency which the DJP hoped to attract) and, as a native of Kyongsang province, he could also offset the DJP's regional appeal. Securing legitimacy required further opening, signs of which came with the initiation of the constitutional dialogue on the post-1988 order and the lifting of the political ban on the 'Three Kims' (including Kim Jong-Pil) on 6 March 1985.

The deaths of individuals under police interrogation and the periodic use of house arrest for opposition leaders were powerful reminders to the public of the regime's origins and of its cynical attitude towards political reform. Without political opening, the regime could not legitimise itself, and yet substantive constitutional reform threatened to generate outcomes beyond its control. Ultimately, the regime's authoritarian impulse proved stronger than its liberalising intent. The suspension of the constitutional dialogue in 1987 confirmed its unwillingness (at least under President Chun) to make the decisive transition from tentative liberalisation to democratisation. With the social and institutional conditions for democratisation having been sown (albeit unwillingly), by 1987 it was too late for the momentum to be reversed.

The social contradictions of economic success

The previous chapter examined the role of labour repression in the economic recovery of the early-1980s. While economically effective in the short term, the anti-labour policy was premised on two unsustainable conditions, namely, authoritarian rule and a slack labour market. The prolongation of the anti-labour policy did not prepare Korean industrial relations for democratisation and the return to tight labour markets that economic recovery would bring. The first revival of labour protest coincided with the beginnings of political liberalisation in 1985. Labour was angry while business had grown used to state intervention in its favour (an attitude that also bred the complacent reliance on low wages and long hours that would later plague competitiveness).

The absence of a tradition of artisanal discontent did not prove to be any obstacle to the rise of labour militancy after 1987, as claimed by some commentators (e.g. Amsden 1989: 135). The explosion of labour discontent into the Great Workers' Struggle in the aftermath of democratisation was symptomatic of more than two decades of repressed demands. The impact of the struggle is apparent from Table 3.8, which shows the extent to which manufacturing workers (those at the forefront of the 'miracle') closed the wage gap with the rest of the workforce between 1988 and 1991. Grievances went beyond low wages. Labour protest highlighted two socio-political problems affecting Korea's transition to advanced industrial status, namely, the condition of Korean labour and lagging social development. Like the pressure for democratisation, these problems highlighted both the successes and the limitations of past development policies. For them to be accommodated (for they could no longer be so effectively repressed) required a redistributive approach from government towards social problems that would represent a significant departure from the growth-first priority that had dictated economic policy for almost three decades.

Sources of the Great Workers' Struggle

Even after a quarter of a century of sustained wage increase, the condition of many sections of the population still hovered perilously close to the subsistence level. Apart from those employed in the 'informal' sector of the economy (and who were omitted from official statistics; on social marginals, see Chung-Sik Kim 1983: 38–43), ample evidence of inadequate remuneration, even within the formal workforce, can be cited. For example, the average wages of production and service workers remained below the average urban household consumption expenditure. The ratio of earnings to consumption expenditure[4] for all manufacturing workers was 87 per cent in 1986; in textiles it was only 57 per cent; and in electronics-based industries it was 88 per cent (which helps explain the drift of workers away from the textiles industry during the 1980s). These crude estimates suggest that the typical low-income household could survive only with a supplementary source of income to the main breadwinner, and then only just.

Case studies reveal the existence of pockets of poverty where wages lower even than these averages actually prevailed. Being concentrated in the industries and firms of low productivity, female workers fared particularly badly. For example, one study estimated that, without wage discrimination, female wages should have been as high as 80 per cent of the male manufacturing wage in 1989, instead of being around 50 per cent (Bai and Cho 1995: 160; for an anecdotal treatment based on a case study of the Masan Free Trade Zone, see Seung-Kyung Kim 1997). In contrast to their male counterparts, women employed within the heavy industries did not enjoy significantly better wages compared to those employed in light industry (Shim 1994: 70–2). For much of the 1980s, attempts to establish a minimal wage were successfully resisted by the business sector, which played up fears of the erosion of export competitiveness. In December 1986, minimum wage legislation was enacted based on an estimation of a monthly subsistence wage of 100,000 won for an individual male worker (although the legislation was not immediately put into effect) (MOL 1987: 68). Official estimates tended to be on the conservative side. For example, the 1988 official estimate for monthly subsistence of an individual male worker was 133,376 won compared to the estimate of 154,597 won by Seoul National University (MOL 1989: 45–6).

Apart from the persistence of inadequate pay, and of considerable variation in the ability to meet basic needs between different sections of the workforce, labour discontent was generated by work-related issues (for a study based on Hyundai car workers, see Bae 1987). Working conditions in Korea continued to be among the most regressive of the East Asian NICs. In contrast to other NICs where the length of the working week was being reduced as a result of industrialisation, Korean industry was moving in the opposite direction. Between 1981 and 1986, the length of the working week was hardly reduced. In 1981–2 (in conjunction with the most repressive phase of the anti-labour policy and sharply rising productivity), hours actually returned to the levels of the mid-1970s. The lengthening of the working week after 1981 was especially pronounced in the manufacturing sector, where the proportion of workers doing at least fifty-four hours per week rose from 59.6 per cent in 1981 to 70.6 per cent in 1982 (see Table 3.10). The proportion of workers (all industries) doing at least 54 hours per week was higher in 1986 (50.8 per cent) than in 1981 (49 per cent). The sharp rise of the average number of hours worked and the proportion of the workforce putting in 54 hours weekly or more were evidence of the effect of labour repression on the work process in the early-1980s.

Complementary to the harsh working conditions was the system of labour discipline designed to suppress the slightest manifestations of labour autonomy. The repression of labour initiated after 1980 helped to drastically curb the incidence of strikes. It helped bring about a sharp growth in productivity. Such a policy certainly enhanced managerial flexibility. It put firms in a stronger position to enlarge the variable component in their workers' wage packets – the 'bonus' – enabling adjustment costs to be passed on to labour in the form of smaller bonuses. The state's anti-labour bias meant that management could, with the tolerance (even the connivance) of the authorities, behave arbitrarily. Human rights organisations catalogued numerous cases of abuse involving wage claims, working conditions and the right of workers to form their own unions (Asia Monitor 1987: 28–32). The absolute refusal of management or the state to countenance independent labour organisation meant that there were no channels through which the discontent could be peacefully articulated.

Recognising the potential strength of organised labour brought about by continued industrialisation (production workers and equipment operators made up 32 per cent of the workforce in 1987), the regime sought to establish official institutions through which labour discontent could be defused. Labour activation in the late-1970s was a sign that the maintenance of stable industrial relations would have to depend on strategies of labour incorporation or accommodation. This meant shifting away from the coercive approach that marked the rise of the Chun regime. For example, decrees passed in 1981 prohibited the intervention of 'third parties' (e.g. student and social activists) and in an attempt to reorganise the union structure away from the national–industrial level, the government promoted the formation of labour-management committees at the company level. Given the parallels in industrialisation experience, Korean policy-makers in the 1980s became attracted to the Japanese pattern of labour incorporation in which the most articulate sections of labour were co-opted into pro-management structures. Characteristics popularly ascribed to the Japan Inc. pattern of industrial relations include cooperative labour–management relations, employee loyalty to the company (in exchange for lifetime employment and welfare provision), flexible working practices and company unionism. Korean and Japanese companies had practices in common, notably their use of the bonus system. But the benefits of Japanese company unionism, such as the company provision of welfare and the security of employment, were absent from the Korean system, where the use of force and the suppression of legitimate grievances remained at the heart of managerial practice. Even very large and relatively high-paying companies in Korea (e.g. Hyundai), which might have been expected to emulate Japanese practice, instead relied heavily on coercion and state intervention as their method of settling industrial disputes (Asia Monitor 1987: 63–5). Consequently, Korea lacked the core of privileged permanent employees that exercised a stabilising force on Japanese industrial relations. Relatively privileged workers in Korea tended to be militant. It meant that the potential for labour–management polarisation and confrontation was also much greater (on the subtle coercive features of Japanese management, see Tabb 1995: 140–68).

The failure to develop a pattern of effective labour incorporation pointed to the likelihood of a resurgence of labour activation coinciding with political opening (as had occurred in 1979). Although many attempts to form independent unions were forcibly stifled, containment could not be translated into legitimacy for the company-controlled or manipulated structures of labour 'representation'. Attempts by companies to impose their stooges on the workforce triggered many of the disputes of the 1980s. Labour discontent was aroused also by the contradiction between the ostensibly liberal labour laws and the reality of continuing repression. The suicide of the labour activist Chun Tae-Il by self-immolation in 1971, an event which greatly raised public consciousness of labour grievances, was in protest against the government's failure to abide by its own labour code. The restrictions on legitimate dissent at the workplace served only to encourage unofficial action, which often swept the official representatives into making bolder demands in order to avoid being outflanked by more militant activists, just as in the later years of the Park regime. Moreover, relatively well-paid workers were not immune from taking militant action. The strikes at Daewoo Motors and Songwon Steel in 1985 were examples of this, and these incidents were symptomatic of the grievances harboured by even highly paid workers over working conditions such as food, hours and safety (Asia Watch Committee 1986: 258–9 [Daewoo Motors], 222–3 [Songwon Steel]). Many white-collar workers (with the exception of the highest administrators, managers and professionals) also harboured grievances against the excessive managerial power sanctioned by the government. If harmonious Japanese-style industrial relations was the instrument of the state in its aim of pacifying labour, government and managerial attitudes and tactics in dealing with the workforce in the 1980s did not foster the appropriate conditions for such peaceful incorporation to prevail in Korean industry for the immediate or foreseeable future.

To sum up, the Great Workers' Struggle of Korean labour that took place in the summer of democratisation was the product of alienation born of deeply pent-up grievances, not only over pay but over the whole framework of authoritarian management. Overall improvements in pay concealed the continuing impoverishment of many sectors of the workforce. But discontent went beyond the economic and was prevalent also in many sections of labour that were comparatively well remunerated, revealing the limits of attempts at garnering political legitimacy on the basis of economic performance. It was noted in the previous chapter that the re-imposition of tight labour controls was not incompatible with rising wages but that its significance was rather that it gave management great leeway not only over wage determination but over the conditions of employment. The movement for independent labour organisation during the 1980s challenged a fundamental assumption of the Korean development strategy, namely, that labour was not entitled to any intrinsic rights and that improvements in its position (whether it be wages or conditions) was a matter for managerial dispensation. It showed that the workers were becoming increasingly aware of the absence of such rights and were determined to see such claims legally established, an aspiration facilitated by the student movement which dedicated itself to raising the consciousness of labour (Asia Monitor 1987: 35–41). Just as the pressure for democratisation could not be contained by the instrumental appeal of rising wages (for the poorly paid, the frustration born of workplace authoritarianism was added to the daily struggle for survival). The state's anti-labour bias and widespread use of coercion could only suppress the symptoms of a deeper change in labour expectations. The years 1980–7 demonstrated the limits of the old style of labour control rooted in coercion. The Great Workers' Struggle highlighted the necessity of stabilising a new pattern of state–labour relations in which democratisation and labour assertiveness could be reconciled with the traditional state–business concern for growth and flexibility.

Social development and equity

A stated priority of development for the 1980s was the elimination of absolute poverty and other social problems accumulated from the Park era. A passage that summed up the government's recognition of the sources of social discontent is worth quoting at length:

> Up to the Fourth Plan ... the concern for social development had been overshadowed by the emphasis on industrial development. For the next five years, however, fundamental changes in policy direction will occur, namely, [an] *active government role in social development to meet the basic needs of the people* ...
>
> Concerning policy implementation, efforts will be made to enhance fairness and justice in the administrative system. As a result, *any*

> *non-labour income accrued by leisure groups as a result of administrative favoritism or speculation investment will be considerably curtailed*, but fair rewards will be ensured to conscientious workers. Concurrently, since the eradication of absolute poverty will be of the foremost importance in social development, *the provision of decent housing and appropriate medical care will be the primary policy pursued.* In view of the fact that education is a source of sustained growth for the economy and at the same time a major factor determining the level of individual earnings, the government will increase its efforts to provide more equal educational opportunities, with better quality, especially for the low income segments of the population. *All these policies are designed for the formation of a solid middle-income group*, hoping that this group would eventually become the majority of total population.
>
> (Government 1981: 97–8 [italics added])

More than two decades of export-led development had undoubtedly boosted the living conditions of the majority of the population by creating jobs and by generating rapid real wage rises. These improvements were the results of policies designed to maximise growth rather than of social investment or redistribution. But there were limits to the trickle-down effect: the persistence of vast pockets of poverty within the overall context of rising wages; huge rewards from corruption and speculation for a few; and the lack of resources devoted to social development in spite of the country's growing affluence. It was seen in Chapter 2 that the official avoidance of pro-active redistribution policies became a source of popular grievance against the state. By avoiding pro-active redistributive measures, the state was seen to be favouring special interests such as the *chaebol* (even though the investment-first priority had transformed mass living standards through employment generation). The official emphasis on social development after 1980 was designed to demonstrate the Chun government's commitment to correcting past failures in this politically sensitive area.

Measurements of the decile distribution of income show that distribution improved after 1980 (see Table 2.2). Within the overall figures there were disparities (e.g. as seen for the manufacturing sector discussed above) and controversies over the methods of accounting. Of the critical studies, one estimated that welfare and income inequality declined only briefly, between 1969 and 1974, and that, on the whole, growth was accompanied by rising inequality, especially if the ownership of land and financial assets is taken into account (see below). Studies cite the neglect of the following elements for producing findings biased towards equality: the under-reporting of income by the high income groups; income accruing from property; and the pay-offs from the underground economy (Jong-Goo Yoo 1990: 388). While not undermining Korea's reputation for relative equality from an international standpoint, the existence of elements of inequality overlooked in standard accounts certainly helps to explain the pressures for redistribution that the Roh government faced from 1987–8.

While income distribution improved and was, by international standards, equitable, negative public perceptions were shaped by other visible facets of maldistribution. These included spiralling property costs, homelessness, economic concentration and corruption. Housing was a particularly serious problem. The supply ratio deteriorated during the 1980s; despite the greater share of the public investment devoted to housing construction (on public housing programmes in the 1980s, see Suh and Yeon 1986: 15–16). The burden of housing costs was evident from its growing share of consumption expenditure. Given the concentration of land ownership and the rapid appreciation of land price, it was not surprising that even middle-class people had difficulty entering the property ladder. The problem was serious enough for the Roh administration to establish a Commission on the Public Concept in Land. While the value of land appreciated fourteen-fold between 1974 and 1989 (three times faster than GNP), the Commission found 77 per cent of land to be owned by 1,080 persons (cited in S. Kwon 1990: 31). One study estimated the extent to which the picture of distribution was distorted by the exclusion of financial and real assets. Adjusting income data on earnings to include investment income shares as well as capital gains, the study found a marked skewing of income distribution with the income share of the top decile growing from 27 to 41 per cent in the process (Jong-Goo Yoo 1990: 382–5; Leipziger *et al.* 1992).

The land situation and labour grievances highlighted the social costs of authoritarian industrialisation led by the government–*chaebol* nexus. The austere image that President Chun tried to cultivate (beginning with the 'purification campaign' of 1980) was soon tarnished by the disclosure of dubious dealings on the underground financial market (the kerb market scandal of 1982) involving his wife and her uncle. Another scandal, the collapse of the Myongsong (literally, shining star) business group in 1985, whose chairman had built a $150 million empire by dubious means, under-lined the extent of the corrupt relationship between business and the state – a link often described as *chongkyong yuchak* (literally, the cohesion of politics and economics) (Clifford 1994: 194–200). With his own inner circle compromised, Chun would not initiate 'purification' measures after the 1982 kerb scandal.

Deliberately suppressed under Park, the affluent lifestyles of the well-to-do became more visible under Chun (symbolised by e.g. the acquisition of imported cars and luxury apartments, and lavish corporate entertainment expenditures). Scholars have argued that the bitter strikes that occurred in the late-1980s were directed at such perceived economic injustices, with workers striking out at the company managers as their most accessible targets (e.g. Choong-Soon Kim 1992: 193–4). The failure to implement the 'real name reforms' (a measure to prevent individuals from holding bank accounts under assumed names) was an indication of the secret incomes accruing to public officials. Measured by the share of the national product accruing to the *chaebol*, distribution of wealth had deteriorated during the 1980s. The *chaebol* were also clearly resistant to the dilution of their power. For example, after having been required to list company shares on the stock exchange, the chairman of Hyundai, Chung Ju-Yung, established the so-called Asan Foundation which became a principal holder of group shares. (In the 1970s, the founder of the Samsung group, Lee Byung-Chull, established the Samsung Cultural Foundation as a holding company.) The windfall profits made by the *chaebol* (e.g. from land speculation and monopoly profits) strengthened the opposition case for the tighter regulation of business power.

The limits of political change

In Chapter 2, it was argued that Korea's military-led authoritarianism was less penetrating than the quasi-Leninist type that prevailed in Taiwan. As such, Korea's military-dominated regimes had closer affinities with Latin American bureaucratic authoritarianism. As a result, there was space in the political arena for conservative opposition while social discontent fed the development of non-communist forms of radical opposition (e.g. the student movement, labour groups led by church activists). These two levels of opposition connected effectively in the cause of anti-authoritarianism but they would diverge once more in the aftermath of democratisation. Having concentrated on specific issues such as social or labour reform and having thrown their weight behind the conservative opposition in the cause of constitutional reform, the radical opposition groups were in no position to launch a credible electoral alternative of their own. This opened the way for the conservative dominance of the electoral politics in the new democracy. The immediate rift between the two main opposition leaders, Kim Young-Sam and Kim Dae-Jung, was symptomatic of the onset of the ideological vacuum once the goal of constitutional reform had been realised. Divided opposition parties had allowed President Park an electoral clear run in the 1960s, something that was about to be repeated.

In the December 1987 presidential election, Roh Tae-Woo secured victory with a plurality of just over one-third of the votes cast. There was something ironic about the result since it was Roh's nomination by Chun in April that had sparked the democratic uprising. Roh's success at retaining power without an overall majority, but merely by preventing one from being formed against him, was by no means surprising once the two veteran opposition leaders, Kim Dae-Jung and Kim Young-Sam, resumed their old rivalry (just as they had done in 1979–80). Paradoxically, democratisation threw a political lifeline to Roh and other recent democratic converts in the leadership. The next section will further examine why the opposition fragmented and why the political activation (as expressed in the broad-based democratic movement and the emerging labour movement) unleashed in 1987 did not translate into a more thoroughgoing political change.

Sources of fragmentation

The legacies of authoritarian rule, economic growth and political control helped to shape the scope and limitations of the democratic transition. Official prohibition of left-wing ideas (reinforced by the security situation) as well as their own conservative outlooks confined the mainstream opposition leaders within very narrow ideological limits. During the campaign for democracy, they had been able to turn this moderate approach to their political advantage. Moderation on economic and foreign policy issues enabled them to reassure potential veto groups (such as the army) about their intent. Instead, they emphasised constitutional reform, an issue on which they could submerge their personal differences and rally broad-based support. The democratic coalition encompassed diverse elements (the Kims and their provincial followings, middle-class, workers and students) with potentially conflicting post-democratic interests. Having realised the common objective of constitutional reform, latent divisions (including their rival regional backgrounds) soon turned into open disunity.

The discontent over the social costs of authoritarian industrialisation, identified above, appeared to offer the potential for effecting a more thorough leadership change, but this was inhibited by a number of factors. For many (the middle class, especially), the feeling of discontent with state–*chaebol* economic domination had to be balanced against the positive economic gains made during the 1980s, a tension for which Erik Olin Wright's concept of 'contradictory class location' seems highly appropriate (Koo 1987: 390–3). With their moderate, reformist, pro-capitalist platforms, the mainstream opposition parties were well placed to capitalise on the social discontent of a public not yet ready for social-democratic alternatives. This was reinforced by other advantages: renowned leaders, established organisation and financial resources. Combined with four decades of official persecution, these factors limited the electoral prospects for the success of more progressive politics in the new democratic polity (on the merits of Centre–Right governments for democratic consolidation, see Kaufman 1986: 105–7). Having helped trigger the nationwide protests of 1987, the influence of the radical student movement remained trapped within campus confines thereafter. The nationalist radicalism (pro-North Korea, anti-America, anti-capitalist and rejection of the legitimacy of the fledgling democracy which they called the '5½ Republic') which it acquired in the 1980s ensured that the movement would find little support from the wider public once the constitutional issue had been settled (on student radicalism, see Sung-Chun Kim 1986; Yun 1986; Bond 1988). Of those who threw their weight behind the mass democratic protests of June 1987, the majority was not yet ready to step beyond the moderate confines of conservative democracy (even the industrial workers were reluctant to support the students' politically motivated demonstrations) (Dong 1988: 178–9).

Emergence of the Democratic Liberal Party

Having narrowly survived its first test of public opinion in 1987, Roh's government had to operate within highly restrictive political constraints. With a core voting constituency of about one-third, the government remained vulnerable to potential oppositional alliances. The DJP's loss of its national assembly majority in the election of 1988 (as a result, the government was forced to open hearings into the Kwangju Incident) and Roh's decision to cancel the mid-term referendum the following year underlined this point. Democratisation also provided enormous political leeway to the *chaebol* and the nascent labour movement. In order to govern effectively, the DJP had to reach some form of understanding with the opposition parties.

Roh took a number of initiatives to broaden the basis of his support and to prepare the conditions for coalition with the other parties. To

Table 4.2 Composition of government expenditure by function 1971–98 (%)

	Total public spending/ GNP	General admin- istration	Defence	Social develop- ment	Educa- tion	Economic develop- ment	Local govern- ment	Other
1971		9.6	26.0	na	na	42.4	12.8	9.4
1975	24.6	11.3	28.8	19.4*	–	26.7	7.7	6.2
1976	24.3	10.4	32.9	6.2	14.8	25.0	7.1	3.7
1980	29.1	9.7	35.6	6.4	17.7	21.5	6.3	2.7
1985	28.1	10.1	30.6	6.8	20.1	16.1	8.1	8.1
1986	24.9	10.1	31.4	7.9	20.0	16.5	9.4	4.8
1987	22.9	9.9	30.4	8.2	19.8	19.4	10.2	2.0
1988	22.2	9.9	30.7	7.8	20.5	14.6	9.5	6.9
1989	23.7	10.3	28.5	8.9	20.0	14.9	10.1	7.2
1990	25.0	10.2	25.0	8.9	20.4	14.1	10.1	11.3
1991	25.8	11.2	25.4	10.2	17.7	16.4	11.0	8.0
1992	26.5	12.5	25.9	9.7	19.4	18.6	11.8	2.2
1993	26.7	12.0	24.6	9.2	19.8	20.7	11.7	2.1
1994	28.1	11.1	23.7	9.0	19.3	23.1	11.1	2.7
1995	26.6	10.6	22.1	8.1	18.8	22.3	10.6	7.3
1996	27.9	10.7	22.1	8.6	18.9	22.4	10.9	6.3
1997	30.9	10.7	21.3	9.2	18.9	25.4	10.7	3.8
1998ᵖ	34.3	9.5	19.0	9.1	16.0	26.9	9.3	10.2
1999ᵖ	34.4	8.9	17.9	10.7	13.8	25.3	8.2	15.1

Notes: *Includes educational expenditure; ᵖ = provisional

Source: EPB–NSO (several issues) Major Statistics

emphasise the break with the past, former president Chun was forced to make a public apology for past misdeeds and a number of DJP hardliners were purged. On the issue of the legacy of the Fifth Republic, agreement with the opposition was reached in 1989. To demonstrate the government's commitment to redistribution and the alleviation of deprivation, social development spending was accorded higher priority. It reached a new peak of 10.2 per cent of government expenditure in 1991 (see Table 4.2).

Political opportunism and lack of ideological differentiation allowed Kim Young-Sam and Kim Jong-Pil to merge their parties with the DJP into a new political formation, the Democratic Liberal Party (DLP) in 1990.[5] There were obvious parallels with the Liberal Democratic Party (LDP), the dominant force of post-war Japanese politics (Roh 1990: 171–5). The exclusion of Kim Dae-Jung's Party of Peace and Democracy (PPD) was logical: of the three opposition leaders, he was the most populist and radical (by Korea's conservative standards, anyway) with a record of advocating fairer redistribution and a more constructive approach to North Korea. He certainly elicited more blue-collar and student sympathies. To many senior army officers and conservative members of the DJP, Kim Dae-Jung remained unacceptably radical. To the better educated as well as to the people of the majority Kyongsang Province, he appeared demagogic and authoritarian (e.g. in the way in which he ruled his followers) (Lee 1990: 55–8). By contrast, the other two Kims had stronger establishment backgrounds. Kim Jong-Pil had served as premier under Park Chung-Hee and founded the Korean CIA in 1961 while Kim Young-Sam was a professional politician renowned for moderacy. Superimposed on this ideological compatibility was regional affinity, as Kim Young-Sam came from the same province (albeit the southern half) as many senior DJP functionaries and military top brass (who represented the so-called 'T-K' [Taegu-Kyongbuk] network of North Kyongsang). An alliance between the two halves of Kyongsang Province was consistent with the prevailing economic geography of the country, since they had benefited disproportionately from the export platform (see S. Kang 1985 and Yea 1994). The Kwangju Massacre of 1980 had also made it unlikely that a leader from Cholla (especially Kim Dae-Jung) could share power with Roh Tae-Woo, one of the architects of that action. And, on a personal level, neither Kim Young-Sam nor Kim Dae-Jung could yield to the other even in the aftermath of their 1987 defeat.

The DLP now extended itself to social and regional bases beyond the reach of its constituent parties acting alone. The governing party could now count on solid regional support in Kyongsang and the much smaller Chungchong Province (Kim Jong-Pil's home province). In the key population centres outside the regions of the principal protagonists (especially Seoul and Inchon), the inclusion of the RDP extended the appeal of the governing party to those target middle-class voters (such as small-business

Table 4.3 Perceptions of social class (%)

	Upper	Middle	Lower
1980	2.6	41.0	56.4
1985	4.4	53.0	42.6
1991	1.6	61.3	37.1
1994	1.4	60.4	38.2

Source: NSO (1986 and 1995) *Social Indicators*

owners, and the aspiring 'new middle class') who had prospered under Chun and Roh but harboured grievances about specific aspects of authoritarian industrialisation, such as monopolisation and the lack of freedom. The perception of middle-class status was strong in Korean society (see Table 4.3). Being untainted by the authoritarian past, Kim Young-Sam's brand of conservative reformism could appeal to those liberal elements of society wary of the DJP. The new party could also capitalise on the sense of middle-class unease at the excesses of democratisation such as labour militancy, falling growth and rising inflation after 1989.

Roh Tae-Woo's election success in 1987, the conservative merger between the DJP and two opposition parties in 1990 and Kim Young-Sam's emergence as the DLP's presidential candidate for the 1992 election underlined the moderate nature of political change in Korea. In contrast to Latin America and Eastern Europe, democratisation in Korea was followed by the survival of the authoritarian leadership in a weakened form, forced into a pact with a section of the opposition. The gradual nature of political change points to the double-edged effect of authoritarian industrialisation. While rapid growth and its social costs fuelled the expectations for democratisation and economic reform, the legacy of authoritarianism (economic success, political centralisation and anti-communism) channelled mass and elite opinion towards constitutional reform with mild redistributive measures rather than towards radical reform. Against this background, the fragmentation of the opposition and the subsequent merger of two of its parties with the DJP was not a surprising outcome.

Democratisation and the developmental state: institutional features of the fragile miracle

The institutional basis of Korea Inc. was the state–*chaebol* developmentalist alliance. The key decisions were taken by state elites (leaders of the military, senior civilian bureaucrats, top policy specialists) in close collaboration with the top business leaders. Without having to be accountable to short-term electoral pressures, economic decisions could be made on the basis of strategic and long-term economic considerations.

As a result of democratisation, economic policy became subject to the pressure of previously excluded forces and short-term electoral considerations. The basis of development policy now had to be extended beyond the confines of state and business elites to achieve a broader consensual basis. First, the state had to win broad public backing by reversing the relative disparities that had accumulated as a result of a generation of growth-first policies. Here, redistributional objectives such as popular capitalism and housing construction were aimed particularly at winning over the middle class. Expanding that stratum was expounded explicitly in the Fifth Plan. Second, the institutional basis of development had to be reformed to make way for a new relationship of cooperation between state, business and the newly empowered labour movement. It was against the background of these considerations (with their implications for long-term economic performance) that development policy took on a redistributional emphasis (that included attempts to bring labour into formal collaborative arrangements with the state and with employers) after 1987.

Redressing the problems of relative inequality and anti-labour bias was tied up with the issue of the *chaebol* and their growing economic dominance. In the previous chapter, it was seen how the importance of the *chaebol* to economic recovery and the state's long-term economic plans had the effect of nullifying pro-competition measures (e.g. financial liberalisation, business de-concentration policies). Many aspects of the state's redistributional and consensus-building initiatives after 1987 (e.g. the extension of popular capitalism, land policies, tentative openings to organised labour) threatened to curb the power of the *chaebol*. Given their economically powerful position, democratisation opened the way for the *chaebol* not only to resist those redistributional initiatives that confronted their interests but to advance their own alternative economic agendas. In some areas, like housing construction, the *chaebol* even became the biggest gainers of the ostensibly redistributive measures. The inability of the state to tackle the problem of the *chaebol* was a sign of the state's eroded autonomy in the democratic context (a context that made public officials far more susceptible to bribery). The added inability to win over organised labour (partly a function of the state's continuing intimacy with the *chaebol*) meant that there would ultimately be no consensual basis for facing the difficult economic tasks of the 1990s. In the transition to advanced industrial status, Korea would face more difficult economic problems (see Chapter 3) than those faced by Japan a generation earlier. Her institutional framework was also more conflict-ridden than Japan's. The institutional features of the fragile miracle would persist.

Continuing advance of the chaebol

The 1980s saw the transformation in the balance of the state–business relationship from state dominance to interdependence. The business sector's economic influence became even more pronounced in the 1980s given its lateral expansion and leading role in the frontier industries. An aspect of the *chaebol*'s growing leverage was the development of informal ties by marriage with members of the ruling DJP and bureaucracy (many of whom went on to political careers and the running of public enterprises) (Kong 1989; Suh 1989). The combination of size and financial vulnerability also gave the most powerful *chaebol* considerable leverage over the state. Political stability and the survival of the government became closely intertwined with the economic survival of the major conglomerates. Concomitant with economic dominance was the widening of the political possibilities available to the *chaebol*.

The origins of big business's discontent with government policy and its subsequent dissent can be traced to the period of President Chun's leadership (1980–7). Discontent intensified after democratisation. Being close to the government yielded considerable benefits for the *chaebol*: funds for restructuring; funds for developing the frontier industries; and labour control. But there were burdens as well as gains. The demands for political donations from the governing DJP were becoming irksome (Woo 1991: 198–200), especially since much of the money was going straight to the First Family. Unlike his predecessor, Chun did not have the same hands-on interest in economics and so was perceived by leading industrialists as being insufficiently pro-business. And given his unpopularity with the public, Chun did not seem to be the safest guarantor of business interests.

If democratisation posed dangers for the *chaebol* (e.g. labour unrest and pressures for redistribution), it offered advantages as well (e.g. less official meddling in corporate affairs and the opportunity of translating economic resources into direct political influence). In the area of economic policy, financial liberalisation (first announced as an official objective in 1981), promised to provide big business with abundant external funds for expansion and for lessening their dependence on the government-controlled policy loans. External and domestic conditions were making financial liberalisation increasingly attractive to the *chaebol*. The confidence of commercial lenders was given a tremendous boost by the Plaza Agreement in 1985. Domestically, the Korean government set about reducing policy loans after 1985, a change that would make foreign borrowing (at competitive rates and without political strings) increasingly attractive to the *chaebol*. Moreover, liberalisation would facilitate the *chaebol* in achieving their ultimate objective of controlling their own banks and becoming global enterprises akin to western and Japanese TNCs. The stronger the *chaebol* became (they were greatly strengthened by the three boom years of 1986–8), the more they identified their interests with financial liberalisation (manipulating the booming stockmarket or 'financial-tech' replaced the kerb market in the late-1980s as the means of easy money-making for the *chaebol*) and became discontented with the unwillingness of government to accelerate the pace of reform (see below). Increasingly capable of standing by themselves, the *chaebol* were emerging out of the shadow of the developmental state.

Developmental agenda: conflict and consensus

During the 1960s and 1970s, the state was strong enough to resist the societal pressures that might have undermined its long-term economic priorities. Under Park, the priority was simple: to use subsidised credit to maximise export growth and develop the next generation of export winners. By the early-1980s, with the heavy industrial base established, the leading issue became that of achieving efficiency, for which market forces had to be given freer rein. Heavy industrialisation transformed big business and labour from instruments of the state's development strategy into economic interests with the resources to support their own agendas. Democratisation transformed this potential into a stronger business assertion of independence. It also enhanced the influence of electoral considerations in economic policy-making, an area in which big business could make its influence felt. The cost of political campaigning (party organisation, publicity and vote-buying) meant that politicians of all parties would have to depend heavily on business support. And through the direct bribing of public officials, the *chaebol* could circumvent those governmental regulations (e.g. in areas as diverse as credit limits, land use and environmental protection) designed to control their activity. The changing character of corruption under democracy will be further discussed in the Chapter 5.

Under Presidents Park and, to a lesser extent, Chun, there was a very close coincidence of economic objectives between state and big business in which the former was the senior partner. The ambitious official pursuit of full-range industrialisation necessitated the concentration of resources around a few giant conglomerates. For their part, the *chaebol* required extensive government support: subsidised credit; readjustment loans (especially during the difficult early-1980s); protection of the home market to compensate for export expansion based on low profit margins; and labour control. By the late-1980s, however, this relationship was being transformed as a result of the accumulation of economic power by the *chaebol* and the divergence of their interests from those of the government in key policy areas. Divergence was reflected in the *chaebol*'s demands for faster financial liberalisation and in the state's redistributive initiatives.

Financial liberalisation

Though reduced in scope after 1985, subsidised credit remained an instrument with which the government could influence the development of the private sector in the absence of a liberalised financial system. Even during the boom period of 1986–8 the government was guiding the banks into making substantial restructuring loans to the *chaebol*. In spite of the disappearance of the kerb market by the early-1990s, recipients of policy loans (for government-designated projects) got their credit at a significantly lower rate than the market rate (as represented by the corporate bond yield). But the dependence now ran both ways. Interrupting the flow of credit to one of the super *chaebol* (Samsung, Hyundai, Daewoo, Lucky–Goldstar) was no longer a viable option. For example, when Kukje, the sixth-largest *chaebol*, went bankrupt in 1986, the government ensured that its facilities would be absorbed by other *chaebol*. Their indispensability to national development (in terms of production share and their dominance in the frontier industries) gave the *chaebol* considerable leeway to pursue their own agenda.

High on that agenda was accelerated financial liberalisation. Financial liberalisation would provide big business with direct access to the foreign sector, offering the prospect of ample funds for expansion as well as independence from government control. Fearing further monopolisation – an unintended result of the limited liberalisation of 1981–6 (see Chapter 3) – as well as financial instability, the government adopted a cautious approach to financial liberalisation. In response to the official line that liberalisation would be accelerated (Government 1986: 26–7), the business sector argued that deregulation was not proceeding rapidly enough. Signalling deep dissatisfaction with the Roh administration, Hyundai chairman Chung Ju-Yung launched his own political party (the Unification National Party) in 1991 with the aim of contesting the presidency in December 1992. Chung's intervention did not result in the realignment of Korean politics, as perceived by some commentators (e.g. Back 1994) and it was even explained as a 'victory' for the government in its containment of the *chaebol* (Yeon-Ho Lee 1996: 165–6). If anything, what the incident demonstrated was the political potential of the *chaebol* under democratic conditions and the inherent instability within the ruling coalition (and of the rift that had emerged between Korea's most eminent industrialist and the ruling party). After a symbolic punishment (in the form of a small fine) of Hyundai by the Kim Young-Sam government in 1993, the new president soon made peace with the top tycoons, and the economic power of Hyundai and other top *chaebol* groups would thereafter expand.

If democratic conditions enhanced the political options available to big business, the need to garner electoral support (as well as strictly economic considerations) also resulted in government–business divergence in the areas of agricultural liberalisation and share ownership. Having no direct stake in the agricultural sector, big business supported import liberalisation for the purpose of lowering food prices (to help keep down wage costs as well as to deflect US pressure for reciprocity in the manufacturing sector). Fearful of the electoral repercussions (for urbanites sympathised with the plight of the country's farmers), the Roh government resisted US pressure for agricultural import liberalisation in the late-1980s (Jin-Hyun Kim 1988).

Share ownership

Differences existed also over share ownership. In its 1986 summary of the Sixth Development Plan (1987–91), the government had served notice of its intention to counteract economic concentration by the promotion of share ownership:

> To curb economic concentration in a limited number of large companies, excessive borrowings by such business will be prohibited. The conglomerates and many other Korean enterprises will instead be urged to list their shares on the Korea Stock Exchange and to increase their capital by allotting new shares to the public. This should help separate business management from its ownership.
>
> (Government 1986: 27–8)

Democratisation increased pressure on the government to be seen acting against the *chaebol* and promoting wider ownership.

The boom of the late-1980s was reflected in the appreciation of the Korean stock market (see Table 3.4). Apart from improving the debt–equity ratios of Korean companies, the government also favoured the spreading of 'popular capitalism' as a means of garnering political support, especially from the lower-middle classes. From 1987, the government stipulated that 20 per cent of any rights' offering should be allocated to employees. Shares in profitable public companies such as POSCO and KEPCO were sold for this politically motivated purpose in the late-1980s. Share ownership was also a means of instilling corporate loyalty by linking the welfare of the employee to the performance of the firm. One study notes that by 1991 some 1.4 million employees belonged to the Employee Share-Ownership Programme out of an investing population of some 3.9 million (Young-Ki Lee 1992: 14). While appreciating the advantages of stock market listing, the *chaebol* owners were also concerned with maintaining their majority holding (often through cross-holdings and ownership by proxy). Despite the rise of mass share ownership after 1987, the founding families still retained substantial equity holdings by indirect means (within non-transparent corporate structures). For example, in 1990, the 1 per cent of shareholders owning at least 10,000 shares also accounted for 79 per cent of all shares owned. On the other hand, some 80 per cent of shareholders had less than 500 shares (accounting for less than 4 per cent of the total shares owned) (see Table 3.7). Given the unpopularity of the *chaebol* and their close association with the DJP during the Fifth Republic, being seen to confront them made good political sense for an administration seeking to break with its authoritarian past. The dispute between the Roh government and Hyundai could thus be seen in the light of the conflicting economic and political objectives of the business sector and the government.

Land policy

Pressure to remedy another problem associated with the *chaebol*, land spec-ulation, also intensified after democratisation. The government had given notice of its intention to tackle this problem in 1986 (Government 1986: 44) but the boom aggravated the problem of speculation as surpluses found a profitable outlet in land. For example, a study found that the top thirty *chaebol* held more than 438 million square metres of land and building with a book value (i.e. a fraction of the real value) of 13,139 billion won (about $18 billion) in 1989. Of this amount, the top five owned 192 million square metres with a book value of 7,130 billion won (Kang *et al.* 1991: 35, 156). Data from the business sector put the figures at 10,053 billion won and 5,130 billion won for the top thirty and top five respec-tively (see Table 4.4). In response, the government inaugurated a Commission on the Public Concept in Land. This was followed by the implementation of various counter-measures in 1989–90 such as compul-sory land registration, tighter limits on residential land ownership and capital gains tax. In an attempt to force the *chaebol* to liquidate their excess land holdings, the government enacted the '5–8' Measure on 8 May 1990. Under its provisions, the fifty largest conglomerates were required to sell any land holdings not used for immediate purposes (T. Lee 1994: 236–45). Like previous efforts by the Chun government, these ran into the familiar problems of distinguishing between productive and excess land holding within the web-like internal structures of the *chaebol* (Dong-Kun Kim 1991: 15–26). And even as they were forced by the government to relinquish land (at favourable prices), the *chaebol* were the principal beneficiaries of the massive housing construction programme launched by the Roh govern-ment. The *chaebol*'s perspective was that the shortage of residential land was the result of the green-belt policies in Seoul and advocated the policy alternative of land deregulation. Indeed, the Suso Scandal (the building of a luxury apartment complex in a protected area) of 1990 demonstrated that it was well within the capability of the *chaebol* to circumvent these regulations by corrupt means. The abatement of the land-price accelera-tion from 1991 was related to the macroeconomic slowdown as much as to the government's land measures.

Labour incorporation: expanding the developmentalist alliance?

For big business, the sacrifices imposed by the government's develop-mental priorities were compensated for by massive financial rewards. For labour, the benefits of subordination were always less tangible. During the 1980s (as noted above) labour estrangement from the government was made worse by staunch official support for management, harsh working conditions and the application of heavy coercion at all levels. That labour had achieved greater autonomy against a background of unrelenting

Table 4.4 Securities, real estate holdings and cross-payment guarantees of the top 30 *chaebol* (billion won)

Group	Securities holdings (June 1989)	Book value of real estate holdings	Cross-payment guarantees (April 1988)
Samsung	487	1,339	9,300
Hyundai	907	1,374	5,596
Daewoo	870	947	6,175
Lucky–Goldstar	568	1,163	1,648
Hanjin	153	307	5,379
Ssangyong	456	334	1,758
Sunkyong	272	370	207
Korea Explosives	265	498	330
Dong Ah	77	104	2,458
Lotte	149	686	264
Kia	120	276	589
Daelim	139	123	726
Hyosung	77	203	710
Doosan	96	322	1,205
Dongkuk	94	264	425
Hanil	316	293	1,212
Kumho	167	232	1,139
Kolon	84	168	802
Sammi	109	134	723
Kukdong Const.	173	61	460
Miwon	31	88	177
Dongbu	150	159	1,118
Tongyang	68	47	76
Hanbo	2	85	306
KOHAP	36	18	324
Kukdong Oil	28	33	280
Haiati	34	71	221
Tongil	6	124	116
Halla	30	83	311
Poongsan	5	149	95
Total	5,967	10,053	44,130

Source: Business Korea (1991 III: 3)

governmental and managerial hostility foreclosed the possibility of gradual accommodation immediately after democratisation.

Democratisation represented a watershed for a development strategy hitherto grounded on the political exclusion of labour (on the traditional model, see Ogle 1990). The labour challenge was manifested in rising unionisation and strikes (see Tables 2.5 and 3.9) and the inception of a radical labour umbrella organisation, the National Trades Union Congress, in 1990 (the forerunner to what later became the Korean Confederation of Trades Unions). The established FKTU also asserted its independence from the state. The impact on the developmental agenda was apparent not only in wage concessions, but in the prominence accorded to the plight of labour as a political issue by all the parties. In an attempt to shed their anti-labour image, Roh Tae-Woo and the ruling DJP did a *volte-face* on labour issues and donned an ultra-reformist mantle (no doubt with an eye to the presidential and National Assembly elections) in 1987–8 as previous legal restrictions on the labour movement were repealed or diluted (Bognanno 1988: 33–4, 75–82).

Double-digit growth rates in 1987 and 1988 concealed the economic impact of labour autonomy as politicians embraced the populist tide. But the disappointing growth rate of 6.8 per cent in 1989 brought home to government and business the economic dilemma posed by accelerating unit labour costs. Strikes were particularly serious in the *chaebol*-owned heavy industry plants located in the southeastern cities of Pusan and Ulsan while the transport strikes in Seoul eroded public sympathy for the strikers. The seriousness of the situation could be seen in the return to a tougher line against strikers and student activists in 1990 (e.g. in punishing those involved in political strikes and third-party intervention). Although the level of labour disputes abated after the initial years of democratisation, the sources of labour–management conflict continued to cast a shadow over the economy. Since democratic conditions limited the scope and effectiveness of coercion, peaceful labour relations could be consolidated only on the basis of an economic consensus that brought apparent benefits to labour as well as to the business sector. The creation of the Presidential Commission on Economic Restructuring, whose 1988 report emphasised the need to balance social and economic priorities, was a step in this direction. This was followed by the formation of a tripartite round-table in 1991.

State efforts to incorporate labour into an expanded developmentalist alliance was demonstrated in the expansion of social expenditure programmes beneficial to labour after 1987. In the past, Korean governments had avoided redistributive measures, preferring instead to alleviate poverty by means of high growth and employment generation. From 1987, there was a switch to a higher priority for social development expenditure (see Table 4.2). To overcome the endemic shortage in housing supply, the Two Million Housing Construction Plan was launched in 1988. Some 17.6 trillion won of public money was allocated between 1988 and 1991, a fourfold increase on the amount spent during 1983–7. Within the total expenditure, 190,000 rental units (costing 4.2 trillion won) were constructed for the lowest income group. During 1991–2, 36,000 units of workers' sale and company-rental housing were built (Bae 1995: 389–400). The overall impact (including the contribution of the private sector) can be seen in Table 2.6. There remained, however, evidence that housing provision continued to be skewed in favour of the builders (*chaebol*) and middle-class purchasers (Yoon 1994: 131–49). Apart from higher real wages and positive social development measures, the improvement in the conditions for labour was evident also in the reductions in both the length of the working week and the incidence of industrial accidents from their peak levels of the mid-1980s. Even so, in its study of urban poverty, a Korea Development Institute report estimated that the informal sector accounted for 39 per cent of the total labour force in 1991 compared to 35.7 and 32.6 per cent in 1986 and 1981, respectively (Jong-Gie Kim *et al.* 1993: 34).

By stressing the need to bolster labour's stake in economic perform-ance, the Presidential Commission on Economic Restructuring recognised that sustained development would have to be built on a new pattern of consensual relations between labour, business and the state (Presidential Commission 1988: 101–48). Yet, for all the undoubted reforms effected between 1988 and 1992, this was a difficult transformation to bring about in the light of the long legacy of confrontation and suppression by the state. One scholar has summarised the difficulties of transition from the employers' perspective thus:

> [S]ince few Korean employers have yet been willing to allow their unilateral authority to be checked, the possible various channels for the expression and resolution of employee concerns are unable to func-tion properly. The implication is that most Korean employers still adhere to labour relations policies that emphasize the minimization of labour costs and the maintenance of strict labour control over the cultivation of employee commitment and cooperation.
>
> (Rogers 1993: 77)

Contrasts with Japan Inc.

Japanese influence on Korean modernisation has been profound. The origins of Korean capitalism can be traced to the colonial era, and the growth strategy based on selective and gradual integration into the world economy was also pioneered by Japan. The movement of Korean industry into sectors (or, at least, stages of production) vacated by Japan provides further evidence of the latter's influence. In the aftermath of the 1987 democratisation, there were affinities between the Korean and Japanese political economies. Parallels with post-war Japanese political economy included the continuing role of the bureaucracy in economic guidance, the deliberately slow pace of economic opening and an institutional frame-work based on the ruling conservative political coalition. Apart from the apparent parallels in levels of economic development between Korea in the late-1980s and Japan of a generation earlier (as symbolised by the Seoul and Tokyo Olympics), features of Japan Inc. represented a bench-mark according to which Korea's institutional basis of development could be compared: coexistence of a developmentalist state–business alliance, placid company labour unions, liberal-democratic constitutional framework dominated by a single conservative party.

The political economy of post-war Japan can be characterised in terms of the following institutional features:

1   *State–business partnership.* Private sector cooperation with government priorities arose from a combination of nationalism and shared interests (e.g. control of labour, development of frontier industries, protection of the domestic market), and from the instruments of official direction inherited from the authoritarian industrialisation phase (on post-war state–business relations in Japan, see Johnson 1981).

2   *Exclusion of labour influence over economic decision-making.* The structure of employment precluded the emergence of powerful labour organisations. Coercive labour controls of the pre-1945 and Red Purge periods were replaced by economic ones in which the affluent sectors of labour were co-opted by management (e.g. by the division between core and peripheral workers and the segmentation of the labour market) (on the 'classic' pattern of post-war corporatism of Japan Inc., see Pempel 1978: 145–57; Pempel and Tsunekawa 1979).[6]

3   *Emergence of a dominant political party that mediated between business and bureaucratic priorities* (with overlapping personnel networks linking the three). Political continuity provided the foundation for the formulation and implementation of long-term economic objectives. Developmental priorities could thus be perpetuated in the presence of a liberal-democratic framework.

A number of the above features can be seen in post-1987 Korea: shared interests between the government and big businesses over the development of the frontier industries; the attempt by the state and business to minimise radical labour influence by measures of incorporation; conservative merger and the emergence of an apparently dominant Centre–Right party, the DLP. But the conflicts over the pace of financial liberalisation, the strikes and the bitter factional disputes within the ruling party that affected Korea after democratisation were reminders of the contrasts between the two cases. They suggested that Korea's ascent to advanced industrial status was unlikely to be as smooth as had been Japan's.

The contest for economic leadership in Korea illustrates the different conditions under which the state–business partnership was forged in Japan. Japanese democratisation took place against the background of the weakening of the *zaibatsu* (conglomerates) by the Occupation authorities, credit scarcity and popular left-wing appeal (for a comparison between the *chaebol* and modern Japanese business groups, see Hattori 1989). By contrast, thirty years of sustained capitalist development, economic centralisation and the rise of global financial markets created the conditions for the Korean conglomerates to assert their independence from state control beginning from the late-1980s. Confident of their indispensability to national development (and that the government would not dare to withdraw their economic supports), the *chaebol* demanded the speedy liberalisation of finance.

The legacy of repression and the resultant labour activation militated against the emergence of the Japanese pattern of labour incorporation in post-democratisation Korea. In spite of the affinities between the employment structures of the two countries, such as the bonus system and the core–peripheral workforce division, the non-coercive mechanisms of labour control were underdeveloped in Korea. Even the very large Korean conglomerates did not dispense benevolence (e.g. permanent employment, welfare benefits and pensions) to their core employees, a practice at the heart of stable labour relations in post-war Japan (at least, prior to the 1990s' economic downturn). Consequently, Korea lacked the mechanisms that underpinned the pacification of industrial relations and the exclusion of labour influence in the post-war Japanese political economy (e.g. legitimate enterprise unions beholden to the company, fragmentation of the workforce between a privileged core and an exploited but politically inert periphery).

Superficially, parallels between the Korean DLP and the Japanese LDP were evident: a governing party linking the developmentalist bureaucracy to big business, and underpinned by a mass electoral base consisting of the middle classes and the party bosses' own provincial followings. The opposition leader Kim Dae-Jung appeared to be trapped within his regional base and condemned to permanent minority status. But the DLP's consolidation as a hegemonic party was far from assured, as it remained an unstable coalition. The instability of the DJP–RDP–NDRP merger of 1990 may be seen from the fierce opposition from the DJP conservatives (the DLP's *minjung* faction) to the prospect of Kim Young-Sam (leader of the *minju* faction of the party) assuming the presidential candidacy, and from the appearance of independent conservative candidates for the 1992 National Assembly elections. Even though Chung Ju-Yung had no hope of capturing the presidency in 1992, his intervention in politics was a sign that discontented industrialists were capable of mounting effective spoiling tactics against the DLP.

The intra-DLP wrangling and state–big business tensions can be traced to the differing circumstances under which the Japanese and the Korean conservative mergers took place in 1955 and 1990, respectively. The Japanese merger took place between equal partners drawn together by the presence of a popular left-wing movement and international conditions (the Cold War was in an intense phase). The absence of a popular Left in Korea, together with the ending of the Cold War, meant that there were less powerful forces holding the conservative partners together. Elements of the DJP were still coming to terms with power-sharing with forces which they had previously excluded. Apart from the intra-DLP conflicts, the task of simultaneously binding the DLP to big business and consolidating mass support was also more problematic in Korea. In contrast to Japan, democratisation and the conservative merger coincided with the *chaebol*'s economic ascendancy in Korea. But the *chaebol*'s unpopularity made it necessary for the DLP to accommodate public expectations for social and economic reform. At the same time, however, the *chaebol* now had much greater capacity for resisting government directives.

Conclusion

This chapter has examined the relationship between democratisation and the evolution of development policy. Democratisation was the consequence of the success of past development policies implemented by authoritarian regimes. In transforming the social structure, these policies created the typical prerequisites for democratisation (e.g. high literacy, a well developed middle class, material affluence) identified by modernisation theorists. In that sense, it could be said, authoritarianism was the victim of its own success.

Korea's democratisation, however, did not signal a dash to the complete political and economic liberalisation seen elsewhere. In those countries where democratisation had led to far-reaching political and economic transformation, authoritarianism was the victim of its own failure, a failure that led to public demands for radical economic alternatives under new leadership. In contrast to the former authoritarian regimes of Eastern Europe or Latin America, Korea's was not discredited by economic failure, and its representatives (i.e. Roh Tae-Woo and the DJP) were in a strong position to survive the test of open political contestation. Apart from enjoying the benefits of buoyant economic conditions (on the basis of which redistributional demands could be accommodated), the ruling party had the benefit of its own solid electoral base in the most populous region. Moreover, the legacy of anti-communism and the electoral appeal of the conservative professional politicians (and the corresponding electoral weakness of the radical forces such as the student movement) helped to ensure that there would be a high degree of continuity in post-democratic political and economic arrangements. Economic success did not sustain authoritarian rule (as President Chun Doo-Hwan might have hoped), but it did steer the transition from authoritarianism along a gradualist route distinct from the radical transitions to liberal capitalist democracy attempted elsewhere.

Within the model of gradualist economic reform initiated in 1981, democratisation brought with it a new official emphasis on redistribution. In not diverting resources away from investment, the absence of pro-active redistributive policies was a strength of the Korea Inc. development model. On the other hand, in light of the growing affordability of social programmes and the disproportionate benefits obtained by those who controlled the economy (e.g. *chaebol* families and senior government officials), the absence of pro-active redistributive measures was a source of de-legitimisation for the authoritarian regime. The consolidation of the new democratic regime depended on its ability to placate the social and economic grievances that stemmed from the authoritarian era. With the democratic state no longer having the capacity to impose changes on a reluctant society like its authoritarian predecessor, it was officially recognised that sustained development would have to be based on greater popular consensus (in particular between organised labour and business) than previously. It was against the background of such considerations that the democratic regime (headed by reconstructed former authoritarians) implemented redistributional policies and then made tentative openings to organised labour.

The gradualist model of economic and political reform also had its costs. In the previous chapter, it was shown how the vital role of the *chaebol* in leading the post-1980 recovery resulted in the extension of their economic dominance (in the process nullifying the effectiveness of business de-concentration measures). Democratisation would shift the power balance in the developmentalist alliance further in the *chaebol*'s favour. This would undermine the state's efforts at counteracting business concentration and the *chaebol*'s involvement in unproductive activities (e.g. land speculation) and corruption. These failures underlined the depth and persistence of the collusive ties between the state and the *chaebol*. Organised labour remained alienated from the state–business nexus and would not be integrated into an expanded developmentalist alliance. This lack of basic consensus – one of the institutional aspects of the 'fragile miracle' – would make it difficult to implement crucial structural reforms of the labour market. In spite of the superficial similarities (e.g. state–business collusion, three-party conservative merger, mechanisms of labour incorporation), the institutional framework of Korean development of the late-1980s cannot really be likened to the Japanese framework (Japan Inc.) of a generation before.

5 Rise and fall of the 'globalisation' project

The political economy of 'high cost, low efficiency'

Korean political economy in the 1990s was marked by remarkable contrasts. In spite of worries about structural economic weaknesses (the term 'high cost, low efficiency' was prevalent in economic policy circles), achievements at the macroeconomic level were impressive. The achievement of the $10,000 per capita GNP in 1995 was another milestone. The country gained accession to the OECD as its twenty-ninth member in December 1996, becoming one of Asia's two representatives (Japan was the other). On the political front, the election of the civilian Kim Young-Sam in 1992 heralded a break with the military past. The break was underlined by the pursuit of 'clean government', a drive that brought about anti-corruption measures such as the long-awaited Real Name Reform of 1993. The conviction of former presidents Chun Doo-Hwan and Roh Tae-Woo in September 1996 (for corruption and for mutiny) suggested a decisive step towards the dismantling of the *chongkyong yuchak* (political–business cohesion) that lay behind Korea's *chaebol*-dominated economy. The economic and political reform efforts of the Kim government came to be represented by the term 'globalisation' (*segye hwa*). Used at every opportunity (though its precise meaning was never specified) to highlight the new government's reformist zeal, the term came to be associated with the completion of economic liberalisation and democratisation. President Kim declared that his reforms would create a 'New Korea with a New Economy'.

Within a year of joining the OECD, however, these achievements had all but evaporated.[1] The balance of payments was already under pressure from the collapse of semi-conductor prices in the summer of 1996. That December exporters were further hit by strikes triggered by the abortive labour reform. Several leading *chaebol* (including the leading car maker, Kia) went bankrupt in 1997. The spate of *chaebol* bankruptcies and the corruption cases involving high-ranking public officials (including a member of the First Family) were signs that the malpractices associated with the state–*chaebol* developmentalist alliance were still prevalent. On top of these structural problems, the shockwaves from the Southeast Asian financial crisis sent Korean currency and share values crashing in November 1997.

Burdened by debt-servicing problems, Korea came under the sway of tough IMF conditionalities in December 1997 (just as she had done in 1981). Per capita GNP in 1998 dipped to $6,500. In spite of their early promise, the achievements of 'globalisation' had proven more illusionary than real; Kim Young-Sam left office the most unpopular leader in Korean history (even more so than the disgraced Chun Doo-Hwan).

This chapter locates the persistence of the fragile miracle in the failure of the state to reshape the institutional basis of Korea Inc. By that I mean putting the state–conglomerate relationship on a legal and transparent basis (in the absence of which malpractices such as obtaining bank loans by irregular means thrive), while extending the developmentalist alliance to include labour. This is illustrated by an examination of five key areas of economic and political reform under the Kim Young-Sam government's 'globalisation' project: financial liberalisation; the shift from direct to functional intervention; business de-concentration; labour; and anti-corruption. The origins and fate of policy reform in these areas will highlight observations that have emerged in previous chapters. First, the political imperative of maintaining high growth rates was as prevalent under Kim Young-Sam as under previous governments. By preventing radical liberalisation or business de-concentration measures the government helped to perpetuate the dominance of the *chaebol*. Second, the *chaebol* were poised to take advantage of the selective liberalisation measures in finance to expand on the basis of debt-led growth (perpetuating the traditional vulnerability to external shocks). Consistent with the trends of the 1980s, the *chaebol* insinuated themselves into domains vacated by the state. Moreover, as direct intervention was pared back, the *chaebol* emerged as the principal beneficiaries of the new functional intervention. Third, growth and democratisation continued to shift influence within the developmentalist alliance towards the *chaebol*. This was evident from their vocal articulation of alternative agendas on the issues of business deregulation and labour reform, and in their circumvention of financial regulations as exposed by the corruption and bankruptcy cases of 1996–7. Fourth, the failure to bridge the historical enmity between business and the newly empowered labour movement prevented the implementation of much-needed labour market reforms. Fifth, the formal shift towards 'globalisation' in 1993 underlined the rapid pace of international changes since 1985, changes that were making the traditional developmentalist practices untenable.

Sources of the globalisation project

Contents of the globalisation agenda

Kim Young-Sam's assumption of the presidency in February 1993 gave a fresh impetus to economic and political reform. The ongoing Seventh Five-Year Economic and Social Development Plan (1992–6) (Government

1992) formulated under the Roh government was superseded by a revised economic programme. First, a 100-Day Plan for ameliorating the short-term problems of the economy was introduced in March (KIEP 1993). This was followed in July by the launching of the New Economy Plan (1993–7) (Government 1993). The stated aims of the plan consisted of three main parts: to liberalise the economy to levels approximating those of the advanced industrialised economies; to consolidate the democratic system by eliminating the vestiges of authoritarian rule (especially the corruption and iniquities flowing from the state–big business cohesion); and to improve the quality of life to a degree commensurate with the country's economic advance. Like the Seventh Plan it superseded, the New Economy Plan expected high rates of growth to be maintained. For example, by 1998 it aimed to boost total and per capita GNP to $650 billion and $14,000, respectively, while the balance of payments deficit would be eliminated (Government 1993: 352–3). The new government's aim of completing the transition from state to market-led development was stated in the 100-Day Plan:

> The engine of economic growth adopted by previous regimes can no longer contribute to continued growth in Korea's new democratic environment and in the rapidly changing international economic scene. A new engine must be developed in order to sustain Korea's growth especially in the context of the new setting which advocates a market economy and market opening policies. In the new environment, voluntary participation and initiatives of private economic agents will be essential elements for economic growth. The cornerstone of the New Economy lies in increasing productivity based on voluntary participation and private-sector initiative and in sharing burdens and benefits of growth.
>
> The year 1993 will be a fundamental turning point, marking a change from the development mechanism under a government-led regime to a new mechanism under democracy. The fundamental change will require institutional reforms in may fields, including reforms in administrative, fiscal, and financial areas, intended to reduce government control over private economic activities.
>
> (KIEP 1993: 4)

From its outset, the Roh government had recognised the necessity for the reform of economic policy and institutions (Presidential Commission 1988). In fact, the intensification of the international and domestic pressures for accelerated reform called for under the revised economy plan was also acknowledged in Roh's Seventh Plan (1992–6):

> Korea is now at a crossroads and must consolidate its foundations before it can enter the ranks of the advanced countries. However, the

rapidly changing environment surrounding the Korean economy poses difficult challenges. Internationally, the developed countries have increased their pressure to open the Korean market and have become more protective of their technologies. At the same time, international competition has become fiercer. Domestically, demands for growth that is regionally balanced and more social welfare are growing.

To overcome these domestic and international challenges, the following three development strategies will be pursued during the Seventh Five-Year Plan: 1) strengthen industrial competitiveness, 2) enhance social equity and spur balanced regional developments, 3) implement internationalization and liberalization and pave the way for national unification.

(Government 1992: 26–7)

In a similar vein, the New Economy Plan emphasised four interrelated areas: private initiative replacing the government as the new engine of economic growth; structural economic reform (wealth, finance and public government); reform of economic consciousness; and crucial areas of economic policy (strengthen growth potential, expand international market foundation, improve citizens' welfare) (Government 1993: 13).

The renewed emphasis on accelerated reform under the New Economy Plan and its predecessor could be attributed to international and domestic circumstances: the changing international economic context of the 1990s; the transformation of Korean civil society after the 1987 democratisation; and the recognition that the slowness of past reform (complacency was bred by the externally induced boom of 1986–9) was now affecting economic performance. Based on recognition of these changes, the New Economy Plan implied far-reaching restructuring away from the policy instruments (e.g. policy loans, trade protectionism and the semi-closure of the financial system) and institutional relationships (e.g. the collusive state–*chaebol* relationship, the political exclusion of labour) that once underpinned economic success. Not only was the incoming Kim Young-Sam government receptive to the economic case for change but, as Korea's first democratic civilian leader in thirty years, economic reform suited the new president's bid to make his mark on history by breaking decisively with the authoritarian past.

Patterns of gradualist reform 1981–92

Recovery first 1981–5

In accelerating economic reform, the Kim Young-Sam government's globalisation project was acknowledging the limits of the gradualist pattern of economic reform initiated in 1981 (Chapter 3). The 1979–80 crisis had exposed the structural weaknesses of the Korea Inc. model of

development: inefficiency of government intervention (subsidisation, pick-
ing winners, etc.); high levels of business concentration around financially
fragile *chaebol*; and the limits of a labour control policy dependent on
coercive control and labour abundance. The need to maintain growth
and the presence of powerful interests associated with authoritarian industrialisation ensured that prior policies would not be reversed rapidly.

Liberalisation (especially of trade and finance) was designed to enhance
the efficiency of a private sector heavily dependent on state support.
Although the new economic team advising President Chun consisted of
US-trained advocates of liberalisation, there was less enthusiasm among
big business and sections of the bureaucracy for the dismantling of
policy instruments that had served the Korean economy (and themselves)
well for almost two decades. The umbrella organisation for the *chaebol*,
the Federation of Korean Industries, expressed its reservations against
rapid liberalisation in the early-1980s. Neo-mercantilism was prevalent in
the economic ministries such as the Ministry of Commerce and Industry
and the Ministry of Finance. These agencies waged a campaign of opposition against the liberalising technocrats in the Blue House (B.-S. Choi
1989). This mind-set was nurtured by the decades of US indulgence of
Korean protectionist practices, a reward for loyalty to US foreign
policy. Economic nationalism became embedded as a result. Not surprisingly, the idea that domestic firms should have to surrender market
share or even face bankruptcy for the sake of some notion of competitiveness defined by abstract economic models found few supporters in the
economic ministries.

The practical problems involved with rapid liberalisation were real
enough. By 1980, monopolisation had advanced to the point that the fate
of the economy was tied up with the survival of the *chaebol*, especially the
powerful ones. Over-exposure to competitive forces threatened the viability
of these fragile giants with the fearful social and economic consequences
that collapse would entail. The priorities of growth, restructuring without
losing jobs or capacity, and the development of new export sectors ensured
that financial supports from the state would have to continue for the foreseeable future.

Similar constraints also applied to business de-concentration measures.
They could not be applied too rigorously for fear of undermining the
chaebol. It was noticeable that the Chun government's zeal for reform of
the chaebol (e.g. by the Monopoly Regulation and Fair Trade Act passed
in 1980) wavered once it fully appreciated the extent of the interdependence
between state and conglomerate and the costs to both sides of any rupturing
of the relationship. Given the importance of the *chaebol* to economic revival,
the implementation of effective measures to reduce the concentration of
economic power took lesser priority. The effect of the weak application
of business de-concentration measures, the continuing financial supports
and general economic recovery was further concentration. The *chaebol* had

now also established themselves in the frontier industries and in the partially liberalised domains such as finance. On the labour front, the recovery of competitiveness between 1980 and 1985 was achieved by the intensification of the anti-labour policy; temporary success was bought at the expense of longer term reconciliation.

The missed opportunity 1986–8

In the absence of effective anti-monopoly measures, it was not surprising that the partial financial liberalisation measures resulted in further concentration rather than competition. It was considered that far-reaching reform (full-scale liberalisation and rigorous anti-monopoly measures) would have to await the economy's return to conditions of stable growth. The conditions for far-reaching economic reform seemed to have arrived in the late-1980s. So long as the economy was growing rapidly, however, there was little incentive for the government to implement difficult reform measures to correct the economy's fundamental weaknesses: dominant *chaebol* with unsound financial structures; weak small and medium-sized enterprises; technological dependence on Japan; and an outmoded institutional environment founded on authoritarian politics. Economic bureaucrats were reluctant to give up their remaining important economic powers (e.g. regulation of financial institutions, setting of the interest rate). The growth of conglomerate power consequent of previous partial liberalisations reinforced their reluctance. On the other hand, the attitude of the *chaebol* had changed. Rapid growth, the improvement of internal financial structures and the potential gains from deregulation all contributed to the intensification of the *chaebol*'s demands for more liberalisation and opened up differences in the state–business relationship.

The boom of 1986–8 also altered the economic perceptions of both the Korean elite and public. It looked as if affluence had finally arrived. The surpluses were squandered as each section of society took its share. The emphasis on redistributional policies by the Roh government was an important break with past development policy. At the same time, however, the government failed to tackle a root cause of maldistribution, the *chaebol*-dominated economy. Attention was focused instead on gaining short-term political advantage. The accumulation of substantial trade surpluses, the rise of mass consumerism, a booming stock market and the capacity of industry to absorb hefty wage increases in 1987–8 were signs of the complete economic turnaround since 1980. The economy appeared to be firmly set along the trajectory of self-sustaining growth towards advanced industrial status.

For a time, Korea was on show and the feeling of triumphalism was evident. In the self-congratulatory atmosphere of the late-1980s, confident *chaebol* executives boasted that Korea would overtake the US while Korean basketball fans cheered the Russians and booed the Americans at the 1988

Olympics. The favourable economic environment bred complacency on all sides. With democratisation unleashing pent-up labour demands, all politicians rode the populist wave and gave little thought to the long term. Insecure in its legitimacy, the Roh government tried to buy popularity by raising social expenditures and building homes. On top of the massive wage hikes for labour and the middle-class consumption boom (fuelled by a spiralling stock market), the government joined in the euphoria and poured money into an ambitious housing project to build 2 million homes in five years. Instead of upgrading its competitiveness by investing in new plant and technology, big businesses adhered to the low skill model. They obtained artificial profits from land acquisition and government-funded construction projects. Financial liberalisation also opened up the way for the *chaebol* to make easy money from the stock market and other such institutions (so-called 'financial-tech' or '*chae*-tech'). The democratic transition was certainly being celebrated in style.

The consequence of slow-down 1989–92

The delusions of superiority would soon be exposed for what they were. The slow-down of growth in 1989 and the return to trade deficits in 1990 were shocking reminders of the economy's underlying weaknesses. These reverses were proof of the illusory nature of the affluence caused by the 'Three Blessings' (low oil prices, low international interest rates and appreciated yen). The failure to take advantage of the boom for structural reform and reinvestment in industrial competitiveness was now evident:

> The illusion that Korea was becoming an advanced country also began to loosen the work ethic of entrepreneurs and workers, alike, causing rapid wage hikes, the degradation of product quality, and a slowdown in the development of technology.
>
> (KIEP 1993: 2–3)

Pressures for reform again resurfaced. These pressures were now of a social as well as an economic nature. Big business and the middle classes blamed the blue-collar wage hikes for making the economy uncompetitive (and for dampening the stock market, which fell from 919 to 587 points between 1989 and 1992). This prompted a return to tougher anti-labour measures. Everybody resented the *chaebol* for their involvement in land speculation, and so the government tried to force the *chaebol* to sell off their non-industrial land from 1989. In turn, the *chaebol* blamed their loss of competitiveness not only on labour but actually on the government for not having deregulated quickly enough. Once again, the subjective and the practical circumstances for *chaebol* reform were out of synch. The anti-monopoly measures (e.g. the Second Amendment to the Monopoly Regulation and Fair Trade Act, 1990) coincided with the slowing of the economy. The impulse for reform, however, was over-ridden by the public clamour for recovery. Naturally, only the *chaebol* could spearhead that recovery.

It had long been recognised that the injection of foreign competition (trade and financial liberalisation) combined with properly policed regulatory measures (e.g. restrictions on diversification, the enforcement of transparency and internal accountability to outside shareholders) would promote efficiency. With democratisation, the dangers associated with such reform (slower growth, unemployment, middle-class dissatisfaction) weighed even more heavily on the minds of the political leaders. How, then, did the support for reform fall into place? Something fundamental had changed in 1989, the year of the 'slow-down' (actually the economy grew by 7 per cent). The changing nature of the international linkages after 1989 created pressures for the accelerated reform of the Korean development model.

Sources of policy change

International context of globalisation

This study has emphasised the role of the US in effecting previous changes of policy direction in Korea. It was argued in previous chapters that, up to 1985, the US involvement in Korea was supportive of the developmental state. Motivated by strategic concerns, this support extended to tolerance of Korea's illiberal trading policies. With the decline of the Cold War from 1985, the US began to shift from her previously benign attitude. The shift was accelerated with the end of the Cold War in 1991. Economic issues, in particular the establishment of a supranational framework of institutions favourable to international trade and capital flows, came to displace security issues from the diplomatic agenda. As in previous episodes, changes in US global orientation brought pressure for corresponding adaptation on the part of Korea.

The ending of the Cold War brought latent economic differences to the fore. Strategic location no longer shielded Japan and Korea from strict US scrutiny of trading practices. Both countries were judged to be exponents of protectionism and put under pressure to open their markets. Dismantling the pockets of protectionism provided not only access to growing markets for competitive US industries (e.g. banking, agricultural products, pharmaceuticals, aerospace, software, entertainments) but facilitated the restructuring of those sectors burdened with high domestic labour costs (e.g. cars, electronics). Having lost much ground to East Asian rivals during the 1970s and early-1980s, these sectors responded by implementing aggressive efficiency measures, central to which was the transnationalisation of production via foreign investment (the formation of NAFTA in 1993 consolidated such ties with Mexico and Canada). In both respects, Japan, Korea, Taiwan, and, increasingly, China presented enormous opportunities for US business (whose manufacturing sector was now resurgent after the restructuring of the 1980s).

US competitiveness did not depend only on achieving an open trading environment. It depended also on an environment that would afford protection of intellectual property rights to key American exports of 'intangible products', products that were sensitive to copyright violation – e.g. software, the film industry – (Evans 1997: 77–8), a practice with which East Asia was commonly associated in the US. These factors underpinned the high profile of US economic diplomacy towards Northeast Asia in the 1990s, consisting of pressure for faster liberalisation (e.g. by threats of unilateral retaliation) combined with multilateral engagement (e.g. via the Uruguay Round/WTO and APEC). Some commentators (e.g. Cumings 1989) have even associated the US support for democratisation with these economic motives.

In an international economic order dominated by neo-liberal principles or 'Washington Consensus' (Williamson 1989 and 1993),[2] there could be no place for the traditional Korean instruments of industrial promotion such as policy loans and import tariffs. In October 1989, Korea graduated from the General Agreement on Trade and Tariff's Balance of Payments conditions that allowed agricultural import restrictions on the grounds of trade deficits. It was a precursor to further liberalisation pressure. Even in the absence of full trade liberalisation, the trade balance was in deficit. This was a sign of the persisting weakness of Korean industry (especially in its dependence on Japanese suppliers) and the dangers associated with full exposure to foreign competition. On the other hand, it was apparent that trade liberalisation was unavoidable and Korea would have little choice other than to adapt. Besides, external pressures for full market access had their advantages. First, signing up to the rules of international free trade would facilitate access to target markets. Fettered by a maze of official regulations (from procedural red tape to the major instruments of government control such as entry–exit barriers and financial regulations), Korean business was in dire need of liberalisation anyway. Competing on 'level playing fields' with US, Japanese and European TNCs was seen as a means for exerting discipline on the *chaebol*. Domestic labour and land prices had been steadily pushing Korean producers outwards ever since 1985. Second, for the new government, difficult decisions could now be blamed on external pressure.

From a strategic angle it was necessary for Korea to be congruent with the evolving international economic trends. An ever-present consideration in South Korea's external orientation was the rivalry with the communist North. This also extended to economic diplomacy. By the late-1980s, the economic race with the North had effectively been won, and this superiority was translated into diplomatic dominance by the Roh Tae-Woo government's *Nordpolitik*. Through the lure of economic incentives, the capitalist South progressively diluted Russian and Chinese support for the

North (Russian support for North Korea had ceased with the dismemberment of the USSR in 1991). In spite of economic inferiority, the North Korean military still posed a formidable threat. The globalisation project would help to meet this challenge in two ways. First, economic internationalisation would help to deepen Korean interdependence with the advanced countries. Second, the South could use its economic potential to help stabilise the North. It was likely that the South would have to provide economic assistance to forestall the dangers associated with the collapse of the North's ailing planned economy. North–South economic cooperation could also contribute to the development of a dynamic Northeast-Asian growth zone involving the two Koreas, China, Russia and Japan.

Represented in terms of the completion of economic liberalisation and the overhaul of the institutional structure of development, popular economic terms of the 1990s such as 'internationalisation' (*kukje hwa*) 'globalisation' (*segye hwa*) also carried strong nationalistic connotations associated with the enhancement of Korean economic power and diplomatic influence. The terms were conveniently ambiguous. With their connotations of economic openness, they appealed to the liberal observers outside. On the other, hand, the terms also drew on Koreans' deep-rooted desire for international recognition of their economic achievement and to be thought of as an 'advanced' society, second in Asia only to Japan. Such sentiment lay behind the bid by the Kim government to achieve OECD membership, a move actually initiated by its predecessor (EPB 1992: 434–6). While belonging to the 'club' of industrialised nations brought no immediate tangible benefits to the national economy, for Korea to remain outside while Mexico, the Czech Republic and Turkey gained membership would have been an affront to national pride.

Changing orientation of the chaebol

The New Economy Plan was also a consequence of the intense liberalisation pressure applied by business from the late-1980s. The *chaebol* also appreciated the challenges and opportunities of liberalisation, and they came to reassess the institutional foundations of the development model. In the early-1980s, the *chaebol* reacted against the government's liberalisation proposals. Having become financially more self-sufficient with the 1986–8 boom, the confidence and political clout of the *chaebol* grew. As the potential benefits were recognised, the fear of liberalisation gave way to demands for faster reform. They argued that if they were to compete effectively with foreign TNCs, they would have to enjoy a flexible operating environment like their rivals, one in which governmental controls (over crucial areas such as entry and exit, financing, employment practices and movement of capital overseas) would be greatly diminished.

With their high growth rates, the *chaebol* had the potential to borrow directly from international sources to finance their ambitious expansion plans. Capital could be borrowed much more cheaply from external sources (e.g. see US and Japanese interest rates in Table 2.1). They also argued that in order to take advantage of the most efficient factors of production on a world scale, Korean industry would have to become internationalised. This explained their insistence on the dismantling of government barriers via speedy deregulation to bring about a 'level playing field'. Expansion overseas represented the *chaebol*'s survival strategy in the face of the potential 'squeeze' on Korean industry from first world producers and new NICs. Each conglomerate's internationalisation strategy resembled in microcosm the government's strategy for raising Korea's economic status. The parallels were evident: attract inflows of funding and technology; relocate production overseas to utilise lower cost labour and improve proximity to target markets; reorganise local labour to improve its productivity; and branch out into new areas of activity while exiting from the declining ones.

Change of political leadership

It was against the background of economic reversal and international pressure that the Seventh Five-Year Economic and Social Development Plan (1992–6) was formulated by the Roh government. The government once again made the familiar pledges about promoting economic internationalisation, industrial competitiveness, de-concentration of economic power and equity. But 1992 was an important election year, and so the objectives set out in the Seventh Plan had to await the transition to a new government. The outgoing President Roh Tae-Woo was in no position to take any fresh reform initiatives. His personal credibility had been tarnished by the Suso Scandal of 1990, while the ruling DLP was wounded by Hyundai founder Chung Ju-Yung in the National Assembly elections of 1992. And, as his tenure of office drew to a close, influence within the party started to ebb away from Roh and flow towards DLP presidential hopeful Kim Young-Sam.

A professional politician not noted for his specialist knowledge, the new president Kim, Young-Sam, sought to make his mark on the economy. He labelled his brand of economics 'Y-S NOMICS'. The new president pledged to end the old collusion of *chaebol* (rival candidates pledged to do the same) and the politics practised by his military predecessors as part of the wider drive to transform Korea into an advanced democratic society ('New Korea'). The commitment to reform was signalled by the new administration's launch of a 100-Day Reform that included a vigorous anti-corruption drive. In July 1993, a New Economy Plan (1993–7) was launched to supersede the ongoing Seventh Plan, and the government announced the intention of entering the OECD within President Kim's term of office (1993–8). Liberalisation would be an integral part of a government that wanted to be identified with political and economic openness. Since admittance into the OECD was also conditional on advancing the liberalisation agenda, it too was a spur to reform.

Gradualist aspects of the globalisation project

While the principle of accelerated liberalisation was accepted, there remained questions about how the project would be implemented. Here, the continuities with the gradualist pattern of reform of the previous dozen years become evident. In the design and implementation of the globalisation project, three aspects of continuity with past reforms stood out. First, to minimise its socially disruptive impact, liberalisation would be completed in a phased (albeit accelerated) manner. Second, the dismantling of the old instruments of intervention did not mean the withdrawal of the state from the economic arena. Instead, the state would develop new market-conforming forms of intervention in areas where the business sector could not provide leadership (functional needs of industry, redistributional and social aspects of development, regulation of the business environment). Third, in contrast to the neo-liberal opposition to corporatism, the opening of the developmentalist alliance to labour would be one of the defining features of the New Korea. These continuities contrasted the Korean globalisation project with the radical neo-liberal programmes being conducted almost simultaneously in parts of Latin America and Eastern Europe. The need for a modified developmental role for the state becomes apparent from a consideration of the potential dangers involved in the globalisation project.

Instabilities of globalisation and their policy implications

The history of liberalisation in Korea and elsewhere suggested that serious instabilities could arise. First, trade and financial liberalisation could give rise to macroeconomic instabilities detrimental to the real economy: the growth of imported consumer goods widening the trade deficit; short-term financial inflows stoking up inflation (much of the economic debate within institutions such as the KDI centred around this issue); and increased sensitivity to external interest rate fluctuations. Second, while partial liberalisation worked to accentuate the power of the *chaebol* (see below), full liberalisation threatened to expose the competitive disadvantages of vulnerable sectors, resulting in local companies' loss of domestic market share or even in their takeover by more efficient foreign competitors. Financial liberalisation threatened to plunge profitable Korean firms into the world of the hostile takeover. Unemployment posed a serious dilemma for a political and bureaucratic elite whose legitimacy had long been defined by its ability to deliver growth. Growth was the basis of the conservative political hegemony. Electoral considerations now made this an even more sensitive issue for the government.

Third, instead of fostering competition, Korea's piecemeal liberalisations of the past accentuated the concentration of economic power as the *chaebol* captured the economic domains vacated by the state. The removal of industrial entry barriers risked aggravating the problem of concentration since the *chaebol* could dominate emerging sectors by their financial power, one such method being the acquisition of smaller but more dynamic companies (e.g. Samsung's attempt to enter the car market by acquiring Kia Motors). The reinvigoration of the competitiveness of local firms was one possible outcome of foreign entry into the Korean market. Another was the reinforcement of monopolistic tendencies if the *chaebol* and foreign TNCs colluded to carve up the market (e.g. by licensing agreements that allowed locally made products to carry prestigious foreign brand-names). Instead of freeing up the economy, deregulation had the potential to strengthen monopoly power.

This concern would mean a difference between the *chaebol* and the state in their perspectives on the meaning of globalisation. While both government and *chaebol* sought enhanced international competitiveness via accelerated liberalisation reforms, the two also differed over the pace and scope of deregulation. Disagreements between state and business over liberalisation first surfaced in the 1980s. The *chaebol* supported the dismantling of the barriers to entry and exit, a measure that would allow them to discard or relocate their loss-making sectors and facilitate their movement into promising fields (e.g. take control of the lucrative public monopolies set to be privatised). Many unprofitable sectors within the *chaebol* were originally taken over at the insistence of the government but became highly burdensome at a time when foreign competitors were ruthlessly downsizing or using cheaper labour. The *chaebol* hoped to follow a corresponding strategy. They resisted business de-concentration measures that sought to define their scope of operation (which they argued was for the deregulated market to decide). For the government, the dangers of monopolisation pointed to a pro-active role aimed at effecting business de-concentration. Given the declining importance of the policy loan, financial controls and entry–exit regulations constituted the remaining instruments of government leverage over the *chaebol*. Not surprisingly, senior economic bureaucrats (the Ministry of Trade and Industry being particularly committed to maintaining some type of industrial policy) were unwilling to relinquish their residual powers.

The globalisation project implied that the state had to assume a proactive role in other areas too. The possible domains for government intervention and leadership were those that had been neglected in previous development plans. Because of the importance to competitiveness, such domains (e.g. transport, regional development and technology) could not be left to the private sector alone. The dismantling of instruments of direct intervention was opening up space for functional ones. There was the question of social displacement caused by rapid liberalisation. It raised the question of what residual role the state should play in sustaining social cohesion. For a country with Korea's legacy of government economic leadership, growth orientation, interventionism, and fragile political stability the neo-liberal path did not appear so suitable. Such considerations opened the way towards an enhanced social development role for the state in managing the tensions of restructuring (e.g. social safety-net, retraining) and building a consensus for smoother reform (e.g. by improving industrial relations and the quality of government). These wider considerations and their policy implications were evident from the Seventh Plan and its successor.

The status of organised labour

The rise of organised labour also shaped the development agenda of the 1990s. For nearly three decades of industrialisation, the presence of an authoritarian political system precluded the emergence of economic alternatives and, in particular, the advocacy of fairer distribution in favour of labour and other disadvantaged elements. Since rapid industrialisation was accompanied by the concomitant growth of the industrial workforce and as the harshness of early capitalism engendered social discontent, the state expanded its mechanisms of control in the attempt to prevent labour mobilisation. Not surprisingly, despite all the efforts of the authoritarian state (coercion, incorporation, bureaucratic obstacles, propaganda), labour's potential (especially of the 'proletarianised' workers in large enterprises) to assert its interests independently was enhanced by economic development. Even the ferocious state repression of the early-1980s proved to be only a temporary reverse. The easing of the dictatorship after 1983 and the controlled liberalisation thereafter provided the opportunity for labour to regain and extend its strength.

The significance of the economic crisis of the late-1970s was that it marked the limits of the model of development based on cheap labour and its subordination. The labour situation has since become a central feature of the crisis facing the Korean development model. In spite of numerous declarations of intent (e.g. Government 1981), governments both authoritarian and democratic were unable to move beyond the pattern of coercive labour control established during the 1960s and 1970s but which no longer suited the more open political environment of the 1990s. If the economic crisis of the late-1970s signalled the end of the development model based on an unlimited supply of cheap labour, the political repression of the early-1980s represented a last-ditch attempt at preserving that model. For a period of time labour was effectively demobilised, and this was instrumental in the improvement of competitiveness during the 1980s. In the longer term, however, its effect was to make the transition towards improved industrial relations more difficult by deepening labour's grievances. The exponential surge in strikes and in unionisation after democratisation in 1987 indicated just how deeply felt labour's grievances were, and not only over pay but over working conditions and the authoritarian style that typifies Korean management. In spite of the wage concessions won by labour in 1987–8, the Roh government returned to a tougher line in 1990 in support of business and capitalised on public unease (especially from the middle class) over the economic slow-down. Elements of the authoritarian regime survived the transition to democracy. For example, the Labour Law continued to prohibit 'third-party' intervention in industrial disputes, while the new democratic union (*minju nochong*) was not accorded official recognition.

The state's strong anti-labour bias prolonged the dependence of Korean business on growth achieved through cheap labour working long hours (a strategy once suited to the country's high level of basic literacy). As a consequence of market factors and the growth of labour's organisational strength (achieved in spite of official discrimination), Korean labour by the 1990s was expensive by the standards of newly industrialising countries. Maintaining competitiveness called for a transition involving the relocation of low-wage production overseas, and the adoption of flexible and skill-intensive production processes at home. Successful reform of employment practice depended on labour and business being prepared to accept gains and concessions, but the legacy of confrontational industrial relations hardened both sides' reluctance to compromise.

The contribution of strikes and wage hikes to the economic problems after 1988 demonstrated that sustained growth in a non-authoritarian context depended on stable industrial relations. This, in turn, depended on the establishment of some sort of understanding between labour and capital. In spite of the Roh government's return to more coercive anti-labour policies in 1990, it was recognised that such methods were fast losing their effectiveness. Establishing such a social consensus was likely to be difficult, given the background of confrontation. Yet the economic context of the 1990s made it imperative that such a reconciliation be realised. As mentioned above, to become internationally competitive the *chaebol* had to become transnationalised like their rivals. Apart from the relocation of productive processes abroad, greater flexibility had to be imparted to the labour market and workplace organisation at home. The Korean labour market was governed by rules (dating back to 1953) which made for an ostensibly very liberal labour code, but the non-enforcement of those rules was part of the state's anti-labour policy during the authoritarian years. Democratisation and labour's demands for the enforcement of existing labour laws and the overturning of the repressive measures introduced under the military regimes (as implied by Korea's entry into the OECD) threatened to make the labour market very rigid.

The state remained the only force capable of managing the divisive effects of democratisation and accelerated economic reform. The task of the government was to reconcile two competing demands: to reform the labour code in the interests of competitiveness; and to enhance labour rights in line with OECD requirements and the pressure being exerted by Korea's now active labour movement. The background of government–business hostility to labour made this a difficult task, but the cause of reform was perhaps helped somewhat by President Kim Young-Sam's history as an opponent of authoritarianism. Even so, the sensitivities of the issue led the government to delay labour reform until the latter part of its term of office, after the National Assembly election of April 1996.

Summary

The globalisation project embodied in the New Economy Plan responded to the growth limits of the authoritarian industrialisation model of development. The controls with which the Korean state had nurtured the *chaebol* (e.g. policy loans, trade and capital flow restrictions, anti-labour policy) were incompatible with the liberalised world trading order and the existence of a democratised polity. Traditional economic controls fettered the outward expansion of Korean business. To compete with the TNCs of the first world, Korean firms also had to maximise their efficiency by taking advantage of opportunities for globalised production. For the *chaebol*, excessive state control impeded their competitiveness by limiting their access to foreign capital. Politically, the Kim Young-Sam regime's pursuit of 'clean government' (here, the corrupt links between public officials and business consequent of decades of intervention were the obvious targets) and Korea's formal promotion to 'advanced status' (membership of the OECD) gave new momentum to the major economic reforms that the New Economy Plan signified. If liberalisation of the economy and the outward movement of Korean capital represented a break with the old-style developmental state, the government's concern with mitigating the economically and socially destabilising effects of the transition (e.g. in establishing a consensual approach to employment reform) represented continuity with the pattern of gradual systemic change begun in 1981.

Liberalisation of capital flows

Capital flows were strictly controlled under Korea Inc. By the early-1990s, both business and government recognised the benefits of further liberalisation. Without the opening of the domestic economy to trade and capital flows, Korean firms could not acquire the foreign finance, the technology, the labour and the production sites needed for them to become internationally competitive. This became one of the principal aspects of economic policy change under the globalisation project. In outlining the main contours of liberalising reform, this section highlights continuities with the themes already raised in Chapter 3: the continuing caution of the authorities over the relaxation of control (what Dalla and Khatkhate (1995) called the 'regulated deregulation' of finance); the persistence of the sources of the 'fragile miracle' in the onward march of the *chaebol* (occupying domains vacated by the state) and in the structural dependence of Korea on Japanese capital.

Financial liberalisation

For almost three decades, the cornerstone of Korean state-directed indus-trialisation was the government's control of the financial sector. In spite of the formal privatisation of the banks in 1982, finance continued to be subordinated to the demands of industrial policy. The legacy of massive loans (many of them non-performing) to the business groups, made at the behest of the government, had left the banks financially vulnerable and dependent on support from the central bank. The current accounts surpluses and stock market boom that accompanied the robust industrial performance of 1986–8 led to an improvement of the financial structures of the *chaebol* and their supporting banks. These conditions favoured the gradual liberalisation of the financial sector. From 1985, the government began the gradual reduction of policy loans as a share of commercial bank lending, while low inflation enabled the banks to charge real rates of interest. Financial developments of the 1980s (development of the NBFIs, rise of the corporate bond and stock markets shown on Table 3.4) led to the decline and disappearance of the kerb market by the early-1990s. While the decline of the policy loan after 1985 signalled the state's inten-tion of reducing direct financial support for big business, this support could be reduced only gradually. In spite of the favourable circumstances of 1986–8, the government could not quickly relinquish its control of the financial sector. By international standards, Korean manufacturing compa-nies still stood out by their high debt–equity ratios and their low technology. To effect an orderly restructuring of the declining sectors and to provide the emerging industries with the needed infusion of funds, the government continued to make use of the policy loan (see 'preferential credit' in Table 3.1). It also made use of administrative or 'window' guidance through the banks to achieve its industrial policy. Because of these residual controls exercised by the government, the liberalising effect of the 1988 interest rate deregulation was only limited. In any case, the state was forced to reassume its leadership role once economic growth started to falter in 1989. The decline in the rate of growth followed by the crash of the stock market in 1990 (which reversed the previous three-year improvement in the corporate financial structure) and the reversion of the current account into deficit were not conditions favourable to financial liberalisation. The favourable window of opportunity for reform that existed in the late-1980s appeared to have been wasted.

Nevertheless, there were factors which made accelerated financial liber-alisation attractive to government and industrialists alike, some of which have already been cited: external pressure for financial opening; the abun-dant funds available from international capital markets; the necessity of strategic alliances with foreign TNCs; and opportunities of overseas invest-ment. Given the decline in government financial support after 1985, the *chaebol* were no longer so insulated from the effects of high domestic interest rates. Industrialists complained that their competitiveness suffered as a result (e.g. of high local interest rates). It has been argued that the 1988 interest rate deregulation was soon reversed after the business sector complained about the damaging impact on manufacturing (Jwa 1992: 8). But the ability to borrow cheaply from foreign sources without being fettered by the state also led to a significant shift in the attitude of big business to financial reform from around that time. From being threat-ened by financial liberalisation, industrialists came to demand more rapid reform and criticised the financial constraints imposed by the government (see e.g. FKI 1992: 61–6). Such demands were reinforced by the poor growth performance (5 per cent) of the economy in 1992.

In response to domestic and external pressures for liberalisation, a four-stage interest rate deregulation plan was announced in 1991 (in the previous year the government had adopted a market-average foreign exchange system for the determination of exchange rates). To build on the previous liberalising measures, and to bolster Korea's chances of joining the OECD, a five-year plan of accelerated financial liberalisation was announced in July 1993 with schedules for the completion of deregulation in key areas of the financial system (interest rates, deposits, policy loans, external capital account) (see Figure 5.1). The priorities of reform are clear from Figure 5.1: to shift the responsibility for commercial lending decisions from the government to the private financial institutions themselves. Instead, the government would assume an increasingly regulatory role responsible for maintaining the stability of the financial system, especially during the opening stage. The phasing of the liberalisation plan over four years was aimed at giving local financial institutions a sufficient adjustment period to prepare for the entry of foreign competition. In spite of the accelerated pace of reform after 1992, the process of financial liberalisation was never-theless consistent with the guiding principles behind the pragmatic approach to liberalisation adopted over the previous decade, namely the concern with the growth and stability of the real economy.

The run on the peso triggered by the capital flight from Mexico's liber-alised financial market in 1994 showed that financial opening carried a real risk of macroeconomic destabilisation (the currency was stabilised only after heavy buying from the Federal Reserve Bank) (Edwards 1996: 301–2). Apart from the danger of capital flight, opening to the foreign sector carried other risks, notably the destabilising impact of sudden capital flows, the vulnerability of listed Korean companies to predatory takeovers and

	Interest rates of financial institutions	Deposits	Policy loans	External capital account
1990–1	Most short-term lending rates of banks and NBFIs deregulated Interest rates on money and capital market instruments (including issue rates on corporate bonds with maturities of over two years) freed	Deposit rate liberalisation extended only to deposits with maturities of at least three years		Introduction of market average foreign exchange-rate system Foreign investors allowed to invest directly in Korean stocks subject to ceilings (1992)
Phase 1 1993	Deregulate interest rates on all loans of more than two years of banks and non-banks, except for policy loans	Liberalise interest rates on all long-term deposits	Establish limit on policy loans Setting up of Policy Loan Coordinating Committee	
Phase 2 1994	*Policy loan:* liberalise interest rates on policy loans; terms and conditions for loans undertaken by commercial banks to be determined by market conditions *Commercial loans:* lending rates offered by financial Institutions to reflect credit standing of borrower		Abolish policy loans which provide income supports Transfer policy finance to specialised financial institutions or to the government budget BOK or government will redeem non-performing loans with special loans	Foreign purchase of government and public bonds permitted

	Interest rates of financial institutions	Deposits	Policy loans	External capital account
Phase 3 1994–5	Continue reduction of interest rate subsidy on policy loans Expand the scope of deregulation of short-term market-type products	Liberalise interest rates on short-term deposits, excluding demand deposits	Deregulate interest rate on loans subject to BOK discounts Deregulate discount rate for policy loans; reduce or terminate policy finance by commercial banks and/or privatise specialised banks Phased reduction of policy loans of general banks Activation of short-term financial markets	Liberalise the holding of foreign exchange by resident abroad Move towards liberalisation of the won
Phase 4 1996–7	Continue reduction of interest rate subsidy on policy loans Terminate the preferential interest rate for the manufacturing sector	Introduction of deposits at market interest rates Gradual liberalisation of short-term deposits Consider abolishing controls over short-term market products	No policy loans Terminate ratio of mandatory loans to SMEs and regions Full implementation of open market operations	Exchange rate to reflect market conditions Permit indirect investment by foreigners in listed bonds

Figure 5.1 Blueprint for financial reform 1990–7

Sources: BOK (1996: 41–64); Dhalla and Khatkhate (1995: 22–3); Asia-Pacific InfoServ, Inc. (1996: Section VII)

the poor competitiveness of domestic financial institutions. To avert the danger of hostile takeover, the financial liberalisation plan retained the limits on foreign equity holding: up to 15 per cent foreign equity holding per Korean company and up to 5 per cent holding for each individual foreign investor. Nevertheless, the reform by the Kim Young-Sam government represented a significant step in the liberalisation of finance. This was evident from the six-and-a-half-fold increase in portfolio and other non-direct investments between 1993 and 1996 (Table 3.3). The economy was now well placed to mobilise vast amounts of foreign capital. The price would be greater susceptibility to externally induced financial shocks.

The lack of competitiveness of domestic financial institutions meant that the opening of the financial sector to direct foreign participation had to be gradually phased in. Plagued by problems caused by the lack of autonomy and exposure to competition (overmanning, lack of managerial skills, absence of overseas operations and inexperience at risk assessment), the domestic financial sector needed to equip itself for market opening by restructuring and consolidation. Under the Act Concerning the Merger and Conversion of Financial Institutions of 1991, some consolidation of local financial institutions had already taken place.[3] Reorganisation had several advantages. By consolidating into larger units, the international competitiveness of domestic financial institutions would be improved. This would help reduce the dangers of foreign domination of the local financial industry. Consolidation raised the question of the concentration of economic power. With their experience at international business and resources, the *chaebol* were the obvious candidates (apart from foreign financial institutions) to take over and consolidate domestic financial institutions. Having established a solid presence in the local banks and NBFIs, it was logical that the next area into which the *chaebol* would extend their activity would be the nationwide commercial ('city') banks. This would have meant abolition of the 8 per cent shareholding restriction. In spite of the reservations about the concentration of economic power, the direction towards financial consolidation was clear. To encourage mergers, tax incentives were introduced in 1995 (Asia-Pacific Infoserv. 1996: section VII-15). To accelerate the reforms, a Presidential Commission on Financial Reform was set up in December 1996 (*Korea Herald* 9 January 1997).

Liberalisation of direct investment flows

Another policy for attracting foreign capital was the liberalisation of the strict rules governing foreign direct investment (FDI). A Five-Year Foreign Direct Liberalisation Plan was announced in 1993 followed by rolling plans (May 1994 and November 1995) to expedite and broaden the scope of the previous plan. By May 1996, the number of restricted business categories amounted to just 120 out of the 1,148 listed in the Korean Standard Industrial Classification, a liberalisation ratio of 90 per cent. In order to match the liberalisation ratios of the OECD members, the MOFE announced a plan for accelerated liberalisation in late 1996 according to which the liberalisation ratio would reach 98.4 per cent by the year 2000 (up from the original projection of 97.5 per cent) (MOFE Press Release December 1996).

Declining competitiveness meant many sectors of the economy would be seriously threatened by accelerated liberalisation of FDI and imports. This applied not only to traditional weak spots like agriculture and services (apart from financial services, the potentially lucrative sectors such as entertainment and advertising) but even the mainstays of Korean exports (e.g. consumer electronics, cars, semi-conductors) that previously enjoyed the benefit of local monopoly. In spite of the severe import restrictions on directly competitive products (e.g. consumer durables, tobacco), the Korean economy experienced persistent trade deficits, mostly with Japan). These deficits were signs of Korean dependency on imported Japanese machinery and core components. Contrary to design, the ambitious HCI policies of the 1970s aggravated rather than corrected this serious weakness of the Korean development model. The 'localisation' drives of the 1980s were no more successful.

Entry into the OECD in 1996 was preceded by the worsening of the balance of payments deficit (mainly due to the slump in semi-conductor prices). Attempts by the press and government to blame the excessive import consumption by Korean citizens for trade deficits could not detract from the real problems of declining competitiveness. The further liberalisation consistent with OECD membership and other international pressures meant that deficits were set to grow. The US government, in particular, was exercising liberalisation pressure on Korea through international[4] and bilateral channels. The nominal opening of the Korean market since the 1980s did not quieten US dissatisfaction at Korean trade practices. Targets of American criticism included high tariffs on imports, the failure to protect intellectual property rights and even the denial of primetime television advertising to foreign products. Continued pressure reflected the shift in the US emphasis from 'market opening' to 'market access', a criterion change directed against secondary non-tariff barriers of the Northeast-Asian type (Chung 1996: 52). Substantive opening of the domestic market was not something that could be delayed for long. If American pressure was forcing open the Korean market, the most dangerous competitive threat came from the Japanese. Korea's most successful products in international markets overlapped with Japanese products, and the very high Japanese import content (e.g. engines for cars) ensured that even successful Korean exports were not so profitable.

From $484 million in 1985, the value of accumulated overseas investment increased to $2.3 billion in 1990 and $10.2 billion in 1995 (EPB *Major Statistics* 1996). This showed the rising trend of direct investment overseas by Korean business. Korean direct foreign investment could be divided into two categories. First, there were the small and medium-sized companies producing labour-intensive goods, able to compete only by utilising cheap labour in China and the ASEAN area. Between 1992 and 1994, the share of foreign direct investment (FDI) accounted for by small and medium-sized firms increased from 16.5 to 24.1 per cent – from $200 million to $864 million (MOTIE 1995: 152). (Here, North Korea represented a huge investment opportunity constrained by political difficulties.) These investors resembled the Japanese companies attracted to the Korean export processing zones during the 1970s.

Then there were the *chaebol* with their larger and more diverse investments ranging from simple assembly operations (that now took them as far afield as the former Soviet republics) to integrated semi-conductor plants even larger than those of Japan. The *chaebol* responded to the looming 'squeeze' crisis with a strategy of foreign investment and strategic alliances. By extending their presence globally, they would be able to absorb new technologies and utilise the most efficient factors of production worldwide. The top *chaebol* announced ambitious strategies for establishing their international presence. India alone was projected to receive $3 billion worth of investments, mainly from the *chaebol*, by 2000 (*Korea Herald* 30 April 1997).

There were important differences between Korean and Japanese FDI. In contrast to the earlier wave of Japanese investments to Europe and North America in the 1980s, Korean FDI to those areas occurred at a less advanced stage of technological development and stood to gain more from collaboration with foreign partners. Apart from the attraction of cheaper labour, the foreign investments of the *chaebol* were motivated by other considerations. Trade imbalances in favour of Korea and allegedly unfair practices had resulted in friction with both the EU and US in recent years and direct investment in those areas was a way of forestalling retaliatory sanctions. Investments in the industrialised countries also provided other advantages for the *chaebol*. Apart from proximity to their target markets, they also derived the benefits of superior sub-contracting, collaborative R&D with local companies (whereas Japanese companies kept their core technologies at home), local contribution to financing and marketing services and a more orderly labour relations environment. In effect, the Korean *chaebol* were investing in the industrialised economies to learn whereas Japanese companies were primarily relocating the lower value added stages of production. It was part of a policy to escape the structural dependence on Japan.

To overcome their technological weakness, the *chaebol* adopted strategic alliances with foreign TNCs (Y.S. Hong 1996). Such linkages assumed various forms and involved many of the leading producers in each field: joint-production; reciprocal licensing; and even the attempted acquisition of financially troubled foreign firms possessing core technologies (a strategy that was encountering technological protectionism from Northern

Industry	Type of alliance	Alliance firms	Content of alliance
Automobile	Technology and capital	Hyundai–Mitsubishi	Capital participation and technology introduction
	Technology	Daewoo–Nissan	Technology alliance related to commercial automobile
	Complex	Kia–Mazda–Ford	Production–technology–sales complex alliance
Electronics	Technology and production	Samsung Electronics–US TI	Joint-production of semi-conductors by technology alliance
	Technology	Samsung Electronics–Toshiba	Joint-development of memory semi-conductors
	Technology and production	LG–Hitachi	Efficient combination of technology and production equipment
	Capital	LG–Zenith	Joint-technology development and transfer by capital alliance

Figure 5.2 Status of alliances with foreign firms in the automobile and electronics sectors

Source: adapted from Hong (1996: 104)

governments).[5] Apart from acquiring the advanced technology that would assure their survival, these linkages enabled the *chaebol* to enhance their brand-name recognition and gain access to the home markets of their collaborators. The interactions between domestic and foreign firms are summarised in Figure 5.2.

Unlike their counterparts in the industrialised countries, SMEs in Korea lacked the resources that gave them the complementarities necessary to forge strategic alliances with foreign TNCs. For example, whereas dynamic small companies in the US attracted top-class researchers preferring to operate outside the confines of bureaucratic corporations, leading talents in Korea were invariably drawn towards the *chaebol* or the government by material reward and prestige. Because of their financial and other resources accumulated from decades of state support, the *chaebol* were well placed to gain from the opportunities of strategic linkages with TNCs and from outward investment.

These openings to the world market were likely to bolster the dominance of the *chaebol* and aggravate economic disparities. The *chaebol*'s pursuit of strategic alliances, and outward investment by companies large and small, reflected the unfavourable operating conditions posed by the domestic 'high cost, low efficiency' economic structure. The plan for financial liberalisation discussed above was designed to alleviate the problems of capital shortage and high borrowing rates, commonly identified as core elements of the 'high cost, low efficiency' structure. While facilitating the flight of domestic companies overseas, financial liberalisation was a necessary but insufficient measure for attracting significant long-term foreign investment (as opposed to speculative funds) into Korea. Without reforming other aspects of the 'high cost, low efficiency' economic structure (e.g. a backward transport infrastructure, uncompetitive wage levels, high land price and excessive bureaucratic controls), the operating environment would remain unfavourable for domestic and foreign investment. The typical response of Korean business was to take flight. Whereas the spread of Japanese FDI in the 1980s was characterised by the retention of core production processes at home, the tendency of the Korean *chaebol* was to transplant entire industries overseas with its implications of domestic industrial 'hollowing out' (Heong-Jong Kim 1996: 401). That there was some substance to these concerns was evident from the net outflow of direct investment (see Table 3.3). The private sector was incapable of resolving the problems posed by the 'high cost, low efficiency' economic structure. It pointed to new areas for governmental economic leadership.

The turn towards functional intervention

The main elements of the 'high cost, low efficiency' structure that deterred domestic investment were the high interest rate, high land price, high transport cost and high labour cost. The lowering of the cost of borrowing was the objective of the financial liberalisation reforms discussed above. Together with R&D, land and transport were the main elements of Korea's economic infrastructure, those public goods on which the long-term competitiveness of the private sector depended. Impressive by developing country standards, Korea's infrastructure lagged well behind those of the advanced industrialised countries. Infrastructural investment did not keep pace with the development of the economy as a whole, and this deficiency was harming Korean competitiveness. The promotion of infrastructural development showed the shift that was taking place from direct to functional intervention. Permissible within the strict rules of the WTO, functional intervention became the market-conforming intervention of the 1990s (see also Leipziger and Petri 1993: 20–31). The globalisation project built on the policies initiated in the later years of the Roh government.

The effectiveness of such policies on competitiveness can be evaluated only by technical analysis over the long term. The purpose here, by contrast, will be to illustrate how functional intervention reinforced the pro-*chaebol* bias that typified previous interventions. Public investment in economic infrastructure was strongly supported by the *chaebol*. While they favoured deregulation, the *chaebol* encouraged the government to take an active role in the development of the economic infrastructure. This was motivated by their own inadequacies and by the prospects of contracts in expensive government-funded projects. In all aspects of economic infrastructure, the Korean economy faced serious shortcomings. These serious problems demanded government-led responses, for the reaction of Korean business was to relocate to countries where conditions were more favourable. To improve the economic infrastructure and make the operating environment for local industry less costly, the government announced policy initiatives for R&D, land use and transportation.

Infrastructural development policies

One obstacle hindering the *chaebol*'s ambition of matching the leading producers in the frontier sectors was access to state of the art technology. The persistence of trade deficits with Japan in capital goods and critical components was a sign of this deficiency in the industrial structure. Korea's past efforts at developing a domestic industrial technology capacity had been impressive by the standard of LDCs (e.g. Lall 1990). In the past, indigenous R&D efforts were supplemented by the purchase of mature technology and by the copying of foreign designs (frequently in breach of intellectual property rights) through reverse engineering. But stricter conditions of technology transfer prevailed in the 1990s, and IPRs were now more strictly enforced under the terms of the WTO and OECD. Moreover, Korea's previous success in the field of emulation had made market leaders wary of the long-term competitive threat posed by technology transfer to Korea (the case of steel illustrated the potential for 'boomerang' effects).

Approaching the standards of the most advanced countries was proving to be a difficult process. A passage from an OECD report succinctly sums up the technological problems facing Korean development in the 1990s:

> The country can no longer simply afford to import technology – which foreigners are in fact more reticent to introduce on concessional terms – and it will have to raise the value added and technological intensity of what it produces. In the more or less distant future, it will find itself in a stranglehold, squeezed, on the one side, by the production of the more advanced countries which it is catching up with and, on the other, that of the more recently industrializing countries, particularly in Asia, which are following in its footsteps. Korea is obliged to innovate by developing and exploiting creatively its own R&D assets.
>
> (OECD 1996: 136)

An example of Korean technological dependence quoted in the report was the stability in the expenditure ratios of technological imports to R&D: 21 per cent (1977–81); 20 per cent (1982–6); and 18 per cent (1987–93). By contrast, as long ago as 1975, the figure for Japan was only 5 per cent (OECD 1996: 139). Part of the problem lay in the internal structures of the *chaebol* themselves. Although the top *chaebol* ranked among the largest corporations in the world in terms of overall size, their technological capacity in individual sectors was adversely affected by diversification into unrelated ones (including non-productive pursuits such as land speculation) and also by the relatively low priority accorded to R&D. Instead of taking the initiative by investing in future technological capacity, the years of boom (1986–8) proved to be a disincentive for modernisation. According to Amsden, business 'leadership' of the economy did not prove to be very energetic (Amsden 1992 and 1994a).

In response to Korea's continuing weakness in core technologies, a series of R&D initiatives were launched under the Roh government within the context of a rising R&D : GDP ratio (see Table 2.4). The most important of these was the Higher Advanced National Project (or HAN Project) established in 1992 (on the pre-planning and preparation for the launch of the project, see Yoon-Chuel Lim 1995). The aim of the HAN Project (or G-7 Project) was to raise the standard of Korea in selected core technologies to the standard of the G-7 countries by 2001. To do this, $5,069 million would be invested. To the nine projects identified in 1992, another eight were added between 1993 and 1996 (MOST 1996: 20–2). Besides the HAN Project, Strategic National R&D Projects were announced in biotechnology, computer software, aerospace, nuclear energy and ocean development (MOST 1996: 23–7). Strategic R&D projects involved close collaboration between government ministries and the business sector. Given their dominance in private sector R&D activity, the *chaebol* were the principal participants from the business sector. In 1993, the top five and top twenty firms accounted for 31 and 51 per cent of private sector R&D, respectively, while large enterprises accounted for 83 per cent (OECD 1996: 93–4). Another study calculated the concentration ratio of private sector R&D expenditures for the top five and top twenty firms in Korea in 1992 at 30.1 and 49.8 per cent, respectively. The corresponding ratios for the US in 1987 were 17 and 30.6 per cent, respectively while the Japanese figures were 17.1 and 36.3 per cent, respectively (Yang 1996: 16).

Apart from technology capacity, competitiveness was affected by other weaknesses in the economic infrastructure. Land prices in Korea were even higher than those in densely populated competitors such as Japan and Taiwan. Small and medium-sized companies were hardest hit (*Business Korea* 1993: 24–8) and many went abroad as a result (the 'runaway shop' phenomenon). The growth of domestic car ownership in Korea easily outstripped the capacity of the transport network. The clogged roads were not only an inconvenience for commuters but they also adversely affected industry's distribution costs. For example, between 1986 and 1993, the number of automobiles increased 2.6 times whereas the length of roads increased by only 1.2 times (Kwon 1992: 126). Land shortage and traffic congestion were also symptomatic of a regional development bias that had consistently favoured Seoul and the Kyongsang region (the home region of all presidents between 1961 and 1998) while leaving the Cholla region underdeveloped in spite of its convenient access to the Asian Continent.

The persistence of development bias

Infrastructural problems were the results of the lopsidedness of the Korean model of development. Traffic congestion and the price of land were symptoms of regional concentration while the weakness of technological capability reflected the priority accorded to capacity expansion. But without correcting the underlying social causes of uneven development, the programme aimed at resolving infrastructural problems lacked effectiveness. For example, the attempt by the Roh government to control land speculation by the *chaebol* was scuppered by the difficulty of different-iating between productive and non-productive holdings. Infrastructural projects even had the potential of reinforcing the disparities of the development model. For example, the development of the transportation network showed a continuing bias toward the traditionally dominant Seoul–Taegu–Pusan axis under the Kim Young-Sam government. As a result, it reinforced the economic and political prevalence of the Kyongsang Province, the traditional base of regime support. To illustrate this phenomenon, on a trip to Taegu in December 1996, President Kim announced 10 trillion won (*c.* $12.5 billion) worth of projected infrastructural investments for the following year. Key projects included the extension of the Seoul and Taegu subways, airport expansion at Taegu, and the improvement of the Seoul–Taegu–Pusan high-speed rail link. Taegu was also designated as the site for the development of a new special industrial zone. The priority accorded to Taegu demonstrated President Kim's concern with winning back voters alienated by the prosecution of former Presidents Chun and Roh, both natives of North Kyongsang. In an attempt to win back the people of the province, he reminded them of their importance. The president reportedly said: 'I plead with you Taegu citizens to take the lead in national development one more time' (*Korea Herald* 20 December 1996a). Thus the aim of alleviating transport and industrial congestion was constrained by the need to maintain regional political alliances, the persistence of which reinforced further regional economic and political division.

In turn, the *chaebol* followed the political logic by concentrating their investments in the already developed regions. For example, Samsung intended to locate both of its proposed car and steel plants in President Kim's native South Kyongsang Province. That same area was to be the site of Hyundai's proposed steel plant. By giving huge construction contracts to the *chaebol* (in the process, sapping the contractors' competitive instincts), the programme of infrastructural development also conflicted with the government's stated aim of promoting business de-concentration and competition. Similarly with the problem of overpriced land as a factor raising industry costs: the speculative activity of the *chaebol* was a major causal factor behind the phenomenon. Having played a role in pushing up land prices in the first place, the *chaebol* stood to benefit from government policies for making more land available for industrial use such as the dismantling of environmental zoning regulations.

Not unlike the set of policies it replaced, functional intervention also contained a built-in bias in favour of the *chaebol*. Ironically, the sectors of the economy that benefited from old-style intervention were also becoming the principal beneficiaries of the new. If improvement of the infrastructure contributed to the attractiveness of investing in Korea, it was doing so by reinforcing the *chaebol*, with consequences that tended to be unfavourable to domestic competition. Reform of the other two elements of the 'high cost, low efficiency' structure of the economy – high labour costs and excessive bureaucracy – implied a fundamental reorganisation of the pattern of state–business–labour relationships of Korea Inc. in accordance with the changed economic conditions and power configurations of the 1990s. It is to these reorganisations of the developmentalist alliance and their socio-political implications that I now turn.

The regulatory framework of state–business relations

The shift towards functional intervention showed that the old style of industrial policies was being replaced by new instruments of market-conforming intervention. Complementary to these technical changes were government efforts to reform the business regulatory framework and employment relations. A stated goal of the Kim Young-Sam government was the ending of the system of collusive state–business relations and their replacement with a competitive market system based on clear and consistent rules. This meant removing those bureaucratic obstacles that undermined business efficiency while at the same time strengthening the rules against anti-competitive practices. Having once been the cornerstone of developmental success, state–business collusion was now viewed as the source of corruption and economic inefficiency. These concerns pointed to a necessary reform of the legal framework by which business was regulated (a task for which the Committee for Economic Deregulation was responsible). In their bid to become free from governmental controls, the *chaebol* also espoused transparency and the replacement of official discretion by the rule of law. They criticised the timidity of the government's deregulatory reforms and offered an alternative agenda of reform, one which had some support from within official policy circles. The course of the deregulation debate during the Kim Young-Sam government was consistent with themes already articulated in this study. First, the gradualness of deregulatory reform (in contrast with the official publicity) reflected the residual bureaucratic caution about dismantling controls too rapidly. Second, the growing independence of the *chaebol* could be seen from the active campaign for faster deregulation. Third, despite institutional reforms, it was proving difficult to make business de-concentration measures effective, the result of which was that deregulatory reform favoured the continuing advance of the *chaebol*.

Business de-concentration reforms

If deregulation promised to lower business costs by removing red tape and other bureaucratic barriers, it also carried the risk of accentuating business concentration as the *chaebol* took over domains vacated by the state (e.g. newly privatised industries, entering sectors from which they were previously excluded). The Fair Trade Commission, the government's anti-trust agency, was concerned not only with the efficiency aspect of deregulation but also with redressing the imbalance between the *chaebol* and the rest of the domestic business sector. It viewed *chaebol* demands for rapid deregulation in light of these concerns. The FTC viewed the monopolistic tendencies as being deeply embedded and capable of surviving market opening, and as something that could be redressed only with active policies to counter the *chaebol*'s economic dominance (Interview FTC 5 July 1996). (For example, even under a liberalised trade regime, importers and producers could collude to control the price of imported products and keep them high at the expense of the consumer).

Previous chapters have explained the origins of the concentration of economic power and the factors hindering effective reform. What, then, were the characteristics of reform under the Kim Young-Sam government? As a sign of the new government's commitment to reform, the status of the FTC was upgraded. It was made independent of the Economic Planning Board in December 1994. In March 1996, its chairman was elevated from vice-ministerial to full ministerial status (FTC March 1996: 2). The FTC described its mission in the following terms:

> The competition policy aims to encourage free and fair competition by prohibiting abuses of market-dominating positions, excessive concentration of economic power, unreasonable collaborative activities and unfair trade practices. Ultimately, the policy stimulates creative business activities, protects consumers and promotes a balanced development of the national economy.
>
> (FTC March 1996: 10)

The FTC proposed a series of measures aimed at equalising the conditions of competition between the *chaebol* and non-*chaebol* sectors. The Kim Young-Sam government reinforced the legal measures for counteracting *chaebol* economic power. These measures extended the scope of previous jurisdiction, the powers of enforcement of the FTC and the severity of punishments on transgressors. Internal relations between *chaebol* group affiliates and diversification were key areas targeted for reform.

The financial liberalisation policies of the 1980s failed to arrest the growth of *chaebol* economic power. One source of this power was the advantage enjoyed by the *chaebol* in their access to bank lending. With the system of mutual debt guarantees and cross-holdings between group affiliates, it was not surprising that banks favoured *chaebol*-affiliated borrowers. The *chaebol* groups' collateral was also inflated by the real estate boom of the late-1980s. Apart from aggravating the problem of concentration, such asset- or collateral-based lending also impaired the competitiveness of the banks by preventing them developing the appropriate experience of risk analysis based on project viability rather than the status of the borrower. The Third Amendment (December 1992) to the Monopoly Regulation and Fair Trade Act was passed in order to limit the size of cross-holdings and mutual debt guarantees between *chaebol* affiliates. Intra-group subsidisation through trade (e.g. sales to group affiliates at low prices) was also prohibited under this principle. The Fourth Amendment (December 1994) targeted *chaebol* expansion by reducing an affiliate's equity ceiling in a non-affiliated company from 40 to 25 per cent (FTC 1996: 12–14). The FTC reported signs of progress. For example, the number of cases of abuse reported, investigated and acted upon during the 1990s increased on that of the previous decade (FTC March 1996: 22–8).

Effecting business de-concentration also necessitated concurrent support for small and medium-sized enterprises which, despite numerous grand sounding initiatives, continued to be plagued by the problems identified in Chapter 3 (*Business Korea* 1993: 24–8). The FTC was responsible for the enforcement of the Fair Subcontract Transactions Act (FSTA) of 1984. The FSTA was amended again in January 1995 to improve the position of small and medium sub-contractors in their dealings with business groups (e.g. pricing of goods, compulsory purchasing) (FTC 1996: 241–60). A further sign of the government's commitment to promoting SMI came in March 1996 when the Office for SMI was given independent status from having previously been a bureau within the Ministry of Trade and Industry. Data from the FTC show that the agency became more active during the 1990s.

The ultimate aim of policies curtailing intra-group support was to facilitate the transition of the *chaebol* into more profit-oriented smaller groups or independent firms. Because the *chaebol* originated relatively recently, the influence of the founder or his immediate descendants remained strong. There were reasons for expecting the dilution of familial control with time: as members branch off to form their own independent companies (e.g. establishment of the Halla group by the younger brother of the Hyundai founder); as talented outsiders got promoted into senior managerial positions; and as the dependence on stock market finance grew. According to this type of reasoning, the prospect of efficiency gains was the driving force for internal reform. Drawing on trends showing the diminution of the founding families' direct shareholding and cross-subsidisation over the span of a decade, one commentator predicted the separation of ownership and management within 10–15 years – when the founding families' stake would diminish to 1–2 per cent (Jung 1996: 17–18).

Another trend that had the potential for reducing the degree of market power of the *chaebol* was that towards greater competition in the system of distribution brought about by the rise of mass merchandising and discount sellers (e.g. the New Core group), a change that would separate ownership in the spheres of production and distribution. Such arguments had their limitations. At best, such trends could be expected to take effect only in the long term, and they assumed that the *chaebol* would not take active measures to maintain concentration and familial dominance. Such measures included: grooming select family members while disinheriting others; associating with the political elite by intermarriage; intensified lobbying; and extension into the distribution sector.

Apart from intra-group support, the *chaebol* could finance their diversification using incomes derived from unproductive activities, such as investment in land. The *chaebol* claimed that their acquisitions of land represented investments for future industrial sites rather than speculative purchases since land prices had stabilised by the mid-1990s. Even though land prices had fallen from their boom levels of the late-1980s, acquisition continued to be a highly profitable activity. With the general recovery of the economy in 1993, land prices resumed their upward movement. Because of the land shortage, real estate prices rose much more rapidly than the general price level. To counter this activity (it was also highly unpopular with the public), the government in 1995 implemented a real name system for land holdings that prohibited the holding and sale of land under false names.

The emergence of an alternative agenda

The *chaebol* expressed dissatisfaction with what they perceived to be excessive official caution and articulated an alternative agenda for the correction of market distortions. As opposed to control by anti-monopoly measures, the *chaebol* alternative looked to rapid deregulation and competitive pressure. The Korea Economic Research Institute (KERI), the think-tank of the Federation of Korean Industries (FKI) – the *chaebol*'s umbrella organisation – was particularly active in its critique of the slowness of deregulation under the Kim Young-Sam government. One such author characterised the deregulatory effort under way as 'quantitatively abundant' while claiming that 'actual change is not being felt in the area of enforcement' (Il-Joong Kim 1995: 171). Especially targeted for criticism was the unwillingness of the government to extend the principle of deregulation to the 'sacred precincts' of the economy (e.g. by dismantling the controls for curbing wealth concentration, land ownership, finance) (ibid.: 190–1). According to this theoretical perspective, deregulation would provide the 'level playing field' needed by Korean business to compete on equal terms with foreign TNCs.

Following on from this (so the KERI's argument went), with the domestic market liberalised, talk of monopoly would no longer make any sense, for market dominance would denote superior efficiency rather than official favouritsm (Interview KERI 14 June 1996). This view contrasted with the FTC's fears for the persistence of monopolisation in liberalised markets (see above). It formed the basis for the *chaebol*'s case for sweeping deregulation. Based on the principles of neo-classical political eonomy, the KERI argued that the problem of government–business collusion (*chongkyong yuchak*) was rooted in the state's power to meddle in business affairs, in response to which they advocated sweeping deregulation. Anti-monopoly measures were seen to be perpetuating government over-regulation. Far from promoting competition, anti-monopoly policies worked for the protection of inefficient special interests (ironic, given the *chaebol*'s history of reliance on state support). Sweeping deregulation leading to the exposure of the private sector to competition would therefore remove much of the necessity for anti-monopoly measures (Seung-Cheol Lee 1995: 256). Some economists associated with the government-sponsored Korea Development Institute (the EPB–MOFE think-tank) were also sympathetic towards such arguments for accelerated deregulation:

> [A] search for an alternative to the existing mass production system should not be the responsibility of government . . . instead, the Korean government should lift all entry barriers, domestic as well as at border, and deregulate [the] Korean economy. Moreover, a search for or a discovery of a new optimal industrial organisation should be the responsibility of the private sector given the undistorted market incentive structure provided by a rational government.
>
> (Jwa and Kim 1997: 44)

Counter-arguments also emerged stating that the dangers of business concentration were exaggerated. Such arguments have challenged the empirical bases of the claims about family ownership and excessive diversification. Instead it is argued that the separation of ownership and management in the US, Japan and Germany took a long time to achieve and so the pace should not be forced in Korea (Yoo 1995).

The preference for the promotion of competition by market discipline rather than control also had its supporters within the economic bureaucracy. Differing from the FTC approach of trying to control the size and diversification of the *chaebol*, the Ministry of Finance and Economy (formed from the merger of the EPB and the Ministry of Finance in 1994) took a less pessimistic view of the *chaebol* phenomenon and advocated more market-oriented solutions to the problem of economic concentration. Rather than direct controls, the emphasis here was on corporate governance and disciplining the business groups by a combination of transparency regulations and exposure to competition (Interview KDI 12 June 1996). Instead, the stress was on allowing the *chaebol* to make their own decisions (e.g. about diversification and exit) within a competitive environment governed by clear rules of corporate governance. To improve corporate governance, rules concerning the use of funds and the rights and responsibilities of managers and shareholders (especially smaller investors) would have to be stipulated and enforced against illegal activities (e.g. bid rigging for government contracts, price fixing). The establishment of clear rules would pave the way for the lifting of entry and exit barriers. By emphasising the need for companies to take responsibility for themselves, the MOFE approach (as articulated by the KDI) represented a liberally oriented stream within the government and showed clear affinities with the pro-deregulation perspective favoured by the KERI (cf. e.g. Seung-Cheol Lee 1995). This was a sign that the *chaebol*'s perspective on the future of industrial organisation in Korea coincided with intellectual currents within the semi-official KDI. It suggested that the emergence of a pro-conglomerate approach to deregulation was probable.

The government recognised that enhancing industrial competitiveness called for the lifting of exit and entry barriers and other deregulatory measures. At the same time it was concerned with balancing efficiency-enhancing deregulation measures with the stated official goal of improving economic equality, objectives that the *chaebol* believed should be separated (their view was that the government should use measures other than restrictions on business growth in order to realise equity objectives). In their respective versions of deregulation with de-concentration, the emphases of the government agencies differed. For their part, the *chaebol* (via the FKI) favoured a type of deregulation that would allow them to take advantage of the new opportunities offered by deregulation: to enter new sectors; vacate old ones; and to buy up public utilities set for privatisation[6] without corrective measures for the concentration consequent of decades of official pro-conglomerate bias. In the area of privatisation, major industries had been targeted by the Kim government, including highly lucrative monopolies such as Korea Gas, Korea PC Telecom, Korea Tobacco and the Ginseng Corporation (Kye-Sik Lee and Hyung-Pyo Moon 1996: 179). The economic dominance of the *chaebol* was set to be enhanced with the control of these industries. While favouring deregulation on the one hand, the *chaebol* favoured the maintenance of legal safeguards against hostile takeovers by foreigners in the event of financial liberalisation on the other (*Korea Herald* 20 December 1996b). In effect, they sought deregulation that would strengthen their position on the domestic market in readiness for intensified foreign competition.

From the analyses and policy prescriptions discussed above, the problems of de-concentration and deregulation become apparent. Effective competition promotion measures depended not only on the dismantling of unnecessary red-tape, but also on the existence of clear rules and an apparatus capable of enforcing them. The enforcement apparatus as it existed in the mid-1990s was not yet up to the task. In spite of having been strengthened, the sanctions available to the FTC were either limited (e.g. small fines) or, as in the case of severe measures (e.g. imprisonment), extremely difficult to apply against powerful offenders, while FTC officials themselves on occasions succumbed to bribery. Effective enforcement was also compromised by the persistence of illegal collusion between senior public officials (including senior presidential advisers, and defence and health ministers) and *chaebol* (more on politics and corruption below). These cases suggest that the government still exercised great discretion and that its rulings affected the prospects of individual *chaebol*. The diversification of the leading *chaebol* into controversial areas continued to forge ahead (e.g. Hyundai's plans for steel production, Samsung's plans for cars and steel).

By undermining the barriers to entry, further deregulation threatened to accentuate the dominance of the *chaebol*. In contrast to the claims made by the KERI (rooted in the NPE), the available evidence on the experience of deregulation measures did not point to the elimination of government–business collusion and corruption. That sanctions for the breaches of anti-monopoly legislation tended to be light reflected not only the vested interests of officials but the government's reliance on the *chaebol* to be successful. De-concentration measures (e.g. the FTC's proposal to eliminate debt guarantees among subsidiaries by 2001 – see *Korea Herald* 27 November 1996) that crossed the path of these broader considerations stood little chance. The continuing success of the economy called for a deregulation strategy that would be favourable to the *chaebol*. For example, the credit restrictions on the *chaebol* outside of the top ten were relaxed in July 1995 (BOK 1995: 29–30). Not surprisingly, deregulation accentuated the dominance of the *chaebol*. This is evident from the growth in the number of affiliates of the top five during the 1990s (see Table 3.6). The sales of the top thirty *chaebol* were estimated at around 82.2 per cent of GNP in 1994, while they accounted for 30 per cent of bank credit in 1995 (Dae-Hwan Kim 1996: 54). The cross-payment guarantees of those groups amounted to 67.5 trillion won or $84.4 billion (cf. 44 trillion won in 1988) in 1996 (*Korea Herald* 27 November 1996). These indicators suggested that the goals of deregulation and de-concentration of economic power were not so compatible in Korea's circumstances of the mid-1990s. If deregulation was contributing to the *chaebol* becoming more internationally competitive and transforming the old-style of *chongkyong yuchak* characteristic of Korea Inc. (as the state power was weakened), it was doing so at the price of accentuating the dominance of the *chaebol* (see below).

Labour market reform

While temporarily helping the return to export competitiveness, the harsh labour policies of the Chun Doo-Hwan regime were wholly unsuited to the conditions of democratisation and the return to tight labour markets. From the recession of 1989–91 and the return to a more coercive stance by the Roh government, the rising trend in labour organisation and industrial disputes was reversed. Even so, labour markets remained tight (with workers now having to be imported from lower waged Asian countries) while the advances gained by Korean labour in the Great Workers' Struggle of 1987–8 weakened the autonomy that management had previously enjoyed. As a result, labour came to be identified in government and business circles as a component of the 'high cost, low efficiency' economic structure.

The labour-repression model deadlocked

The availability of quality manpower (from production worker to engineer) that was a hallmark of the Korean economic miracle (Amsden 1989: 221–7) had given way to the serious labour shortages of the 1990s. The

lack of workers ready to take on the lowest-paid or 'three-D' (dirty, difficult, dangerous) jobs, because of rising incomes and economic growth,
followed the pattern experienced in the industrialised countries. The
shortage of highly skilled workers, on the other hand, owed much to the
over-reliance on labour repression of earlier decades and the consequent
neglect of manpower development. Responsible for lowering the rate of
female participation, the traditional gender segmentation of the Korean
labour market was another contributing factor (see e.g. Heong-Jong Kim
1996: 396–7). The inadequacy of the manpower development was also a
result of a development mentality that prioritised the expansion of productive capacity, as well a higher-education system dominated by the
humanities (reflecting the prestige and financial reward associated with
employment in government and big business bureaucracies).

Then there was the issue of labour flexibility. The gains made by Korean
labour in the 1980s coincided with the opposite trend in the industrialised
countries. In the latter, inflexible labour markets arising from union
power and corporatist arrangements were reformed under the neo-liberal
economic agenda. For the purpose of attracting highly mobile TNCs,
governments of all industrialised countries implemented measures to
promote greater labour flexibility. By contrast, even though the incidence
of industrial disputes had declined drastically from the high point of 1987–9
(see Table 2.5), Korean conditions were not conducive to the appearance
of collaborative industrial relations. The post-democratisation decade
was a period when the Korean labour movement emerged from the shadow
of the authoritarian state and asserted its independence. The development
of flexible labour markets and their associated shopfloor practices (e.g.
flexible working hours) was inhibited also by labour shortages in a growing
economy and by the official policy of avoiding mass redundancies. For
example, the labour code still provided for the mandatory employment of
given numbers of safety workers in factories while the government ensured
that insolvent companies belonging to the *chaebol* would be absorbed by
other *chaebol*. Workers in sectors protected from foreign competition (e.g.
banking) also enjoyed stability of employment.[7]

Not surprisingly, the most privileged workers were those most highly
unionised, concentrated in the core export enterprises of the *chaebol* (e.g.
auto and semi-conductor plants, shipyards). While they had achieved some
benefits similar to those enjoyed by their Japanese counterparts (benefits
in the process of being dismantled in Japan), their gains were attained in
the face of employer opposition. Given the recent history of industrial
conflict, the mechanisms of labour–management cooperation were underdeveloped (even at its peak, Japanese company unionism incorporated only
one-third of the industrial workforce). Until labour relations were improved,
the benefits of technical responses to the problems of human resources
(e.g. administrative reorganisations of the relevant government ministries,
revamping of the educational and training systems) were unlikely to be

effective. Without improving the overall context of industrial relations, the potential for labour resistance would make it difficult to introduce the flexibility reforms much needed by the labour market.

The road to the 1997 reform

As part of the competitive drive of the 1990s, the *chaebol* and the government sought to make the employment system more flexible. Democratisation and labour activism after 1987 transformed the business attitude towards the old labour regulations and conventions that were established during the authoritarian era. In the past, such procedures (e.g. the company's responsibility for paying full-time officials) had enabled the employers to manipulate the union structure. Moreover, the convention that employers paid for wages lost during a dispute was not problematic when there were few disputes and when the labour unions were not in a position to back up their claims with industrial action. With the rise of independent labour unionism, employers came to see such conventions as heavy burdens.

On behalf of the *chaebol*, the KERI persistently criticised government regulations on business activities as manifestations of special-interest group power (as derived from neo-classical political economy) that distort the operation of the free market. Together with unsuccessful businessmen and public officials, labour unions were identified by the KERI as the main special interests behind the excessive regulation (Interview KERI 14 June 1996). Accordingly, deregulation of the labour market would eliminate such 'rents' to organised labour. One KDI report saw such rents as a share of the monopoly profits resulting from government–business collusion (Ju-Ho Lee and Dae-Il Kim 1997: 36). The FKI and the KEF expressed their opposition to the legalisation of plural unions and third-party intervention while reiterating their demands for greater employment flexibility.

While the FKI (via the KERI) argued against the extension of labour union rights from an abstract theoretical viewpoint, the KEF articulated the employers' practical reservations over the extension of labour rights. Among these were the unions' expectations of automatic increases in the annual 'bonus' irrespective of productivity (Interview KEF 25 June 1996), the intensification of wage demands backed up by industrial action and the development of disruptive demarcation disputes between rival unions. Employers sought to dismantle what they saw as an excessively rigid employment system. Changes sought by employers included: the right to control the bonus and impose redundancies in line with profitability; an end to the practice of paying striking workers (decided on a case-by-case basis in the courts under the existing labour code); increased worker mobility between group industries; and the establishment of flexible working hours based on a monthly ceiling. In support of its case, the KEF produced statistics showing that at the GNP per capita level of $10,000, Korean monthly wages were higher than those of the US, Japan, UK, Singapore and Taiwan in the corresponding phase of development. The implication was that wages were very high in relation to productivity, and the two trends had to be brought back into line for the sake of improving national competitiveness (KEF 1996a: 34). Also based on the trends of advanced industrialised societies, the $10,000 per capita national income mark was identified by some labour commentators as the point at which the maintenance of lifetime employment becomes problematic (as growth starts to slow) (Kyung-Soo Choi 1997: 174).

The government faced the difficult task of balancing labour rights and efficiency. On the one hand, it needed to pare away the security and restrictive practices enjoyed by the most powerful sections of labour. On the other, it had to enhance the formal rights of labour organisation in accordance with OECD requirements[8] and growing labour pressures for the repeal of the remnants of the former authoritarian regime's anti-labour laws (e.g. the prohibition of plural unions and third-party intervention). The political concessions, however, strengthened labour's potential to resist labour market reform. Government attempts to control wages by setting pay guidelines (backed up with threats against rogue companies) in the final years of the Roh government had proven ineffective. It was now clear that organised labour could be reconciled with broader economic priorities only on the basis of consent. In pursuit of this end, the government tried to extend the collaborative structures developed under the previous government. President Kim Young-Sam was also determined to complete his programme of reform before the end of his term of office in 1998. In April 1996, he announced his 'Vision for New Industrial Relations' and set forth five guiding principles of reform:

1   maximising the common good;
2   participation and cooperation;
3   self-rule and responsibility for both labour and management;
4   respecting individual persons with a high priority on education and training; and
5   globalising rules and mindsets.

To encompass the broadest consensus, the government announced the formation of the Presidential Commission for Industrial Relations Reform in May 1996, a discussion group consisting of 220 representatives from business, labour (including the as yet illegal but influential KCTU) and civic groups (MOL 1996). This consultative forum was designed to allow each affected group some input into reform and at the same time to encourage compromise by putting both labour and employers in a minority position. The role of the civic groups was to mediate between the potentially mutually exclusive positions of union and employer

(Interview with Academic Representative of Presidential Commission for Industrial Relations, 27 June 1996).

Negotiating a new set of labour laws that would satisfy the demands for enhanced competitiveness while at the same time improving labour rights was proving to be a difficult task. The aforementioned KDI paper summarised the neo-classical case for reform:

> [T]he need for a new legal framework that can provide a competitive and productive environment for both unions and employers has been repeatedly raised since 1987. On the other hand, the regulation of employment and wages in Korea is argued to be too restrictive especially when the Korean labour market is undergoing structural changes. Consequently labour reform in 1996 aims to attain labour market flexibility and [a] new legal framework in industrial relations.
>
> (Ju-Ho Lee and Dae-Il Kim 1997: 2, 43–5)

Each side became entrenched in its position. Encouraged by an opposition eager to embarrass the government (but which stopped short of endorsing strike action), the unions' position was the reverse of the employers'. In a climate of unfavourable economic indicators (a slump in semi-conductor prices and the doubling of the trade deficit to $23 billion), a new labour law was finally passed in December 1996. On the face of it, the bill contained provisions favourable to both sides. For the unions, the legal scope of their activities would be extended under the new provisions. This included the legalisation of the KCTU (by 2000), of multiple unions (by 2002), of unionists' participation in political activities, of third-party involvement in industrial disputes; while schoolteachers would be accorded 'partial' (non-striking) labour rights. The act also promised concessions for the employers by legalising the practice of the lay-off system, flexible working hours within the fifty-six-hour week and the use of substitute labour in the event of strikes (in effect, recognising the principle of 'no work, no pay') (*Korea Herald* 21 December 1996).

Passed (along with a new national security bill) in the National Assembly by the ruling NKP in the absence of the opposition legislators, the new law provoked the most sustained labour strikes for a decade (*Korea Herald* 28 December 1996; 7 January 1997; 14 January 1997). There was broad public sympathy with the strikers, who reversed the post-1989 trend of declining strikes (see Table 2.5). The core export industries were severely affected while white-collar workers (e.g. from bank to hospital to broadcasting workers) were also drawn into the fray. For their part, the employers expressed dissatisfaction with the new law for giving too much to the unions during a period of declining competitiveness. The government responded with a combination of threatening and conciliatory gestures: while threatening to arrest strike leaders (especially those from the more radical KCTU), the government (and the KEF) also emphasised that the new laws would not be used irresponsibly to bring about mass lay-offs (which would take effect only when there was no alternative and after consultations with the unions). To sweeten the new policy, the government also announced that it intended to strengthen social development measures to support those displaced. A revised bill was supported by the opposition parties and passed in March 1997 (MOL 1997).

Reformed labour legislation along the lines of the bill passed in December 1996 had important implications for employment practice in Korea. In theory, labour would enjoy more political rights in exchange for greater economic flexibility. In spite of the conciliatory tones of the government and the employers, such legislation threatened to fundamentally weaken the position of Korean labour. By enabling employers to hire substitute workers during strikes, the legislation weakened the effectiveness of industrial action, the lever effectively used by the unions in their demand for better wages and conditions since 1987. The new legislation was also paving the way for the introduction of the more flexible working practices (e.g. flexible shifts and the employment of more irregular and foreign workers[9]) that Korea's competitors enjoyed. By providing for the ending of guaranteed employment and strike pay, the new law also made unionised workers more alert to the possibility of relocation overseas (leading to the much talked about 'hollowing out' of Korean industry). While the reforms allowed the unions to be more vocal, the economic basis of their group power – the ability to restrict the supply of labour – would be diminished. Although only a minority of the Korean labour force was unionised, this minority provided the benchmark for others to follow, and its success encouraged the spread of labour activism. By curtailing the bargaining power of this sector, the new laws were likely to have a wider effect in weakening labour influence. But the legislation was untested, and key provisions (e.g. the process for lay-offs) were interpreted differently by employers and by trades unionists. The problems inherent in these ambiguities would be tested in the coming recession (see Chapter 6).

State and labour: extending the developmentalist alliance?

By reforming labour legislation, the Kim Young-Sam government aimed to move closer to achieving labour market flexibility akin to the levels enjoyed by the industrialised economies. In pursuit of competitiveness, however, the latter have had to pay high social costs in terms of unemployment, growing inequality and social marginalisation. Aggressive implementation of structural adjustment measures from the early-1990s brought the Latin American NICs like Brazil and Argentina back on to the path of renewed growth, but with even more painful social results. By the early-1990s, labour-intensive jobs in Korea were being exported to lower waged economies, and even advanced industries were taking flight (see above). The introduction of greater automation and flexible working practices which the labour reform was designed to facilitate also threatened job security. But industrial restructuring threatened to reach beyond the shopfloor level and into the clerical and management grades, a trend that carried ominous implications for middle-class security. The experience of the US, where flexible working practices were highly developed, showed that in due course downsizing would extend beyond the shopfloor level. In Korea, where heavy over-manning existed at these levels (e.g. in banks and corporate offices), such a transition threatened the 'new middle class', among whom the Kim Young-Sam government enjoyed political popularity.

Korean policy-makers in the 1990s had to balance the demands for competitiveness and flexibility that were being made by business with the broader political and developmental priorities. Rapidly rising productivity within low overall growth rates in the industrialised countries was associated with widening inequalities and high unemployment (in the North the most dire social effects of neo-liberal policies were mitigated by the presence of well developed systems of social welfare, something Korea did not possess). On economic and social grounds, the neo-liberal pathway did not appear to suit Korea. First, Korea was not experiencing the deep failures of developmentalism that had propelled the Latin American NICs along that route. Second, Korea was still a developing country in pursuit of the economic standards of the most developed. To do so successfully, Korea had to maintain high growth rates for maybe another two decades. This meant fully utilising all human and other resources. Third, not only would high levels of unemployment be economically wasteful, but they would have threatened the social cohesion on which sustained industrialisation depended. Moreover, the implementation of drastic programmes of downsizing and restructuring (as was occurring in the Anglo-Saxon economies) relied heavily on the stewardship of professional executives dedicated to achieving high dividends through corporate leanness and operating with the blessing of neo-liberal governments. By contrast, the mindset of the public officials who made up Korea's economic policy elite held a different ethos in which growth (with its connotations of prestige and power) ranked alongside efficiency in importance. In contrast to their counterparts in the West, the leaders of Korean business could concentrate on improving long-term market share, for they did not face short-term pressures from shareholders to maximise dividends. In spite of the renewed emphasis on liberalisation by the Kim Young-Sam government, the approach to labour reform suggested that a political economy of 'catching up' remained very much in place.

Labour in the globalisation project

Industrial discipline in post-war Japan was maintained by a system of labour–management cooperation (built on the anti-communist purges of 1945–55). Workers and their unions exchanged loyalty in return for company-provided benefits. Labour unions were excluded from national economic decision making. For the US, industrial discipline was achieved by the benefits of high productivity coupled with the historical absence of socialist ideological influence. The threat of unemployment was central to the creation of flexible labour markets in the US and the UK during the 1980s. For nearly three decades, the source of Korean industrial discipline was the power of the authoritarian state. With the ending of authoritarian rule in 1987, Korea was in search of a new source of industrial discipline capable of combining the flexibility of the Anglo-Saxon, or neo-liberal, pattern with the cooperative features of the Japanese one. The former was conducive to efficiency but, given its socially exclusive nature, did not allow for the full utilisation of human capital. Proposed reform of the labour law was designed to equip Korean industry with greater labour flexibility.

But it was also recognised that cooperative industrial relations could not arise from the negative pressure of redundancy alone. In all of the industrialised countries, the transition to industrial maturity after 1945 coincided with the transformation of industrial relations from labour repression to some form of labour–capital accommodation – e.g. western European societal corporatism, Japanese company unionism, US business unionism (for Korean perspectives on industrial relations in advanced countries see Choe *et al.* 1995: 120–55). On the basis of the parallels between the Korean and the Japanese development model, commentators have argued that the Japanese path of transition from labour repression to labour–capital accommodation was the most appropriate course for Korea. Drawing on the Japanese experience, Chalmers Johnson (1994) has suggested 'soft authoritarian societal corporatism' to be the appropriate institutional form for Korea, a view endorsed by some Korean writers (Lee and Lee 1992: 20–2). Effecting such a transition successfully, however, required the implementation of positive measures of social consensus building. This consisted of three types of policy: the development of cooperative mechanisms within the workplace; support for those displaced by market forces; and social development programmes in support of the disadvantaged.

While paring away at the economic basis of union power, reform of the labour law was expected to advance the political rights of labour. For example, the legalisation of third-party intervention would facilitate the entry of lawyers, civic groups and others helpful to the union cause in the event of a dispute. The enhancing of labour rights was designed to encourage labour–management cooperation, on which many types of efficiency reform (e.g. the introduction of more flexible working shifts) would depend. President Kim's announcement of April 1996 emphasised the contribution of labour reform towards a definitive break with authoritarianism and the interdependence of economic performance with labour–management cooperation. The extent and effectiveness of that cooperation depended on the scope of the company issues open to discussion and on the nature of the consultation process. Some issues, such as the policy for older workers and the criteria for remuneration (e.g. the transition from a seniority- to a performance-based system), were amenable to labour–management cooperation. The appropriate forum for consultation was more problematic though. The labour unions' preferred mechanism of consultation was collective bargaining (which carried with it the implicit threat of industrial action), and, with the increasing threat to regular employment, the unions wanted more issues translated into this arena. By contrast, employers preferred to channel issues through the existing labour–management councils and to keep the most sensitive issues (especially the traditional managerial prerogatives like personnel management) within that mechanism (KEF 1996a: 18–19). This was not surprising, given that the labour–management councils were established in 1980 for the purpose of bolstering managerial power (Hwang-Joe Kim 1994: 11–12). Correspondingly, it was difficult to imagine the unions having much confidence in such a forum.

Whether a basis for cooperation could be established depended on the extent to which either side was prepared to shift from its maximum position. The attitude of the KEF exemplified the authoritarian culture of Korean management and the techniques by which its past success was achieved. While the labour unions were learning about the economic limits to strike action (the interdependence of competitiveness and livelihood), the employers were adjusting to the opposite problem, that of not having a fiercely anti-labour state capable of resolving disputes in their favour. The absence of compromise in past industrial relations encouraged both sides to adhere to inflexible maximum positions between which it was difficult to find common ground. For example, the KEF vehemently opposed the extension of labour rights, claiming that it would lead to more disputes and the further erosion of competitiveness (e.g. as competing unions vied for members by escalating militancy; see KEF 1996b: 11–12) while in late 1996 the FKI called on the government to impose a pay freeze. On the other hand, the labour unions, especially the more radical KCTU, remained highly suspicious of the Kim Young-Sam government's neutral-sounding rhetoric of 'manpower development' and 'labour–management cooperation', believing it to be a ploy to strengthen the position of the employers. They rejected the economic basis of the employers' arguments that attributed declining competitiveness to rising real wages and instead drew attention to the impact of the high land price, transport cost and interest rate (Uh 1995: 52–3). In its shopping list of demands, the Korea Labour and Society Institute (the think-tank of what eventually became the KCTU) culled the most favourable aspects of employment legislation prevailing in the industrialised countries (much of it derived from the 'golden age' of Western capitalism rather than its contemporary manifestation):

making it subject to union agreement such matters as relocation of factory, change of industry, liquidation of company; take-over of employees by the new employer in case of merger or transfer of company; automation and strengthening of labour intensity; guarantee of equal working conditions for foreign workers; recruitment and maintenance of labour force on natural reduction in [labour] force.

(KLSI 1995: 15)

The KCTU's maximum agenda called for co-determination in industry but with no mention of concessions to flexibility, and even the less militant FKTU took a similar view on the appropriate response to globalisation pressures:

The FKTU views job security and good working conditions as a most important way of improving the competitiveness in concern. Job security makes easier human capital being accumulated in a company level, or even in a national level. And good working conditions are the base for workers to increase labour productivity through voluntary participation and cooperation. These points seem to be already proved in such countries as Germany and Japan being evaluated to have strong competitiveness in the world markets.

(Uh 1995: 67)

Strategies of labour inclusion

To close the gap between the two sides the state had to demonstrate its neutrality and show a readiness to forgo its past pro-business bias. Labour grievances in the past emanated not just from the absence of labour rights (which were abundant in the labour code; see MOL 1995) but from the failure of government to enforce them, a failure first tragically highlighted by the Chun Tae-Il Incident of 1971. Having grown in power in spite of official hostility, the unions were in no hurry to enter into a consensual arrangement with their long-time adversaries. Not only were official promises considered unreliable (e.g. the Kim Young-Sam government waged a campaign of arrest and harassment against unofficial unionists in 1993–4, soon after passing legislation restraining the security services, see KLSI 1995: 27–33), but the unions took the state's concessions as the baseline for further pressure. For example, in response to the new labour law of December 1996 the unions campaigned against the 2002 deadline for the legalising of plural unions and demanded that the date be moved forward.

The consolidation of pro-business unionism required more than legal concessions to labour. Cooperative industrial relations could arise only on the basis of an economic order that was perceived by labour to be fair.

Business was expected to contribute towards the improvement of industrial relations through the introduction of company welfare schemes. Such schemes included forms of profit sharing (e.g. employee share ownership, discussed in Chapter 4) and help with workers' living expenses (e.g. health, education, housing and recreation). Legislation towards the end of the Roh government's tenure provided the basis for the expansion of company welfare. For example, the Corporate Welfare Fund Act of 1991 (building on a recommendation of 1984) provided tax incentives for the foundation of a company fund based on a rule of 5 per cent of pre-tax profits, while the Korea Labour Bank (or Peace Bank) was founded as a workers' welfare scheme by the government and employer–union representatives in November 1992 (KEF 1996a: 40–1). There were also limits to company provision. Because of its great cost, the provision of company welfare varied between employers, with the large enterprises being able to contribute more to their workers' welfare. One report found that the average welfare expenditure per employee for companies with 30–99 employees was 67.6 per cent of that of companies with 500 or more employees in 1990 (KEF 1996a: 41). In contrast to the neo-liberal model, Korea's globalisation project envisaged a continuing regulatory and a financially demanding expansionary role for the state in social development (on Taiwan, see Cheng and Schive 1997).

The combination of sustained growth with improvements in popular welfare earned Korea lavish praise from mainstream development observers (a view to which dependency critics in the West were also converted by the 1980s). The improvement in popular welfare during the authoritarian industrialisation period (1961–87) was largely the result of employment generation against a background of relative equality. Deliberate policies of social development (with the exception of the Saemaul Undong; see Chapter 2) played virtually no role. Since 1987, government pronouncements have shown greater awareness of the importance of giving labour a stronger stake in economic performance and have stressed the importance of balancing economic and social priorities (see e.g. Presidential Commission 1988: 101–48). Taking active steps to redress the social disparities consequent of the legacy of pro-business bias also helped to reduce the unions' distrust of the state, a necessary condition for the emergence of a new pattern of consensual industrial relations (within which the state could assume an arbitration role). Social development expenditure continuously increased and as a share of the government budget reached new highs in the late-1980s (see Table 4.2). Such economic measures reinforced the anti-corruption drive in the government's attempt to cultivate a more neutral image of the state. The setting up of the Employment Insurance System (EIS) in December 1993 exemplified the agenda of social development with economic flexibility. Consisting of three main elements (employment security promotion, vocational skill development, unemployment benefit) the EIS was characterised as follows:

> Unlike other unemployment insurance systems, the system was designed to enhance labour market flexibility with the aim of assisting employment adjustment, thus leading to employment security in the wider sense. Its purpose is made explicit in its name 'Employment Insurance System' as opposed to 'Unemployment Insurance System'.
>
> (Kyung-Soo Choi 1995: 28)

Similarly, to soften the impact of job insecurity in the wake of the December 1996 labour law, the government announced its intention of enlarging the retraining fund to help those displaced to find new work. It also announced that employers would not be allowed to abuse the new lay-off system.

The slow-down of economic growth in the 1970s cast doubt on the viability of the extensive systems of social provision that underpinned labour–capital accommodation in the industrialised countries after 1945. Their enormous costs and disincentive effects required governments in both North America and Europe to make efforts to pare down social expenditures since the 1980s. This Anglo-Saxon model of paring back social expenditures became a powerful trend even in those Western European societies with strong corporatist traditions. In recent years, Japanese companies have also tried to reduce welfare provision as part of their retrenchment. At her level of development in the mid-1990s, Korea could not afford social provision on the same comprehensive scale. Apart from affordability, the course of Korea's social development strategy was influenced also by her own experience of poverty alleviation and by the problems associated with Western systems of comprehensive social provision (e.g. disincentives and the creation of entitlements). In policy terms, this pointed to an anti-poverty strategy that would be carefully targeted, consisting of the expansion of the welfare safety-net for the poorest, some subsidies of the cost of living (e.g. provision of low-cost housing) and the widening of mobility opportunities (e.g. via educational and training programmes). In effect, the state would play a more active role in helping individuals adapt to the rapidly changing conditions of the modern labour market. Thus Korea's emerging pattern of social intervention was to be market-conforming. It would be designed to contribute to the development of growth infrastructure (e.g. by expanding training opportunities) and to be consistent with the established national habits of diligence and family support.

Comparative 'models' of state–labour relations

Economic opening threatened to undermine the cohesiveness of Korean society. While exposure to market forces tends to enhance efficiency, experience has shown that it is usually achieved at the short-term cost of lost growth and intensified social instability and resistance. The concern with simultaneously realising efficiency, growth and social stability lay behind the Korean government's social consensus building policies, central to which was the achievement of a new labour–business consensus brokered by the state. The experience of adjustment to globalisation of the industrialised countries suggested that Korea had to avoid both the excessive institutional rigidity of Continental Europe's 'social capitalism' and the divisiveness characteristic of the Anglo-Saxon model. In Continental Europe, the slow introduction of industrial restructuring measures was attributed to the cosiness of neo-corporatist relationships. By contrast, the disregard for labour interests shown by the Anglo-Saxon model of capitalism, while it was associated with greater efficiency and (arguably) long-term growth, also brought widening disparities and exclusion. Korea's social consensus building policies, described above, were designed to give workers a stronger stake in economic performance and to encourage them (e.g. via consultation mechanisms and social development programmes) to be more sensitive to the needs of their company and to accept more flexible work patterns. By implementing policies of social development, the government hoped to bolster its image as a credible arbiter between labour and management.

On the face of it, the Korean state was steering industrial relations towards the Japanese pattern. Historically, Japanese industrial relations were built on cooperative labour–management relations. More recently, the Japanese state has also been active in the promotion of more flexible work patterns while softening the pain of economic opening through enhanced public expenditure. The consensual network that connected Japanese government, business and labour was a pattern to which Korea also aspired. But significant differences existed between the two countries. First, the Japanese practice of labour–management accommodation was well established before the imperative of downsizing and 'flexibilisation' came to dominate the corporate agenda. Second, operating with the most modern technology and having been a recent pioneer of flexible production methods (e.g. Toyota's 'Just-in-Time' production), Japanese companies were already highly experienced in redeploying labour in response to market fluctuations. By contrast, Korea was trying to realise both labour–management accommodation and flexibility simultaneously but with little prior experience in either (or of the advantage of having the most productive technologies).

How realistically could Korea avoid the trade-offs between efficiency, growth and social cohesion? How adequately could threatened interests be assuaged and persuaded on to the path of compromise? The prospects for successful labour–management accommodation were mixed. There were indicators that a positive-sum relationship was evolving. Apart from reducing the unionisation and strike rates, the experience of the recession of 1990–2 had brought home to the unions the link between living standards and competitiveness, encouraging greater restraint in their wage demands. Furthermore, the embryonic mechanisms of cooperation (e.g.

the tripartite National Council for Economic and Social Affairs) built up under the Roh government had the potential for further development. The KEF and the FKTU agreed to fix wage increases within narrow bands for 1993 and 1994, and the government was widening its social development programmes to support and re-equip workers displaced by restructuring. On the other hand, given the history of labour repression, state–business collusion and unfulfilled promises, the unions remained deeply suspicious of the ulterior motives of the rhetoric of cooperation. That there was support not only for defending the post-1987 gains but for extending labour rights on the pattern of the industrialised countries could be seen from the formation of the KCTU. But the difficulty of effecting a convergence of state, business and labour in the interest of managing economic opening and industrial restructuring lay not only with the unions but owed much to the internal structures of the Korean *chaebol*.

While the Korean development model is frequently likened to the post-war Japanese model, the structure of the Korean *chaebol* in the 1990s more closely resembled that of the pre-war Japanese *zaibatsu* rather than the reformed companies at the forefront of Japan's post-war company unionism. The transition towards forms of labour–capital accommodation in all the industrialised countries after 1945 coincided with the separation of ownership and management and the diluting of the power of the business tycoons. These phenomena were clearly absent from the Korean *chaebol*, where the founding families remained dominant in both respects. The cohesiveness which accompanied the transfer of authority from the founding generation of *chaebol* owners to their successors from within the family suggests that a diluting of the dominant family's control would remain a distant prospect for most groups. The rhetoric of free competition notwithstanding, they fiercely resisted official proposals to dilute their market power and instead sought to extend it under the cloak of deregulation. The means by which the *chaebol* expanded (diversification on the basis of loans, cross-holdings, mutual debt guarantees between group affiliates and the issue of non-voting stock) allowed them to combine growth with the maintenance of family control. Given this concern with maintaining familial control, it was difficult to imagine the owners of the *chaebol* reforming their internal power structures in a manner that would diminish their own authority.

In their relationship with labour and the state, the Korean *chaebol* clearly fitted the classic late-industrialisation pattern observed for Germany and Japan, where highly repressive systems of labour control existed before 1945. In those cases, labour–capital accommodation emerged only in the wake of military defeat and the forcible restructuring of capital by the occupying power (e.g. the reform of the *zaibatsu* system by the US Occupation authorities). By contrast, the conditions for such a redistribution of power within Korean business did not exist in the mid-1990s, and this inhibited the movement of industrial relations onto a more consensual plane (as evidenced by the controversy surrounding the labour reforms of 1996–7).

On top of the unwillingness of the founding families to accept the diluting of their power, the *chaebol* did not share many aspects of the government's broad developmental agenda. Whereas the government's concern with accommodating labour was motivated by worries about the socially disruptive costs of economic opening, no such reservation existed on the part of the *chaebol*. In *their* scheme of things, the *chaebol* hoped to vacate or streamline the unprofitable sectors and enter rapidly into promising ones with a minimum of government restraint. Thus the FKI and the KEF were dissatisfied with the Kim Young-Sam government for making too many concessions to the unions in its reform of the labour law. The transition towards a more consensual style of industrial relations was hindered not only by the *chaebol*'s lack of concern for wider social priorities but by the nature of the new interdependence between state and business, to which I now turn.

State and business interdependence in the 1990s

In Chapter 4 we saw how democratisation altered the structural interdependence of the state and the *chaebol* in favour of the latter. This interdependence could be seen in the continuing economic support for the *chaebol* as well the close interconnections between the *chaebol* and (elected and appointed) public officials at all echelons. Corruption was regarded as a symptom of the inter-penetration of the business and political spheres. Its elimination therefore would be a measure of the Kim government's break with the authoritarian past. Even though anti-corruption was accorded high priority, the persistence of corruption was a sign of the resilience of the relationships forged over three decades. The nature of corruption in the 1990s also pointed to the growing influence of business in its relationship with the state. Corruption takes many forms and definitions. Here, I define it as the following practices: the extraction and acceptance by public officials of payment from private interests (be they individual or organisational); and the misappropriation and abuse of public funds for the personal benefit of public officials.

Corruption and democratisation

Superficially, the reforms of the Kim Young-Sam government made deep inroads into the elimination of state–business collusion. President Kim pledged to eradicate corruption and to accelerate the liberalisation of the country's dirigist economy. He categorically stated that he would refuse any money offered to him by business (Roh Tae-Woo made a similar pledge at the start of his presidency). Much heralded by the international liberal media (e.g. FEER 1993a and 1993b), the anti-corruption drive appeared to have some substance when a number of senior military men (notably, those most closely associated with Chun) and functionaries of the ruling DLP were dismissed from office in 1993. More significantly, after almost ten years of deliberation, a real name system of financial transaction was enacted in August 1993. A Bank of Korea report describes in the following terms the Emergency Presidential Decree Concerning Real Name Financial Transactions and the Protection of Confidentiality:

> [I]ts provisions stipulated that all financial transactions including those involving deposits, installment savings, checks, CDs, stocks and bonds were to be made only in the actual names of the transacting parties.
>
> Depositors holding accounts at financial institutions were obliged to confirm that these were in their actual names prior to making their first transaction after August 12 with their institutional counterparts. Those holding financial assets under pseudonyms had to register them in their real names by October 12, two months from the date of emergency decree, or face punitive sanctions.
>
> (BOK 1993: 32–3)

Failure to comply would result in the cumulative confiscation of up to 60 per cent of the holder's assets. By outlawing the holding of bank accounts under false names (a practice synonymous with corruption and tax evasion) the reform was designed to make it more difficult for illicit payments to be concealed by public officials using aliases. The same Bank of Korea report stated that high rates of conversion (from false to real names) and confirmation (accounts where holders had confirmed their identities) were recorded in the two months after the enactment of the legislation (BOK 1993: 34). A law placing limits on electoral campaign expenditures was also passed that year (although there were no limits on the amount that party headquarters could spend on a candidate's behalf). Such measures led two Korean academics to conclude: 'Events clearly showed that Kim Young-Sam was a man with a sense of mission to end corruption and to put the society on a righteous path' (Chong-Sik Lee and Hyuk-Sang Sohn 1994: 8).

After the initial momentum, however, public confidence in the government was rocked by a series of major disasters that resulted in heavy loss of life in 1994–5.[10] Then in the autumn of 1995 came the confirmation that former President Roh Tae-Woo had amassed a secret political fund amounting to 500 billion won (approximately $650 million) during his presidency (1988–93). While the exposure of Roh was apparently a triumph for the government's real name reform, the ensuing disclosures about how the political money was circulated underlined the extent to which illicit funds had permeated the Korean polity. Korean newspapers had long been speculating about this 'secret' fund (in 1990, Roh's daughter received a one-year suspended sentence for violating US currency regulations by entering that country with $250,000 in cash). Significantly, veteran opposition leader Kim Dae-Jung also admitted to having received (albeit indirectly through his campaigners' fund-raising activities) a 'modest' $2.5 million from Roh during the 1992 presidential election. It was subsequently disclosed that the other leading figure in Korean politics, Kim Jong-Pil (who broke away from Kim Young-Sam in early-1995 to form his own opposition party), had received $10 million from the same source. Attention then turned to the originator of the money, Roh's predecessor Chun Doo-Hwan and his financial benefactors from the business community (including the chairmen of such *chaebol* as Daewoo and Hanbo, both of whom received suspended prison terms). This slush-fund scandal did not leave President Kim Young-Sam's reputation untarnished either, for he was widely believed to have been the principal beneficiary of Roh's political financing. On top of the slush-fund scandal, cases of improper financial involvement with business by top public officials (e.g. the Defence Minister's acceptance of money from Daewoo Heavy Industries in connection with military procurements) continued to unfold in late-1996.

Then, in January 1997, the insolvency of Hanbo (one of Korea's top twenty *chaebol*) raised the question of how the conglomerate managed to raise 5 trillion won (*c.* $6 billion) without adequate collateral for an ambitious steel project when, in theory, strict supervisory guidelines existed under the General Banking Act (BOK 1996: 96–8). The alleged source of influence peddling was President Kim Young-Sam's second son. If the disasters undermined public confidence in the government, then the slush-fund and bribery scandals cast doubt on the integrity of civilian politicians, government and opposition alike. These happenings highlighted the persistence of illicit collusion between public officials and the business sector (Hanbo boss Chang Tai-Soo had already been implicated in incidents in 1991 and 1995–6) and the extent of the saturation of the political system by business money.

Given that corruption is associated with the existence of a cosy relationship between public officials and their favoured producers, one might expect democratisation and economic liberalisation to erode the conditions on which corruption thrives. By opening up the political process, democratisation should, in theory, subject officials to the gaze of public scrutiny. It should also facilitate the establishment of countervailing powers to the state and its clients. Economic liberalisation should lead to the separation of government and business. The motivation for collusion – the exchange of financial favours for market advantage – should also disappear with the regulated competition that liberalisation brings.

Such optimistic expectations however, were yet to be borne out by the Korean experience of economic and political reform. A decade since the fall of authoritarianism, and despite repeated pronouncements about liberalisation and the separation of the spheres of business and politics, corruption appeared to remain deeply rooted in both the private and public domains. While disasters could be seen as legacies of the authoritarian past or even as the failure of enforcement at the local level, the persistent allegations of financial impropriety surrounding senior officials and national legislators of all parties could not be so easily explained away. The strict regulations which existed on paper were not rigorously enforced. For example the rumours about the Roh slush-fund had been circulating for some time, but were not investigated. This suggests the persistence of money politics and the difficulties of seriously pursuing allegations of wrongdoing. How should we account for this pattern of behaviour, and what were its implications?

It can be argued that corruption persisted because democratisation and liberalisation were in their infancy in the 1990s and that it would take a long period of reform for the decades of established malpractices to be reversed. Clearly, political reform still had some way to go before Korea could measure up to the standards of a mature liberal-democracy. To begin with, the democratic transition was incomplete, even in the formal procedural sense. On the positive side, the power of the security agencies such as the army and the Agency for National Security Planning (successor to the KCIA) had been drastically pared back after 1987 (Paik 1994). But even well into the Kim Young-Sam government's term of office, democratisation had not been consolidated, and many aspects of authoritarian practice remained: the National Security Law; the semi-censorship of the press; and legal prohibitions on organised labour. In October 1994, the government reaffirmed that the National Security Law, which proscribes 'pro-North Korean activities', was to be maintained (while political prisoners from the 1950s continued to languish in prison). In 1996, the Kim Young-Sam government even made preparations for its strengthening.[11] Such conditions hindered not only the emergence of effectively organised countervailing powers (such as a political party based on the backing of organised labour) but the emergence of critical standards by which governance and the quality of life (e.g. of consumer choice and standards) could be judged. If Korea was a democracy in the formal sense, the substance of a pluralistic society had yet to be developed.

The publicly stated goal of eradicating corruption and the state–business collusion that underpinned it was, from the start, compromised by the exigencies of power, as President Kim Young-Sam could not afford to endanger the coalition that had brought him to power. The personnel turnover witnessed at the beginning of the Kim government could be interpreted as a move directed against potential leadership rivals rather than as a genuine attempt at eradicating corruption.[12] Previous presidents (Park in 1961 and Chun in 1980) engaged in similar manoeuvring under the guise of fighting corruption at the beginning of their terms of office. While much publicity was given to the heavy sentencing (since commuted) of Chun and Roh in August 1996, it should also be noted that the initial proceedings against the two were halted in July 1995 due to the statute of limitations (a mechanism designed by Chun and Roh to extricate themselves safely from power). Furthermore, the most serious charges (of mutiny, abuse of power, corruption) were confined to only a very small coterie of the former presidents' closest associates. In the action against Chun and Roh, President Kim Young-Sam was constrained by the need to maintain the cohesiveness of his ruling DLP-NKP. This meant keeping on board the former presidents' *minjung* faction (the old DJP). The 1990 merger with the DJP was a condition for Kim Young-Sam's subsequent victory but it was also an obstacle to the thorough reform of the authoritarian legacy.

The impact of leadership style

Yet the problem went beyond the expediency of making a compromise 'pact' with erstwhile authoritarians for the sake of governing. The similar methods by which the so-called 'Three Kims' controlled their parties reflected the deeply ingrained political habits that made the emergence of more accountable (and, by extension, less corruptible) government difficult, regardless of the party in power. All three ruled their parties on a personal authoritarian basis and motivated electoral support by fanning regional rivalry (e.g. by appealing to some sense of regional superiority or victimhood). The dominance of such political bosses, rooted in personal and regional appeals, was not conducive to democratic consolidation. It was a style of leadership that did not encourage questioning on the part of followers. The leaders themselves were not accountable to any type of intra-party democracy and nor were they bound by any policy platforms. At any time, any of these leading lights could desert a party and take almost its entire following with him (as Kim Dae-Jung did with the Democratic Party). Aspiring leaders owed their positions first and foremost to their bosses rather than to party or principle. Consequently, parties and legislatures, the central institutions of representative democracy, failed to develop credibility as the central arenas of political interaction, but remained appendages of the dominant individuals' pursuit of power.

There was another way in which such a culture of personality as perpetuated by the Three Kims, fed corruption. Because the political bosses enjoyed great power and prestige, there was strong incentive for those who were socially ambitious to become close to them or to their associates. The system of personal loyalty thus replicated itself at lower levels, as sub-leaders were apt to cultivate the same type of relationship with their subordinates. In such a situation, those with apparent access to the political bosses (e.g. as revealed by the activities of the uncle of President Chun's wife in the kerb market scandal of 1982) were well positioned to extract rents or to become attractive targets for bribery.

But why were the dominant leaders interested only in the pursuit and maintenance of power for its own sake? Why were 'principles' so readily disregarded and mechanisms of accountability so weak? The origins of these phenomena could be traced to the history of the South Korean Republic. Staunch anti-communism of successive authoritarian regimes eliminated moderate social-democratic parties as well as the anti-democratic communists. For ambitious politicians eager to distinguish themselves within the narrow ideological confines of the conservative regime, emphasising personal qualities and locality were obvious strategies. Within the authoritarian civilian regime of Syngman Rhee, leaders and factions of the ruling Liberal and opposition Democratic Parties jockeyed for power and engaged in the exchange of favours with the business community (e.g. granting of import licences in exchange for 'donations' to individual politicians, officials or parties). The arrival of the military power in 1961 intruded on that relationship. The military priority on growth reinforced but also transformed the nature of the exchange of favours between public officials and businessmen. Performance now became an added criterion for continued official support for business while business's financial contribution was directed away from the ineffectual civilian politicians and towards the ruling parties created by the military (first Park's DRP and then Chun's DJP).

Excluded from power and its benefits for quarter of a century, the civilian politicians finally turned the tables on the military usurpers and triumphantly returned on the bandwagon of the mass democratic uprising of 1987. Both Kim Young-Sam and Kim Dae-Jung belonged to the generation of civilian politicians whose formative years were under Syngman Rhee and who would have risen to national leadership sooner but for the military. The fierce determination of Kim Young-Sam and Kim Dae-Jung to seek and preserve power (even at the cost of letting Roh Tae-Woo hang on in 1987 or, more tragically, for Chun to seize power in 1979) reflects the belief of each that the mantle or 'prize' of leadership rightfully belonged to him by seniority, inheritance and merit (e.g. the record of long-time opposition to authoritarian rule and hardships thereby endured). Originally a military man, Kim Jong-Pil inherited Park's DRP and adapted to civilian politics. Belonging to the same generation as the other two Kims, he made a belated conversion to democratic politics in the 1980s and encountered persecution from the new military rulers. As a potential successor to Park and an opponent of the Chun-Roh regime, he too could stake a claim to national leadership after 1987. Democratisation re-opened a path to power that had been frustrated for so long. Having realised the one and only principle to which they were dedicated, anti-authoritarianism, the scene was set for the trio to return to the old game of manoeuvring for power. The style of the politics associated with the leading governing and opposition politicians, of personality and office seeking above all else, lent itself to expediency (e.g. the alliance and fallout between Kim Young-Sam, Roh

Tae-Woo and Kim Jong-Pil, followed by the latter's alliance with Kim Dae-Jung). One aspect of this expediency was the acceptance of business money in the pursuit of power. In this sense, there was continuity between the democratic and pre-military styles of elite politics.

Such elite machinations could thrive only on the basis of public toleration and inertia. That the style of opportunistic elite politics prevalent in 1990s' Korea survived was evidence of the continuation of conservative ideological dominance. Given the extent of popular enthusiasm for democratisation in the 1980s, it seems surprising that the procedural changes of 1987 did not result in a more effective challenge to that dominance. How could this apparent contradiction be explained? The popular rejection of authoritarianism and the economic gains made by organised labour after 1987 were very real achievements. Yet labour was unable to translate its militant economism into support for a wider social-democratic political agenda and transcend the politics of regional personalities with one based on social and economic issues. As of the mid-1990s, attempts to form alternative political parties to displace the dominance of the Three Kims had been unsuccessful. Committed to this objective, the Democratic Party fared badly in the April 1996 National Assembly elections. This was followed by the defection of many of its legislators to the Kims. The climate of public opinion (especially of the much-expanded middle class) remained deeply suspicious of socialistic ideas especially when presented in the shape of the radical nationalism of the students. The identification with middle-class status was very prevalent in Korean society (see Chapter 4 and Table 4.3). The tension with North Korea reinforced such suspicion and provided powerful justification for the state of national security. Added to this was the appeal of the reformed conservatism being sold by the political bosses. Against a background of growing affluence and relatively full employment, it was difficult for social-democratic parties to make headway on the distributional issue, especially when that issue was also being integrated into the conservative agenda (e.g. the expansion of social development programmes under the Roh and Kim governments). Like the land reform of the 1950s, the effect of conservative reformism of the 1980s and 1990s was to forestall the conditions in which popular social-democratic alternatives could emerge. By accommodating the pressures for social reform, conservative reformism helped to perpetuate the existing style of elite politics and the state–business collusion that went with it.

Structural interdependence of the state and big business

But explanation for the persistence of state–business collusion goes beyond the style of elite politics and the climate of public opinion upon which it thrives. The previous discussion linked the persistence of corruption and other malpractices of the authoritarian industrialisation era with the incompleteness of political and economic reform. A complete explanation for the endurance of corruption and the limited effect of reform also has to consider the existence of a deeper structural interdependence between the state and business. What was the nature of this structural relationship in the 1990s, and how did it compare with previous patterns?

Under military rule, economic performance was added to the process by which business and state exchanged favours. The capacity of military-based governments to extract donations from the business community was total, and resistance brought swift retribution (as happened to Kukje, the conglomerate dissolved by Chun). If corruption under authoritarian rule was characterised by the capacity of the government to extract, then democratisation and liberalisation (however incomplete) accentuated the potential for corruption from the other side by enhancing the capacity of big business to bribe. Whereas authoritarian rule enabled the government to extract finance from the business sector (e.g. in donations to the ruling party), democratisation enhanced the independence of the latter. Given the cost of fighting elections (e.g. publicity, campaign staff, distribution of largesse to potential electors) aspiring politicians of all persuasions needed to attract business support. It was therefore advantageous for politicians to cultivate relations with big business and seek its financial support. By implicating politicians from across the political spectrum (including the two opposition Kims) as well as many *chaebol* heads, the Roh Tae-Woo slush-fund scandal was evidence of the extensive dependence of all politicians on business donations for their campaign activities. An insider from the ruling DLP alleged (*Korea Herald* 1 May 1997) that the party had spent 312.7 billion won (*c.* $370 million) in the 1992 presidential election (against the 28.4 billion won declared and the legal limit of 36.7 billion won). The 1993 electoral laws placed strict limits ($112,000) on candidates' campaign expenditures but not surprisingly, they did not prevent the irregularities that were alleged to have marked the April 1996 National Assembly election (in which it was widely believed that candidates spending under two billion won – *c.* $2.5 million – were likely to be defeated) (Koh 1997: 4).

Democratisation presented the *chaebol* with more political options in their bid to influence policy. A less well publicised source of *chaebol* influence was their extensive control over the elements of the media network (especially the press). Moreover, the *chaebol* had become more resilient to the effects of state sanctions: their size made them resistant while effective sanctions would impose electorally unpopular social costs (e.g. lower growth, lost jobs if a group subsidiary collapsed). The direct entry of business into politics in 1992 (when Hyundai founder Chung Ju-Yung's launch of a breakaway conservative party garnered 16 per cent of the popular vote) did not signify the demise of the close state–business relationship.[13] It was, however, a sign of the potential damage a disgruntled business tycoon could inflict on the government of the day. In exchange for political donations (to individual politicians, to party coffers, to bureaucrats) and growth, the Kim government effected policies beneficial to the *chaebol* despite its intentions of fostering competition: tolerance of monopolistic practices; liberalisation strategies designed to favour the *chaebol*; infrastructural investments from which the *chaebol* benefited as contractors and end-users. Indeed, the rhetoric of reform disguised the lack of real change. For example, little headway was made on the problem of concentrated land ownership amid the serious shortage of industrial and residential land; ironically, the *chaebol* themselves complained vocally about the land price as a contributor to high production costs. Thus the state–business nexus persisted, but in a modified form: business remained reliant on state support, but democratisation widened its channels of influence over the incumbent government (with the formation of breakaway conservative parties being an extreme option). The slush-fund scandal that came to light in 1995 also highlighted another type of state–business adhesion, namely the connection by marriage between the children of senior government officials and *chaebol* families (e.g. the Sunkyong group's rise to become the fifth-largest *chaebol* was allegedly as much due to the chairman's daughter's marriage to President Roh Tae-Woo's son as it was to enterprise). Not surprisingly, such structural interdependence between politicians and business made effective enforcement of anti-corruption policies difficult. The prosecution of the former presidents could not extend much beyond their immediate associates without damaging powerful individuals still active in politics. The sentencing was also of limited severity to avoid alienating the voters of the North Kyongsang region. For these reasons, the apparently harsh initial verdicts on Chun and Roh were always going to be commuted, as they were in December 1996. Even this limited reckoning with the erstwhile authoritarians brought discontent among the people of their native North Kyongsang region. For economic reasons, the businessmen implicated with the former presidents (including the chairmen of the Daewoo and Samsung groups) had their prison sentences suspended.

Money politics thus survived the transition to democratisation. The basis of that relationship, the interdependence of state and business, altered in favour of business but interdependence remained nevertheless. In spite of their leading role in the transformation of 1987, the students, organised labour and civic groups had yet to develop the resource base, cohesiveness and political voice (beyond the opportunistic encouragement sporadically given by members of the established political elite) to establish an effective countervailing power to the state–*chaebol* nexus. Even after almost a decade, procedural democracy had neither displaced the old forms of elite competition nor ushered in a more effective brand of popular politics. In that sense, Korea's democratic development could be characterised as one of *arrested democratisation*.

Corruption is commonly associated with the unaccountability of public officials and the existence of a cosy relationship between officialdom and its favoured producers. On that basis, we should expect democratisation and economic liberalisation to remedy the problem by making officials more accountable to the law and by replacing discretionary bureaucratic allocation of resources with impersonal market allocation. With the political system having democratised, and with economic decisions increasingly taken by the market, public officials should in theory have become less attractive as targets for bribery. The Korean experience of democratisation suggests that there are grounds for expecting the persistence of state–business collusion (and its associated illicit dealings) in spite of reform. First, the toppling of authoritarian regimes, or popular anti-militarism, should not be identified with the rejection of the habits formed during (or pre-dating) authoritarian rule. Indeed, those habits may even become more prevalent as a consequence of political opening. For example, the completion of the military's overthrow accelerated the democratic leaders' reversion to the politics of personality and regional rivalry. This rift was deepened by the military's uneven development of the regions, but was capitalised on by civilian politicians after 1987. The exchange of favours that once existed between the military and business became generalised to include all politicians seeking to finance their electoral ambitions.

Second, the strength of the popular desire for a clean break from the practices of the past also depends on the achievements of the authoritarian rulers. Where the authoritarians presided over relatively successful economies, incoming democratic governments have to tread carefully. In targeting abuses, they have to avoid endangering economic performance. This point goes to the nub of the Korean situation and the problems of reform faced by the Kim Young-Sam government. The exchange of favours between government and business was the institutional foundation of thirty years of high growth. Interdependence between public officials and businessmen was fostered on the basis of mutual interest and the shared ideology of growth. Attempts to root out corruption were thus constrained from the start by these considerations and, in particular, by the threat of economic decline. The determination with which the Kim Young-Sam government pursued its anti-corruption and anti-monopoly programme diminished as its term of office wore on and as the warnings of slower growth from the *chaebol* became more serious (e.g. *Korea Herald* 27 November 1996). While the clamping down on corruption and other abuses of business power went down well with the public, slowing the economy by jeopardising the viability of the *chaebol* did not. This reflected not only the worry about jobs but the Korean people's pride in the *chaebol* as symbols of national success. In this sense Korean capitalism and its industrialists had established a legitimacy that they lacked when industrialisation first started.

Third, in the absence of a deeply ingrained democratic culture, it was unlikely that there would be much popular will to make use of the newly acquired democratic procedures to bring state–business collusion to account (except when public opinion was fired up by major disasters that could be traced directly to corporate greed and regulatory negligence).

This was especially so at times when the public was not economically dissatisfied. In such conditions, instead of the public bringing corrupt state–business dealings to book, it was business's leverage over the government that was strengthened. This was evident in Korea after 1987 when the *chaebol* became more assertive in their demands for speedy deregulation.

What of economic liberalisation? Was it not its incompleteness that was behind the persistence of the state–business adhesion? Even the more radical of the Three Kims, Kim Dae-Jung, continued to subscribe to this diagnosis of Korea's social and economic ills a decade on from when it was first systematically articulated in his writings. In essence, his proposals for economic reform (e.g. of the tax system) and cooperative industrial relations differed little from those of Kim Young-Sam (Dae-Jung Kim 1996). The evidence from Korea suggested this to be an unrealistic belief. Economic liberalisation weakens the extent of direct influence that the state can exert over economic outcomes (e.g. via industrial policy) but even in a liberalised economy there are other opportunities for state–business collusion. In the Korean case, direct support was being replaced by the growth of government spending on infrastructural development. Rather than intensifying competition, liberalisation could end up bolstering economic concentration among those *chaebol* which had international strategic alliances with TNCs (since foreign TNCs entering the Korean market would need local partners).

In liberalised economies, competition depends on the zeal with which public officials enforce anti-monopolistic regulations. Such officials and the politicians who control them are likely to become the targets for lobbying activities. We saw in Chapter 3 that the limited liberalisation of the financial sector in the 1980s extended the influence of the *chaebol*. Instead of promoting competition and the erosion of collusive state–business ties, further liberalisation in Korea fostered new potentials for monopolisation, collusion and corrupt practices (foreign corporations may well get sucked into this web). Since the *chaebol* sought to enhance their dominance (e.g. by acquisition of financial institutions and outward movement), it was not surprising that they (via the FKI) subscribed to the NPE perspective on liberalisation as a justification for faster deregulation. Just as neo-classical representations of the nature of Korea's development success were inaccurate in the 1960s and 1970s, liberal-inspired beliefs about the effects of democratisation and economic liberalisation were similarly misguided in their understanding of the Korea's globalisation project. The institutional foundations of corruption (such as a close big business–state relationship, the dominance of the conservative political agenda and an interventionist bureaucracy) may well have survived Korea's greater congruence with international democratisation and liberalisation trends.

The congruence with those international trends also brought destabilising elements into the state–business relationship. I have argued above that, besides efficiency, the globalisation project was driven by the concern for growth (or 'catching up') and for social stability. The state's broader concerns with these three objectives brought frictions with the *chaebol*. The outward movement of the *chaebol* was highly significant for Korea's development path. While the advantages of foreign direct investment by the *chaebol* were officially acknowledged, there was also official unease over the loss of domestic jobs and the 'hollowing out' effect on local industry. Not surprisingly, the *chaebol* gave globalisation (the maximisation of borrowing and investment opportunities worldwide) a higher priority than they did local jobs. They lobbied vigorously for more labour flexibility at home. As the *chaebol* were becoming increasingly diversified internationally, they were becoming less 'Korean'. Accordingly, their allegiance to the goals of national welfare diminished along with the state's capacity to regulate them in the national interest. The *chaebol* themselves recognised that for the benefits of the productive potential of technical changes (e.g. higher expenditure on R&D) to be realised, the organisation of production would also have to be transformed (e.g. from mass production to flexible production and managerial rationalisation). This trend was likely to be reinforced by the policy of forging strategic alliances with foreign firms. Such internationalisation could not but alter the character of Korean capitalism, creating new tensions with the Korean state in the process. Like other states, Korea's was facing the tension between the national basis of political legitimacy and the internationalisation of economics.

The impressive growth rates and the maintenance of high rates of employment in the first half of the 1990s meant that the social costs of the internationalisation of Korean capital (and, indeed, their reckless patterns of international investment financed by debt) had not yet become a major political issue. This depended on high growth and employment rates being maintained. Even though the Kim government had passed a pro-business labour law in March 1997, business did not immediately make use of those laws to implement the mass lay-offs so feared by the labour unions. Much depended on how the state would respond to proposed lay-offs and how much it was prepared to intervene to assist the displaced. Another factor was the livelihood of the articulate middle class (the prospects for white-collar unemployment were also rising). As in other East Asian societies, the family unit remained a powerful source of support, helping the unemployed to relaunch themselves without adding to the burden of the state. But the potential was there for conflict between the *chaebol* sector, driven by its concerns for workforce reduction and international expansion, and a Korean state having to balance these efficiency concerns against other priorities. The conditionalities of the IMF-supervised rescue package of December 1997 would bring these latent tensions out into the open.

Conclusion

The structural weaknesses (weak technology base and SMEs, over-diversified *chaebol* weaned on official favouritism) of Korean capitalism were evident by the end of the 1970s. In the early-1980s, the Korean economy achieved stabilisation without deep structural reform. Reforms in response to these problems were slow in coming because of the vulnerability of the economy. Many heavy industries that later became export winners were in their infancy and depended on government support for their survival. Because the government implemented its heavy industrialisation through the financially vulnerable *chaebol*, liberalisation and anti-monopoly measures could be introduced only gradually. The effectiveness of labour repression in controlling wages during the early-1980s was another factor working against the restructuring of the development model. As the economy recovered, and moved into the (externally induced) boom phase of 1986–8, the political incentives for structural economic reform, with all the uncertainties involved, were further diminished. Instead, the development policy took on a redistributional emphasis. This chapter has attempted to explain why the structural economic reform was once more accelerated by the Kim Young-Sam government (under the theme of 'globalisation'). This was done from an assessment of the changing relationships between state, business and labour, the particular nature of which was said to define the Korean developmental state.

Changing external and domestic circumstances brought renewed pressures for the acceleration of economic restructuring. The Plaza Agreement of 1985 (under which the Japanese yen was appreciated) was a foretaste of the US counter-measures that would be taken against countries deemed to be using protectionistic trading practices. Attention shifted from Japan to other major surplus countries such as Korea and Taiwan. The end of the Cold War in 1989–91 exacerbated these latent trade frictions. US criteria for fair trade became more demanding, and bilateral pressure for the opening of the Korean market was reinforced through the multilateral GATT–WTO.

In their pursuit of freer access to foreign finance, technology and production bases, the *chaebol* also lent their powerful voices to the liberalisation cause. Without such access, their prospects (and Korean industry as a whole) looked bleak. They risked being squeezed between the labour-abundant new NICs and the advanced industrialised economies (regaining their competitiveness after a decade of painful restructuring). On the domestic front, democratisation in 1987 and the rise of independent organised labour (concentrated at the large-scale production facilities of the *chaebol*) diminished the economic effectiveness of labour repression and forced the *chaebol* to look for cheaper and more flexible labour. With the externally induced boom over in 1990, it was clear that economic reform had to be accelerated. The economy had become too large and society (*chaebol*, organised labour, consumers) too resistant to be directed in the old way. In response to these pressures, and in seeking to establish the reformist reputation of his government, President Kim Young-Sam announced a plan of reform designed to bring about a transition from the semi-reformed developmental state to a 'New Economy' consistent with changed domestic and international conditions. The 'globalisation' project of the Kim Young-Sam government came to be identified with the completion of economic liberalisation and democratisation.

As commonly used, the term 'globalisation' denotes growing worldwide economic interconnectedness in which production, consumption and financial intermediation take place at the international level. Corresponding to these trends is the diminishing effectiveness of the traditional policies of governmental economic intervention like industrial policy and demand management (e.g. in controlling the economic shocks caused by international financial instability). Yet the state remains a significant actor on three levels. First, it can determine the speed and scope of the national economy's opening (e.g. through economic diplomacy and (de)regulatory measures). Second, through indirect interventionary measures it can affect the prospects for domestic firms own internationalisation strategies. Third, the degree of social disruption accompanying economic liberalisation will depend on the speed of liberalisation and the nature of governmental action to relaunch the displaced. At all three levels, the Korean state played an active role in managing the integration of the national economy with the global mainstream. This was a defining feature of the Kim government's globalisation project. This showed the state's concern with balancing efficiency and other gains of liberalisation with the traditional priorities of Korean development, namely 'catching up' (maintaining high growth rates) and social stability. Even if liberalisation accelerated after the inception of the Kim Young-Sam government, the transition remained graduated especially when compared with the 'big bang' approach of Eastern Europe and the spasmodic character of change in parts of Latin America (from heterodox stabilisation to neo-liberalism). That Korean policy-makers enjoyed such room for manoeuvre was a legacy of the past success of the authoritarian industrialisation pattern and the cohesive bureaucracy–business alliance fostered by it.

That is not to say that there were no problems associated with the reform of the Korean developmental state. Accommodating domestic and international liberalisation pressures with the traditional priorities for national development and social stability highlighted the areas of tension and consensus in the state–business relationship. There was difference between the state and the *chaebol* on the deregulation issue. The *chaebol* sought faster deregulation that would afford them the advantages (low interest rates, technology, flexible labour, inexpensive land) enjoyed by foreign competitors. For the state, on the other hand, the type of deregulation favoured by the *chaebol* would have brought unwelcome consequences: rising unemployment with the lifting of exit barriers; further economic concentration (as the *chaebol* moved to take over financial institutions); and the 'hollowing out' of domestic industry as business rushed to relocate overseas. In spite of the *chaebol*'s assertiveness, they still relied on state support. While calling for faster deregulation, what they actually sought was a type of partial liberalisation that would maximise their opportunities for expansion without losing their traditional benefits (e.g. dominance of the local market, control of newly privatised state monopolies, and state support in moments of crisis). Full and rapid liberalisation would have exposed their deficiencies and rendered them susceptible to hostile takeovers, dangers that could be averted only by government regulation (e.g. safeguards against such predatory takeover actions). The *chaebol* also depended on government intervention (e.g. via land policy, infrastructural development and labour reform) to alleviate the problems of the 'high cost, low efficiency' structure that was said to characterise Korean industry. For the government's own legitimacy, it was vital to maintain the viability of the *chaebol*.

Such interdependence explains why the collusive state–business relationship (and one of its by-products, corruption) remained entrenched and impervious to the reforms enacted by the Kim Young-Sam government of 1993–8. Rather than eliminate the state–business collusion established under authoritarian industrialisation, the effect of economic liberalisation was to provide new opportunities and incentives for collusion. Instead of strengthening accountability, democratisation gave business more leverage over the state (e.g. by extending the web of money politics to opposition politicians) and made the prospects for economic de-concentration very dim indeed. Neo-liberal predictions (to which the *chaebol* officially subscribed as part of their lobbying offensive) that economic and political liberalisation would lead to the separation of state and business failed to materialise under Kim Young-Sam's globalisation project. Economic concentration and the politico-economic relationships that arose from it were core features of the Korean model of late-industrialisation development. These features appeared to have survived the 1990s' consolidation phase of democratisation and liberalisation.

Economic liberalisation also threatened popular interests. The shift towards internationalised production threatened jobs. Domestically, enhancing competitiveness entailed more flexible and less secure forms of employment, a situation threatening to reverse the gains made by organised labour since 1987. While the well-paid manual workers (e.g. in shipyards, auto plants) of the *chaebol* and clerical workers in the service sector (e.g. in highly overmanned sectors such as finance and distribution) were the most at risk from these trends, the white-collar new middle class (including managers) would not be exempt from the dangers of downsizing either. This helps to account for the scale of the protests against the labour laws of December 1996.

Reconciling popular interests with the drive for increased efficiency was another defining feature of the Kim Young-Sam government's globalisation project. In promoting social development, improving organised labour's legal status and providing facilities to help re-equip those displaced for re-employment, the state was seeking to bring labour into an expanded developmentalist alliance. On the basis of such a consensus, difficult decisions vital to Korea's future competitiveness could be taken and smoothly implemented. This was not proving to be an easy task (one of the reasons why it was left until the latter part of the government's term of office). The legacy of hostile industrial relations did not facilitate the development of consensual relations between labour and its former enemies (who were clearly still colluding). Both business and labour became entrenched in their maximal demands. It was not until the economy slipped into deep recession in the autumn of 1997 that the agenda for consensus building for restructuring would resurface.

6 The twilight of developmentalism?

Korea in the 'IMF era'

Symptoms of the crisis

In the autumn of 1997, Korea felt the force of the Southeast Asian financial crisis. Against a background of major corporate insolvencies, corruption scandals, and heavy short-term borrowing due to mounting trade deficits, intense speculative pressures forced repeated depreciations of the won. From October, the descent of the won was rapid. From about 900 won per dollar, it slumped to 1,650 won per dollar by December. The currency collapse was matched by the slump in the stock index. In the attempt to defend the won, Korea's foreign exchange reserves were depleted from $22 billion to $7 billion between October and November. The most immediate impact of the won's collapse was that it exacerbated the servicing burden on Korea's short-term dollar-denominated external debt. The lack of foreign confidence raised the spectre of default. On 21 November 1997, the Korean government made a request to the IMF for financial assistance, a move justified on the following grounds:

> Despite the sound economic fundamentals in terms of economic growth, price stability and the external balances, the Korean economy has recently been suffering from a temporary liquidity shortage. The declining confidence in the Korean economy, triggered by a series of large corporate insolvencies, has undermined the overseas borrowing capability of domestic financial institutions, making the roll-over of short-term debt difficult.
>
> (MOFE 21 November 1997)

Given the heavy exposure of Japanese banks in Korea, the response of the international financial community to the Korean financial crisis was swift. By 3 December, an IMF-supervised rescue package worth $57 billion had been assembled (MOFE 3 December 1997). Korea's importance was underlined by the fact that it received a loan worth 2,000 per cent of its country quota (against the ordinary credit limit of 300 per cent) (MOFE 19 December 1997). From 21 December, the World Bank also made available $10 billion.[1] In spite of some initial reservation on the part of Kim Dae-Jung, all the candidates in the ongoing Korean presidential election contest soon accepted the conditionalities and pledged to implement the terms faithfully. Business leaders gave their support to the programme and the labour unions did not express opposition to the need for fundamental economic reform. The Korean economy thus entered what is now commonly known as the 'IMF era'. A sense of national humiliation pervaded the country.

Narrowly elected to the presidency at the fourth time of asking,[2] Kim Dae-Jung pledged to implement the international rescue plan negotiated by his predecessor, a medicine that entailed negative growth for 1998 (with uncertain prospects for recovery thereafter). The new president also promised to eradicate the root causes of the 1997 crisis by completing the political and economic reform started by his predecessors (Dae-Jung Kim 1998). The financial crisis and the corrective policies prescribed by the IMF were exacting a heavy toll on the real economy. By the time of Kim Dae-Jung's inauguration in February 1998, the unemployment rate had jumped to 5.9 per cent from the 1997 average of 2.6 per cent (from 934,000 to 1,235,000). There was prospect of worse to follow.

This chapter places the economic meltdown of 1997–8 in the context of the evolution of the state–business–labour relationship that has been the main concern of this book. Specifically, it evaluates the causes of the crisis from the perspective of the institutional relationships raised in previous chapters. First, I argue that the regulatory weaknesses that led up to the crisis of 1997 were consistent with patterns of state–business interaction that *pre-dated* the 1993–7 wave of accelerated liberalisation. Far from being the consequence of the dismantling of the developmental state, the vulnerability to crisis was implicit in the *chaebol*-dominated economy created under Park Chung-Hee. Second, despite the shift towards redistribution from 1987 (Chapter 4) and social consensus building from 1993 (Chapter 5), democratic governments were unable to transform the pattern of confrontational industrial relations inherited from their authoritarian predecessors. A consequence of this was the failure to reform the inflexible labour market, one of the components of the 'high cost, low efficiency' economic structure.

Only twelve months earlier, Korea had entered the OECD as Asia's second representative. In that same year, Seoul had been chosen as the venue of the 2000 ASEM summit and Korea had obtained the right to co-host the 2002 football World Cup. The country was brimming with a self-confidence reminiscent of the late-1980s. In 1996, however, there had been a major deterioration in the balance of payments as the current accounts deficit soared from $8.5 billion to $23 billion (Table 6.1). Even so, there was no sense of an overwhelming panic. While the existence of structural problems in economic organisation was acknowledged, the deficit was attributed primarily to external factors, principally the collapse of

Table 6.1 Indicators of Korean economy 1991–8

	1991	1992	1993	1994	1995	1996	1997	1998
GNP ($ billion)	292	306	331	378	453	480	437	304
GNP/capita ($)	6,757	6,988	7,484	8,467	10,037	10,543	9,511	6,750
GNP growth rate (% p.a.)	9.1	5.0	5.8	8.4	8.7	6.9	4.9	−5.8 (GDP)
GNP deflator (% p.a.)	10.2	6.1	5.1	5.5	5.6	3.4	4.3	7.5
Unemployment rate	2.3	2.4	2.8	2.4	2.0	2.0	2.6	6.8
Exchange rate won : dollar	733.8	780.8	802.7	803.6	771.0	804.8	951.1	1,398.7
Current account balance ($US billion)	−8.3	−3.9	1.0	−3.9	−8.5	−23.0	−8.9	40.0
Total external debt ($ billion)	53.6	57.5	62.8	94.0	115.0	(164.3)	(158.1)	(149.3)
Short-term debt (%)	46.8	43.9	44.3	42.7	51.3	49.9	37.5	30.8
Stock price index (annual average)	657.1	587.1	728.2	965.7	934.9	833.4	654.5	409.0

Note: Total external debt for years 1991–8 includes debt contracted by overseas branches of Korean financial institutions

Source: MOFE (based on Bank of Korea data)

world semi-conductor prices and the depreciation of the Japanese yen. By September 1997, several *chaebol* both second-tier (Kia, Halla, Hanbo) and third (Dainong, Haitai, Sammi, Jinro, New Core) as well as their supporting financial institutions, were bankrupt or teetering on the edge of bankruptcy.

While accepting that the economy was in severe trouble, Korean policy-makers at the highest levels apparently failed to detect the makings of the coming financial crisis (e.g. MOFE 11 September 1997). Policy statements continued to reiterate the established schedule for reform and even spec-ulated about Korea's rosy prospects for the new millennium. It was expected that a growth rate of 6–7 per cent could be sustained, enabling the social friction of restructuring to be lessened. The feeling was that the economy would grow its way out of its temporary difficulties, just as it had done in the past. The top tier of super-*chaebol* had their eyes on further expansion (e.g. by taking over the auto division of the troubled Kia group). As late as November, comparisons in the foreign press between Korea's predicament and the financial melt-downs in Mexico (1994) and Thailand (forced to abandon the baht–dollar exchange rate in July 1997) were emphatically rejected. At international economic fora and through press releases, top officials asserted time and again that Korea's economic funda-mentals (growth potential, price level, government expenditure patterns, debt–service ratio) were sound (MOFE 10 November 1997).

The role of state–business relations

It has been argued that the fragile debt structure was the consequence of financial liberalisation without adequate regulatory safeguards in the 1990s. The massive short-term foreign borrowing requirement was said to be the consequence of falling profitability owing to the unregulated expansion of productive capacity. In effect, the crisis was brought about by the erosion of the twin pillars of the developmental state: financial control and indus-trial policy. Corresponding to the weakening of the state's traditional instruments of regulation was the change in the nature of the state–busi-ness relationship from reciprocal to particularistic. While the Park, Chun and even Roh governments were pro-*chaebol*, subsidies and other favours were dispensed on the basis of successful performance. By contrast, it was only under the Kim Young-Sam government that such favours came to be allocated to individual business groups on the basis of private connec-tions with senior officials, or 'cronyism' (Chang *et al.* 1998: 741).

The arguments made in the previous chapters concur with some of the claims made above: accelerated financial liberalisation in response to inter-national and domestic pressures; the transition away from industrial policy to functional intervention; and the growing identification of individual *chaebol* with particular public officials during the 1990s. The vulnerability of the economy to external shocks of the 1997 type, however, *pre-dated* the policy failures of the Kim Young-Sam government and originated in the practice of state–business relations that characterised Korea Inc. First of all, the claim that the Korean economy was fundamentally sound (the basis of the arguments that attribute the Korean crisis to excessive liberalisation and global financial instability) should be dispelled.

The particular vulnerability of the Korean economy to external shocks is apparent from a comparison with the other first-wave NICs of the region. In spite of having more liberalised financial sectors and direct exposure, the epicentre of the 1997 crisis, the Southeast Asian economies, Taiwan, Hong Kong and Singapore did not suffer currency and stock market collapses as severe as Korea's. Hong Kong and Taiwan made use of their superior foreign reserves to maintain the value of their currencies. Korean trade surpluses, on the other hand, lasted for only a brief period: 1986–9. High growth rates had to be maintained by debt-financed investment. Because of her high external indebtedness, Korea was more vulnerable to lapses in international financial confidence. While a 6 per cent growth rate was highly satisfactory for her nearest competitor, Taiwan, this rate only barely sufficed for Korea. The Korean economy needed to achieve comparatively higher growth rates in order to service the external debts generated by its persistent trade deficits. Persistent trade deficits also showed up the basic weaknesses of industrial competitiveness: the heavy imported content of Korean exports (mainly from Japan) and the growing domestic demand for imported consumer goods. These weaknesses undermine the claims for soundness of Korean industrial structure on the basis of Korean debt–equity ratios being comparable to Japanese levels of the mid-1970s (see e.g. Chang *et al.* 1998: 742).

Vulnerability to external shocks of the 1997 type was inherent in the design of the developmental state itself. This goes back to four observations made in previous chapters. First, over-capacity in the basic industries (e.g. cars, electronics, steel, ships, petrochemicals, machinery) was a by-product of the HCI drive of the 1970s. Rejecting the Taiwanese path of the public ownership of heavy industry, the Korean state achieved its aim by stimulating competition between selected conglomerates. Effective at meeting the ambitious targets for expansion and at avoiding the inefficiencies typical of third world nationalised industries, such an industrial policy also started a trend towards excessive diversification and capacity duplication among fierce *chaebol* rivals. The bids to enter new industries by the Samsung (steel and cars) and Hyundai (steel) groups during the 1990s were merely the latest episodes in this long-running saga.

Second, the erosion of the state's disciplinary powers had preceded the Kim Young-Sam government's diluting of industrial policy. Successive efforts by governments both authoritarian and democratic had since 1980 proven ineffective at enforcing a more rational division of labour between the *chaebol*. Rooted in an earlier version of Japanese capitalism, Korean industrial policy in the 1980s was unable to make the transition from all-out expansion to administrative guidance on the Japanese pattern of the 1960s. This could be seen in the rush into semi-conductors in the 1980s by *chaebol* with no previous experience such as Hyundai and Daewoo. The abandonment of industrial policy in favour of market discipline by the Kim government might have made things worse by relaxing constraints. Both approaches, however, were hampered by the reluctance of the state to reduce excessive capacity by shutting down inefficient plants or allowing failing *chaebol* to go bankrupt. In the absence of these sanctions, *chaebol's* loss of managerial control over a failing subsidiary simply meant transferring the burden to the absorbing group (which, in turn, would have to be financially compensated in some way). This could be explained by the priority of maintaining growth and avoiding the spread of bankruptcies within the financially fragile *chaebol*, and by the connections between the *chaebol* and public officials. The leading *chaebol*, at least, had become 'too big to fail'. There is certainly something to Krugman's claims about 'moral hazard' (Krugman 1998a).

Third, it has been argued that the success of the *chaebol* as dynamic international companies had enhanced their influence over the state to the extent of distorting policy-making in the manufacturing sector. By contrast, past corruption (the misuse of public powers and resources for private benefit) was confined to non-strategic domains, and while the state was pro-*chaebol* it was not beholden to particular *chaebol* (Chang *et al.* 1998: 741). While it is undeniable that democratisation and the gaining of international reputations had allowed the *chaebol* to influence economic policy decisions in domains from which they might have previously been excluded, the existence of particularistic connections between senior government officials and business pre-dates the Kim Young-Sam era and goes back to the founding of the developmental state. For example, the Hyundai and Daewoo groups would not have risen so meteorically as 'national champions' in the 1960s and 1970s without the special favour of President Park (e.g. the father of the Daewoo chairman having been Park's teacher). More recently, the growth of the Sunkyong group was not unconnected to the marriage between the group chairman's daughter and President Roh's son. Moreover, even in the heyday of industrial policy, instances of the state's use of its disciplinary powers could be traced to non-economic motives. *Chaebol* were kept going for their political financing of the ruling party as well as their developmental prowess. Insufficient payments to President Chun's DJP allegedly led to the dissolution of the Kukje group in 1985. Political donation was also an issue in the troubles between the Hyundai group and the Roh and Kim Young-Sam governments.

Fourth, even if it is accepted that the exchange of government incentives for business performance under Korea Inc. represented a reciprocal relationship that was qualitatively distinct from cronyism, it can be argued that the transition to cronyistic government–business relations had been taking place well before the arrival of the Kim Young-Sam government. In her study of HCI, Amsden emphasised the importance of the government-engineered 'switch in industrial leadership' in transferring responsibility for the newly prioritised sectors towards select companies (Amsden 1989: 245–7). The wide portfolio of *chaebol* activities that enabled any underperforming *chaebol* subsidiary to be transferred to a rival *chaebol* was also said to be a strength of the system (Chang 1994: 123). The business concentration effected by the HCI drive, however, meant that industrial leadership would become fixed in the hands of the leading *chaebol*. The state's inability to repeat such root-and-branch industrial transformation heralded the decline of its disciplinary powers, and the corresponding rise of business influence. In effect, the reciprocity that lay at the heart of successful performance was starting to erode from the late-1970s. In any case, state discipline over the private sector was predicated on there being clear and effective criteria by which private sector performance could be guided. The excessive investments in HCI during the 1970s showed how misleading such criteria could be. Partial liberalisation measures (all of which served to enhance the economic dominance of the *chaebol*) introduced since 1980 were based on a recognition of the limits of the old 1970s' approach. To recapitulate, cronyism in Korea was not the consequence of the dismantling of industrial policy: it was inherent in the type of monopoly capitalism fostered by such a policy.

IMF-supervised capitalist restructuring

Economic policy veered sharply in the neo-liberal direction as a result of the 1997 crisis. IMF support for Korea was conditional on the implementation of macroeconomic stabilisation measures and the completion of liberalisation (just as development commentators were pronouncing the 'twilight' of conditionality (e.g. Nelson 1996)). The crisis and IMF conditionalities altered the parameters of the economic debate. They impressed upon all sections of Korean society the power of global economic forces, the structural weaknesses of the Korean economy and the need for far-reaching economic reform. In the past, it was assumed that the economy could make the transition from neo-mercantilism gradually and without the social pain associated with liberalisation programmes elsewhere, but the predicament unleashed by the crisis undermined those assumptions. The new reality could be seen from the economic reform programme and its accompanying social pact.

The reform strategy

From 1993 the Kim Young-Sam government had accelerated the pace of economic liberalisation under the slogan of 'globalisation' (Chapter 5). In its concern with maintaining growth and social cohesiveness, the globalisation project actually had greater affinity with the gradual pattern of liberalising reform established in 1981 than with radical neo-liberal-inspired reform strategies attempted elsewhere. The IMF-supervised (in conjunction with the World Bank[3]) reform programme represented a fundamental break with Korea's previous liberalisation efforts in key respects. First, the completion of liberalisation was set within a short time frame that was to be externally determined and supervised. Second, liber-alisation was now reinforced by conditionality as IMF financial support was made contingent on reform. In the previous period of multilateral support (1981–5), by contrast, the IMF did not set such extensive condi-tionalities. Third, the IMF programme was expected to deepen the economic and social pain, a position that reversed the priorities of growth and social stability that had guided previous reforms.

Apart from binding the Korean government to measures of macroeco-nomic stabilisation (of the government budget, prices, currency), the IMF agreement established a schedule for the rapid completion of structural reforms in the key areas of finance, trade, corporate governance and employment (see Figure 6.1). The conditionalities of the IMF rescue package were designed to hasten Korea's transition to liberalisation and business transparency, the lack of which were diagnosed as major causes of the crisis. In accepting the IMF programme, Korea took a crucial step towards adopting core components of the neo-liberal agenda – industrial restructuring, trade and financial liberalisation, labour market reform, reform of corporate governance in favour of shareholder rights (e.g. MOFE 3 December 1997; 18 February 1998).

The mounting pressures of *chaebol* and the bank failure were already forcing the government to take more decisive action in the restructuring of the financial and industrial sectors before the November 1997 crisis. These measures prefigured policies that would be adopted under the IMF-inspired restructuring programme. On 25 August 1997, a financial package was announced to provide assistance to the financial institutions exposed by their lending to *chaebol*. The package consisted of the government purchase of non-performing loans and the issue of government bonds for bank equity. In return for the intervention of the government, the distressed financial institutions were required to make full disclosures of their accounts and to present credible programmes of rehabilitation, including reduction by 1,800 employees, the merger of branches and the sale of real estate (MOFE 8 September 1997).

After the IMF agreement was reached, it was announced that the govern-ment would issue 24 trillion won's worth of bonds (for the management of which the Korea Asset Management Corporation was created) for the purchase of non-performing loans and for the protection of depositors. Incentives were to be given to encourage healthy financial institutions to absorb weaker ones. Foreigners' share of domestic bank share was to be expanded beyond 4 per cent while the two city-banks with unsound financial structures (Seoul Bank and Korea First) were to be sold off to foreigners after the normalisation of their operations (MOFE 16 December 1997). To provide greater transparency, the supervision of the liberalised financial sector was to be enhanced with the formation of a Financial Supervisory Committee (established in April 1998). In effect, the government was intervening to maintain the solvency of the financial institutions in the interests of the industrial firms and the savers dependent on them. At the same time it was promoting consolidation, reorganisation of business operations and exposure to direct foreign competition. The cost of the restructuring of the troubled financial sector was estimated to be 67 trillion won over five years, or 15 per cent of GDP (Shin and Hahm 1998: 59). The IMF programme for financial sector reform was consistent with the thinking on the issue already prevalent (e.g. as recommended by the Presidential Committee for Financial Reform appointed in January 1997) but accelerated under conditions far less favourable than originally anticipated (e.g. Hahm 1998).

What of the restructuring policies for the *chaebol*-dominated industrial sector? The loss of international confidence was due in no small measure to the spate of *chaebol* insolvencies. The restructuring of the troubled conglomerates began with the tentative rescue plan for Kia, implemented in the autumn of 1997. In a misguided attempt to demonstrate its adherence to market principles, the government initially left the matter to Kia and its bank creditors. By failing to step in early, the government ruptured the implicit official guarantee on which external lending was based and further destabilised international confidence. But when, by October, no viable private sector solution was forthcoming, the government was forced to step in to maintain the operations of the country's eighth-largest conglomerate and second-largest car producer. Through the Korea Development Bank, the company's loans were converted into equity. To rationalise the group's operations, it was decided that the subsidaries would be put up for international auction (the successful Kia Motors division was eventually purchased by Hyundai) (MOFE October 1997).

The officially enforced restructuring of Kia marked the beginning of a more aggressive official policy of conglomerate restructuring. On 13 January 1998, a five-point accord was reached between president-elect Kim Dae-Jung and the heads of the top five *chaebol*. Under the agreement, the *chaebol* pledged their commitment to five principles of corporate restructuring: business restructuring focusing on core competence (entailing the reduction of the total of top-five affiliates from 265 to 130); elimination of cross-guarantees (by March 2000); substantial improvement of capital structure (to below 200 per cent by the end of 1999); enhancement of transparency of corporate management; and regular monitoring by government and creditor institutions (MOFE 12 February 1998). The government's commitment to restructuring was underlined by a number of legal revisions enacted on 24 February 1998. In the first round

Policy area	Objectives, policies and schedule for implementation
Overall programme	• Sustain the restoration of confidence and contribute to resolving the external financial crisis • Minimise disruptions to the real economy and support economic recovery in the latter half of 1998 • Macroeconomic projections for 1998: negative to one per cent GDP growth; average inflation rate of 1998 to be below double digits after acceleration in the first half of the year; current account to shift to US$8 billion surplus or possibly more
Macroeconomic stabilisation	*Monetary policy* • Lowering of interest rates envisaged only after the foreign exchange market has durably stabilised *Exchange rate policy* • Exchange rate policy will remain flexible: BOK operations will be limited to smoothing operations • Foreign exchange window of the BOK, opened during the crisis, will be closed as soon as the short-term debt restructuring has been finalised and usable reserves have reached a comfortable level *Reserve management policy* • Usable reserves targeted to increase to US$30 billion by end of June 1998 • Limit on use of foreign exchange window of BOK to repayment of short-term debt. In exceptional circumstances, the BOK would provide support for other purposes such as reductions in foreign exchange deposits, but will shorten the repayment period to 2 weeks from a maximum of 1 month • BOK will reach agreement by 30 June 1998 with domestic financial institutions on repayment schedule for emergency support extended since 1 November 1997 *External debt* • Continue to develop external debt reporting system to enhance debt management and monitoring • Continue to publish detailed data on the outstanding stock and maturity structure of debt on a monthly basis, within 30 days from the end of the previous month *Fiscal policy* • Cuts in public expenditure to yield 1.2 per cent of GDP except budgets related to the social safety net (including unemployment insurance) and SMEs
Small and medium-sized enterprises	• Raised ceiling for Credit Guarantee Fund from W (won) 21 trillion to W57 trillion • BOK rediscount facility for SMEs raised by W1 trillion
Financial restructuring	*Merchant banks* • All banks submit preliminary rehabilitation plans (30 December 1997) • Bridge Merchant Bank established to pay out depositors of suspended banks and to take over, manage, collect or liquidate their assets (30 December 1997) • Closure of 10 suspended banks (30 January 1998) • Remaining banks to submit rehabilitation plans. Those failing their second evaluation to have their licences immediately suspended and revoked by 30 April 1998 • Approved banks to achieve capital adequacy ratio of 8 per cent by 30 June 1998 *Commercial banks* • Government recapitalisation of Korea First and Seoul banks with 94 per cent stake (31 January 1998). Appointment of outside experts to assist Privatisation Committee for KFB and SB (31 March 1998). To obtain bids by 15 November 1998 • Establish Special Task Force at MOFE with adequate powers to coordinate and monitor bank restructuring and provision of public funds (7 March 1998). Transfer of Special Task Force powers to special unit of Financial Supervisory Board (30 April 1998) • Further loan purchases by Korea Asset Management Company to be subject to recapitalisation plans as approved by supervisory unit or as part of liquidation process (11 February 1998) *Information* BOK/MOFE will record all public support for financial sector restructuring on a transparent basis
Capital account liberalisation	*Money market* • Full liberalisation of money market instruments issued by non-financial institutions (16 February 1998) • Full liberalisation of money market instruments issued by financial institutions (31 December 1998) • Deepen treasury bill market by issuing treasury bills of more than W1 trillion (30 April 1998) *Corporate borrowing* • Lift restrictions on borrowing up to US$2 million for venture companies (15 February 1998) • Review the removal of restrictions on corporate borrowing of 1–3 year maturities for large firms and SMEs (15 May 1998) • Comprehensive review and announcement of all remaining restrictions on corporate borrowing (31 December 1998)

Figure 6.1 Highlights of the 1998 IMF programme

Sources: MOFE press releases at www.mofe.go.kr

Policy area	Objectives, policies and schedule for implementation
	Financial sector • Issue of Presidential Decree to provide transparent guidelines governing foreign investment in domestic financial institutions (28 February 1998) • Allow foreign banks and brokerage houses to establish subsidiaries (31 March 1998) *Foreign borrowing* • Place prudential controls on short-term external borrowing of financial institutions (31 March 1998) *Equity market* • Eliminate aggregate ceiling on foreign investment in Korean equities (31 December 1998)
Trade liberalisation	*Trade-related subsidies* • Elimination of four trade subsidies (January–March 1998) *Import liberalisation* • Phase out Import Diversification Programme covering 113 items (committed to WTO). Liberalise 97 items (December 1997–December 1998) and remaining items by June 1999 • Reduce number of items subject to tariffs from 62 to 38 (1 January 1998) • Review existing import certification procedures and present a plan to streamline them and bring them in line with international practice (15 August 1998) • Review all existing subsidy programmes and their economic rationale. Present proposal for rationalising existing subsidy programmes (15 November 1998) *Financial services* • Binding of Korea's OECD commitments on financial services liberalisation in WTO (announced in WTO Financial Services Committee 30 January 1998)
Labour market reform and social safety net	*Labour market flexibility* • In the context of the Tripartite Agreement, amend legislation to clarify the circumstances and procedures for lay-offs • Relax restrictive legal provisions relating to private job placement and manpower leasing services *Social safety net* • Budget allocation for the employment insurance fund including for more training support and employment stabilisation, will be trebled from W0.7 trillion to W2 trillion • Social welfare assistance, including income support to persons without own incomes, to be protected and increased by at least 13 per cent compared to 1997 • Additional social expenditures will be provided in the context of the Tripartite Agreement *Unemployment benefits scheme* • Expanded coverage of benefits to firms with 10+ workers (from previous requirement of 30+ workers) from 1 January 1998; and to firms with 5+ workers from 1 July 1998 • Increase in the minimum benefit level to 70 per cent of the minimum wage (from 50 per cent) from 1 March 1998 • Increase in the minimum duration of benefits to 2 months (from 1 month) from 1 March 1998 • Temporarily extend eligibility to benefit by reducing the minimum period of contribution from 1 year to 6 months (1 April 1998 to 30 June 1999)
Corporate governance and restructuring	*Transparency* • Require financial statements of listed companies to be prepared and audited in accordance with international standards • Require publication of combined financial statements for associated companies • Further reduce the use of mutual guarantees by affiliates/subsidiaries • Introduction of mandatory auditor selection committees for listed companies and large conglomerates. The committee should be composed of internal auditors, shareholders, and if applicable, outside directors and the representatives of creditors *Accountability to shareholders* • Require listed companies to have at least one outside director • Remove restrictions on voting rights of institutional investors in listed companies (investment trust companies and trust accounts of banks) • Strengthen minority shareholders' rights by lowering substantially the thresholds on exercising these rights (e.g. the right to file a representative suit and the right to make a proposal) • Review the possibility of allowing for class action suits against corporate executive and auditors *Corporate restructuring* • Ensure that all corporate restructuring is voluntary and market oriented • Liberalisation of the domestic mergers and acquisitions by removing the mandatory tender offer requirement • Permit take-overs of non-strategic Korean corporations by foreign investors without government approval • Raise the ceiling on the amount of stock foreigners can acquire in non-strategic companies without approval by the company's board of directors to one-third from one-tenth *Bankruptcy procedures* • Amend bankruptcy law to facilitate more rapid resolution of bankruptcy proceedings

Figure 6.1 (continued)

of reform, the closure of fifty-five *chaebol* affiliates (including twenty belonging to the top five) was announced in June 1998 (Dong-Chul Park 1998: 12–13). A number of second- and third-tier *chaebol* (dubbed the '6 to 64' group according to their ranking) were reported to have made vigorous attempts to restructure (the most high profile being the Doosan group, which reportedly reduced its number of industries to four and its debt–equity ratio to a healthy – by Korean standards – 200 per cent). The core industries of the top five *chaebol* (Hyundai, Daewoo, Samsung, LG and Sunkyong), however, were not included in this first wave.

In order to rationalise the leading industries (petrochemicals, aircraft, railroad vehicles, power-generating equipment, ships' engines, semiconductors, electronics and automobiles) of the top five *chaebol*, the Kim Dae-Jung government encouraged the conclusion of so-called 'swap deals' or 'big deals'. Under such arrangements, leading *chaebol* would negotiate the transfer of whole industries to more efficient rivals. In requiring *chaebol* to concentrate on their core industries, it was similar to past consolidation policies. In contrast to previous efforts, however, the leading *chaebol* were now financially hard-pressed. Their international credit ratings were down and the government's grip on the financial institutions was much tighter. Even so, rationalisation of these sectors was a slow process, pointing to the reluctance of leading *chaebol* to vacate core industries (and the belief that they could weather the crisis in much the same way as they had done previously).

To inject momentum into the swap deals, the government had to assume an active role. In spite of repeated declarations of intent from the *chaebol*, there were no concrete steps taken in the swap deals until 7 December 1998, when it was announced that the Samsung group would vacate the car industry (it had actually not yet exported a car) in favour of the more experienced Daewoo group. In return, Daewoo's consumer electronics business would be transferred to Samsung. Later that month (after an assessment by US consulting firm Arther D. Little), it was decided that LG would transfer its semi-conductor facilities to Hyundai (a surprising deal, given LG's status as a pioneer of Korean electronics). With these swaps agreed in principle, the new government's pressure seemed to be paying off.

The context of acute recession and strict external conditionality meant that the financial and industrial restructurings in the wake of the 1997 crisis would be marked by features distinct from previous efforts. First, effecting structural reform took precedence over the traditional concerns about employment and growth. Second, that the economy was already in freefall when the IMF moved in was a condition favourable to restructuring, since there was no longer any growth left to be endangered. In effect, the *chaebol* could no longer thwart reform with their traditional threat of slowing down the economy. Third, the presence of international supervision made it more difficult for troubled financial institutions and *chaebol* to resist long-proposed (but never actualised) reforms including corporate transparency, external auditing of accounts, merger (swaps), liquidation of non-productive assets and exit from peripheral activities (and their transfer to small and medium-sized firms or to the foreign sector). Fourth, whereas foreign capital was previously integrated in Korea on local terms, it was now destined for a much freer role within the IMF-supervised reform (e.g. equity holdings, direct investments and even some hostile acquisitions). Korea was now under greater external pressure to make a rapid transition to the internationalised development model than at any point since 1980.

Social pact for transition

The industrial strife that followed the passage of the new labour law in December 1996 (the revised version was passed in March 1997) was another short-term factor in the deterioration of the economy in the run up to the 1997 crisis. But the new labour law itself was an attempt to resolve the deeper problem of labour inefficiency. The cost of labour and its inflexible working practices was a source of the Korean economy's 'high cost, low efficiency' structure. Even those accounts that attributed the prime responsibility for the 1997 crisis to global financial instability recognised the deteriorating competitiveness of Korean industry in the 1990s (see e.g. Wade 1998). The inability of the democratic governments to overcome the authoritarian legacy of confrontational labour relations would exact a heavy price on competitiveness. Chapter 5 explained why, despite the shifts away from the anti-labour policies of the past (towards redistribution from 1987 and political reform and consensus building from 1993), democratic governments were unable to secure labour consent for the much-needed employment reform. Two main stumbling blocks were identified: the irreconcilability of the alternative models of labour relations favoured by business and labour; and labour's mistrust of the state. One consequence of such polarisation was that Japanese-style corporatism (referred to as 'soft authoritarian societal corporatism' by Johnson) favoured by foreign and domestic experts (Johnson 1994: 64, 82; see also K. Lee and C.H. Lee 1992: 20–2) was bypassed.

The 1997 crisis appears to have accelerated the forging of the new social consensus that had proven elusive for most of the Kim Young-Sam government's duration. On 15 January 1998, the Tripartite Commission for Fair Burden-Sharing was inaugurated in response to the crisis. Its signatories included representatives from government, labour, business and the political parties supporting president-elect Kim Dae-Jung. On 20 January, the Commission released a joint-statement of cooperation, the Tripartite Agreement for Fair Burden Sharing (TAFBS) (MOFE 20 January 1998). The labour unions reluctantly accepted the necessity of lay-offs and greater employment flexibility. In return, the business sector agreed to put its own financial house in order and to implement lay-offs only in the last resort and after the appropriate consultation with the unions. The TAFBS built upon the revised labour law of March 1997. That legislation had in principle reformed the labour market in the direction of greater flexibility, but it contained loopholes and was untested. For example, while making dismissal for 'managerial reasons' easier, the 1997 law also provided for a two-year grace period of employment adjustment. Under TAFBS, the two-year grace period was abolished and replaced with a more flexible system of sixty days' notice to the affected employees. The role of the government was to ensure that neither side would take advantage of the crisis. To cushion workers' economic hardship, the government agreed to extend the social safety-net and to provide schemes for the relaunching of those displaced by restructuring. The share of government expenditure devoted to social development projected for 1999 was an all-time peak (see Table 4.2). The unions also got concessions extending their organisation in the government sector and their rights of political participation.

While not removing the underlying differences, the financial crisis restored some sense of shared interest between state, organised labour and business, the result of which was TAFBS. Essentially TAFBS was a social pact whereby organised labour accepted redundancies in exchange for state social counter-measures and structural reform of big business, including its internal governance. If the labour unions and big business could not agree on an arrangement for the sharing of the benefits of growth, circumstances appeared to be forcing them into an uneasy understanding on the principle of burden sharing for recovery (MOFE 20 January 1998). Also important was the role of president-elect Kim Dae-Jung (although he had first opposed the IMF conditionalities in the run up to the election). Closely associated with the cause of fairer distribution throughout his political career, he lent populist credibility to the agreement.

The inclusion of the structural reform of the *chaebol* was a crucial step in facilitating TAFBS. The labour unions had previously resisted labour market reforms, pointing instead to corruption, land acquisition and other business malpractices as the root causes of the Korean economy's declining competitiveness. On the other hand, democratic governments (like their authoritarian predecessors) were wary of the risks of attempting to carry out deep structural reforms of the conglomerates (Chapter 5). Deep structural reforms threatened to jeopardise economic growth (at least in the short term), and presiding governments risked losing public sympathy, not to mention financial support. But the financial crisis put reform back on the agenda. Not only was the reform of business practices a condition of the IMF rescue package, but the economic recession triggered by the financial crisis altered the political parameters of reform. It was clear that the erosion of foreign confidence that led to the financial crisis could in no small part be traced to *chaebol* insolvency amid the accumulation of massive short-term external debt. Public opinion held the government and the *chaebol* responsible for the crisis and expected reform of business practices. TAFBS, therefore, stipulated deep structural reform of the *chaebol* to prevent the recurrence of similar failures. In particular, practices traditionally associated with the *chaebol* (e.g. cross-guarantees, expansion on low equity, concentration of decision-making powers, accumulation of real estate) were targeted for reform under the terms of the new social consensus (MOFE 20 January 1998).[4]

The involvement of the IMF also helped the Korean government establish the January 1998 social accord for recovery. First, dependence on IMF support gave the government leverage in persuading both business and organised labour to abandon their rigid negotiating positions of the past. Second, the association between economic recovery and sacrifice (e.g. loss of jobs, falling wages, enforced transfer of subsidiaries to rivals, reduced executive autonomy) was strongly impressed upon both labour and business by the IMF. Third, by supporting the reform of corporate governance and by posing as a convenient scapegoat for the painful social adjustment, the IMF helped to deflect popular wrath away from the incoming Kim Dae-Jung government.

A turning-point?

A constant theme running through the recent history of Korean economic reform is the resilience of the practices and interests of the developmental state. The record of success ensured that the transition away from Korea Inc. would follow a gradualist course (within which two changes of rhythm occurred, in 1987 and 1993). The decision to initiate liberalising reform occurred in the context of deep economic crisis in 1979–80. Given the prevalence of similar conditions of deep economic and social distress, it is logical to ask whether the 1997 crisis marked a crucial turning-point akin to the 1979–80 watershed. How was President Kim Dae-Jung's 'DJ-nomics' transforming Korea's development trajectory?

Internationalised model of development

As the condition of IMF support, the Korean government was forced to accept a programme of macroeconomic stabilisation and sweeping liberalisation. Reminiscent of other debt-embattled third world states, the Korean government accepted the IMF programme without reservation. Although the IMF programme was consistent with the liberalising sentiments expressed in Korean policy statements over the previous two (if not more) decades, the context of the 1997 IMF programme pointed to the most concerted push for liberalisation since 1981. In the previous phase of IMF conditionality (1981–5), external supervision did not extend into the microeconomic practices of Korea Inc. Once prices were stabilised and growth restored, the Koreans were permitted to effect structural reforms at their own gradual pace. By contrast, the IMF programme of 1997 insisted on the completion of liberalisation within a tight schedule. The more extensive conditionalities of 1997 showed how changing external perceptions narrowed the Korean side's freedom of manoeuvre. In its infancy during the early-1980s, the neo-liberal analysis was widely accepted by 1997 (under the label of the 'Washington Consensus'). Korea's position within the foreign policy thinking of the US had also changed. With the ending of the Cold War, US political worries about the dangers of a protracted Korean recession were subordinated to economic concerns about debt repayment and open markets. In this sense, Korea's situation had become Latin Americanised.

Similar to the programmes imposed by the IMF elsewhere, the reform programme for Korea was based on an analysis that traced the crisis to the existence of distorted financial markets. From this perspective, distortion enabled borrowers to get funding for unsound projects by colluding with domestic creditors or by lowering foreign creditors' perceptions of risk (such as fostering the illusion of the semi-controlled system being state guaranteed). Ultimately, it was interpreted by the IMF as a problem of incomplete liberalisation:

> Although private sector expenditure and financing decisions led to the crisis, it was made worse by governance issues, notably government involvement in the private sector and lack of transparency in corporate and fiscal accounting and the provision of financial and economic data.
>
> (IMF 1999: sub-section 'Origins of the crisis')

It followed therefore, that liberalisation accompanied by the appropriate institutional reforms would eliminate the market distortions that lay at the root of the crisis. In demanding an overhaul of the system of corporate governance itself, the IMF programme went well beyond the partial liberalisation that had benefited the Korean conglomerates since the 1980s.

The neo-classical basis of the IMF programme provoked criticisms from influential commentators. These critics alleged that the IMF's prescription of painful and inappropriate medicine was based on a mis-diagnosis of the crisis. According to Sachs (1997), for example, in accelerating the liberalisation of their financial sectors in the run up to the crisis, the Asian countries were actually following IMF advice. Rather than financial liberalisation being incomplete, as in the view of the IMF, the critics countered that the crisis was the consequence of over-hasty liberalisation in such a highly volatile and sensitive sector. Heavily leveraged owing to their historical role of industrial finance, liberalised Korean banks became highly vulnerable to the herd-like behaviour of international capital. Drawn to the image of 'miracle Asia', such capital took flight at the first sign of downturn (Wade 1998: 696-7).

According to Krugman (1998b), the recovery of the real economy after Britain's 1992 devaluation, compared with capital flight (triggering recession and contagion) in the aftermath of the Mexican (1994) and Thai (July 1997) devaluations, pointed to investors' lack of confidence in the capacity of third world economies to absorb shocks. And yet the unsatisfactory halfway house of liberalisation with dollar-pegged currencies practised through much of Asia made such shocks more likely by attracting speculative flows. This analysis was consistent with the perspectives of both the IMF and its critics. It was reflected in Krugman's suggested policy alternatives: reintroduction of financial controls; or full liberalisation with floating exchange rates (see Krugman 1998b, especially sections 5–8).

Critics argued that the IMF's prescriptions for recovery show the basic misunderstanding of the causes of the crisis. By deepening the recession, the macroeconomic stabilisation instruments of high interest rates (e.g. the corporate bond rate reached a peak of 24 per cent in December 1997 against an annual inflation rate of 2.3 per cent) and reduced government expenditures (when the budget was in surplus for the four consecutive years 1993–6) were more likely to deter rather than attract the entry of foreign capital (e.g. Wade 1998: 700–1). Moreover, the targeting of the public sector for expenditure cuts was cited as clear evidence of the IMF's misinterpretation of the Korean crisis in Latin American terms (i.e. as a balance of payments crisis caused by excessive deficit spending) (see e.g. Kregel 1998: 45–6; Palma 1998: 799–802). Warning that deflationary policies would aggravate the global crisis of confidence, such critics drew ominous parallels with the Great Depression (Wade 1998: 700).

What of the longer term effects of the IMF requirement for structural reform? Was it likely to be effective for recovery and other developmental goals? For the supporters of structural reform, the IMF programme of liberalisation would facilitate recovery by easing the entry of investment capital, competition and technology transfer. The deep recession provided a rare opportunity to enforce streamlining and governance reform of the *chaebol*, attempts at which had always been thwarted by the dangers of provoking growth slowdown. Moreover, in their weakened state, and with strengthened supervision, the *chaebol* would not be able to extend their monopoly powers (e.g. by acquiring the liberalised financial institutions) as they had done in previous partial liberalisation drives. It has been argued that Korean policy-makers have successfully taken advantage of the crisis conditions to decisively modernise (by insisting upon measures such as corporate restructuring that went beyond the recommendations of the IMF) and create a 'new' market-conforming development model consistent with neo-liberal conditions (see e.g. Mathews 1998).

Those unconvinced of the promises of neo-classical-inspired recovery programmes voiced serious doubts about the 'big bang' approach that was being proposed by the IMF. Although the sweeping liberalisation of the economy called for under the IMF programme was consistent with the direction of Korean economic policy since the early-1980s, critics worried about the rapid implementation of reform under difficult circumstances. Some have argued that the recession could have been avoided altogether. Proponents of this view point out that the deterioration of Korea's liquidity crisis (caused by the mismatch between short-term borrowing and long-term investment) into a currency crisis and full-blown recession could have been avoided by more decisive IMF assistance to reassure creditors, and that such a move would have allowed the needed structural reforms to proceed in a more orderly fashion (Nam 1998: section entitled 'An appraisal'). In light of the resistance to structural reform (see below), it is questionable that there would have been much impetus for reform had the crisis been contained in its infancy.

Other criticisms predicted that the IMF medicine would bring about an extended recession and impair the long-term capacity for recovery. First, critics argued that the deflationary stabilisation policies were unlikely to attract foreign capital to Korea. They contrasted this with the expansionary response to the US savings and loans crisis of the 1980s (e.g. Akyüz 1998: 35–6). This point could be answered by pointing to the extensive conditional re-capitalisation of the financial institutions through the establishment of the Korea Asset Management Corporation (with a proposed fund of 24 trillion won) in late-1997. This arrangement led to the closure of five non-viable banks (acquired by other banks) and the conditional approval of seven others in June 1998 (H.-S. Kim and C.J. Kim 1998).

Second, the further financial liberalisation that was being proposed was as likely to promote destabilising short-term capital flows as to introduce the much-needed long-term investment. The experience of financial liberalisation of the advanced economies themselves (e.g. the US savings and loans debacle) pointed to the difficulties of developing effective regulatory safeguards. Here, critics cited the lessons of Chile, the shining example of neo-liberal success. Having suffered a financial sector boom-and-bust during 1979–81 (Diaz-Alejandro 1985), the Chilean authorities decided that speculative financial flows were sufficiently destabilising to warrant the retention of capital controls (despite extensive deregulation elsewhere) (Akyüz 1998: 36). Through such safeguards, speculative flows would be curtailed and long-term investment encouraged. The problem of persistently high rates of unemployment despite impressive growth rates was another negative lesson from Chile (Foxley 1987; Mizala 1997: 99–101).

A third criticism was that the IMF opened the way to the foreign take over of Korean industry, the prospect of which would nullify decades of economic policy dedicated to the aim of autocentric development (e.g. investment restrictions, preference for borrowing over direct investment, gradual liberalisation). Some commentators and politicians (e.g. Malaysia's Prime Minister Mahathir Mohamed) even alleged that the 1997 crisis was part of a grand US scheme aimed at subverting Asia's economic sovereignty. Foreign auditors' probing of Korean corporate accounts and foreign purchases of Korean companies at knock-down prices were cited as instances of such economic colonisation. The IMF agreement was labelled the 'trojan horse' of international liberalism (Bullard *et al.* 1998: 130). Another critic labelled Kim Dae-Jung 'the IMF's man in Seoul' (Cumings 1998: 60). Concerning the IMF programme's effect on recovery, only time will tell. The economic-sovereignty-type critiques of the IMF, however, lack credibility. Previous chapters have shown that behind the nationalism of Korean ownership was dependence on Japanese suppliers (this paradox was a consequence of what I called 'hyper-developmentalism'). The infusion of Japanese methods and technology was instrumental to the Korean take-off being so rapid. If the claim of 'autocentric development' was weak for Korean development, it was even less tenable for the other troubled Asian economies. It is ironic that such commentators should have considered the Korean developmental state (and its creation, the *chaebol*) the last line of defence against rampaging global liberalism when they had spent decades criticising the Korean phenomenon as a manifestation of US–Japanese sponsored dependent development.

Transformation of the chaebol *sector*

In applying resolution plans that linked assistance to tough conditionalities, the government was preparing the domestic industrial and financial sectors for foreign competition by enforcing consolidation, specialisation and sound financial structure. The fate of the Seoul and Korea First Banks showed that, in some cases, the government was now prepared to contemplate the previously unthinkable action of enforced rationalisation followed by sale to foreigners. The liquidation of Kukje (1985) and half-a-dozen other *chaebol* in 1997 showed that Korean governments have long been prepared to sacrifice lesser conglomerates for efficiency and other motives. In urging the leading *chaebol* to specialise in three to six of their best industries, the 1997 programme had echoes of previous failed restructuring efforts. On previous occasions, the imperative of renewing growth prevented the reforms from being vigorously implemented. The key to successful restructuring lay in the government's readiness to enforce tough measures against the dominant super-*chaebol*. Without the economically and socially painful restructuring of these entities, there could be no successful transition from the unstable *chaebol*-centred growth model.

Traditionally, the super-*chaebol* themselves represented the major obstacle to industrial restructuring in Korea. Previous chapters discussed the difficulties of industrial rationalisation programmes since 1980. While resisting the genuine rationalisation that entailed divestiture of pet projects, the *chaebol* campaigned for a type of liberalisation that would facilitate their ambitious programmes of expansion. There were grounds for expecting the restructuring and consolidation measures arising in response to the 1997 crisis to be more effective than previous attempts. In its ambitious plans for the restructuring of the industrial and financial sectors and the overhaul of corporate governance, the IMF programme signalled the most concerted economic policy change since the 1981 decision to liberalise. There were grounds for expecting the reforms to be pursued more vigorously than in the past.

To begin with, the seriousness of the 1997 crisis highlighted the urgency for reform and the inadequacy of past efforts. In contrast to post-1981 reform initiatives, the 1997 crisis seemed to bring about a more generally accepted view of the limits of the unreformed *chaebol* model (e.g. financial insolvency of the import-intensive *chaebol*, their vulnerability to shifts in Japanese economic trends such as the yen value and semi-conductor output[5]). It was becoming clear that for structural reasons, the economy could not grow its way out of crisis as it had done in the past. For example, the import intensity of the *chaebol* was such that any sustained export recovery was likely to fuel another resurgence of the trade deficits with Japan, one of the triggers behind the short-term debt explosion. Recovery from the 1997–8 crisis was also predicted to be slower than in the past.

The unlikelihood of any swift upturn in growth recovery meant that the political position of the *chaebol* was weaker than at any time since the early-1980s. Facing insolvency, with the economy already in the doldrums and the public angry at their mismanagement, the *chaebol* had less leeway to resist industrial rationalisation measures. Crisis conditions favoured the imposition of tighter discipline over the *chaebol*. The requirement for full corporate disclosure verified by international auditors was designed to prevent unsound expansions on the basis of collusive connections with bankers and politicians (as exemplified by the Hanbo scandal of 1997) that were responsible for corporate insolvencies. To push the top five *chaebol* towards agreeing swap deals, the government threatened to discontinue credit to recalcitrant groups. The potential effectiveness of this instrument was enhanced by the low credit rating of the *chaebol* after the 1997 crash. Under the swap deal strategy, leading *chaebol* came under pressure to vacate industries they had previously considered vital to their prospects and prestige (e.g. LG's agreed transfer of its semi-conductor industry to Hyundai, Samsung's transfer of car production to Daewoo in exchange for electronics). The deals were motivated by incentives as well. In transferring key industries to rivals, leading *chaebol* also stood to reinforce their competitiveness in those industries in which they were required to specialise. Absorbing groups would also get some debt write-off for their new acquisitions. Rationalisation also presented opportunities for discarding or relocating failing industries, and for introducing the flexible working practices the *chaebol* had long lobbied for.

Problems of restructuring

Yet despite being in an unprecedentedly weak position, the *chaebol* could still influence the restructuring process in significant ways. To assess the extent of transformation in the *chaebol* sector since the 1997 crisis, it is necessary to look beyond the successfully concluded swaps that have caught the headlines since late-1998. Also it is important to examine the conditions in which such swaps have taken place and their effect in aiding the recovery of both *chaebol and* non-*chaebol* sectors. The restructuring programme was plagued by the difficulty of securing swaps between leading *chaebol*. If the *chaebol* were resistant to the idea of vacating key industries, giving them over to rival *chaebol* was doubly anathema. This was shown up in the difficulties surrounding the swap deals. For example, in the electronics deal involving LG and Hyundai, LG Semicon workers (backed by their employer) demanded employment guarantees for five to seven years after the merger, a condition not surprisingly considered by Hyundai as excessive (*Korea Herald* 1 February 1999). Ostensibly interested in protecting its employees, LG's stance on relinquishing its electronics industry was undoubtedly designed to create difficulties of absorption for its rival Hyundai. The Daewoo–Samsung cars-for-electronics deal got bogged down over the valuation of assets and the apportioning of debts. In the end, the deal failed to materialise.

That the ambition and traditional inter-group rivalry were alive and well, even in the middle of a deep crisis, could be seen from the *chaebol* plans for further expansion. Buoyed by the recovery of semi-conductor sales, Samsung had achieved a (by Korean standards, anyway) relatively healthy debt–equity ratio of 253 per cent at the end of 1998. The two most financially embattled groups in the top five, Daewoo and Hyundai, also announced ambitious plans for expansion. Having absorbed Ssangyong Motors, Daewoo announced it was expanding into the overcrowded Indian car market while Hyundai planned to invest in North Korea (Graham 1999: 37). Having already acquired Kia Motors and Hanwha Energy, Hyundai then showed an interest in the government-owned Korea Heavy Industry and Construction (HANJUNG) that was now set to be privatised, an interest that prompted Samsung to look in the same direction. The pursuit of expansion in the midst of officially decreed rationalisation was a pattern of behaviour familiar to the *chaebol*.

Apart from the leading *chaebol* groups' resistance to rationalisation, there were other grounds for doubt about the extent to which the state could effectively discipline the *chaebol*. First, genuine reform of the *chaebol*'s internal organisation was proving elusive in key areas such as the disclosure of accounts and ownership structure. Without access to accounts, external auditors could not establish an accurate picture of group finances, without which potential investors dared not risk their capital. It was pointed out that the *chaebol* could improve their nominal debt–equity ratios by such

means as asset revaluation and the transfer of cash between group affil-
iances (*Korea Herald* 14 July 1999). This meant that the impressive
improvement in debt–equity ratios of the top five (from 472.9 per cent in
late-1997 to 335 per cent in late-1998) had to be qualified (ibid.: 8 April
1999). Foreign economic commentators questioned the effectiveness of the
swap deals, claiming that they allowed the top *chaebol* to keep their best
assets (and even gain new ones from lesser groups with the use of public
subsidies). They reiterated that without the liquidation and closure of
unprofitable enterprises, the *chaebol* could not be disciplined effectively
(ibid.: 14 October 1998 and 27 April 1999).

Difficulties of effecting a transition in the ownership structure from
familial dominance were also revealed. For example, the Hyundai group
in 1998 announced its intention of splitting into five firms by 2002 but
without any diluting of the founding family's overall control (Graham,
1999: 37–8). The plan was criticised as a move to divide the group prop-
erties up among the sons of the group founder (*Korea Herald* 11 May 1999).
The Samsung boss's transfer of underpriced shares to his son was another
indicator of the determination of leading *chaebol* families to maintain familial
dominance of the group (ibid.: 5 July 1999). It was also disclosed in July
1999 that the government-appointed Committee on Improving Corporate
Governance had redefined its aim of 'drawing up the principles of good
corporate governance' to 'respecting progressive entrepreneurship', a shift
favouring the retention of the corporate status quo (ibid.: 15 July 1999).

Second, although the defeat of the ruling party in the 1997 general
election represented a break with the tradition of the incumbent party
retaining power, the change in substance was less clear. In the campaign,
Kim Dae-Jung pledged to reform the constitution from a presidential to
a parliamentary cabinet system, and to eliminate the last vestiges of authoritarian practices. Democratic accountability was hailed as the solution to
the problem of collusive government–business relations by Korean and
external commentators (e.g. Mathews 1998: 757–8). In spite of the change
at the political apex and the proposals for political reform, there were
reasons for remaining cautious about the capability of the new government to make significant inroads into the old problem of *chonkyong yuchak*.
Previous governments (notably Kim Young-Sam's, which introduced a
whole raft of transparency measures) had also begun with high hopes but
ended up compromised within a bureaucratic environment in which collusive and corrupt ties with big business were deeply entrenched. A number
of senior figures of the Kim Dae-Jung government reportedly already had
links with the *chaebol* (e.g. *Korea Herald* 5 March 1998). Just as they had
appeased previous political masters, the *chaebol* sought to deepen their links
with the new government by targeting investments in the hitherto neglected
Cholla-Do Province, President Kim's home base.

To investigate the issue of constitutional revision, the government
appointed a Second Nation-Building Commission in September 1998. But

the significance of constitutional reform to the elimination of collusive government–business relations was unclear. Seen by some as a transition away from South Korea's traditional politics of division (Na 1998: 178–9), the alliance betwen Kim Dae-Jung and Kim Jong-Pil seemed to be motivated by straightforward political motives. The change to the parliamentary cabinet system was the price of Kim Jong-Pil's minority support that ensured the election of Kim Dae-Jung. And even the most ardent supporters of political reforms acknowledged that a change in the party system towards ideologically clearer choices was also necessary for overcoming the problems of what in Chapter 5, I termed 'arrested democratisation' (e.g. Huh 1999: 93–4). A sign of the persistence of the regional politics was the claim by ex-president Kim Young-Sam that the failure of the Samsung car plant in his hometown of Pusan was caused by the political vindictiveness of the incumbent Kim Dae-Jung government (*Korea Herald* 8 July 1999). That speech signalled the ex-president's return to active politics.

Finally, the restructuring of the *chaebol* had to be evaluated by the extent it deconcentrated economic power. There were grounds for pessimism as the economic policy remained *chaebol*-centred. The pace of restructuring of the top five *chaebol* was markedly slower than that of the second- and third-tier groups. While the successful conclusion of the swap deals would undoubtedly strengthen the competitiveness of the *chaebol* by enforcing greater specialisation, it was not clear what niches were being opened up to SMEs. With the exception of a few high publicity sales to foreign buyers (e.g. Volvo's acquisition of Samsung Heavy Industries), key industries were transferred within rather than outside of the conglomerate sector. Instead of withdrawing from peripheral activities, there was evidence that the *chaebol* were diversifying into areas better suited to SMEs (*Korea Herald* 2 March 1998). Unlike the *chaebol*, SMEs did not have profitable affiliates (e.g. Hyundai's shipbuilding or Daewoo's insurance subsidiaries) to insulate them from the effects of recession induced by high interest rates. While *chaebol* restructuring proceeded slowly, SME bankruptcies were running at 3,000 per month between January and May 1998. This fell to 1,800 in June and about 1,000 in September (similar to the pre-crisis level) (World Bank 1999: section entitled 'Status of SMEs'). The credit crunch for the SMEs continued even after the lowering of interest rates in the autumn of 1998 as banks failed to reach the minimum loan requirements earmarked for SMEs (*Korea Herald* 4 November 1998).

The balance of the evidence suggests that the leading *chaebol* were seeking to avoid restructuring by prolonging the process until the time when the need for change became less desperate (i.e. the return to growth and the end of IMF supervision). The labour unions had longed suspected that the *chaebol* were not prepared to countenance genuine change in governance or expansion strategy. The recovery of GNP growth and the stock market in the first half of 1999 (the projected growth rate for 1999 was 5–6 per cent) was accompanied by another slowdown in the implementation of the swap deals and other reforms such as divestiture of affiliates (sometimes affiliates were simply merged to give the impression of reduction in group size). Speculative investments in the stock market (or 'financial tech'), a route to quick profits originating from the late-1980s, also accompanied the recovery (e.g. use of money raised from new stock issues for speculative purposes rather than debt reduction). Then the blip of the stock market in July 1999 followed by the Daewoo group's liquidity problems led to another round of fevered media speculation that the *chaebol* would finally embrace reform as the group declared that it would sharply cut its number of affiliates from 34 to 9 (*Korea Herald* 21 July 1999 and 22 July 1999).

Social pact and its stability

Experience from Latin American experiments in neo-liberal economics suggests that stability and efficiency are achieved only at the social costs of high unemployment and the widening of income disparities (with little evidence of 'trickle down'). This is evident not only from ongoing experiments (e.g. Argentina since 1989) but from the consolidated neo-liberal models with strong growth records (e.g. Chile). There was a danger that IMF conditionalities would drive Korea also down the route of socially exclusionary development. By October 1998, almost a year into the crisis, the rate of unemployment had risen from 2 to 7 per cent. Would Korea's experience of stabilisation and structural reform also create a Latin Americanised social model? While broadly conforming to principles of the neo-liberal model, there were also significant features of the Korean recovery programme which were more consistent with the developmentalist tradition. The swap deals discussed above demonstrated continuing official commitment to an industrial policy of some sort. Another distinguishing feature of Korea's response to crisis was the negotiation of a social pact for burden sharing.

If Korea was moving from developmentalism towards some form of 'internationalised' developmental model, she was doing so with a distinctly pro-active social role for the state. The negotiation of the social pact was indicative of the official preference for the introduction of socially painful economic reforms by consensual arrangement. Apart from demonstrating strong concern with maintaining social cohesiveness and President Kim Dae-Jung's populist instincts, the introduction of the social pact was also motivated by practical concerns. Given the widely held perception of the role of business malpractice in the crisis, no popular support could be built for socially painful restructuring without there being commensurate sacrifices on the part of business and the affluent. The liberalising economic policies had to be balanced by inclusionary labour and social policies (e.g. consultation with the unions over redundancies and social development measures to counter the effects of unemployment).

By pushing labour and business towards compromise, the 1997 crisis broke the impasse that had previously thwarted much-needed labour market reforms. But how sustainable was the breakthrough? The introduction of a social pact marked a major departure from past practice of labour repression in response to economic crisis. Korea's social pact experiment was also unique within East Asia. Social pacts had been tried in response to the 1980s' crises of debt and inflation in Latin America. In that region, social pacts were situated within more difficult policy environments. First, the Latin American social pacts existed within heterodox stabilisation strategies at odds with the wishes of the multilateral agencies. By contrast, the Korean social pact was introduced alongside an IMF-approved recovery plan and at a time when the Washington institutions themselves had become more sensitive to the usefulness of selective social intervention. Second, behind the failure of the Argentinian and Brazilian social pacts was the inability of the state to maintain the confidence on which labour and business self-restraint depended. This failure was in part due to weak bureaucratic capacities, whereas the Korean state had a history of stronger co-optive capacities. Third, unlike Latin America, the issue of overbloated bureaucracy was not so serious a financial problem for Korea (even though Korea also introduced a plan for administrative downsizing). Public sector overspending was not a source of the 1997 crisis. If it proves to be successful, the experiment with a social pact will mark a step away from Korea's traditional 'corporatism without labour' to President Kim Dae-Jung's vision of a 'democratic market economy'. Even though it was launched against more favourable background conditions than similar experiments elsewhere, the serious obstacles arising from the legacy of the developmentalist past should not be underestimated.

As denoted by its title, the social pact was an agreement whereby labour and business agreed to share the sacrifices necessary for economic recovery. In return for accepting transitional unemployment and more flexible employment regulations, labour would receive concessions in the form of social development measures, enhanced political rights and reform of the *chaebol*'s crisis-prone corporate structures. As such, the pact's workability depended on both sides perceiving the burdens to be fair, effective in the cause of recovery and in their long-term interests. With their members' basic livelihood at stake, the labour unions were in a particularly sensitive situation. The change of leadership in 1998 helped to ameliorate organised labour's traditional mistrust of the state. In Kim Dae-Jung (the self-proclaimed 'economy president' and 'unification president'), the labour unions had a leader with the strongest record of sympathy with the labour cause (while at the same time maintaining an international reputation for being a pro-market economic reformer). President Kim's intention to make the Tripartite Commission a permanent forum was an encouraging sign of the new government's intention of closer policy consultation with the unions.

Government agencies claimed success for the social pact in quantitative terms (e.g. in the completion rate of the points agreed for action under the social pact). The obstacles to the success of the social pact were significantly more formidable than what was conveyed by the meaningless performance measures. The pain felt by labour was severe, as the unemployment rate soared to 8.5 per cent (1.76 million workers) in January 1999, the highest level since 1966. According to one estimate, the true level of unemployment (including the homeless, and daily and part-time workers) probably exceeded 3 million (Chae 1999: 4). For workers accustomed to growth and rising real wages year upon year, the sudden possibility of unemployment was unfamiliar and terrifying. Even though the social pact contained provisions for moderating the social dislocation arising from economic reform (e.g. wider welfare net, retraining schemes, stabilisation of prices for basic consumer goods), the adequacy of the measures in relation to the likely scale and duration of the unemployment problem was questioned by social policy experts (e.g. Sang-Kyun Kim 1998).

Moreover, since the unions also held the domestic economic and political elite (rather than the IMF or foreign speculators) responsible for the crisis, the social consensus could be sustained only if there was evidence of a genuine transformation of business practice (e.g. in corporate governance) and real sacrifice on the part of the affluent. In the latter area, there has been some discouraging evidence pointing to the widening of income disparities in favour of upper- and upper-middle income groups (e.g. Tae-Yol Lee 1999: 11–12). The crisis has coincided with the numerical decline of the middle income groups (S.M. Hong 1999: 13–14), the strata that for a decade propelled the consumer revolution. Given their ownership of foreign currency denominated assets, it is not surprising for the rich to have hedged themselves against the financial crisis (and even to have become better off in terms of their real purchasing power).

Job losses were testing labour support for the social pact to the limit. The more radical umbrella organisation, the Korean Confederation of Trades Unions was particularly uneasy with the prospect of mass lay-offs arising from public and corporate restructuring (it had originally planned a general strike as early as February 1998 to protest against the lay-offs). It soon demanded renegotiation of the IMF deal, the ending of lay-offs and the cessation of employment of temporary workers (in effect, overturning the measures agreed to in the February agreement). In spite of a televised appeal from the president, the KCTU rejected further involvement in the tripartite process (*Korea Herald* 11 May 1998). This was followed by strikes at key export plants that month, including the Hyundai and Daewoo car factories (ibid.: 28 May 1998).

The difficulties of making the social pact work were highlighted by the Hyundai Motors' dispute of June–August 1998. Being a key part of the export industry and a flagship of the biggest *chaebol* group, Hyundai Motors was a test case for other employers. Hyundai management's decision to cut 1,500 jobs at its Ulsan plant (the planned total being 4,800) led to a protracted dispute that paralysed production for the best part of two months. Fearing that management had plans for much deeper job cuts, the plans were bitterly resisted by the plant unions with strong support from the national umbrella unions. The gravity of the situation at one of the country's leading enterprises led to government intervention that forced the company to dilute its redundancy plan (despite the consistency of the lay-offs with the tripartite agreement). In the end, only 277 workers were laid off, and the labour and management sides negotiated a wage reduction deal instead (*Korea Herald* 13 August 1998, 29 August 1998). The inability of Hyundai to apply the labour laws also set a precedent for other *chaebol* planning redundancies. Daewoo Motors reached a similar deal with its workers. Concern with industrial unrest also led the government to pressure Hyundai to provide the job guarantees for LG workers in the semi-conductor swap deal of 1999. Such intervention represented an unsatisfactory half-way house. By permitting overmanning, it seemed to contradict the principle of restructuring, namely to improve competitiveness. By circumscribing their freedom to act on the new labour law, the government alienated employers. On the other hand, such intervention did not reassure trades unionists who feared that employers would renege on their concessions (e.g. Kia; see below). The pattern of reactive labour protest and mutual recrimination, tentative government crackdowns followed by *ad hoc* efforts to placate both unions and management, and the imposition of an uneasy compromise that neither labour nor business had much interest in maintaining, resembled the pattern of events following the previous government's attempted labour law reforms in December 1996.

The tripartite forum would thus follow a stop–go cycle of boycott and discussion: one side would boycott the forum in protest at allegedly unfair gains made by the other; the government would then attempt to redress the imbalance; this in turn would provoke protests and boycotts from the erstwhile gainers that the pendulum had swung too far the other way. This pattern was evident from developments in 1999. It began with Hyundai Motors reneging on its take-over agreement by dismissing 30 per cent of Kia Motors' employees (a move that confirmed trades unionists, worst suspicions about the *chaebol* management). Simultaneous strikes were occurring at the profitable LG Semicon and the moribund Samsung Motors, with groups of striking workers fearing for their job security under new management (*Korea Herald* 26 January 1999). On 24 February 1999, the KCTU announced its intention of withdrawing from the tripartite forum. It demanded an immediate halt to restructuring, the repeal of the legalised lay-off system, and the shortening of legal working hours. The more moderate FKTU followed suit and made similar demands. The two union groups called a series of nationwide strikes in March (ibid.: 29 March 1999). The KCTU then staged extensive strikes in April and May 1999 in protest at the restructuring programme (including the proposed sell-off of Daewoo shipbuilders) (ibid.: 22 April 1999). The collapse of the tripartite forum raised the dangerous spectre of mass strikes joined by the 2 million or so already unemployed. Reacting to a dangerous situation, the government made concessions, having first resorted to a show of force. It agreed to amend the labour laws and allow the minimum working week to contract from 44 to 40 hours and to require companies to pay the salaries of full-time union officials. This in turn was criticised by the KEF and the FKI as excessively damaging to efficiency and contrary to the tripartite forum (the agreement was reached outside the forum, which in turn had been subject to boycotts from one or all of the business and labour participants over the preceding months) (*Korea Herald* 30 June 1999).

What lay behind the difficulties of cooperation and burden-sharing from the perspective of organised labour? The above episodes demonstrated the ability of organised labour to moderate the effect of restructuring on unemployment. On the political front, labour also made significant advances (e.g. the legalisation of teaching trades unions in December 1998). Yet labour organisations remained seriously dissatisfied with the workings of the social pact. The labour organisations felt that they were excluded from serious consultation in the determination of major economic decisions such as the swap deals. They also felt that progress on issues such as the extension of labour rights was being made only very slowly. For example, the right of laid-off workers to join a union, while being acknowledged in principle by the tripartite presidential advisory panel in September 1998, had its implementation postponed until 2000 (ostensibly because of opposition from the Justice Ministry) (*Korea Herald* 8 December 1998). Ultimately, negative labour perceptions could be traced to the polarisation of viewpoints that plagued reform efforts under the previous government. Labour groups rejected the contention of government and business that labour market inflexibility was the main cause of poor economic performance. Instead, they pointed to the failure of the government to overhaul the internal structure of the *chaebol* and politics (ibid.: 19 May 1998). In the labour unions' view, they were already making substantial concessions, as demonstrated by the rising unemployment and downward trend in unit labour costs (by as much as 12.7 per cent in the manufacturing sector for 1998) (Min 1999). They perceived the *chaebol* to be interested only in implementing lay-offs, an impression reinforced by incidents like that at Kia.

The conclusion of a formal agreement was much easier than was making it work. Some of the action was initiated by enterprise unions over which the umbrella organisations like the KCTU and FKTU had little direct control. As in social pacts tried elsewhere, moderate leaders tended to be outflanked by more militant grassroots activists. There were also some structural problems in the social pact originating from the legacies of Korean labour relations that magnified the problems of cooperation traditionally associated with social pacts. For the purpose of labour control, labour unions were historically established by authoritarian regimes on an enterprise basis. As a result, the creation of nationwide industrial labour unions was pre-empted and the umbrella organisations (FKTU and KCTU) had only limited influence over their enterprise-oriented affiliates. Equally, the *chaebol*'s peak organisation, the Federation of Korean Industry, had only limited leverage over its constituent members (especially the powerful ones). Thus even if the umbrella labour groups and business organisations could overcome their disagreements over principles, the tripartite forum had only limited capacity in enforcing compliance at the enterprise level.

A related obstacle to the effectiveness of the tripartite arrangements was the concentration of labour organisations in particular sectors of the economy. The source of Korean organised labour's strength in the post-democratisation period lay not in absolute numbers (the unionisation rate fell to about 13 per cent of the entire workforce by 1996) but in its concentration in key export industries. This concentration, however, also set limits to organised labour's interest in the structural reform of the *chaebol*. While there was interest in boosting labour's bargaining power by reducing the *chaebol* groups' influence with the state and in preventing the recurrence of future crises, the top priority for the labour unions was the protection of their members' jobs. As such, this made them sensitive to those structural reforms that could lead to the contraction of *chaebol*-owned industries (e.g. the labour reaction to the proposed sale of Daewoo shipbuilders): consolidation into leaner companies; internal governance reforms leading to the share value becoming the leading management concern; and absorption by foreign TNCs with more aggressive employment practices. In this regard, the crisis exposed the interdependence of the *chaebol* and the most powerful (and relatively privileged) sections of organised labour (see e.g. J.-H. Lee and D.I. Kim 1997: 36) at the expense of small and medium-sized enterprises (whose underdevelopment was a major structural flaw of the Korean development model) and their politically voiceless workers. Not surprisingly it was the latter who bore the brunt of the recession. For this stratum of labour, the recession persisted despite the macro-indicators of recovery in the first half of 1999 (*Korea Herald* 16 June 1999).

In spite of having to secure power by aligning himself with two leaders associated with the authoritarian past (Kim Jong-Pil and Park Tae-Joon), President Kim Dae-Jung had initially managed to sell the social pact on the basis of his own reputation. This, together with the novelty of having a government formed from the opposition were factors favouring the new government's social consensus building efforts. But the new government was facing not only a difficult objective situation but deeply ingrained attitudes and practices on the part of organised labour. Long accustomed to fighting for a share of the spoils within a high-growth full-employment economy, Korean labour was psychologically unprepared for an extended period of mass unemployment. It was difficult to envisage any genuine restructuring not effecting a significant reduction in manning levels in all sectors (even in the case of growth recovery). Even the most optimistic economic forecasts predicted a slow return to growth. At the slightest sign of economic upturn in the first quarter of 1999, however, the labour unions were demanding compensation for the previous year's sacrifices (while the *chaebol* were reneging on their commitment to restructuring). The with-drawal of the KCTU and its demands for the dismantling of the tripartite deal was a sign of this basic contradiction between organised labour's adherence to the traditional labour aspirations (formed in conditions of robust growth) and the objective needs of restructuring.

Conclusion

In 1997, the Korean economy entered its longest period of slowdown since the late-1950s. The gravity of the crisis in Korea and elsewhere in Asia has dented the image of 'Miracle Asia'. The literature lauding Asian econ-omic and political practices that was prevalent in the early-1990s (e.g. World Bank 1993) has instead given way to much more critical dissec-tions of Asian growth policies and their institutional frameworks. At the forefront of this reappraisal of the Asian miracle has been the IMF to whose conditional rescue packages the Thai, Indonesian and Korean economies became subject in 1997. In an apparent *volte-face*, the IMF now assailed the governments it had previously praised. The pro-growth alliances previously respected in the West were instead repainted as cronyistic relationships that distorted the competitive environment. The liberalisation policies of the crisis countries that were previously praised were now deemed inadequate and a faster liberalisation schedule was called for under the conditions of IMF rescue. In the IMF's view, the crisis was the product of market distortions, distortions that would be removed by full liberalisation and the reform of corporate governance. The IMF prescription became the basis of the Korean recovery programme.

Critics of the IMF, by contrast, stressed the responsibility of under-regulated private entities both domestic and international. By its accelerated liberalisation policies from 1993, the Kim Young-Sam government is said to have prematurely exposed the financial sector, the Achilles' heel of the Korean development model, to the instabilities of international finance. Thus the crisis was not caused by too little liberalisation but rather by over-zealous liberalisation (e.g. Chang *et al.* 1998; Wade 1998). With its prescription for the speedy completion of liberalisation, the IMF was seen as paving the way for further instability (not to mention the effect of the Fund's unwarranted stabilisation measures in deepening the recession).

By setting the recent economic crisis in the context of the long-term reform of the Korean development model, this chapter has argued that the origins of the crisis go deeper than the over-zealous economic liberalisation of the Kim Young-Sam government or the instabilities of unregulated international finance. The origins of the crisis pre-date the accelerated liberalisation policies started in 1993. In fact, those reforms were more consistent with the pattern of gradual reform established in 1981 than with radical neo-liberal experiments practised elsewhere. Far from being caused by the dismantling of state planning, the crisis can be traced to the legacies of the authoritarian industrialisation model: the tendency of the *chaebol* to over-diversify, the confrontational nature of labour relations, and sensitivity to external fluctuations (in particular, the dependency relationship with Japan born of Korean economic nationalism). The decision to initiate liberalisation in 1981 and the changes in rhythm of reform by democratic governments in 1987 and 1993 were made in response to the limits of state-directed development.

The main focus of this chapter was to assess the impact of the 1997 shock on state–business–labour relationships. The previous major economic crisis of 1979–80 resulted in the decision to alter the direction of economic policy towards liberalisation. The over-riding concern of all governments (authoritarian and democratic) with growth, however, meant liberalisation could proceed only gradually. Instead of effecting greater competition, gradual liberalisation enabled the *chaebol* to extend their power by entering domains previously restricted by the state. The 1997 crisis appears to have made effective policy reform in this area more likely. Fearing the slowdown in growth, previous governments' anti-monoplisation and rationalisation measures aimed at the *chaebol* did not prove very effective. By contrast, the conditions for effective reform seemed more favourable in the aftermath of the 1997 crash: an economy already in the doldrums; the public association of the *chaebol* with economic failure; strong IMF pressure for liberalisation and corporate governance reform; and the transfer of political power to a leadership (Kim Dae-Jung's) unconnected with past policy errors. It was against this background that the government made an ambitious bid to restructure the *chaebol* sector by initiating the swap deals in 1998 (involving the eight major sectors of the top five *chaebol*).

With democratisation, the authoritarian legacy of confrontational labour relations became a serious economic problem. Although the mass industrial unrest following democratisation had died down by the early-1990s, continuing labour–business differences (as reflected in their very different visions of growth-enhancing industrial relations) obstructed the implementation of much-needed labour market reforms. The attempt by the government to impose a new set of rules in December 1996 only worsened the economic situation by provoking major strikes. The onset of the economic crisis in 1997 paved the way for an uneasy burden-sharing agreement between labour, business and state (the Tripartite Agreement for Fair Burden-Sharing). Here again, the background of crisis appeared to be more favourably suited to labour market reforms than at any time since democratisation. A number of facilitating factors were identified: the urgent need for reform; the weakening of the veto powers of both business and labour; and the change of leadership to the populist Kim Dae-Jung.

While economic restructuring and labour reform were favoured by the background conditions of economic crisis and leadership change, the success of the reforms in terms of institutional change was by no means guaranteed. It was argued that the state's management of policy change, and the perceptions and responses of the *chaebol* and the labour unions, would have profound effects on the course of reform. The interplay of these variables could be seen in the implementation of the swap deals and labour market reform. As of mid-1999 only one major industrial swap (the Hyundai–LG semi-conductor deal) had been concluded. The protracted wrangling over the terms by which the transfer of facilities took place reflected the continuing rivalry between the leading *chaebol* at the expense of the overall strategy (e.g. LG's agreement to transfer its electronics industry to Hyundai only under very exacting terms and the collapse of the Samsung–Daewoo deal). The preparedness to use the ultimate power of ceasing credit to recalcitrant groups (risking the deepening of the recession) was also open to question, even for this determined government.

In the area of labour reform, the state assumed a more pro-active social role in exchange for organised labour's acceptance of lay-offs. A year into the crisis, unemployment reached 8 per cent. Organised labour's acceptance of lay-offs (meaning the weakening of its position) was contingent on perceptions that the burdens of the crisis would be shared fairly. There were strong indications that disparities were being widened by the crisis. Even more important were the negative labour perceptions of its prospects in the longer term (e.g. the rehiring of displaced workers, the improvement of political rights and the distancing of the state from the *chaebol*). As of mid-1999, the social pact appeared to be stretched to the limit as the tripartite forum became subject to repeated boycotts by some or all parties representing business and labour.

In terms of the content of the IMF programme accepted by the government, Korea since December 1997 has moved from gradual liberalisation towards radical liberalising policies more akin to neo-liberalism (internationalised model). This chapter has shown how an active role for the state could still be consistent with neo-liberal principles. In spite of the official commitment to speedy deregulation, the state has continued to play an active role in industrial rationalisation and in attempts at maintaining some degree of social consensus. These interventions reflect the problems left by the developmental state, problems that had to be tackled directly if the liberalisation programme was to succeed. They also show the deeply embedded belief that the state could still play a purposeful role in economic development. Given that the sources of Korea's fragile miracle were not only institutional but technical (especially from the dependence on Japan established during the take-off stage), the long-term recovery of the Korean economy would depend on state initiatives for overcoming the weaknesses in the neglected areas of economic development: technology, training, social infrastructure and small and medium-sized firms. These aspects of functional intervention were important areas in which the state could still make an important difference to economic outcomes. For some time, they had been recognised in Korea as the appropriate forms of market-conforming intervention in the liberalised world economy. The nature of the recovery strategy discussed in this chapter indicates that these concerns were not forgotten. But the formidable hurdles emanating both from big business and from organised labour's confrontation and resistance to reform meant that there could be no guarantee of success.

7 Conclusion

The fragile miracle 1979–99

In the study of the economic performance of the East Asian NICs, the literature of the past two decades has placed great emphasis on the effectiveness of public institutions in overcoming both market and governmental failure. 'Institutionalist' accounts from both economics and political science have elaborated on the characteristics of East Asian public institutions that facilitated sustained economic growth with relatively egalitarian distributional outcomes. Economic institutionalism has concentrated on explaining how the East Asian bureaucracies managed to competently perform vital functions (functions that third world bureaucracies failed to perform or performed incompetently) that would have otherwise been neglected by the market. The focus of political institutionalist explanations, on the other hand, has been the means by which East Asian bureaucracies surmounted those claims from influential social interests (including from within the bureaucracy itself) that threatened to divert resources away from productive use. Seeking to explain the interaction of market and institutional forces behind Korea's modernisation, institutionalist accounts have drawn largely on empirical evidence from the 1961–87 period of economic take-off, an era defined by strong government leadership in economics and political authoritarianism.

The diluting of state power by economic liberalisation and democratisation ('dual transition') during the 1980s has shifted the institutionalist debate towards a different set of questions. Are there further spaces for 'market-conforming' forms of intervention that are compatible with the neo-liberal precepts that now dominate world trade? How would the empowerment of previously subordinate social forces by democratisation affect economic policy and performance? How would the legacy of statism influence the transition to a more liberal political–economic form? In short, such questions converged on one point, namely, will East Asia's authoritarian-guided capitalism become more like the West's liberal-democratic capitalism? The Asian economic crisis of 1997 has intensified these debates, with the neo-liberals blaming economic failure on the institutional framework of government–business collusion said to be common to Asian economies. In response, many institutionalists put the blame on over-zealous liberalisation in a sector (finance) renowned for its global volatility.

State, business and labour

In line with the political institutionalist method, this study has examined the interaction between state–society relations and economic performance and policy orientation in Korea during the 1979–99 period. Relations between state, big business and labour have often been emphasised in the institutionalist literature for their positive contribution to Korea's economic performance in the early decades of development. This study has highlighted the legacy of those institutional relationships on economic and political reform efforts of the 1980s and 1990s. Two aspects of state–society relations have been emphasised throughout.

First, the discipline exerted by the state over the big business conglomerates (*chaebol*) was eroded as a consequence of economic success. Along with growing interdependence came stronger lobbying pressure from the *chaebol* over the course of economic policy change, first in opposition to all economic liberalisation and, second, from the late-1980s, in support of a partial liberalisation (i.e. one in which business failures continue to be underwritten by the state) consistent with their ambitions. Interdependence also made it more difficult for the state to counteract the non-productive activities associated with the *chaebol*, just when public opinion was becoming sensitive to such practices. Democratisation in 1987 brought more vocal calls for effective public measures to counteract the dominance and abuses of the *chaebol*. It also, however, strengthened the *chaebol*'s leverage over the state by such means as bribery and political funding. Perhaps the most effective lever in the hands of the *chaebol* was their awareness of the importance of a growing economy to elected politicians. This explains the ineffectiveness of anti-monopoly and anti-corruption measures implemented by two democratic governments from 1988 and 1993 (just like the efforts of authoritarian governments before them).

Second, Korean labour relations are distinguished from Japanese and Taiwanese ones by their confrontational nature. The experience of economic take-off in the 1960s and 1970s had rather paradoxical effects on Korean labour. On the one hand, it was marked by harsh repression of labour and the systematic proscription of all forms of independent labour organisation. On the other, Korean labour enjoyed sustained and rapid wage increases after 1961, while the state's ambitious heavy industrialisation policies (especially from 1973 onwards) created a proletariat with the strongest potential in Asia. Wages were never really 'compressed' in the sense associated with Latin American bureaucratic authoritarianism. These paradoxes set the scene for the flare-up in industrial confrontation between 1987 and 1989 (the Great Workers' Struggle). They helped bring about a redistributional shift in government policy after democratisation. While

the level of industrial disputes was sharply reduced after 1990, the democratic governments of both Roh Tae-Woo and Kim Young-Sam were
unable to overcome the legacy of confrontational labour relations (despite
their pronounced shift towards redistribution and other measures of a
societal corporatist kind).

The undoubted persistence of collusion between state and business
played a part in this. The impasse also owed something to the nature of
the Korean labour unions themselves and the timing of their empowerment from the authoritarian state. In the decade since democratisation,
Korean organised labour remained preoccupied with the extension of its
traditional interests (wages, job security, working conditions and political
rights). Based on the ambitious expectations of what democratisation should
bring, Korean labour became locked into an agenda that was being rapidly
overtaken by the demands of international competitiveness. The 1989–91
slowdown and other indicators (e.g. slow productivity growth, financial
fragility, trade deficits) provided unmistakable signs of the continuing
vulnerability of the economy. The labour relations impasse remained
entrenched, with the result that much-needed labour market reforms (high
labour costs being one component of the 'high cost, low efficiency'
economy) were not introduced until 1997, when the economy was already
in dire crisis. Abortive reform efforts followed a standard pattern: business
criticism of labour market inflexibility; labour criticism of big business
malpractices driving up production costs, such as land price; and the
politicians' inertia, born of their fear of slowing down the economy by
provoking either strikes or loss of business confidence.

Economic nationalism and neo-liberalism

Apart from democratisation, the influence of business and organised labour
was enhanced by the unwillingness of the state to countenance major
corporate bankruptcies and redundancies in the pursuit of market reform
(as neo-liberal reformers were prepared to do in Latin America and Eastern
Europe). More resolute measures in both corporate and labour relations
reform were thwarted by the priority of maintaining high growth rates.
Even the Kim Young-Sam government (1993–8), for all its ambitions of
'globalising' Korean society, was constrained within these parameters.
Political sensitivity to economic slowdown affected democratic and authoritarian regimes alike. Lacking intrinsic legitimacy, military regimes were
even more inclined to look towards rapid growth for their legitimacy. This
concern accounts for the repeatedly ineffectual anti-monopoly, industrial
restructuring and anti-corruption measures tried by the Chun, Roh and
Kim Young-Sam governments over an eighteen-year period.

The neo-liberal technocrats ensconced by President Chun at the Blue
House in 1980 had succeeded in convincing the president of the need
for macroeconomic stabilisation and structural reform (e.g. of industrial,

financial and trade policy). The downturn of 1979–80 provided ample proof of the market distortions built up over two decades of intervention. This was recognised in the liberalising direction of policy change from 1981. Even though the pro-market reformers had won the battle for stabilisation, the route to structural reform would follow a gradual course consistent with the traditional priorities of growth, full-range industrialisation and national ownership. Studies have emphasised the stronger capacities of the anti-liberalising factions in intra-bureaucratic policy battles (e.g. B.-S. Choi 1989). This study has concentrated on the structural explanation of why statism dominated liberalism for so long. The embrace of the radical neo-liberal route to the market was constrained by the legacy of Korea Inc. The overall record of 1961–79, followed by the strong recovery from 1981, showed that the old model, subject to adjustments, could still serve the national interest well. By contrast, the neo-liberal doctrines nascent in the 1980s, were by and large untested and found their appeal in those countries where developmentalism had clearly failed. By Korea's historical standards of growth, the roller-coaster performance of even the most successful third world neo-liberal experiment, Chile, was unimpressive. The resilience of the traditional model and the problems associated with rapid liberalisation in Latin America would underpin Korea's post-1981 gradualist pattern of liberalising reform.

Apart from practical considerations, neo-liberalism also ran counter to the deeply ingrained economic nationalism prevalent in Korean policy circles. In Chapter 2, I described the political economy of Korea Inc. as 'mercantilism with market characteristics'. In the pursuit of national strengthening, the modernising elite around President Park copied the economic instruments of colonial and post-war Japan. Korea's successful state-supported export development became a model example of how the world trading system could be used for nationalistic ends. Economic liberalisation also came to be accepted on instrumentalist terms (it was Park himself who gave the green light for liberalisation in the spring of 1979). The official emphasis on economic liberalisation after 1981 did not mean the abandonment of the classic goals of late-industrialisation. Instead, liberalisation came to be seen from the perspective of the traditional goals of enhancing Korean power and security. These considerations ensured that liberalisation would proceed on a piecemeal rather than a doctrinaire basis. Seen in this light, the 'globalisation' project (commonly understood to mean the completion of economic and political liberalisation) of the Kim Young-Sam government (1993–8) was consistent with the tradition of selective opening to the international economy.

The limits of economic nationalism

But the political economy of nationalism also had its contradictions. One such contradiction was the dependency relationship with Japan. This dependence was manifested in the persistence of trade deficits and sensitivity to Japanese economic fluctuations. Given the nationalist aim of catching up with Japan that motivated Korean economic thinking, this was something of a paradox. Moreover Korean development has been widely praised by Western dependency theorists for its autocentric nature and avoidance of dependency traps. The normalisation of relations in 1965 brought with it a new and subtle form of dependency relationship as Japanese funds, technology and advice became instrumental to the Korean economic take-off. Korean plants came to be established according to Japanese blueprints, using Japanese equipment and advisers, links that became very costly for the Korean side to break. In part a consequence of historical complementarity, dependence was accentuated by deliberate Korean policy choices (e.g. to maximise export growth, to enter the very capital-intensive sectors, to compete in international markets on the basis of own brand-names, to strictly limit direct foreign investments that could have counter-balanced the Japanese influence).

The essential components of the Korean-owned industrial structure were literally 'made in Japan'. Because this relationship was consistent with the priorities of rapid growth, industrial diversification and national ownership, counter-measures (ranging from the promotion of 'national champions' in the 1970s to the numerous industrial 'localisation' programmes of the 1980s and 1990s) proved largely ineffectual. Korean economic nationalism's flawed ambition of challenging Japanese economic superiority while relying on Japanese inputs could be seen from the effect of exchange-rate fluctuations on trade patterns. In supplying their Korean counterparts with technology and critical components for export to third markets, Japanese suppliers managed to establish a win–win relationship that persists to this day. Yen appreciation (low Japanese and high Korean end-product competitiveness) stokes up Korean demand for Japanese inputs. This was evident from the 1986–8 boom, when trade deficits with Japan were mirrored by big surpluses with the US (where anti-Korean protectionist sentiments were stoked up). On the other hand, yen depreciation means that Japanese products outperform Korean ones in third markets. In the build up to the 1997 Asian crisis, Yen depreciation was especially damaging to the competitiveness of NIC economies pegged to the US dollar (Cho 1998: 49). It was shown up in the collapse of semiconductor prices and the widening of the Korean trade deficit. I have referred to the paradoxical effect of Korean economic nationalism in deepening the dependent relationship with Japan as 'hyper-developmentalism'.

The other leash on Korean economic nationalism was held by Washington. The experiment in economic nationalism was conducted under the benign protection of the US. Because of the alliance with the US, Korea's economic experience was for a long time misinterpreted in neoclassical terms. But as world-systems interpretations of Northeast Asian political economy (see Cumings 1984; Woo 1991) have pointed out, Korean economic nationalism thrived within the regional hegemony of the US. They pointed out that Cold War necessities (ensuring a stable Korea loyal to the US) resulted in less exacting demands on economic behaviour from crucial allies such as Korea. It has been argued here that, despite her influential role in key economic and political turning-points of recent Korean history, the US tended to reinforce the Korean developmental state until the mid-1980s. US pressure accelerated the reconstitution of the developmental state in the early-1960s and ensured that it would be export oriented. US demands for economic liberalisation could always be met with cosmetic measures from the Korean side (as in the case of the 1965 financial reforms). And even in the aftermath of the 1979–80 crisis, when Korea came under IMF supervision, the external pressure for radical liberalisation was moderated by US strategic imperatives (e.g. resulting in US-inspired Japanese financial aid to Korea when other debtors were left to struggle).

The decline of the Cold War from the mid-1980s was a major blow for the neo-mercantilist model. The US attitude shifted from reinforcement of the Korean developmental state to concerted efforts aimed at its dismantling. This was reflected in the US–Korean trade battles of the late-1980s and the ever-more testing criteria for fair trade applied by the US (backed up by powerful unilateral and multilateral sanctions). Each time, the Korean authorities conceded just enough to placate the US. Globalisation meant there were also very real benefits to be gained from *more* liberalisation (a point also not lost on the Korean government and business sector). Not only that, but in the intellectual contest between advanced economic role models, the traditional appeal of Japan Inc. was dented by the beginning of a protracted Japanese recession from 1992, just when the US was entering its strongest growth phase for a generation. The 'globalisation' project of the Kim Young-Sam government was launched in response to these external trends. I have argued that the project had stronger affinity with previous selective liberalisations than with any radical lurch towards neo-liberalism. Realising the international drift towards the Anglo-Saxon form of economic organisation, the Koreans also appreciated the important legacy of the German–Japanese form (e.g. M.-W. Lee 1999: 374–5). Because of her dynamic economic performance, Korea could afford to experiment with liberalism in a controlled manner. Economic liberalisation occurred at a graduated pace. But the implications of the new international parameters were clear. Once that performance spluttered, as it did in 1997, Korea could not expect another easy rescue from the US or the US-dominated Washington institutions.

The neo-liberalisation of Korea?

The failures of the developmental state in Latin America, in both its populist and authoritarian forms, resulted in the embrace of neo-liberalism.

The heterodox stabilisation programmes of the newly formed democratic governments of Brazil and Argentina between 1985 and 1987 represented the last gasp of the developmentalist approach in Latin America. Their failure to control the twin crises of inflation and debt opened the way for experiments in neo-liberal economics. What started out in Chile as an aberrant economic form in 1973 had become the normal practice of the continent a quarter of a century later. Although the different make up and performance of the Korean developmental state resulted in a gradualist pattern of economic liberalisation, the nature of the 1997 crisis and IMF conditionalities has led some to suggest that Kim Dae-Jung's government may be launching Korea down the neo-liberal route (e.g. Ahn 1999).

The exposure of international banks ensured that a rescue package would be rapidly put in place to avert any Korean debt default. At the same time, however, the IMF conditionalities, if fully implemented, amounted to nothing less than a complete restructuring of the Korean economy along neo-liberal lines. The tough IMF conditionalities imposed on Korea were already familiar to Latin America. No longer restrained by the same degree of strategic sensitivity, the US was now prepared to put Korea through a painful transitional period of recession and high unemployment for the sake of market principles (and, of course, market access). The 1997 crisis showed that Korea no longer had a privileged status with the US. And, unlike China or Japan, Korea had far fewer cards to play. Instead her position was more akin to that of Brazil or Mexico. If anything, with their greater populations and demonstrable commitment to neo-liberal reform, Brazil and Mexico had higher standing than Korea with the authorities in Washington.

Like counterparts in Latin America (Gibson 1997) and elsewhere (M. Moore 1997), Kim Dae-Jung appeared to be leading the populists down the neo-liberal path. The Kim Dae-Jung government has declared its full acceptance of the IMF conditions. It launched a series of reform measures from February 1998: macroeconomic stabilisation; liberalisations in trade and finance and the labour market; big business restructuring and corporate governance reform. In themselves, the reform measures agreed to were nothing new. They had been partially implemented in some cases, and were the subject of ongoing discussion in others. But the gravity of the 1997 crisis meant that there was now greater urgency. It weakened the traditional reservations against reform on the part of big business, organised labour and elected politicians fearful of endangering growth. With the election of the Kim Dae-Jung government, a government untainted by policy failure and with populist inclinations, the political conditions were also favourable to structural reform. The results have so far (as of mid-1999) been mixed. For example, some restructuring of the *chaebol* has occurred but not across as many sectors as hoped (with the lesser *chaebol* having been more cooperative than the top five), while the umbrella labour organisations and business organisations have found it difficult to make compromises on burden sharing. In spite of high expectations, the social pact has not been especially effective thus far in finding common ground between two traditionally hostile forces with very different analyses of the current crisis. Consensus on the principle of burden sharing has not been matched by a similar attitude concerning the actual distribution of economic sacrifices.

Every Korean government claims to be ushering in a new era. While Kim Young-Sam had 'globalisation', Kim Dae-Jung talks of 'democratic market economy' (he used to talk about 'mass participatory economy' in his younger days). If Kim Dae-Jung's government engineers a neo-liberal revolution (as some critics accuse him of attempting), it will be a first for Asia. The experiences of Mexico and Argentina in 1994–5 and of Brazil in 1998 are reminders of the financial instability that neo-liberal economics brings. In addition, given the social costs (notably the stubbornly high rates of unemployment) associated with its practice in Latin America (the 'actually existing' neo-liberalism of the third world), it is difficult to imagine that that sort of neo-liberal model is the outcome envisaged for Korea by the Kim Dae-Jung government.

If not neo-liberalisation in the Latin American trajectory, what does President Kim's 'democratic market economy' hold for Korea? Of the basic IMF requirements for structural reform (liberalisation of trade, finance, direct investment, labour market and the reform of corporate governance), it is only in financial liberalisation (where an international consensus for tighter regulation is emerging after the Asian debacle) that Korea is likely to have any leeway for choice. This will mean that those Korean businesses and labour forces incapable of coping with intensified competition will have to upgrade, merge (as the government is promoting through its swap deals), divest or face elimination from the market. The establishment of the principle that businesses and their employees (rather than the state) are responsible for their own fates will bring Korea into line with economic practice in the rest of the world. The readiness of the government to tolerate major business collapses will do much to restore the discipline over the top *chaebol* that has been eroded over the past two decades. From this perspective there is much that a strong dose of market discipline can do for Korean efficiency.

Besides liberalisation, there is also a pro-active side to the current reform project. The existence of a purposive government agenda for recovery is reflected in the active role played by the government in financial consolidation and industrial restructuring. The limitations of the *chaebol*-led development model has also underlined the importance of small and medium-sized industry (something that was well known but never acted upon with any great urgency as the *chaebol* delivered growth year upon year). Given the strict rules of the WTO and the continuing competitiveness gap, the functional interventions (e.g. R&D, transportation, regional development) initiated by the Kim Young-Sam government are set to receive added emphasis. Although it claims to have ushered in a new era, the basic outlines of the economic reform by the Kim Dae-Jung government are quite similar to those initiated by its predecessor. The crucial differences are that the *chaebol* have been weakened and the government's moral authority is stronger. At any rate, it does not look like the neo-liberal programmes brought on by the demise of developmental states elsewhere.

Such measures suggest that within the 'democratic market economy' the *chaebol* are envisaged as retaining an important role, but they will be made to concede (through restructuring and regulation) more competitive space to SMEs and foreign business. The pattern of *chaebol* resistance also has echoes of past cycles of abortive reform: demanding market solutions when government intervention threatens their dominance; obfuscation in the acceptance and implementation of reform (e.g. as shown in the protracted wrangling over the swap deals); and diverting attention from their own shortcomings by demanding that other sectors (e.g. labour and the government) adjust first. In a weaker position, the lesser *chaebol* have tended to be compliant. The point hinges on whether the government will have the determination to enforce the painful corrective measures on the top five *chaebol* (who hope that pressures will ease with growth recovery and the withdrawal of IMF supervision). To show that it means business, the government may even have to dissolve one of the super-*chaebol*.

Unlike the raw neo-liberalism of the South, the most socially dislocating effects of neo-liberal policies in the North are cushioned by the existence of well-developed social safety-nets. Implemented in response to desperate fiscal deficits, neo-liberal policies in the South pare back the meagre social provisions that exist. The locus of the Korean crisis of 1997 was the overextended big business sector. In contrast to Latin American cases (Fishlow 1990), Korean public sector finances were healthy (ironically, a consequence of the decades of prioritising investment over redistribution). This has allowed the Korean state to extend social provision (in the shape of welfare and retraining) in response to recession, an effort impressive for an NIC. The recent social development measures and the social pact represent the most concerted efforts at societal corporatism in Korean history. Whether or not the labour unions find them adequate (short of giving those displaced their full incomes, such measures can never be adequate), they cannot claim to be the victims of some exclusionist neo-liberal project.

The state of public finances at the time of crisis has led Korea and Latin America to accommodate neo-liberal policies in different ways. Relatively healthy public finances and the existence of several dynamic private (and public) companies have given the Korean government the capacity to pursue a programme of market-conforming intervention parallel to the IMF's neo-liberal programme. That Korea's public finances were in sound shape when the 1997 crisis struck owed much to the discipline ingrained by the previous stint of IMF conditionality (1981–5). That previous crisis also shifted economic policy in the direction of liberalisation and structural reform. In its response to the 1997 crisis, the Kim Dae-Jung government is bringing to completion the most sensitive items of that reform agenda.

Which brings us back to the political context. The recovery programme depends on the cooperation of big business and organised labour. Many policies in the recovery programme had been circulating around the policy community for years, but could not be effectively implemented because of hostility from and between labour and business. The crisis has diminished their capacity of veto and shifted their orientation from in-fighting towards accepting the principle of concessions for recovery (or at least to accepting the principle of shared burdens). To build the widest consensus for the recovery strategy, the government has incorporated the labour unions and the *chaebol* into a formal social pact. In return for their sacrifice and restraint, the labour unions and big business are compensated. After decades of repression, the pact marks an historic advance for Korean labour. For the conglomerates also (and for the super-*chaebol*, in particular), the acceptance of reform (in effect, surrendering their traditional dominance) means the opportunity for survival by salvaging their most dynamic sectors. The consensus is threatened by the mistrust built up by the long period of state–business repression of labour. Perhaps even more debilitating for consensus is the attitude, fostered in the democratic decade, that sustained high growth could be taken for granted. Based on that assumption, exerting pressure on the state (rather than productivity growth) came to be accepted as the method of getting a bigger share of the benefits (e.g. by industrial muscle, by lobbying and corruption). The failure to arrive at a consensus for labour reform was responsible for the steady erosion of competitiveness in the years before the 1997 crisis. Even if the social pact should rupture and the recovery falter, restructuring will nevertheless take place. In that event, however, Korean business and labour will face an externally driven restructuring process over which they will have far less control. In their reluctance to concede anything, they risk losing everything.

Notes

2 Pre-1979 patterns of political economy

1 The New Community Movement had nine major programmes: roof improvement; general village improvement; construction and improvement of rural roads; sanitary water supply; reclamation of idle land; rural electrification; communications; medical facilities; and saemaul industries. The last programme was of particular importance for the generation of supplementary rural incomes with non-farming activities (Hasan 1976: 159–64).
2 The six sectors designated under the Heavy Chemical Industry Plan of 1973 were steel, chemicals, shipbuilding, electronics, cars and machinery.
3 France sustained three major car producers with a population of about 50 million (compared to Korea's 40 million population).
4 For example, the number of people covered by medical insurance rose from 15,426 in 1976 to a staggering 2.5 million by 1979 (see EPB (several issues) *Major Statistics*).

3 Gradualist pattern of transition

1 The most famous example of foreign opinion being swayed by token liberalisation gestures was the interest-rate reform of 1965, which led US economic adviser Ronald Mackinnon to pronounce the end of financial repression.
2 This occurred when one of the biggest private money-lenders (who was also closely connected to President Chun's in-laws) was caught selling vast quantities of promissory notes obtained from firms that were clients on the kerb market. It revealed the unsound financial structure of many enterprises and the sway which money-lenders had in the environment of financial repression (FEER 1982: 13–14).
3 Workforce participation is defined as the proportion of the population of working age (14+) active in the labour force, or the 'economically active' part of the population.
4 The number of vehicles on the road increased as follows: 249,000 (1980); 557,000 (1985); 2,075,000 (1990); 6,006,000 (1995).
5 The percentage SMI shares of bank credit cited in the report were: 38.6 (1973); 26.6 (1978); 39.2 (1984); and 33.6 per cent (1985) (World Bank 1987a: 92–3).

4 From autonomous state to consensual development?

1 Results were as follows (per cent): DJP 35.3, NKDP 29.2, Democratic Korea Party 19.5, Korea National Party 9.2, Others 6.8. The turnout of 87.2 per cent was the highest since 1958.

2 For example, Lee Min-Woo, the NKDP's nominal leader and a rival of the two Kims, was more amenable to constitutional compromise and eventually broke away.

3 Citing a survey from a pro-government newspaper, Dong (1988: 171–2) cites the following dissatisfaction ratings in May 1985 (per cent): all respondents 65.2; above average income 60.7; people in their twenties 73.6; college graduates 85.7 ($N = 1,307$).

4 'Consumption expenditure' denotes only the spending on basic necessities, and excludes discretionary spending (on items such as education, medical services and entertainment), and so it provides a useful yardstick for assessing the adequacy of remuneration.

5 Kim Young-Sam's Reunification and Democracy Party (RDP) and Kim Jong-Pil's New Democratic Republican Party (NDRP).

6 A single pro-business national union (Rengo) was established in Japan in 1987 (Van Wolferen 1989: 71–2).

5 Rise and fall of the 'globalisation' project

1 For an assessment of the first two-and-a-half years of the globalisation project see Gills (1996).

2 Williamson (1993) lists the following items of economic policy and discusses (a) where 'consensus' has been achieved; (b) where controversy still reigns but has become non-ideological; and (c) where ideological debate can be expected to remain. The policy areas (and Williamson's assessments on the degree of consensus that exists) are as follows: financial discipline (a); public expenditure priorities (c); tax reform (a); financial liberalisation (b); uniform exchange rates (a); trade liberalisation (b); foreign direct investment (a); privatisation (a); deregulation (b); property rights (a); land reform (c).

3 Eight investment and finance companies were consolidated into five security companies and two nationwide commercial banks: Hana and Boram in 1991.

4 For example, at the Manila APEC Summit of 1996, the US pushed for the total liberalisation of trade on information technology products by 2000.

5 1996 saw the failure of two such bids: first, a bid by a *chaebol* consortium consisting of Samsung Aerospace, Daewoo Heavy Industries, Hyundai Heavy Industries and Korean Air to acquire Fokker Aircraft (Holland); and, second, a bid by Daewoo Electronics to acquire Thomson Electronics (France). While both bids failed, this was a pointer to future *chaebol* strategy (and its associated difficulties) for the acquisition of core technology and the possibility of their cooperation by mounting of joint bids.

6 Previous major privatisations included Korea Airlines and Korea Shipbuilding (1968), the 'city-banks' (1982–3) (over which the government retained key decision-making controls), and majority shares of POSCO (1988) and KEPCO (1989).

7 For example, while the Korean Employers' Federation argued that Korean wages were the highest in the world in relation to the country's GNP level, the FKTU challenged such 'phantom statistics' with the observation that wage earners made up only 12 million of the country's 23 million labour force – a point that highlighted the segmentation within the workforce between core and peripheral workers (Interview FKTU Research Centre 1 July 1996).

8 On the OECD labour committee, the position of Korean labour rights was recognised to be much better than those of the other recent entrants, Mexico and Turkey.

9 For example, at Hyundai Motors, the wage differentials between in-house and subcontracted labour doing the same work and using the same machinery could

be as much as two to one (Interview FKTU Research Centre 1 July 1996).

10 The collapse of the Songsu Bridge in Seoul (21 October 1994) and an under-ground gas pipeline explosion caused by tunnelling in Taegu (28 April 1995) both did untold damage to the government's image (see FEER 10 November 1994). President Kim's governing Democratic Liberal Party (DLP) suffered a serious reverse in the local government elections of 27 June 1995. The collapse of Seoul's upmarket Sampoong department store on 29 June 1995 occurred just two days after those elections. Sensing the government's vulnerability at mid-term, Kim Dae-Jung soon reversed his earlier decision to retire from politics. Meanwhile the DLP renamed itself the New Korea Party.

11 The ostensible reasons for this were the ferocity of the student demonstrations at Yonsei University in August 1996 followed by the grounding of a North Korean infiltration submarine on the east coast in September.

12 The order for the arrest of Park Tae-Joon, the former head of POSCO and the Roh Tae-Woo faction's candidate for the DLP candidacy in the 1992 presidential election, was a sign of the political utility of Kim Young-Sam's anti-corruption drive.

13 Chung's son Chung Moon-Jong became a legislator with the ruling NKP and gained much public acclaim for his role in bringing the 2002 soccer World Cup to Korea.

6 The twilight of developmentalism?

1 Of the $10 billion package, $3 billion was dispensed as an Economic Reconstruction Loan and $7 billion as a Structural Adjustment Loan (see MOFE 24 December 1997).

2 The results of the presidential election were as follows: Kim Dae-Jung 40.3 per cent; Lee Hoi-Chang 38.7; Lee In-Je 19.2; Kwon Yong-Kil 1.2 (see Chung 1998: 34).

3 The three areas of Bank support for the Korean government's reform programme were financial sector restructuring, corporate sector reform, and the reform of the labour market and development of social safety nets (see World Bank February 1999).

4 See sections: 1 Management transparency and business restructuring; 1-1 Promoting management transparency; 1-2 Improvement of corporate financial structure; 1-3 Establishment of a responsible management system; and 1-4 Promotion of business competitiveness.

5 The world market price of the 16 megabyte DRAM chip fell from $50 to $10 between 1995 and 1996. During the same period, the Japanese yen fell by 15.6 per cent against the US dollar whereas the Korean won depreciated by only 4.3 per cent (Shin 1997: 9).

Bibliography

Adelman, Irma and Robinson, Sherman (1978) *Income Distribution Policy in Developing Countries: A Case Study of Korea*, Baltimore, MD: Johns Hopkins University Press.

Aghevli, Bijan B. and Márquez-Ruarte, Jorge (1987) *A Case of Successful Adjustment in a Developing Country: Korea's Experience During 1980–84*, Occasional Paper 39, Washington, DC: International Monetary Fund.

Aguilar, Francis J. and Cho, Dong-Sung (1989) 'Daewoo Group', in Don-Ki Kim and Linsu Kim (eds) *Management Behind Industrialization: Readings in Korean Business*, Seoul: Korea University Press.

Ahn, Byong-Man, Kil, Soon-Hoom and Kim, Kwang-Woong (1988) *Elections in Korea*, Seoul: Seoul Computer Press.

Ahn, Byong-Young (1999) 'The Kim Dae-Jung government may fall into the neo-liberal trap', *Shing Dong-Ah*, April: 86–92 (in Korean).

Akamatsu, Kaname (1962) 'A historical pattern of economic growth in developing countries', *Developing Economies* (preliminary issue) 1, March–August: 3–25.

Akyüz, Yilmaz (1998) 'The East Asian financial crisis: back to the future', in K.S. Jomo (ed.).

Allgeier, Peter F. (1988) 'Korean trade policy in the next decade, dealing with reciprocity', *World Development* 16, 1: 85–97.

Amnesty International (1977) *Report of an Amnesty International Mission to the Republic of Korea 27 March–9 April 1975*, London: Amnesty International.

—— (1986) *South Korea: Violations of Human Rights*, London: Amnesty International.

AMPO (1977) *AMPO: Japan–Asia Quarterly Review. Special Issue on Free Trade Zones and Industrialization of Asia*, Tokyo.

Amsden, Alice H. (1987) *Stabilization and Adjustment Policies and Programmes: Republic of Korea*, Helsinki: World Institute for Development Economics Research.

—— (1989) *Asia's Next Giant: South Korea and Late Industrialization*, New York: Oxford University Press.

—— (1992) 'The South Korean economy: is business-led growth working?', in Donald Clark (ed.) *Korea Briefing 1992*, Boulder, CO: Westview.

—— (1994a) 'The spectre of Anglo-Saxonization is haunting Korea', in L.-J. Cho and Y.-H. Kim (eds) (1994).

—— (ed.) (1994b) 'The World Bank's *The East Asian Miracle: Economic Growth and Public Policy*', *World Development* 22, 4 (special issue): 614–70.

—— (1997) 'Bringing production back in: understanding government's economic role in late-industrialization', *World Development* 25, 4: 469–80.

—— and Euh, Yoon-Dae (1990) *Republic of Korea's Financial Reform: What Are the Lessons?*, Discussion Paper 30, Geneva: United Nations Conference on Trade and Development.

—— (1993) 'South Korea's 1980s' financial reforms: good-bye financial repression (maybe), hello new institutional restraints', *World Development* 21, 3: 379–90.

Asia Monitor Resource Centre (1987) *Min Ju No Jo: South Korea's New Unions*, Hong Kong: Asia Monitor Resource Centre.

Asia-Pacific InfoServ Inc. (1996) *Korea Company Yearbook 1996/97*, Seoul.

Asia Watch Committee (1986) *Human Rights in Korea*, Washington, DC: Asia Watch Report.

Auty, Richard M. (1994) *Economic Development and Industrial Policy: Korea, Brazil, Mexico and China*, London: Mansell Publishing Limited.

Back, Jong-Gook (1994) 'Elections as transformation: explaining the reorganization of a ruling coalition', in Doh-Chull Shin, Myeong-Han, Zoh and Myung Chey, (eds) *Korea in the Global Wave of Democratization*, Seoul: Seoul National University Press.

Bae, Kyohan (1987) *Automobile Workers in Korea*, Seoul: Seoul National University Press.

Bae, Soon-Suk (1995) 'Impacts of rapid industrialization on housing: problems and responses', in Gun-Young Lee and Hyun-Sik Kim (eds) *Cities and Nation: Planning Issues and Policies of Korea*, Seoul: Korea Research Institute for Human Settlements.

Baer, Werner (1987) 'The resurgence of inflation in Brazil', *World Development* 15, 8: 1007–34.

Bahl, Roy, Kim, C.K. and Park, C. (1986) *Public Finances during the Korean Modernization Process. Studies in the Modernization of the Republic of Korea: 1945–1975*, Cambridge, MA: Harvard University Press.

Bai, Moo-Ki (1982) 'The turning point in the Korean economy', *Developing Economies* 20, 2: 117–40.

—— and Cho, Woo-Hyun (1995) *Women's Wages and Employment in Korea*, Seoul: Seoul National University Press.

Baldwin, Frank (ed.) (1974) *Without Parallel: The US–Korean Relationship*, New York: Pantheon Press.

Ban, Sung-Hwan, Moon, Pal-Yong and Perkins, Dwight H. (1980) *Rural Development. Studies in the Modernization of the Republic of Korea: 1945–1975*, Cambridge, MA: Harvard University Press.

Bank of Korea (1972) *Annual Report 1972*.

—— (1982) *Annual Report 1982*.

—— (1993) *Annual Report 1993*.

—— (1995) *Annual Report 1995*.

—— (1996) *Banking Supervision in Korea*.

—— (several issues) *Economic Statistics Yearbook*.

—— (several issues) *Monthly Statistical Bulletin*.

—— (several issues) *Monthly Economic Bulletin*.

—— (several issues) *National Income in Korea*.

Baran, Paul (1957) *The Political Economy of Growth*, Harmondsworth: Penguin.

—— (1982) 'A morphology of backwardness', in Hamza Alavi and Teodor Shanin (eds) *Introduction to the Sociology of 'Developing Societies'*, London: Macmillan.

Bates, Robert H. (1981) *Markets and States in Tropical Africa*, Berkeley: University of California Press.

Bernard, Mitchell and Ravenhill, John (1995) 'Beyond product cycle and flying geese: regionalization, hierarchy, and the industrialization of East Asia', *World Politics* 47, January: 171–209.

Bloomfield, Arthur I. and Jensen, John P. (1951) *Banking Reform in South Korea*, New York: Federal Reserve Bank of New York.

Bognanno, Mario F. (1988) *Korea's Industrial Relations at the Turning Point*, Working Paper 8816, Seoul: KDI.

Bond, Douglas G. (1988) 'Anti-Americanism and US–Korean relations: an assessment of Korean students' views', *Asian Perspective* 12, 1: 159–90.

Bullard, Nicola, Bello, Walden, and Malhorta, Kamal (1998) 'Taming the tigers: the IMF and the Asian crisis', in K.S. Jomo (ed.).

Business Korea (1984) 'Big business concentration put under a new critical light', July: 51–6.

—— (1985) 'In search of the right stuff', March: 15–19.

—— (1986a) 'A "quick-fix" solution', June: 15–18.

—— (1986b) 'Corporate mergers raise questions', July: 18–20.

—— (1991) *Business Korea Yearbook 1990–91*, Seoul: Business Korea.

—— (1992) 'Focus on workers' morale (Seventh Five-Year Plan)', January: 20–3.

—— (1993) 'Too weak to survive?', February: 24–8.

Cardoso, Fernando (1973) 'Associated-dependent development: theoretical and practical implications', in *Authoritarian Brazil: Origins, Policies and Future*, New Haven: Yale University Press.

—— and Faletto, Enzo (1979) *Dependency and Development in Latin America*, Berkeley: University of California Press.

Catholic Institute for International Relations (1988) *Disposable People: Forced Evictions in South Korea*, London: Catholic Institute for International Relations.

Chae, Chang-Kyun (1999) 'When will recovery begin indeed?', *VIP Economic Report* 3, Hyundai Research Institute: 4–5.

Chang, Dal-Joong (1985) *Economic Control and Authoritarianism*, Seoul: Sogang University Press.

Chang, Ha-Joon (1994) *The Political Economy of Industrial Policy*, London: Macmillan.

——, Park, Hong-Jae, and Yoo, Chul-Gyue (1998) 'Interpreting the Korean crisis: financial liberalisation, industrial policy and corporate governance', *Cambridge Journal of Economics* 22, 6: 735–46.

Chang, Paek-San (1985) 'The phoenix of 1984: a vibrant democratic mass movement erupts in South Korea', *AMPO: Japan–Asia Quarterly Review* 17, 1: 2–25.

Cheng, Tun-Jen and Schive, Chi (1997) 'What has democratization done to Taiwan's economy?', *Chinese Political Science Review*, June: 1–24.

Cho, Hyoung (1986) 'Labour force participation of women in Korea', in Sei-Wha Chung (ed.) *Challenges for Women: Women's Studies in Korea*, Seoul: Korean Women's Institute Series–Ewha Woman's University Press.

Cho, Lee-Jay and Kim, Yoon-Hyung (eds) (1991) *Economic Development in the Republic of Korea: A Policy Perspective*, Hawaii: University of Hawaii Press.

—— (1994) *Korea's Political Economy: An Institutional Perspective*, Boulder, CO: Westview Press.

Cho, Yoon-Je (1998) 'Asian financial crisis and choices for the Korean economy', *Sasang*, Winter: 38–64 (in Korean).

Choe, Boum-Chong (1975) 'An economic study of the Masan Free Trade Zone', in Wontack Hong and Anne O. Krueger (eds) *Trade and Development in Korea*, Seoul: KDI.

Choe, Yong-Ki, Kim, Dae-Hwan and Uh, Su-Bong (1995) *Changing Social and Economic Climate and the Labour Movement*, Seoul: Hanguk Nochong Chungang Yongu Sa (in Korean).

Choi, Byung-Sun (1989) 'The changing conception of industrial policymaking in Korea', *The Korean Journal of Policy Studies* 4, 17–43.

Choi, Jang-Jip (1987) 'The strong state and weak labour relations in South Korea: the historical determinants and historical structure', in Kyong-Dong Kim (ed.).

—— (1989) *Labour and the Authoritarian State: Labour Unions in South Korean Manufacturing Industries 1961–80*, Seoul: Korea University Press.

Choi, Jong-Won (1993) *Implementation Biases of the Anti-Trust System in Korea: Causes and Consequences*, Working Paper 9306, Seoul: KDI.

Choi, Kwang and Kwack, Tae-Won (1990) 'Tax policy and resource allocation in Korea', in J.K. Kwon (ed.).

Choi, Kyung-Soo (1995) *Labour Policies in Korea*, Seoul: Korea Labour Institute, November.

—— (1997) 'Rapid change in the employment system: how to overcome the "unemployment crisis"', *Shin Dong-Ah*, February: 172–7 (in Korean).

Choo, Hak-Chung (1980) 'Economic growth and income distribution', in Chong-Kee Park (ed.) (1980a).

—— (1985) *Estimation of Size Distribution of Income and its Sources of Change in Korea: 1982*, Working Paper 8515, Seoul: KDI.

Chung, Dae-Hwa (1998) 'A draft analysis of the result of the 1997 presidential election', *Labour Society Bulletin* 18, January: 32–9 (in Korean).

Chung, Eui-Yong (1996) 'Korea's economic development and Korea–US trade relations: a Korean perspective', *Korea's Economy in 1996*, Washington, DC: Korea Economic Institute of America.

Clifford, Mark (1994) *Troubled Tiger: Businessmen, Bureaucrats and Generals in South Korea*, Armonk: M.E. Sharpe.

Cole, David C. (1980) 'Foreign assistance and development', in David C. Cole *et al.*

——, Lim, Youngil and Kuznets, Paul W. (1980) *The Korean Economy: Issues of Development*, Berkeley: University of California Press.

—— and Lyman, Princeton N. (1971) *Korean Development: The Interplay of Politics and Economics*, Cambridge, MA: Harvard University Press.

—— and Park, Yung-Chul (1983) *Financial Developments in Korea, 1945–1978. Studies in the Modernization in the Republic of Korea: 1945–75*, Cambridge, MA: Harvard University Press.

Colclough, Christopher and Manor, James (eds) (1991) *States or Markets? Neo-Liberalism and the Development Policy Debate*, Oxford: Oxford University Press.

Collier, David (ed.) (1979) *The New Authoritarianism in Latin America*, Princeton, NJ: Princeton University Press.

Committee for Justice and Peace of South Korea–National Organization of Catholic Priests to Realize Social Justice (1976) 'A fact-finding survey on the Masan Free Export Zone', *AMPO: Japan–Asia Quarterly Review* 8, 2: 58–69.

Cotton, James S. (1989) 'From authoritarianism to democracy in South Korea', *Political Studies* 37, 3: 244–59.

—— (1990) Review of Amsden (1989), *Pacific Review* (typescript).

—— (1991) 'Understanding the state in South Korea: bureaucratic authoritarian or state autonomy theory?', *Comparative Political Studies* 24 (typescript).

—— and van Leest, Kyung-Ha (1992) 'Korea: dilemmas of the "Golf Republic"', *Pacific Review* 5, 4: 360–9.

Cumings, Bruce (1981) *The Origins of the Korean War: Liberation and the Emergence of Separate Regimes 1945–47*, Princeton, NJ: Princeton University Press.

—— (1984) 'Origins and development of the Northeast-Asian political economy: industrial sectors, product cycles, and political consequences', *International Organization* 38, 1: 1–40.

—— (1989) 'The abortive abertura: South Korea in light of Latin American experience', *New Left Review* 173: 5–33.

—— (1998) 'The Korean crisis and the end of "late" development', *New Left Review* 231: 43–72.

Democratic Republican Party (1972) *DRP: Today and Tomorrow*, Seoul: DRP.

Deyo, Frederic C. (1987) 'State and labor: modes of political exclusion in East Asian development', in Deyo (ed.).

—— (ed.) (1987) *The Political Economy of the New Asian Industrialism*, Ithaca, NY: Cornell University Press.

—— (1989) *Beneath the Miracle: Labour Subordination in the New Asian Industrialism*, Berkeley: University of California Press.

Dhalla, Ismail and Khatkhate, Deena (1995) *Regulated Deregulation of the Financial System in Korea*, Discussion Paper 292, Washington, DC: World Bank.

Diaz-Alejandro, Carlos (1985) 'Good-bye financial repression, hello financial crash', *Journal of Development Economics* 19: 1–24.

Dong, S.C. (1984) 'Incentives and restraints: government regulation of direct investment between Korea and the US', in Moskovitz (ed.).

Dong, Won-Mo (1988) 'Student activism and the presidential politics of 1987 in South Korea', in Il-Pyong Kim and Young-Whan Kihl (eds).

Dore, Ronald (1998) 'Asian crisis and the future of the Japanese model', *Cambridge Journal of Economics* 22, 6: 773–87.

Drucker, Peter (1986) 'The changed world economy', *Foreign Affairs* 64, Spring: 768–91.

Economic Planning Board (1973) *Heavy and Chemical Industry Plan* (in Korean).

—— (1979) *Comprehensive Measures for Economic Stabilization* (in Korean).

—— (1982) *The Twenty Year History of the Economic Planning Board* (in Korean).

—— (1984) *White Paper on Fair Trade* (in Korean).

—— (1992) *Economic White Paper 1992* (in Korean).

EPB–NSO (several issues) *Korean Economic Indicators*.

—— (several issues) *Korea Statistical Yearbook*.

—— (several issues) *Major Statistics of Korean Economy*.

—— (several issues) *Social Indicators in Korea*.

Edwards, Sebastian (1996) *Crisis and Reform in Latin America: From Despair to Hope*, Oxford: World Bank–Oxford University Press.

Enos, John L. and Park, Woo-Hee (1988) *The Adoption and Diffusion of Imported Technology: The Case of Korea*, London: Croom Helm.

Evans, Peter B. (1979) *Dependent Development: The Alliance of Multinational, State and Local Capital in Brazil*, Princeton, NJ: Princeton University Press.

—— (1994) *Embedded Autonomy: States and Industrial Transformation*, Princeton, NJ: Princeton University Press.

—— (1997) 'The eclipse of the state? Reflections on stateness in an era of globalization', *World Politics* 50, October: 62–87.

——, Rueschemeyer, Dietrich and Skocpol, Theda (eds) (1985) *Bringing the State Back In*, New York: Cambridge University Press.

Fair Trade Commission (1984) *White Paper on Fair Trade* (in Korean).

—— (1996) *Fair Trade Laws and Regulations*.

—— (March 1996) *A Guide to the Competition Policy of Korea*.

Fajnzylber, Fernando (1990) 'The United States and Japan as models of industrialization', in Gereffi and Wyman (eds).

Far Eastern Economic Review (1982) 'Search for a scapegoat', 11 June: 13–14.

—— (1985a) 'Time runs out for the conglomerates', 12 December: 70–2.

—— (1985b) 'Scaling down promises a big boost to growth', 12 December: 76–9.

—— (1986) 'Boom masks a near bust', 21 August: 61–5.

—— (1988) 'Appearances are deceptive', 11 February: 57–62.

—— (1993a) 'Cleaning up the act', 27 May: 40–4.

—— (1993b) 'Whirlwind honeymoon', 24 June: 18–19.

—— (1994) 'Honeymoon's end', 10 November: 14–15.

Federation of Korean Industries (1992.10) *New Government Policy Suggestions*, Seoul: FKI (in Korean).

Federation of Korean Trade Unions (1979) *History of the Korean Labour Movement*, Seoul: FKTU (in Korean).

Fishlow, Albert (1990) 'The Latin American state', *Journal of Economic Perspectives* 4, 3: 61–74.

Foster-Carter, Aidan (1987) 'Standing up: the two Korean states and the dependency debate – a bipartisan approach', in Kyong-Dong Kim (ed.) *Dependency Issues in Korean Development*, Seoul: Seoul National University Press.

Foxley, Alejandro (1987) 'Latin American experiments in neo-conservative economics', in J.L. Dietz and J.H. Street (eds) *Latin America's Economic Development*, Boulder, CO: Lynne Rienner.

Frank, André Gunder (1967) *Capitalism and Underdevelopment in Latin America*, New York: Monthly Review Press.

Fransman, Martin (1984) 'Explaining the success of the Asian NICs: incentives and technology', *IDS Bulletin* 15, 2: 50–6.

Fruin, W. Mark (1992) *The Japanese Enterprise System: Competitive Strategies and Cooperative Structures*, Oxford: Oxford University Press.

Gereffi, Gary (1990) 'Big business and the state', *Asian Perspective* 14, 1: 5–29.

—— and Wyman, Donald L. (eds) (1990) *Manufacturing Miracles: Paths of Industrialization in Latin America and East Asia*, Princeton, NJ: Princeton University Press.

Gerschenkron, Alexander (1962) *Economic Backwardness in Historical Perspective*, New York: Bellknap Press.

Gibson, Edward L. (1997) 'The populist road to market reform: policy and electoral coalitions in Mexico and Argentina', *World Politics* 49, 3, April: 339–70.

Gills, Barry K. (1996) 'Economic liberalisation and reform in South Korea in the 1990s: a "coming of age" or a case of "graduation blues"?', *Third World Quarterly* 17, 4: 667–88.

Gold, Thomas B. (1986) *State and Society in the Taiwan Economic Miracle*, Armonk: M.E. Sharpe.

Government of the Republic of Korea (1962) *Summary of the First Five-Year Economic Development Plan 1962–1966*.

—— (1967) *Summary of the Second Five-Year Economic Development Plan 1967–1971*.

—— (1981) *Summary Draft of the Fifth Five-Year Economic and Social Development Plan 1982–1986*.

—— (1986) *Summary Draft of the Sixth Five-Year Economic and Social Development Plan 1987–1991*.

—— (1992) *The Seventh Five-Year Economic and Social Development Plan 1992–1996.*

—— (1993) *The Five-Year New Economy Plan 1993–1997* (in Korean).

Graham, Edward M. (1999) 'Restructuring the *chaebol* in Korea', in *Korea's Economy 1999*, Washington, DC: Korea Economic Institute of America–Korea Institute of International Economic Policy.

Griffin, Keith and Gurley, John (1985) '"Radical Analyses of Imperialism, The Third World, and the Transition To Socialism": a survey article', *Journal of Economic Literature* 23, September: 1089–143.

Gurley, John G. (1965) *The Financial Structure of Korea*, Seoul: Bank of Korea.

Haggard, Stephan (1990) *Pathways from the Periphery*, Ithaca, NY: Cornell University Press.

—— and Moon, Chung-In (1983) 'The South Korean state in the international economy: liberal, dependent, or mercantile?', in John G. Ruggie (ed.) *The Antinomies of Interdependence*, New York: Columbia University Press.

—— and Kaufman, Robert R. (1992) *The Politics of Economic Adjustment: International Constraints, Distributive Conflicts, and the State*, Princeton, NJ: Princeton University Press.

—— and Webb, Steven B. (eds) (1994) *Voting for Reform*, Washington, DC: World Bank–Oxford University Press.

——, Cooper, Richard N., Collins, Susan, Kim, Chongsoo and Ro, Sung-Tae (1994) *Macro-economic Policy and Adjustment in Korea, 1970–1990*, Cambridge, MA: Harvard University Press.

——, Kang, David and Moon Chung-In (1997) 'Japanese colonialism and Korean development: a critique', *World Development* 25, 6: 867–81.

Hahm, Joon-Ho (1998) *Financial System Restructuring in Korea: The Crisis and its Resolution*, Working Paper 9802, Seoul: KDI.

Hamilton, Clive (1986) *Capitalist Industrialization in South Korea*, Boulder, CO: Westview Press.

Han, Sang-Jin (1987) 'Bureaucratic-authoritarianism and economic development in Korea during the Yushin Period: a reexamination of O'Donnell's theory', in Kyong-Dong Kim (ed.).

—— (1988) 'Which is the major agent of social change today: the *Minjung* or the middle strata?', *Shin Dong-Ah* 350: 168–81 (in Korean).

—— (1993) 'The social and political character of the Korean middle classes', in Hsiao (ed.).

Han, Sung-Joo (1974) *The Failure of Democracy in South Korea*, Berkeley: University of California Press.

—— (1990) 'South Korea: politics in transition', in Larry Diamond, Juan J. Linz and Seymour Martin Lipset (eds) *Politics in Developing Countries: Comparing Experiences with Democracy*, Boulder, CO: Lynne Rienner.

Harris, John, Hunter, Janet and Lewis, Colin M. (eds) (1997) *The New Institutional Economics and Third World Development*, London: Routledge.

Hasan, Parvez (1976) *Korea: Problems and Issues in a Rapidly Growing Economy. A World Bank Country Economic Report*, Baltimore: Johns Hopkins University Press.

—— and Rao, D.C. (co-ordinating authors) (1979) *Korea: Policy Issues for Long-Term Development. The Report of a Mission Sent to the Republic of Korea by the World Bank*, Baltimore: Johns Hopkins University Press.

Hattori, Tamio (1989) 'Japanese *zaibatsu* and Korean *chaebol*', in Kae H. Chung and Hak-Chong Lee (eds) *Korean Managerial Dynamics*, New York: Praeger.

Hayek, F.A. (1993) *The Road to Serfdom*, London: Routledge (first published 1944).

Henderson, Gregory (1968) *Korea: The Politics of the Vortex*, Cambridge, MA: Harvard University Press.

Hirschman, Albert O. (1979) 'The turn to authoritarianism in Latin America and the search for its economic determinants', in David Collier (ed.).

Hoekman, Bernard and Kostecki, Michel (1995) *The Political Economy of the World Trading System: From GATT to WTO*, Oxford: Oxford University Press.

Hong, Seong-Min (1999) 'Korea's dwindling middle class', *VIP Economic Report* 5, Hyundai Research Institute: 13–14.

Hong, Wontack (1979) *Trade, Distortions and Employment Growth in Korea*, Seoul: KDI Press.

—— (1981) 'Trade, growth and income distribution: the Korean case', in Wontack Hong and Lawrence B. Krause (eds).

—— (1988) *Market Distortions and Trade Patterns of Korea 1960–85*, Working Paper 8807, Seoul: KDI.

—— and Krueger, Anne O. (eds) (1975) *Trade and Development in Korea*, Seoul: KDI Press.

—— and Krause, Lawrence B. (eds) (1981) *Trade and Growth of the Advanced Developing Countries in the Pacific Basin*, Seoul: KDI Press.

—— and Park, Yung-Chul (1986) 'The financing of export-oriented growth in Korea', in Tan and Kapur (eds).

Hong, Yoo-Soo (1996) 'International strategic alliance for promotion of global competitiveness', in Kap-Young Jeong and Mahn-Soon Kwack (eds) (1996) *Industrial Strategy for Global Competitiveness of Korean Industries*, Seoul: KERI.

Hsiao, Hsin-Huang Michael (ed.) (1993) *Discovery of the Middle Classes in East Asia*, Taipei: Institute of Ethnology, Academia Sinica.

Hughes, Helen (ed.) (1988) *Achieving Industrialization in East Asia*, Cambridge: Cambridge University Press.

Huh, Young (1999) 'Not much time left for DJ's reforms', *Shin Dong-Ah*, January: 90–5 (in Korean).

Hutton, Will (1995) *The State We're In*, London: Merlin.

Im, Hyug-Baeg (1987) 'The rise of bureaucratic authoritarianism in South Korea', *World Politics* 29, 2: 237–57.

International Labour Organization (1998) *Yearbook of Labour Statistics*, Geneva: ILO.

International Monetary Fund (17 January 1999) *The IMF's Response to the Asian Crisis* (www.imf.org).

Interview (12 June 1996) KDI Fellow.

—— (14 June 1996) KERI Fellow.

—— (25 June 1996) KEF.

—— (1 July 1996) FKTU Research Centre.

—— (5 July 1996) FTC Divisional Director.

—— (27 June 1996) Presidential Commission for Industrial Relations, Academic Representative.

—— (18 July 1996) MOTIE Divisional Director.

Johnson, Chalmers (1981) *MITI and the Japanese Miracle*, Stanford, CA: Stanford University Press.

—— (1987) 'Political institutions and economic performance: the government–business relationship in Japan, South Korea, and Taiwan', in F.C. Deyo (ed.) (1987b).

—— (1988) 'Studies of Japanese political economy: a crisis in theory', *Japan Foundation Newsletter*, 16, 3: 1–11.

—— (1989) 'South Korean democratization: the role of economic development', *Pacific Review* 2, 1: 1–10.

—— (1994) 'What is the best system of national economic management for Korea?', in Lee-Jay Cho and Yoon-Hyung Kim (eds).

Jomo, K.S. (ed.) (1998) *Tigers in Trouble: Financial Governance, Liberalisation and Crises in East Asia*, London: Zed Books.

Jones, Leroy P. (1981) 'Jaebul and the concentration of economic power in Korean development: issues, evidence and alternatives', in Sakong (ed.).

—— and Sakong, Il (1980) *Government, Business and Entrepreneurship in Economic Development: The Korean Case. Studies in the Modernization of the Republic of Korea: 1945–1975*, Cambridge, MA: Harvard University Press.

Jung, Hee-Nam (1994) 'Land policies in South Korea: a political economy approach', in Koppel and Kim (eds).

Jung Ku-Hyun (1996) 'The ownership and control structure of Korean conglomerates', *Sasang*, Spring: 10–29 (in Korean).

Jwa, Sung-Hee (1992) *Korea's Interest Rate and Capital Controls Deregulation: Implications for Monetary Policy and Financial Structure*, Working Paper 9218, Seoul: KDI.

—— and Kim, In-Gyu (1997) *Globalization and Domestic Adjustments in Korea*, Working Paper 9702, Seoul: KDI.

Kang, Chul-Kyu *et al.* (1991) *The Chaebol*, Seoul: Beebong Publishing Company (in Korean).

Kang, Sun-Jae (1985) 'The Park regime and regional antipathy', *Shin Dong-Ah* 309: 230–45 (in Korean).

Kaufman, Robert R. (1986) 'Liberalization and democratization in South America: perspectives from the 1970s', in Guillermo O'Donnell *et al.* (eds) *Transitions from Authoritarian Rule: Comparative Perspectives*.

—— (1991) 'Stabilization and adjustment in Argentina, Brazil and Mexico', in Nelson (ed.).

Khan, Mushtaq (1996) 'A typology of corrupt transactions in developing countries', *IDS Bulletin* 26, 4: 12–21.

Kihl, Young-Whan (1985) *Politics and Policies in Divided Korea*, Boulder, CO: Westview Press.

—— (1988) 'Party politics on the eve of a gathering storm: the constitutional revision politics of 1986', in Il-Pyong Kim and Young-Whan Kihl (eds).

Kim, Ae-Sil (1990) 'Economic status and labour conditions: sexist practices and habits continue', *Koreana* 4, 2: 24–33.

Kim, Bun-Woong and Rho, Wha-Joon (eds) (1982) *Korean Public Bureaucracy*, Seoul: Kyobo Publishing, Inc.

Kim, C.I. Eugene (1978) 'Emergency, development, and human rights: South Korea', *Asian Survey* 18, 4: 363–78.

Kim, Chang-Soo (1977) 'Marginalization, development and the Korean workers' movement', *AMPO: Japan–Asia Quarterly Review* 9, 3: 20–39.

—— (1980) 'A new phase of the struggle for democratization in South Korea', *AMPO: Japan–Asia Quarterly Review* 12, 2: 2–29.

Kim, Chi-Ha (1974) *Cry of the People and Other Poems*, Hayama: Autumn Press.

Kim, Chong-Soo (1994) 'Wage policy and labour market development' in Haggard *et al.* (ed.).

Kim, Choong-Soon (1992) *The Culture of Korean Industry: An Ethnography of Poongsan Corporation*, Tucson: University of Arizona Press.

Kim, Chuk-Kyo (ed.) (1977) *Industrial and Social Development Issues*, Seoul: KDI Press.

Kim, Chung-Sik (1983) 'The people who live at the bottom of the society', *AMPO: Japan–Asia Quarterly Review* 15, 1: 38–43.

Kim, Dae-Hwan (1985) 'Rapid economic growth and national economic integration in Korea 1963–78', unpublished DPhil thesis, University of Oxford.

—— (1987) 'Changes of international circumstance and the development of heavy and chemical industries', in Hyun-Chae Park *et al.* (eds) *Economics of Korea*, Seoul: Kkachi (in Korean).

—— (1987) 'Inequality: the adverse effect of "growth policy"', *Shin Dong-Ah* 336: 520–32 (in Korean).

—— (1996) 'Industrialization and the course of democratization', in Dae-Hwan Kim *et al.*, *Half a Century of Liberation. Korean Society: Reflections and Prospects*, Seoul: Hyunam Sa (in Korean).

Kim, Dae-Jung (1985) *Mass Participatory Democracy: A Democratic Alternative for Korea*, Cambridge, MA: Harvard University–University Press of America.

—— (1996) *Mass Participatory Economy: Korea's Road to World Economic Power*, (revised and updated), Lanham: University Press of America.

—— (1998) 'Let us open a new era: overcoming national crisis and taking a new leap forward', Inaugural Address by President Kim Dae-Jung (25 February 1998), *VIP Economic Report* 3, Hyundai Research Institute: 23–8.

Kim, Dong-Kun (1991) 'Tax reform to combat land speculation in Korea', *The Korean Journal of Policy Studies* 6: 15–26.

Kim, E. Han (1990) 'Financing Korean corporations: evidence and theory', in J.K. Kwon (ed.).

Kim, Hee-Song and Kim, Chan-Jin (1998) 'Five banks finally closed down in Korea', *VIP Economic Report* 7, Hyundai Research Institute: 16–17.

Kim, Heong-Jong (1996) 'Saving the Korean economy: severing the chains of the "three highs" structure of high interest rates, high wages, high land prices', *Shin Dong-Ah*, August: 394–401 (in Korean).

Kim, Hwang-Joe (1994) *Industrial Relations in Korea*, Seoul: Korea Labour Institute, September.

Kim, Il-Joong (1995) 'The results and future course of Korea's deregulation policy', in Il-Joong Kim (ed.).

—— (ed.) (1995) *The Role of the Three Branches of Government for the Rule of Law and the Free Market in Korea*, Seoul: KERI.

Kim, Il-Pyong and Kihl, Young-Whan (eds) (1988) *Political Change in South Korea*, New York: Paragon House Publishers.

Kim, Jin-Hyun (1988) 'Vortex of misunderstanding: changing Korean perceptions', in Robert Scalapino and Hongkoo Lee (eds) *Korea–US Relations: The Politics of Trade and Security*, Berkeley: University of California Press.

Kim, Jong-Gie, Kwack, Tae-Won, Kim, Ui-Joon and Kim, Yang-Seon (1993) *Critical Issues and Poverty Measures to Address Urban Poverty: Korean Case*, Working Paper 9305, Seoul: KDI.

Kim, Joungwon A. (1975) *Divided Korea: The Politics of Development 1945–72*, Cambridge, MA: Harvard University Press.

Kim, K.W. (1965) 'Ideology and political development in South Korea', *Pacific Affairs* 38: 164–76.

Kim, Kwang-Suk and Roemer, Michael (1979) *Growth and Structural Change. Studies in the Modernization of the Republic of Korea: 1945–1975*, Cambridge, MA: Harvard University Press.

Kim, Kyong-Dong (1976) 'Political factors in the formation of the entrepreneurial elite in South Korea', *Asian Survey* 16, 5: 465–77.

—— (ed.) (1987) *Dependency Issues in Korean Development* Seoul: Seoul National University Press.

—— (1993) 'Studies on the middle classes in Korea: some theoretical and methodological considerations', in Hsiao (ed.).

Kim, Sang-Kyun (1998) 'Problems in Kim Dae-Jung government's unemployment counter-measures', *Shin Dong-Ah*, May: 220–32 (in Korean).

Kim, Seung-Kyung (1997) *Class Struggle or Family Struggle? The Lives of Women Factory Workers in South Korea*, New York: Cambridge University Press.

Kim, Sung-Chun (1986) 'Where is the anti-Americanism coming from?', *Shin Dong-Ah* 322: 408–23 (in Korean).

Koh, B.C. (1997) 'South Korea in 1996: internal strains and external challenges', *Asian Survey* 37, 1: 1–9.

Kohli, Atul (1994) 'Where do high growth political economies come from? The Japanese lineage of Korea's "developmental state"', *World Development* 22, 9: 1269–93.

—— (1997) 'Japanese colonialism and Korean development: a reply', *World Development* 25, 6: 883–8.

Kong, Chung-Ja (1989) 'A study of the marriage networks among big businessmen's families in Korea', unpublished PhD thesis, Ewha Women's University (in Korean).

Kong, Tat Yan (1995) 'From relative autonomy to consensual development: the case of South Korea', *Political Studies* 43, 4: 630–44.

Koo, Hagen (1984) 'The political-economy of income distribution in South Korea: the impact of the state's industrialization policies', *World Development* 12, 10: 1029–37.

—— (1987) 'Dependency issue, class inequality, and social conflict in Korean development' in Kyong-Dong Kim (ed.) *Dependency Issues in Korean Development*, Seoul: Seoul National University Press.

—— and Hong, Doo-Seung (1980) 'Class and income inequality in Korea', *American Sociological Review* 45: 610–26.

Koppel, Bruce and Kim, Dai-Young (eds) (1994) *Land Policy Problems in East Asia: Toward New Choices*, Seoul: East–West Centre and Korea Research Institute for Human Settlements.

Korea Herald (at www.koreaherald.co.kr) (27 November 1996) 'Government softens tough stance on local business conglomerates'.

—— (20 December 1996a) '10 trillion won earmarked for infrastructure'.

—— (20 December 1996b) 'Supplementary steps needed for hostile takeover bids'.

—— (21 December 1996) 'New Reform Bill could bring significant changes: draft tries to keep labour–management situation balanced, unbiased'.

—— (28 December 1996) 'Strikes spread nationwide: FKTU urges 1.2 million members to extend walkouts'.

—— (7 January 1997) 'Labour crisis heightens: more than 200,000 enter second strike'.

—— (9 January 1997) 'Financial firms bracing for government-initiated M&As'.

—— (14 January 1997) 'One million workers to join strikes today. Tomorrow: subway, taxi, bus, bank unions threatening 2-day walkouts'.

—— (30 April 1997) 'Overall Korean investments in India expected to total $3 billion by 2000'.

—— (1 May 1997) '1992 Campaign Fund re-emerging as issue of contention'.

—— (2 March 1998) 'Chaebol muscle into sectors exclusive to smaller companies'.

—— (4 March 1998) 'Concern grows as austerity campaign loses momentum'.

—— (5 March 1998) 'Daewoo exploits close ties with new government'.

—— (5 May 1998) 'Government, labour differ on cause of nation's falling credibility'.

—— (11 May 1998) 'Kim ready to accept layoffs as cost of business reform'.

—— (19 May 1998) 'Government, labour differ on cause of nation's falling credibility'.

—— (28 May 1998) 'Workers start strikes against layoffs'.

—— (13 August 1998) 'Editorial: Daewoo and Hyundai Motors'.

—— (29 August 1998) 'Government vows not to intervene in labour feuds'.

—— (14 October 1998) 'Chaebol reforms delayed by lack of incentives, says French banker'.

—— (4 November 1998) 'News analysis: banks turn blind eye to smaller cash-strapped companies'.

—— (8 December 1998) 'Government to allow unemployed workers to join trade unions in 2000'.

—— (30 December 1998) 'Assembly panel approves bill allowing teachers' union'.

—— (21 January 1999) 'Fresh obstacles cloud "big deal" talks'.

—— (26 January 1999) 'Job security emerges as biggest obstacle to "big deals"'.

—— (1 February 1999) 'Government close to finalizing chip merger'.

—— (29 March 1999) 'Workers intensify call for job security: KCTU, FKTU protest against corporate restructuring, layoffs'.

—— (30 March 1999) 'Hyundai under pressure to make more concessions in semi-conductor talks'.

—— (8 April 1999) 'Editorial: the invincible chaebol'.

—— (22 April 1999) 'Militant labour umbrella group urges government to come to negotiating table'.

—— (27 April 1999) 'Foreign economists cast doubt on effects of "big deal" business swaps'.

—— (11 May 1999) 'Hyundai chairman under fire for anti-reform remarks'.

—— (4 June 1999) 'Big 5 reform efforts questioned as total debt increased last year'.

—— (16 June 1999) 'Straddling the income gap'.

—— (30 June 1999) 'Business organizations revolting against government–labour deals'.

—— (5 July 1999) 'Samsung case calls morality of chaebol back into question'.

—— (8 July 1999) 'Kim Y.S. says closure of Samsung Motors part of "political vendetta"'.

—— (14 July 1999) 'Chaebol can easily get around government 200 per cent debt-equity policy'.

—— (15 July 1999) 'Corporate governance reform faces stiff opposition'.

—— (21 July 1999) 'Daewoo's success to depend on the market'.

—— (22 July 1999) 'Daewoo crisis turns up heat on chaebol'.

Korea Housing Bank (several issues) *Housing Finance*.

Korea Institute for International Economic Policy (1993) *The Beginning of Korea's New Economy: The Kim Administration's 100-Day Plan*, Seoul: KIEP, May.

Korea Labour Institute (1996) *Labour Statistics*.

Korea Labour and Society Institute (1995) *Labour Situation in Korea*, Seoul: KLSI, February.

Korea Stock Exchange (several issues) *Stock*.

Korean Employers Federation (1996a) *Industrial Relations and the Labour Market in Korea 1996*, Seoul: KEF.

—— (1996b) *KEF Quarterly Review* 17, 61.

Krause, Lawrence B. and Park, Fun-Koo (eds) (1993) *Social Issues in Korea: Korean and American Perspectives*, Seoul: KDI Press.

Kregel, J.A. (1998) 'East Asia is not Mexico: the difference between balance of payments crises and debt inflation', in K.S. Jomo (ed.).

Krueger, Anne O. (1974) 'The political economy of the rent-seeking society', *American Economic Review* 64, 3: 291–303.

—— (1979) *The Development Role of the Foreign Sector and Aid. Studies in the Modernization of the Republic of Korea: 1945–1975*, Cambridge, MA: Harvard University Press.

—— (1990) 'Government failure in economic development', *Journal of Economic Perspectives* 4, 3: 9–23.

Krugman, Paul (1998a) *What Happened to Asia?* (http://web.mit.edu/krugman/www/DISINTER.html)

—— (1998b) *Currency Crises* (http://web.mit.edu/krugman/www/crises.html)

—— (1994) 'The Myth of Asia's Miracle', *Foreign Affairs* 73, 6: 62–78.

Kuk, Minho (1988) 'The governmental role in the making of the chaebol in the industrial development of South Korea', *Asian Perspective* 12, 1: 107–33.

Kuznets, Paul W. (1977) *Economic Structure and Growth of the Republic of Korea*, New Haven: Yale University Press.

Kwon, Hyuck-Chang (1992) 'A study on the long term investment strategies of social overhead capital', *The Korean Journal of Policy Studies* 7: 125–37.

Kwon, Jene K. (ed.) (1990) *Korean Economic Development*, New York: Greenwood Press.

Kwon, Soonwon (1988) *Social Insurance in Korea*, Working Paper 8808, Seoul: KDI.

—— (1990) *Korea: Income and Wealth Distribution and Government Initiatives to Reduce Disparities*, Working Paper 9008, Seoul: KDI.

Lal, Deepak (1983) *The Poverty of Development Economics*, London: Institute of Economic Affairs.

Lall, Sanjaya (1990) *Building Industrial Competitiveness in Developing Countries*, Paris: OECD.

Lee, Chong-Sik (1980) 'South Korea 1979: confrontation, assassination and transition', *Asian Survey* 20, 1: 63–76.

—— (1981) 'South Korea in 1980: the emergence of a new authoritarian order', *Asian Survey* 21, 1: 125–43.

—— and Sohn, Hyuk-Sang (1994) 'South Korea in 1993: the year of the great reform', *Asian Survey* 34, 1: 1–9.

Lee, Chung H. (1979) 'United States and Japanese direct investment in Korea: a comparative study', *Journal of Economic Development* 4, 2.

—— (1992) 'The government, financial system, and large private enterprises in the economic development of South Korea', *World Development* 20, 2: 187–97.

—— and Ramstetter, Eric D. (1991) 'Direct investment and structural change in Korean manufacturing', in Eric D. Ramstetter (ed.) *Direct Foreign Investment in Asia's Developing Economies and Structural Change in the Asia-Pacific Region*, Boulder, CO: Westview.

Lee, Duk-Hoon, (1992) *The Korean Economy: Prospects and Financial Reforms*, Working Paper 9202, Seoul: KDI.

Lee, Eddy (ed.) (1981) *Export-Led Industrialization and Development*, Kuala Lumpur: International Labour Organization–Asian Employment Programme.

Lee, Hahn-Been (1982) *Korea: Time Change and Administration*, Honolulu: East–West Centre Press.

Lee, Jeong-Taik (1988) 'Dynamics of labour control and labour protest in the process of export-industrialization in South Korea', *Asian Perspective* 12, 1: 134–58.

Lee, Ju-Ho and Kim, Dae-Il (1997) *Labour Market Developments and Reforms in Korea*, Working Paper 9703, Seoul: KDI.

Lee, Keun and Lee, Chung H. (1992) 'Sustaining economic development in South Korea: lessons from Japan', *Pacific Review* 5, 1: 13–24.

Lee, Kye-Sik and Moon, Hyung-Pyo (1996) 'Competitive environment: introduction of market-type mechanisms in Korea', in Kye-Sik Lee and Il-Ho Yoo (eds) *Fiscal Reform in Korea and OECD Countries*, Seoul: KDI.

Lee, Kyu-Uck (1986) *The Concentration of Economic Power in Korea: Causes, Consequences and Policy*, Working Paper 8602, Seoul: KDI.

—— and Lee, Jae-Hyug (1990) *Industrial Group and the Concentration of Economic Power*, Seoul: KDI (in Korean).

Lee, Man-Woo (1990) *The Odyssey of Korean Democracy: Korean Politics 1987–1990*, New York: Praeger.

—— (1999) 'Is privatization of public enterprises satisfactory as it stands?, *Shin Dong-Ah*, February: 368–76 (in Korean).

Lee, Seung-Cheol (1995) 'The results and future course of anti-trust policy in Korea', in Il-Joong Kim (ed.).

Lee, Suk-Chae (1991) 'The heavy and chemical industries promotion plan (1973–9)', in Lee-Jay Cho and Yoon-Hyung Kim (eds).

Lee, Tae-Il (1994) 'Recent urban land reforms in Korea: goals and limitations', in Koppel and Kim (eds).

Lee, Tae-Yol (1999) 'Domestic consumption and household economies', *VIP Economic Report* 4, Hyundai Research Institute: 11–12.

Lee, Won-Young (1988) 'Direct foreign investment and transfer of technology in the Republic of Korea: a survey', in KDI, *Industrial Policies of Korea and the Republic of China: Papers and Discussions from the 1988 Joint KDI/CHIER Conference*, Seoul: KDI.

Lee, Yeon-Ho (1996) 'Political aspects of South Korean state autonomy: regulating the chaebol, 1980–93', *Pacific Review* 9, 2: 149–79.

Lee, Young-Ki (1992) *Korean Capital Market Development: Major Characteristics and Policy Implications*, Working Paper 9206, Seoul: KDI.

Leipziger, Danny M., Dollar, David, Shorrocks, Anthony F. and Song, Su-Yong (1992) *The Distribution of Income and Wealth in Korea*, Washington, DC: World Bank.

—— and Petri, Peter A. (1993) *Korean Industrial Policy: Legacies of the Past and Directions for the Future*, Discussion Paper 197, Washington, DC: World Bank.

Lenin, V.I. (1975 [1916]) *Imperialism: The Highest Stage of Capitalism*, Beijing: Foreign Language Publishing House.

Lim, Hyun-Chin (1984) *Dependent Development in the World System: The Case of South Korea*, Seoul: Seoul National University Press.

Lim, Yoon-Cheol (1995) 'Establishment of the Korean national R&D program in the 1980s and its development in the 1990s: its content and role in building the Korean system of innovation', in Science and Technology Policy Research Institute, *Review of Science and Technology Policy for Industrial Competitiveness in Korea*, Seoul: STEPI.

Lindauer, David L. (1984) *Labour Market Behaviour in the Republic of Korea*, Staff Working Paper 641, Washington, DC: World Bank.

——, Kim, Jong-Gie, Lee, Joung-Woo, Lim Hy-Sop, Son Jae-Young and Vogel, Ezra F. (eds) (1997) *The Strains of Economic Growth: Labour Unrest and Social Dissatisfaction in Korea*, Cambridge, MA: Harvard University Press.

—— and Vogel, Ezra (1997) 'Toward a social compact for Korean labour', in David Lindauer *et al.* (eds).

Lipset, Seymour Martin (1959) 'Some social requisites of democracy: economic development and political legitimacy', *American Political Science Review* 53: 69–105.

Luedde-Neurath, Richard (1984) 'State intervention and foreign direct investment in South Korea', *IDS Bulletin* 15, 2: 18–25.

McGinn, Noel F., Snodgrass, Donald R., Kim, Yung-Bong, Kim, Shin-Bok and Kim, Quee-Young (1980) *Education and Development in Korea. Studies in the Modernization of the Republic of Korea: 1945–1975*, Cambridge, MA: Harvard University Press.

Mabe, Yoichi (1984a) 'Korean conglomerates: their power and strategy–(1) Excessive concentration of economic power', *The Oriental Economist*, November: 24–30.

—— (1984b) 'Korean conglomerates: their power and strategy–(2) ROK–Japan–US friction in the offing', *The Oriental Economist*, December: 14–19.

Martins, Luciano (1986) 'The "liberalisation" of authoritarian rule in Brazil', in Guillermo O'Donnell *et al.* (eds) (1986).

Marx, Karl (1977 [1853]) *The Eighteenth Brumaire of Louis Bonaparte*, Moscow: Progress Publishers (first published 1853).

Mason, Edward S., Kim, Mahn-Je, Perkins, Dwight H., Kim, Kwang-Suk and Cole, David C. (1980) *The Economic and Social Modernizaton of the Republic of Korea: 1945–75*, Cambridge, MA: Harvard University Press.

Mathews, John A. (1998) 'Fashioning a new Korean model out of the crisis: the rebuilding of institutional capacities', *Cambridge Journal of Economics* 22, 6: 747–59.

Matsuzaki, Tadashi (1985) 'The development of South Korea's steel industry', *Journal of International Economic Study*, March: 73–9.

Michell, Tony (1981) 'What happens to economic growth when neo-classical policy replaces Keynesian? The case of South Korea', *IDS Bulletin* 12, 1: 60–7.

—— (1984) 'Administrative traditions and economic decision-making in South Korea', *IDS Bulletin* 15, 2: 32–7.

Migdal, Joel S. (1988) *Strong Societies and Weak States*, Princeton, NJ: Princeton University Press.

Mills, Edwin and Song, Byung-Nak (1979) *Korea's Urbanization and Urban Problems. Studies in the Modernization of the Republic of Korea: 1945–1975*, Cambridge, MA: Harvard University Press.

Min, Ju-Heong (1999) 'Unit labour cost trends in the IMF era', in *VIP Economic Report* 7, Seoul: Hyundai Research Institute: 16–17.

Ministry of Finance and Economy (at www.mofe.go.kr) (December 1996) press release: 'Foreign Direct Investment Liberalization Plan'.

—— (8 September 1997) 'Korea's economic reforms: implications for Korea–US relations in the new millennium – a presentation by Ki-Hwan Kim, Ambassador-at-Large for Economic Affairs at the American Enterprise Institute, Washington, DC'.

—— (11 September 1997) 'Recent economic developments and future cooperation – speech for the Foreign Bankers Group Meeting by Vice-Minister Man-Soo Kang'.

—— (October 1997) 'Resolution plan for Kia'.

—— (10 November 1997) 'Korean government's view on recent foreign press release'.

—— (21 November 1997) 'Statement by Deputy Prime Minister and Minister of Finance and Economy, Mr Chang-Yuel Lim'.

—— (3 December 1997) 'IMF programme for Korea'.

—— (16 December 1997) 'IMF programme implementation plan – meeting of the Emergency Economic Advisory Council'.

—— (19 December 1997) 'Results from 18 December meeting of the IMF Council'.

—— (24 December 1997) 'IBRD (World Bank) and the Republic of Korea conclude negotiations for loan agreement'.

—— (20 January 1998) 'Tripartite joint statement on fair burden-sharing as a means of overcoming the economic crisis: statement of the Tripartite Commission on Fair Burden-Sharing'.

—— (12 February 1998) 'Agreement for the restructuring of the top five chaebol'.

—— (18 February 1998) 'Letter of intent sent to the IMF (including a comprehensive review of implemented actions and plans for the IMF programme as of February 7 1998)'.

—— (19 February 1998) 'Government announces measures to implement policy recommendations of the IBRD'.

Ministry of Labour (1987) *Labour White Paper 1987* (in Korean).

—— (1989) *Labour White Paper 1989* (in Korean).

—— (1995) *Labour Laws of Korea*.

—— (1996) *President Kim Young Sam's Vision for New Industrial Relations*.

—— (1997) (at www.molab.go.kr) *New Labour Law*.

—— (several issues) *Yearbook of Labour Statistics*.

Ministry of Science and Technology (1996) *Science and Technology in Korea*.

Ministry of Trade, Industry and Energy (1995) *Annual Report on Small and Medium Industry 1995* (in Korean).

Mizala, Alejandra (1997) 'Two decades of economic policy in Chile', in Akio Hosono and Neantro Saavedra-Rivano (eds) *Development Strategies in East Asia and Latin America*, London: Macmillan.

Moon, Chung-In (1988) *The Korean Economy in Transition: Political Consequences of Neoconservative Reforms*, Working Paper in Asian-Pacific Studies 88–03, Durham, NC: Duke University.

Moon, Pal-Yong and Kang, Bong-Soon (1989) *Trade, Exchange Rate, and Agricultural Pricing Policies in the Republic of Korea*, Washington, DC: World Bank.

Moore, Barrington (1984 [1966]) *The Social Origins of Democracy and Dictatorship*, London: Penguin (first published 1966).

Moore, Mick (1984) 'Agriculture in Taiwan and South Korea: the minimalist state?', *IDS Bulletin* 15, 2: 52–64.

—— (1997) 'Leading the Left to the Right: populist coalitions and economic reform', *World Development* 25, 7: 1009–28.

Moskovitz, Karl (1982) 'Korean development and Korean studies: a review article', *Journal of Asian Studies* 42, 1: 63–90.

—— (ed.) (1984) *From Patron to Partner: Issues in US–South Korean Economic Relations*, Lexington, MA: Lexington Books.

Myrdal, Gunnar (1970) *The Challenge of World Poverty*, London: Pelican.

Na, Chong-Il (1998) 'From politics of division to politics of unity: tasks facing President-Elect Kim Dae-Jung', *Shin Dong-Ah*, January: 176–81 (in Korean).

Nahm, Andrew C. (ed.) (1973) *Korea Under Japanese Colonial Rule*, Michigan: Kalamazoo.

Nam, Chon-Hyun (1981) 'Trade, industrial policies, and the structure of protection in Korea', in Wontack Hong and Lawrence Krause (eds).

Nam, Duck-Woo (3 October 1998) *Some Observations on the Reform Policies in Korea*, IMF–World Bank Group (www.worldbank.org*)*.

Nam, Sang-Woo (1992) *Korea's Financial Reform Since the Early-1980s*, Working Paper 9207, Seoul: KDI.

—— and Kim, Dong-Won (1993) *The Principal Transactions Bank System of Korea and its Comparison with the Japanese Main Bank System*, Working Paper 9312, Seoul: KDI.

National Statistical Office, see EPB–NSO.

Nelson, Joan M. (ed.) (1991) *Economic Crisis and Policy Choice: The Politics of Adjustment in the Third World*, Princeton, NJ: Princeton University Press.

—— (1996) 'Promoting policy reforms: the twilight of conditionality?', *World Development* 24, 9: 1551–9.

Nordlinger, Eric (1981) *On the Autonomy of the Democratic State*, Cambridge, MA: Harvard University Press.

North, Douglass C. (1981) *Structure and Change in Economic History*, New York: W.W. Norton & Company.

O'Donnell, Guillermo (1973) *Modernization and Bureaucratic-Authoritarianism: Studies in South American Politics*, Berkeley: Institute of International Studies, University of California Press.

—— (1978) 'Reflections on the pattern of change in the bureaucratic-authoritarian state', *Latin American Research Review* 13, 1: 3–38.

—— and Schmitter, Philippe C. (1986) *Transitions from Authoritarian Rule: Tentative Conclusions about Uncertain Democracies*, Baltimore, MD: Johns Hopkins University Press.

——, —— and Whitehead, Laurence (eds) (1986a) *Transitions from Authoritarian Rule: Comparative Perspectives*, Baltimore, MD: Johns Hopkins University Press.

——, —— and —— (eds) (1986b) *Transitions from Authoritarian Rule: Latin America*, Baltimore, MD: Johns Hopkins University Press.

Office of Planning and Coordination (Office of the Prime Minister) (1972) *Evaluation Report of the Second Five-Year Economic Development Plan (1967–1971) 1972*.

—— (1973) *Evaluation Report of the First Year Programme: The Third Five-Year Economic Development Plan 1973*.

—— (1977) *Evaluation Report of the Third Five-Year Economic Development Plan (1972–1976)*.

Ogle, George E. (1974) 'Korean labour unions in the 1960s', *International Journal for Korean Studies* 1: 23–56.

—— (1990) *South Korea: Dissent Within the Economic Miracle*, London: Zed Books.

Oh, Suek-Hong (1982) 'The counter-corruption campaign of the Korean government (1975–1977): administrative anti-corruption measures of the Seojung-shaeshin', in Bun-Woong Kim and Wha-Joon Rho (eds).

Ohtsuka, Shigeru (1981) 'Improvement of the technical capabilities of the small enterprises supplying parts and components to the large assembly industries: expansion of exports and domestic sales of Korean machinery and equipment', in Sakong (ed.).

Olson, Mancur (1982) *The Rise and Decline of Nations*, New Haven, CT: Yale University Press.

Organization for Economic Cooperation and Development (1996) *Reviews of National Science and Technology Policy: Republic of Korea*, Paris: OECD.

Paik, Young-Chul (1994) 'Political reform and democratic consolidation in Korea', *Korea and World Affairs* 28, 4: 730–48.

Palma, Gabriel (1998) 'Three and a half cycles of "mania, panic and [asymmetric] crash": East Asia and Latin America compared', *Cambridge Journal of Economics* 22, 6: 789–808.

Park, Chong-Kee (1980) 'The organization, financing, and cost of health care', in Chong-Kee Park (ed.) *Human Resources and Social Development in Korea*.

—— (ed.) (1980a) *Human Resources and Social Development in Korea*, Seoul: KDI.

—— (ed.) (1980b) *Macroeconomic and Industrial Development in Korea*, Seoul: KDI.

Park, Chung-Hee (1970) *Our Nation's Path: Ideology of Social Reconstruction*, Seoul: Hollym Corporation.

—— (1977) *Korea Reborn: A Model for Development*, Englewood Cliffs, NJ: Prentice-Hall.

Park, Dong-Chol (1996) 'The characteristics of the First Five-Year Economic Development Plan', in Seoul Kyongje Sahoe Yongu So [Seoul Institute for Economic and Social Research] *Korean Industry: Towards Structural Change*, Seoul: SIES (in Korean).

Park, Dong-Chol (1998) 'Government announces first list of non-viable firms', *VIP Economic Report* 7, Hyundai Research Institute: 12–13.

Park, Eul-Yong (1984) 'An analysis of the trade behaviour of American and Japanese manufacturing firms in Korea', in Moskovitz (ed.).

Park, Funkoo and Castenada, Toriscio (1987) *Structural Adjustment and the Role of the Labour Market*, Working Paper 8705, Seoul: KDI.

Park, Jong-Kyu (1997) 'Business–labour confrontation caused by extremism', *Chosun Wolgan*, February: 90–9 (in Korean).

Park, Yung-Chul (1981) 'Export growth and the balance of payments in Korea, 1960–78', in W. Hong and L. Krause (eds).

—— (1994) 'Korea: development and structural change of the financial system', in Patrick and Park (eds).

Patrick, Hugh T. and Park, Yung-Chul (eds) (1994) *The Financial Development of Japan, Korea and Taiwan*, New York: Oxford University Press.

Pempel, T.J. (1978) 'Japanese foreign economic policy: the domestic bases for international behaviour', in Peter J. Katzenstein (ed.) *Between Power and Plenty: Foreign Economic Policies of Advanced Industrial States*, Madison: University of Wisconsin Press.

—— and Tsunekawa, Keiichi (1979) 'Corporatism without labour: the Japanese anomaly', in Philippe Schmitter and Gerhard Lehmbruch (eds) *Trends Towards Corporatist Intermediation*, Beverly Hills, CA: Sage.

Peterson, Wallace C. (1994) *Silent Depression: Twenty-Five Years of Wage Squeeze and Middle Class Decline*, New York: W.W. Norton & Company.

Presidential Commission on Economic Restructuring (1988) *Realigning National Priorities for Economic Advance: Presidential Report on Economic Restructuring*.

Rao, D.C. (1978) 'Economic growth and equity in the Republic of Korea', *World Development* 6, 3: 383–96.

Repetto, Robert, Kwon, Tai-Hwan, Kim, Son-Ung, Kim, Dae-Young, Sloboda, John E. and Donaldson, Peter J. (1980) *Economic Development, Population Policy, and Demographic Transition in the Republic of Korea. Studies in the Modernization of the Republic of Korea: 1945–1975*, Cambridge, MA: Harvard University Press.

Rhee, Yung-Whee, Ross-Larson, Bruce and Pursell, Gary (1984) *Korea's Competitive Edge: Managing the Entry into World Markets*, Baltimore, MD: Johns Hopkins University Press.

Rhee, Sung-Sup (1987) *Policy Reforms of the Eighties and Industrial Adjustments in Korean Economy*, Working Paper 8708, Seoul: KDI.

Rogers, Ronald A. (1993) 'The role of industrial relations in recent national and enterprise level industrial strategies in the Republic of Korea', in Krause and Park (eds).

Roh, Tae-Woo (1990) 'Joint declaration on creating a new era: launching a new national political party (Speech 22 January 1990)', in Tae-Woo, Roh *Korea: A Nation Transformed: Selected Speeches*, Oxford: Pergamon.

Rueschemeyer, Dietrich, Stephens, Evelyne Huber and Stephens, John (1992) *Capitalist Development and Democracy*, Oxford: Polity Press.

Rustow, Dankwart A. (1970) 'How does a democracy come into existence?', *Comparative Politics* 3, 2: 337–63.

Sachs, Jeffrey D. (3 November 1997) 'The wrong medicine for Asia' (http://equity.stern.nyu.edu/).

Sakong, Il (ed.) (1981) *Macroeconomic Policy and Industrial Development Issues*, Seoul: KDI.

Schive, Chi (1990) 'The next stage of industrialization in Korea and Taiwan', in Gereffi and Wyman (eds).

Science and Technology Policy Institute (1995) *Review of Science and Technology Policy for Industrial Competitiveness in Korea*, Seoul: STEPI.

Shaw, Edward S. (1973) *Financial Deepening in Economic Development*, New York: Oxford University Press.

Shim, Young-Hee (1994) 'Women's wage labour in Korean heavy and chemical sectors', in Hyoung Cho and Pil-Wha Chang (eds) *Gender Division of Labour in Korea*, Seoul: Ewha Women's University Press.

Shin, In-Seok and Joon-Ho Hahm (1998) *The Korean Crisis: Crisis and Resolution*, Working Paper 9805, Seoul: KDI.

Shin, Sang-Dal (1997) *The Korean Economy: Confronting the New Challenges*, Working Paper 9707, Seoul: KDI.

Silva, Patricio (1991) 'Technocrats and politics in Chile: from the Chicago Boys to the CIEPLAN Monks', *Journal of Latin American Studies* 23: 385–410.

Soh, Byung-Hee (1997) 'The merits and demerits of the chaebol: evaluation and future issues', *Sasang*, Spring: 242–60 (in Korean).

Sohn, Hak-Kyu (1989) *Authoritarianism and Opposition in South Korea*, London: Routledge.

Song, Byong-Nak (1980) 'Economic development and rural–urban transformation', in Chong-Kee Park (ed.) (1980b).
—— (1990) *The Rise of the Korean Economy*, Hong Kong: Oxford University Press.
—— and Struyk, Raymond J. (1977) 'Korean housing: economic appraisal and policy alternatives', in Chuk-Kyo Kim (ed.).
Song, Dae-Hee and Ryu, Byung-Seo (1992) 'Agricultural policies and structural adjustment', in Vittorio Corbo and Sang-Suh Mok (eds) *Structural Adjustment in a Newly Industrialised Country: The Korean Experience*, Baltimore, MD: Johns Hopkins University Press.
Steers, Richard M., Shin, Yoo-Keun, and Ungson, Gerardo R. (1989) *The Chaebol: Korea's New Industrial Might*, New York: Harper & Row.
Steinberg, David I. (1982) 'Development lessons from the Korean experience: a review article', *Journal of Asian Studies* 42, 1: 91–104.
Stepan, Alfred (1985) 'State power and the strength of civil society in the southern cone of Latin America', in Evans *et al.* (eds).
Stern, Joesph J., Kim, Ji-Hong, Perkins, Dwight H. and Yoo, Jung-Ho (1995) *Industrialization and the State: The Korean Heavy and Chemical Industry Drive*, Cambridge, MA: Harvard University Press.
Suh, Jae-Jean (1989) 'The social and political networks of the Korean capitalist class', *Asian Perspective* 13, 2: 127–34.
Suh, Nam-Pyo (1981) 'An assessment of critical issues confronting the Korean machinery industries', in Sakong (ed.).
Suh, Sang-Chul (1978) *Growth and Structural Change in the Korean Economy 1910–45*, Cambridge, MA: Harvard University Press.
Suh, Sang-Mok (1980) 'The pattern of poverty', in Chong-Kee Park (ed.) (1980a).
—— and Yeon, Ha-Cheong (1986) *Social Welfare During the Adjustment Period in Korea*, Working Paper 8604, Seoul: KDI.
Sumiya, Mikio (1963) *The Social Impact of Industrialization in Japan*, Tokyo: Japanese National Commission for UNESCO.
Tabb, William K. (1995) *The Postwar Japanese System: Cultural Economy and Economic Transformation*, New York: Oxford University Press.
Tan, Augustine H.H. and Kapur, Basant (eds) (1986) *Pacific Growth and Financial Interdependence*, Sydney: Allen & Unwin Press.
Toye, John (1989) *Dilemmas of Development*, Oxford: Blackwell.
Uh, Soo-Bong (1995) *International Competitiveness in Trade and Investment: Challenges and Opportunities for Trade Unions. The Case of Korea*, Seoul: Research Centre of the FKTU.
Van Wolferen, Karel (1989) *The Enigma of Japanese Power*, London: Macmillan.
Von Hayek, Frederick (1986) *The Road to Serfdom*, London: Routledge & Kegan Paul (first published 1944).
Wade, Larry L. and Kim, Byong-Sik (1978) *Economic Development of South Korea: The Political Economy of Success*, New York: Praeger.
Wade, Robert (1982) *Irrigation and Agricultural Politics in South Korea*, Boulder, CO: Westview Press.
—— (1988) 'The role of government in overcoming market failure: Taiwan, Republic of Korea and Japan', in Hughes (ed.).
—— (1991) *Governing the Market: Economic Theory and the Role of Government in East Asian Industrialization*, Princeton, NJ: Princeton University Press.

—— (1992) 'East Asia's economic success: conflicting perspectives, partial insights, shaky evidence', *World Politics* 44, January: 270–320.

—— (1998) 'From "miracle" to "cronyism": explaining the great Asian slump', *Cambridge Journal of Economics* 22, 6: 693–706.

Warren, Bill (1980) *Imperialism: Pioneer of Capitalism*, London: New Left Books.

Westphal, Larry E. (1978) 'Korea's experience with export-led industrial development', *World Development* 6, 3: 347–82.

—— (1979) 'Manufacturing', in Hasan and Rao.

Wideman, Bernie (1974) 'The plight of the South Korean peasant', in Baldwin (ed.).

Williamson, John (1989) 'What Washington means by policy reform', in John Williamson (ed.) *Latin American Adjustment: How Much Has Happened?*, Washington, DC: Institute of International Economics.

—— (1993) 'Democracy and the "Washington consensus"', *World Development* 21, 8: 1329–36.

Woo, Jung-En (1991) *Race to the Swift: The Role of Finance in Korean Industrialization*, New York: Columbia University Press.

World Bank (1979) *Korea: Policy Issues for Long-Term Development. A World Bank Country Report*, Washington, DC: World Bank.

—— (1984) *Korea: Development in a Global Context. A World Bank Country Report*, Washington, DC: World Bank.

—— (1987a) *Korea: Managing the Industrial Transition*, volume 1: *The Conduct of Industrial Policy*, Washington, DC: World Bank.

—— (1987b) *Korea: Managing the Industrial Transition*, volume 2: *Selected Topics and Case Studies*, Washington, DC: World Bank.

—— (1989) *World Development Report 1989*, New York: Oxford University Press.

—— (1991) *World Development Report 1991: The Challenge of Development*, Washington, DC: World Bank.

—— (1993) *The East Asian Miracle: Economic Growth and Public Policy. A World Bank Policy Research Report*, Washington, DC: World Bank.

—— (February 1999) (at www.worldbank.org) *The Republic of Korea and the World Bank: Partners in Recovery*, Korea Country Management Unit, East Asia and the Pacific Region, Washington, DC.

—— (1999) (at www.worldbank.org) *Update on Korea*, Washington, DC.

—— (several issues) *Global Development Finance: Country Tables*, Washington, DC: World Bank.

—— (several issues) *World Debt Tables*, Washington, DC: World Bank.

Wynia, Gary (1990) *The Politics of Latin American Development*, Cambridge: Cambridge University Press.

Yang, Joon-Mo (1996) 'Technology policies in Korea', paper delivered at the KIET–ESCAP Regional Symposium on Strengthening the Private Sector in Enhancing Manufacturing Sector Competitiveness, Seoul: 19–22 March.

Yang, Sung-Chul (1994) *The North and South Korean Political Systems: A Comparative Analysis*, Boulder, CO: Westview Press.

Yea, Sallie W. (1994) 'Regionalism and political economic differentiation in Korean development: power maintenance and the state as hegemonic power bloc', *Korea Journal* 34, 2: 5–29.

Yoo, Jong-Goo (1990) 'Income distribution in Korea', in J.K. Kwon (ed.).

Yoo, Jung-Ho (1989) *The Government in Korean Economic Growth*, Working Paper 8904, Seoul: KDI.

—— (1996) *Challenges to the Newly Industrialised Countries: A Reinterpretation of Korea's Growth Experience*, Working Paper 9608, Seoul: KDI.

Yoo, Seong-Min (1995) *Chaebol in Korea: Misconceptions, Realities and Policies*, Working Paper 9507, Seoul: KDI.

Yoon, Il-Seon (1994) *Housing in a Newly Industrialised Economy: The Case of South Korea*, Aldershot: Avebury.

Young, Alwyn (1995) 'The tyranny of numbers: confronting the statistical realities of the East Asian growth experience', *Quarterly Journal of Economics* 60, August: 641–80.

Yun, Chae-Kol (1986) 'The radical forces and the anti-establishment groups in South Korea, *Shin Dong-Ah* 321: 462–93 (in Korean).

Zo, Ki-Zun (1978) 'Korean industry under the Japanese colonial rule', in Shin-Yong Chun (ed.) *Economic Life in Korea*, Seoul: International Cultural Foundation.

Zysman, John (1994) 'Korean choices and patterns of advanced country development', in Lee-Jay Cho and Yoon-Hyung Kim (eds).

Index